GW00600757

1492

Literature, Culture and Identity

Series Editor: Bruce King

This series is concerned with the ways in which literature and cultures are influenced by the complexities and complications of identity. It looks at the ways in which identities are explored, mapped, defined and challenged in the arts where boundaries are often overlapping, contested and re-mapped. It considers how differences, conflicts and change are felt and expressed. It investigates how such categories as race, class, gender, sexuality, ethnicity, nation, exile, diaspora and multiculturalism have come about. It discusses how these categories co-exist and their relationship to the individual, particular situations, the artist and the arts.

Published titles:

1492

The Poetics of Diaspora

JOHN DOCKER

CONTINUUM
London and New York

Continuum
The Tower Building, 11 York Road, London SE1 7NX
370 Lexington Avenue, New York, NY 10017–6550

First published 2001

© John Docker 2001

All rights reserved. No part of this publication may be reproduced or transmitted in
any form or by any means, electronic or mechanical, including photocopying,
recording or any information storage or retrieval system, without permission in
writing from the publishers.

An earlier version of Chapter 12 was published as 'Recasting Sally Morgan's *My Place*:
the fictionality of identity and the phenomenology of the converso' in *Humanities
Research*, 1 (1998).

British Library Cataloguing-in-Publication Data
A catalogue record for this book is available from the British Library.
ISBN 0–8264–5131–4 (hardback)
    0–8264–5132–2 (paperback)

Library of Congress Cataloging-in-Publication Data
Docker John.
    1492 : the poetics of diaspora / John Docker.
        p. cm
    Includes bibliographical references (p.) and index.
    ISBN 0–8264–5131–4—ISBN 0–8264–5132–2 (pbk.)
    1. Jews in Literature 2. Docker, John—Family. 3. English literature—History and
criticism. I. Title: Fourteen ninety two.   II. Title.

PR151.J5 D63 2001
809'.9335203924—dc21

                                                                    00–056988

Typeset by BookEns Ltd, Royston, Herts.
Printed and bound in Great Britain by
Biddles Ltd, Guildford and King's Lynn

Contents

Preface and acknowledgements

This book began – no, don't begin like that: at least explain the key elements of the title of the book first –

By '1492' I intend to suggest one of those dates, like 1066 or 1776 or 1789, that have achieved iconic and mythological status in European and Western and perhaps world history. In 1492 three key happenings occurred within a very short time near the beginning of that fateful year: Columbus sailed for the Americas; eight centuries of Moorish Spain finally ended in the surrender by the sultan Boabdil of Granada, with its legendary fortress-palace the Alhambra; and the Jews of Spain, except for those who in perilous circumstances had chosen or had been forced to convert to Christianity (becoming known as the *conversos*), were subject to one of history's recurring crimes against humanity, mass expulsion. In this book I will be focusing mainly on the consequences of the ending of Moorish Spain and the expulsion of the Jews. I explore '1492' as an idea, rich in literary and historical implications, a meeting point for diverse cultural histories and religions: a pivotal moment of world history, for Europe, for the Mediterranean, for India, for Jewish history, for Zionism and Israel, for modern societies influenced and shaped by European nationalism, for contemporary ethnic and cultural identities.

By 'poetics' I intend to suggest that we necessarily understand or try to understand identity and belonging, or not belonging, through cultural forms: through representation as in genre, myth, novel, poem, allegory, parable, anecdote, story, sayings, metaphors, puns, riddles.

By 'diaspora', minimally defined, I mean a sense of belonging to more than one history, to more than one time and place, more than one past and future. Diaspora suggests belonging to both here and there, now and then. Diaspora suggests the omnipresent weight of pain of displacement from a land or society, of being an outsider in a new one. Diaspora suggests both lack and excess of loss and separation, yet also the possibility of new adventures of identity and the continued imagining of unconquerable countries of the mind.

The journeys of this book will be simultaneously intellectual and autobiographical. The book will explore '1492' and 'diaspora' in terms of literary and cultural history, social and political history, and excursions into theology and religious narratives; and by 'theology', minimally defined, I mean the study of religion as religion and not as the reflection of other things. I wish this book to be 'postsecularist'.

I also offer this book as a kind of historical novel, Freud's phrase (in a 1935 letter to Lou Andreas-Salomé) for his last work, the highly idiosyncratic *Moses and Monotheism* (1939). The book will make journeys into fragments of my own diasporic ancestry and being: England, Ireland, Australia, Jewishness. It will involve family stories and memories, mixed with diasporic dreams and imaginings; longings to belong to other times, other places, other sensibilities.

I was brought up in a left-wing, socialist and secular family; indeed, I was a Red Diaper baby. My father, who died in the early 1980s, was of mixed English and Irish descent, his Irish mother having migrated to Sydney town sometime in the 1880s, there to marry an Englishman, Henry Docker. My father lived at his mother's place till his forties, marrying when she died. So I never met my Irish grandmother. But my father would talk in lifelong affectionate terms of his mother Susan, how she came from a tiny town on the west coast of Ireland, Kilrush in County Clare, near the river Shannon. Her family were Protestants, indeed poor Protestants, in that wild area which I visited, ancestor-tracking, on my first time overseas in the early 1970s. He never spoke of his English father; it's my Irish grandmother who lives for me. Yet I have no photos of either of my father's parents.

My mother, who died in the late 1980s, was of London East End Jewish stock. Her family migrated to Sydney sometime in the 1920s, settling in 'perpetually migrant' Bondi. She would talk abundantly of growing up in the East End, and had some striking photos of her parents displayed on the mantelpiece in the Bondi flat where I grew up.

My father, like his father, was a carpenter, my mother had been in the clothing trade. My father had been in the Communist Party since its inception, my mother joined in the 1930s. So I grew up in an atheistical Communist family, knowing no formal religion of any kind. I didn't think of myself as Jewish when I was growing up. I thought of myself as growing up in a Communist family, torn between an extreme desire to conform, to be ordinary, to play football and tennis, and a sense, with such an upbringing, of it being always too late. In my third year of university I met an American anthropologist who, on acquaintance, declared that I was Jewish, that I didn't know how Jewish I was, and that I reminded her of American East Coast Jews.

She demanded to meet my family, and came to dinner. Since my anthropologist friend was quite a few years older than me, my mother produced the family photo albums, turning over and pointing at photos of me as a baby and little boy. My anthropologist friend also insisted on meeting my argumentative Jewish uncles, on which occasion I became, I still recall, childishly jealous of her camaraderie with them; I was the excluded young.

But I did think much more about Jewishness from then on. I thought that the way my mother had visited her mother and father, who lived not far away in Bondi, every single day was perhaps re-creating London East End family life. I got my mother to make whatever Jewish food she remembered her mother making. I realized how characteristically food-centric she was (and I would duly become), and recalled how in our little Bondi flat she would advance from the kitchenette into the loungeroom, holding a large knife while making a point. I realized how Jewish families always try to absorb outsiders into the family, into food-sharing rituals. I realized that as the one boy in the family I had been spoilt silly.

For a postmodern world of multiple, fragmented, contradictory identities, my mixed conception was, I now think, most suitable. But, perhaps like all fragmented identities, it was not without its difficulties. I always felt my claims to any 'identity' were embarrassingly, even contemptibly, thin, inauthentic. I felt uneasy with other Jewish boys at my eastern suburbs high school because they seemed 'really Jewish', obviously from families that knew and perhaps practised the religion (it was much later that I learned of Melbourne Jewish scorn for the laxity and hedonism of Sydney Jews). Also, my south Bondi family, my grandparents and us, were obviously poor, compared to other eastern suburbs Jews, from North Bondi, Dover Heights, Rose Bay: the intricacies of diaspora and class.

Yet I could not comfortably claim 'Irish' descent either. When I was a teenage Leavisite in Melbourne in the late 1960s, I was surprised and slightly amused to encounter in the English department at Melbourne University a phenomenon I'd never witnessed before, a kind of aggressive Irishry, centred on the poet Vincent Buckley and his young followers. Again, I felt uneasy – in the face of such militant identification with their proclaimed Irish Catholic ancestry, how could I weakly meekly mention that I had an Irish Protestant grandmother, who married an Englishman?

A fragmented identity is a strange thing. You always feel other people are more secure and assured in their identity, which they're almost certainly not. And you always have a feeling of not fully knowing yourself, of why strange desires and passions and identifications erupt and endure.

My mother, when I was a child and later, in my latter teens and early twenties, when I became interested in the family's Jewish ancestry, would say that we were possibly of Portuguese descent. As the reader will see, that idea or (in terms of a famous Freud essay) 'family romance' has inspired much of the imaginative journeying of this book, for it connects to '1492'. A significant proportion of the Jews expelled in 1492 proceeded from Spain to Portugal, thence to be baptized as Catholics later in the 1490s. They became known as the New Christians, and in the sixteenth century some of the New Christians were regarded as *marranos*, secret or crypto-Jews.

Books begin in vague thoughts, obscure desires and passions, fantasies and obsessions. More practically and materially, this book began with the award of a five-year Australian Research Council fellowship, which I began in 1993, researching ethnic and cultural identities. I wished to address the challenging debates that had been raging for over a decade, in many ways inspired by Edward Said's *Orientalism* (1978), that discussed issues of colonialism, postcolonialism, migration, diaspora, exile, belonging, identity, ethnicity, 'race'. I felt I could apply my 'cultural history' approach to these issues, an approach I had explored in my *Postmodernism and Popular Culture: A Cultural History* (1994) as well as in my previous writing; the approach of someone trained in literary studies who yet wishes to sustain conversations between literary theory and other fields, cultural theory, the history of ideas, intellectual history, historiography, political theory.

After years of immersing myself in popular culture, especially television, it was with a kind of secret joy that I decided that for my new book I would return to the close study of literary texts, including 'high' texts, and I felt the best place to start would be a detailed rereading of Joyce's *Ulysses*. In his anguish and perplexity, Mr Leopold Paula Bloom, the most famous evocation of a Jewish character in twentieth-century literature, was calling to me, calling to me.

Intellectual work is a curious condition, often involving being alone for long periods writing and thinking and journeying deep within oneself to the scattered islands and mirages; yet also intensely co-operative with other writers and scholars and intellectuals, sharing ideas and interests, mentioning references to follow up, excited conversation. Coffee and the coffee shop are very important both to times when one wants to be by oneself, and to times of sociable exchange of ideas with many and varied interlocutors. I have been fortunate that the notion of 'adventures of identity' – a guiding idea in the writing of this book, and its working title – seems to intrigue people and has led to conversations of the most eccentric, often personal, kind. The writing of the book has also led to 'life' changes for the author, in an interest in body decoration, embarrassing fetishes, the history of cooking and a wealth of new recipes to play with for one who is food-demented, and a sudden, perhaps bizarre, theological turn. It was only after my theological turn, which led to an absorption in the Old Testament stories, that I could appreciate in *Ulysses* Bloom's admiration for Spinoza, their shared critique of the Exodus story, and the significance of whether or not Bloom is circumcised.

During the first part of my fellowship (from 1993 to July 1995) I was attached to the Faculty of Humanities and Social Sciences at the University of Technology, Sydney. I must thank Mairéad Browne, then Dean, for permitting me this attachment. At UTS, Ann Curthoys (who left in January 1995 to go to ANU), Stephen Muecke and Meaghan Morris provided a particularly stimulating 'cultural studies' environment. I also enjoyed many coffee conversations with the doctoral students present at UTS in 1993–95, in particular Marsha Rosengarten, Ann Genovese, Jane Connors, Alison Cadzow and Lynda Parry.

I very much enjoyed my discussions at Mama Maria's (then near the Sydney Powerhouse Museum) with Marsha Rosengarten on a variety of topics, from Zionism and Jewish identity to the relative merits of Foucault and Derrida: Marsha found almost incomprehensible my preferring Derrida to Foucault, eventually putting it down to the textual interests of the literary critic; at coffee or lunch at Mama Maria's, Marsha and I would also try to outdo each other wringing the *shlemiel* comedy of disaster and humiliation out of anything we could think of. Marsha has also observed that she thinks of me 'as neither Jewish nor non-Jewish', a phrase I treasure and ponder and which is perhaps the leitmotif of this book.

I have particularly to thank Caroline Grahame for my interest in analysing Zionism. Caroline was a colleague at UTS teaching politics and Orientalism, and is also a longtime family friend. It was from the mid-1980s that I began to write about Zionism and Orientalism. Caroline was prominent in the Sydney Palestine Human Rights Campaign, and I admired her courage in publicly espousing the Palestinian cause. She would occasionally ask me when I was going to write something about Zionism, perhaps relating it to literature, and in 1986, while on a Literature Board grant, I spent some months painstakingly reading every critique I could get hold of, the eventual first results being talks and essays on Leon Uris's *Exodus* and Blanche D'Alpuget's *Winter in Jerusalem*.

In July 1995 I moved from my home city of Sydney to Canberra and the Australian National University, where I became attached to the English department and the Humanities Research Centre.

I would particularly like to thank the Humanities Research Centre for its informality, friendliness and hospitality, and for hosting an international community of scholars sharing diverse knowledge. In particular, I would like to thank Iain McCalman and Graeme Clarke, the HRC directors, whose welcoming of me when I came from Sydney to ANU has made my stay so pleasant and rewarding. During the writing of this book Iain McCalman was general editor of *An Oxford Companion to the Romantic Age: British Culture 1776-1832* (1999), and I benefited from frequent discussions-over-coffee at the ANU's excellent Calypso café with Iain as well as associate editors Jon Mee and Clara Tuite. I would also like to thank the administrative staff at the Humanities Research Centre – Julie Gorrell, Leena Messina, Misty Cook, Ann Palmer and Judy Buchanan – for their unfailing humour and support.

During these years the book began to take shape as an argument and narrative, with a kind of repository or archive of texts I could work on and worry at. At a conference in 1995 at ADFA (the Australian Defence Force Academy, Canberra) on 'Crossing Cultures', I heard a paper by Ms Debjani Ganguly on 'Salman Rushdie: an Indian view', which talked of the Jewish characters in *The Moor's Last Sigh*. I immediately became excited, felt embarrassed that I hadn't already read it, and decided that it would have to be included. In May 1996 I gave a paper on 'Ethnic and cultural identities in Salman Rushdie's *The Moor's Last Sigh*' to the humanities school at the University of Canberra, hosted by Satendra Nandan. I was particularly struck by the story framing the novel, which connected contemporary India to the fall of the last of Moorish Spain in Granada in 1492.

At some point someone, it must have been a fellow literary critic, told me I must read Scott's *Ivanhoe*, for its ending mentions Moorish Spain. At some other point Jon Mee and the Bakhtin scholar Subhash Jaireth thankfully urged me to read Amitav Ghosh's *In an Antique Land*, and Subhash kindly provided me with excerpts from *The Hindu* on the reception of *The Moor's Last Sigh* in India. Clara Tuite also told me of Marc Shell's 'Marranos (pigs), or From coexistence to toleration', an essay which crystallized further the developing project of this book for me: the importance for European and world history of the fateful events in (and out of) Spain in 1492; and the wealth of connections between European and Indian literatures.

Soon after I arrived in Canberra, Jill Matthews, then of Women's Studies, now in the History department, ANU, lent me her copy of Washington Irving's *Tales of the Alhambra*, and has consistently fortified my interest in questions of Orientalism with the interest we share in Middle Eastern and North African cuisine, especially Moroccan (we help each other with pickled turnips, preserved lemons, sumac, pomegranate syrup and *ras el hanout*).

I would like to acknowledge conversations I have enjoyed over the years with colleagues at the Australasian Middle Eastern Studies Association conferences: with Caroline Grahame (who first invited me), Sami Hajjar, Samar Attar, Ahmad Shboul, Michael Humphrey, Robert Springborg, Patricia Springborg, the late Irwin Hermann, and Ghassan Hage.

In Australia and in England I have benefited from conversations with Miriam Glucksmann.

In Sydney on visits I have benefited from conversations with Barbie Bloch, Marta Romer and Derek Wolfson.

As a city Sydney is dazzlingly beautiful, cosmopolitan, sophisticated, extravagant, brazen, corrupt; as architecture it continually destroys itself. W. B. Yeats's 'The Second Coming' was published in the early 1920s, almost at the same time as *Ulysses*. Remember its apocalyptic aphorism so appropriate for the new millennium: 'The best lack all conviction, while the worst are full of passionate intensity.' Such could be said of Sydney: the more bullying, the more brutally assertive, the more ignorant, the more mediocre, the more severely economical with the truth people in public life are, the more they thrive:

> ... what rough beast, its hour come round at last,
> Slouches towards Bethlehem to be born?

Sydney, the millennial city, is a sign of white Australia – perhaps even of that rough beast the Western-dominated world – writ depressingly large on the stained sky. Yet I miss it, I miss it, especially Bondi where I grew up, and the rumbustiousness of conversational style, the opportunity to extend oneself into the wicked extreme in story, anecdote, comment.

Canberra is a very odd city. It is still too much like a country town, an Australian country town, with all its dangers of parochialism, prejudice, racism, homophobia, conformity, *ressentiment*. Strangers from that conformity seek each other out. Yet Canberra is also the nation's political capital, and its Australian National University continuously attracts scholars from elsewhere, nationally and internationally. There is a breadth of specialized knowledge at ANU, especially in Asian studies and cross-cultural research, that is I think beyond any other university in Australia. At ANU and in Canberra, I have benefited from conversations with resident or visiting scholars, writers, artists: Ien Ang, Bain Attwood, Robert Barnes, Susan Conley, Gavin Edwards, Chris Forth, Andre Frankovits, Debjani Ganguly, Geoff Gray, Tom Griffiths, Subhash Jaireth, Carol Johnson, James Jupp, Philippa Kelly, Rosanne Kennedy, Alison Kibler, Brij Lal, Sarah Lloyd, Jacqueline Lo, Jane Lydon, eX de Medici, Tessa Morris-Suzuki, Kavita Nandan, Satendra Nandan, Katarina Paseta, Senia Paseta, Ben Penny, Craig Reynolds, Gillian Russell, Yuan-fang Shen, Pat Tandy, Christine Winter, Nira Yuval-Davis.

At ANU in 1996 I was fortunate to meet Igor Primoratz, a philosopher from the Hebrew University in Jerusalem, while he was visiting the philosophy department at RSSS, ANU. I read with great interest his essay 'Israel and genocide in Croatia' (in Stjepan G. Mestrovic, ed., *Genocide after Emotion: The Postemotional Balkan War* (London and New York: Routledge, 1996)), and we had fortifying conversations at the Calypso about Israel, sharing judgements and evaluations, reflecting on impending disaster.

In 1997 I benefited from meeting the anthropologist Deborah Bird Rose at NARU, ANU's outstation in Darwin, and two American 'political theory' visitors to ANU, Jane Bennett and Bill Connolly, who severally reassured me that the life of the mind can still involve generosity and adventure, the wayward and the maverick, daring sideways moves, wit and irony and self-irony.

I have to thank Gerhard Fischer, of the German Studies department at the University of New South Wales, for friendship over the last several years, and his challenging conversation on issues of identity, busily pursued on e-mail. Gerhard and I together organized 'Adventures of Identity: Constructing the Multicultural Subject', an international symposium held in late July–early August 1998 in the beautiful setting of the Goethe Institut in leafy Woollahra, Sydney; the conference was sponsored by the Humanities Research Centre and by Gerhard's department in association with the Goethe Institut and the German Research Council. Subsequently, Gerhard and I have edited two collections drawing on papers given at the conference: *Race, Colour and Identity in Australia and New Zealand* and *Multicultural Identities: Theories, Perspectives, Models, Case Studies*.

Early in 1999 the HRC was fortunate to have as a visitor the theologian Roland Boer, who invited me, as a non-biblical scholar interested in the Old Testament stories, to participate, along with biblical scholars, in a Bible and Critical Theory Seminar at tiny St Albans, NSW, in June 1999: being there was a privilege, one of the most enjoyable intellectual occasions I've experienced.

In 1999 I very much enjoyed and learnt enormous amounts from an informal ANU theological discussion group, calling ourselves the Calypso Critters, with Ann Curthoys, Deborah Bird Rose and Christine Winter.

I must especially thank Christine Winter, trained in theology in Germany, for her unfailingly good-humoured assistance in German translations over the last few years. Christine introduced me to the poetry of Paul Celan, gifting me a copy of his *Breathturn* (translated by Pierre Joris).

In 1999 my horizons widened in another way, when I participated in the teaching of the ANU History department's World History course, and listened to fascinating lectures on science and creation stories.

Also in 1999: my thanks to Peter Hulme for suggesting I read Amin Maalouf's *Leo the African*.

Above all, I would like to acknowledge the stimulus of Ann Curthoys, and our son Ned Curthoys. It was Ned who said I must read Walter Benjamin's *The*

Origin of German Tragic Drama, and the results of that reading will be evident throughout the stories told here. Indeed, this book is something of a family affair, with Ann's mother Barbara providing the genealogy that figures in Chapter 2. My uncles Lew Levy and Jock Levy have also greatly contributed with their family stories.

Especial thanks to series editor Bruce King for his encouragement and support: his witty e-mails have been a delight.

In terms of general intellectual influence in the area of ethnic and cultural identity, my surpassing debt has to be to Edward W. Said, especially his brilliant 'Canaanite' reading of the Exodus story in *Blaming the Victims* (1988), the collection of essays Said edited with Christopher Hitchens.

In terms of theories of diaspora, my surpassing debt is to the work of James Clifford, in particular 'Looking for Bomma', his illuminating review-essay on Amitav Ghosh's *In an Antique Land* in the *London Review of Books* (24 March 1994), which alerted me to Ammiel Alcalay's *After Jews and Arabs: Remaking Levantine Culture;* and his synoptic essay 'Diasporas' in *Cultural Anthropology,* 9(3) (1994), reprinted in *Routes: Travel and Translation in the Late Twentieth Century* (1997).

Note: The introductory chapter, 'His slave, my tattoo: romancing a lost world', is an expanded version of an essay written with the same title for Debjani Ganguly and Kavita Nandan (eds), *Unfinished Journeys: India File from Canberra* (1998); another version has been published as 'An unbecoming Australian: romancing a lost pre-1492 world', in Richard Nile and Michael Peterson (eds), *Becoming Australia* (1998).

This book is dedicated to
Barbara Curthoys (1924–2000) and Geoff Curthoys

1

His slave, my tattoo: romancing a lost world

Ye shall not make any cuttings in your flesh for the dead, nor print any marks upon you: I *am* the LORD.

(Leviticus 19:28)

...we have come to the great question of the treatment of slaves. One is tempted to quote the paragraph with which Maimonides concludes the chapter on slavery in his code of law: 'It is both pious and reasonable on the part of a master to be merciful and just towards his slave, not to overburden him with work and not to cause him grief, and to let him share all food and drink taken by himself....He should not humiliate him either by infliction of corporal punishment or even by words. . . . He should not shout at him . . . but talk to him quietly and listen to his arguments....' Similar admonitions could be quoted from Christian and Muslim sources. But, of course, not all people were pious or reasonable. As far as our actual information from the Geniza records is concerned, the male slaves, who normally acted as business representatives, are referred to in the same way as respected merchants and, in case they served also as personal factotums, were greeted in letters as other members of the household, sometimes with the honorable epithet 'the elder'.

S. D. Goitein, *A Mediterranean Society*[1]

In the early 1920s a young scholar, Shlomo Dov Goitein, from a Moravian–Hungarian family of rabbis, trained in Arabic studies in Germany, took up a teaching appointment in Palestine. In subsequent decades he travelled widely in the Levant and in southern Arabian regions like the Yemen, and made it his life's work to investigate and evoke the thousand-year-old interactions between Europeans and Jews and Arabs and Indians in the mercantile world of North Africa, the Mediterranean, Arabia and the Indian Ocean. His writings are increasingly coming to be recognized as major contributions to how we conceive the historical relations between not only Christians and Jews and

Arabs but also Christians and Jews and Arabs and Indians and, more broadly, between Oriental and European histories. Goitein is one of the last twentieth-century scholars to have had intimate contact with an ethnically and religiously plural world that was assaulted by Europe over a very long period, in the medieval Crusades and the events of 1492 and subsequent European maritime expansion. After the Second World War it was sharply disrupted and bifurcated by both Zionist and Arab nationalism.[2]

In 1992 Amitav Ghosh, the Indian anthropologist and novelist, published a wonderful, playful, witty, adventurous and very moving book, *In an Antique Land*, that pays homage to and draws on and supplements the work and research of S. D. Goitein. *In an Antique Land* is a text that crosses and mixes many forms and genres: autobiographical memoir, anthropological treatise, apprentice's woes, traveller's tales, comedy, romance, detective, mystery, utopia, dystopia and anguished conversation with history.[3]

Goitein's histories and *In an Antique Land* touch me personally and intellectually, here, in Australia, as, dismayed by aspects of modernity in relation to ethnic and cultural identities, I make my own quixotic journeys into pasts that now seem impossibly exotic.

In this introductory chapter I will focus on the relationship between Goitein and Ghosh, and in so doing I will treat *In an Antique Land* as a novel, albeit a novel supported by impressive scholarly Goiteinesque research, as is clear from the notes at the end; a novel which creates characters, medieval and contemporary, including the narrator himself, as it tracks back and forth between eras past and present, trying to make them talk to each other; pasts and presents which keep entwining and separating, teasingly.

I will also relate Goitein and Ghosh to the genesis of *1492: The Poetics of Diaspora*, itself inspired by another great Indian diaspora novel, *The Moor's Last Sigh*. And I will relate these thinkers to certain personal events associated with *1492: The Poetics of Diaspora*. I hired a research assistant to do a genealogy of my English Jewish family ancestry (my mother was a Levy). And in 1997, as the book was coming together, I acquired a quite large tattoo, in shades of grey, which sits on my right shoulder as I tap these words, the representation of a figure I refer to puzzled acquaintances and concerned friends as the Veiled Stranger.

From England and Europe to the Levant to the Indian Ocean to India and thence to Australia — this crescent will be my journey in this book.

Egypt

In an Antique Land tells the story of a young Indian anthropologist, only twenty-two years old when in 1978 he arrives in England on a scholarship to begin a doctorate in social anthropology. In the winter of that year, in the library in Oxford, he comes across *Letters of Medieval Jewish Traders*, a book of translations edited by Professor Goitein referring to the Mediterranean Arab and Jewish societies of the Middle Ages, the time of the Crusades in the eastern Mediterranean as well as of a remarkable trading, social and cultural world that extended from southern Europe and Moorish Spain and Morocco and Tunisia in the west through the Levant and East Africa to India and China in the east. The material on medieval Jewish traders and their slaves in Goitein's *Letters* catches the attention of the apprentice anthropologist, so that his doctoral research suddenly takes on for him a personal interest. He reads letters from merchants in the Middle East written in the first part of the twelfth century to their partner and friend, a Jewish trader who lives in India, Abraham Ben Yiju, letters which at the end include greetings to Ben Yiju's Indian slave, a man called Bomma.[4]

His doctoral thesis becomes infused with urgent questions: how could it be that a Jewish trader, speaking Judeo-Arabic and writing in Arabic as well as Hebrew, lived in Mangalore for nearly two decades, with an Indian slave whom he sent on trading voyages back to the Middle East as his trusted business agent? What did slavery mean in those times in that world before modern European plantation experience in the Americas gave slavery its brutal contemporary inflection? What was Ben Yiju like? What was Bomma like? How could it be that their cultural worlds intersected so easily? What did their cultural worlds share, for example, in terms of popular religion? And is there any evidence of such cultural interaction between the Middle East and India in present-day Egypt, now as then the hub of the Arab Mediterranean? He feels that the past presence of Bomma the Indian slave should give him 'a right to be there' in Egypt, 'a sense of entitlement'.[5]

The journey of his thesis takes shape. He first learns Arabic in Tunisia. He then arranges to go to an agricultural village in Egypt he calls Lataifa, southeast of Alexandria, there to practise his European social anthropology on its mostly poor inhabitants, many of whom he comes to respect and admire and value dearly as friends. In part *In an Antique Land* is such an entertaining and provocative novel because it tests and permits the reversal of the usual relationship between ethnographer and informant in the Western anthropological project. In this tradition (at least before the arrival of 'postmodern' self-reflexive ethnographic writing, of which *In an Antique Land* is a very fine example), Western anthropologists might confide doubts, lack of knowledge, puzzlement, bafflement, difficulties of research, chagrin of incomprehension, sense of defeat, to their private notebooks and diaries and in letters home. But in the published scholarly account they will strive to appear imperturbably objective, as if their ethnography is the impersonal unfolding of the total truth of the observed society, garnered from informants' data scientifically sifted. In *In an Antique Land* the anthropologist, the 'I' of the narrative, allows himself to be a vulnerable character in the drama of research and the stories he tells, stories where he frequently becomes the object of his informants' curious gaze and speculation and amusement. As Jabir, a young village boy who befriends him, whispers to people: 'Reads books and asks questions all day long; doesn't have any work to do....'[6]

The devout Muslim villagers in Lataifa, young and old, male and female, ply him with questions about Indian life and religion, often disbelieving or horrified or laughing hilariously at his responses. They can't believe it when he suggests that he is not a practising Hindu. 'What is this "Hinduki" thing? I have heard of it before and I don't understand it. If it is not Christianity nor Judaism nor Islam what can it be? Who are its prophets?' They cannot understand a religion without prophets. They accuse him of worshipping cows. They insistently want to know if Indians are 'purified', if the women receive clitoridectomy, the men circumcision. And the narrator: surely he shaves his armpits? Surely he shaves his genital hairs? They gasp with incredulity at his reluctant answers. 'You should try to civilize your people. You should tell them to stop praying to cows and burning their dead.' 'Everything's upside down in that country.'[7]

He who should be the ever-confident Western-trained observer becomes increasingly discomfited and defensive. On one occasion, when a gathering again demands to know if he's been circumcised, he feels he can stand it no longer, and runs from the room. Nabeel, one of his friends, catches up with him:

'They were only asking questions', he said, 'just like you do; they didn't mean any harm. Why do you let this talk of cows and burning and circumcision worry you so much? These are just customs; it's natural that people should be so curious. These are not things to be upset about.'[8]

Yet the narrator is upset for another reason. That the villagers show such incomprehension at what they take to be the bizarre customs and superstitions of India is a sad sign of how much Egypt and India no longer relate to each other, how much their histories have diverged and become mutually alien. The villagers, who in their turn like and respect and are kind to the strange young man who asks them questions all day and doesn't work, cannot see the narrator as part of their extended world, as once an Indian surely would have been. At least, this is what he infers from the occasional references he follows up and the mysterious clues which he, as scholarly detective, chases and puzzles over that suggest images of the lost world of Abraham Ben Yiju and Bomma. But how can he find out about them?

These references and clues he will seek in the documents of the famous Cairo Geniza. The famous Cairo Geniza?

European and Oriental Jews

In the introduction to the first volume (1967) of his five-volume *A Mediterranean Society: The Jewish Communities of the Arab World as Portrayed in the Documents of the Cairo Geniza*, S. D. Goitein tells the story, deploying terms and metaphors of colonialism no less striking for being unwitting, of a 'discovery' that he feels is becoming increasingly important for European scholarship. Goitein explains that the Hebrew word *geniza*, like the Arabic *janaza* (burial), is derived from the Persian *ganj*, denoting a storehouse or treasure. In medieval Hebrew, *geniza* designated a repository of discarded writings bearing the name of God (Hebrew was regarded as God's own language), writings to be put aside in a special room to await burial in a cemetery. Especially from the eleventh to the thirteenth centuries, a 'long-concealed' 'great treasure', hailing from all over the Mediterranean countries and beyond, was kept in the Geniza in the synagogue in Fustat, in Old Cairo (Fustat was the capital of Muslim Egypt until 969 and the Fatimid conquest). Such writings, which could be and often were secular in nature, ranged from literature and philosophy and medicine to the interpretation of dreams and folktales, to court depositions of marriage contracts and bills of divorce and records of commercial transactions, to deeds of manumission emancipating slaves and slave girls.

What Goitein refers to as the Classical Geniza, the body of documents that flooded in for two and half centuries after the second part of the tenth century, and which reveal the 'eloquence and lucidity of speech of the Mediterranean man', was attached to the synagogue of the Palestinians, those Jews in Cairo who had originally come from Palestine and Syria. Yet, says Goitein, what is surprising is that in the period of the Classical Geniza there was a preponderance of material from people from Tunisia and Sicily, Tunisia at that time being the seat of great Jewish learning. The synagogue seemed to serve the Maghrebi merchants who regularly commuted from the western to the eastern part of the Mediterranean and then beyond. The Geniza provides, in letters back home, detailed illustrations of daily life concerned with travel and seafaring. Goitein also speculates that it may have been the Tunisians, the Maghrebi merchants involved in Mediterranean trade with India, who initiated the idea of a permanent Geniza in Fustat.

For a thousand years, the Fustat synagogue with its remarkable Geniza never ceased to be a house of worship. Then European Jewish scholars and collectors of Oriental Hebrew manuscripts began to hear of its 'treasures'.

Goitein refers to the Karaite scholar Abraham Firkovitch (1786–1874), who in his 'daring travels' managed to acquire some and sold them to the Imperial library of St Petersburg. Goitein also tells us of two English Jewish collectors and scholars, Elkan N. Adler of London and Dr Solomon Schechter of Cambridge, who became key figures in the moving of the Geniza documents late in the nineteenth century and early in the twentieth to Western libraries and private collections.

In Goitein's account, it was Dr Schechter who, in 1896, was pivotal in what he refers to as 'the liquidation of the Cairo Geniza' in terms of its non-printed manuscripts. Schechter 'conceived the bold idea to save, with one stroke, the whole of the Cairo Geniza for scientific research'; he was able to 'transfer' to the University Library, Cambridge, 'a hoard of manuscripts of fabulous dimensions'. Later visitors to the Geniza confirmed that nothing but printed matter remained. Then new Geniza material was unearthed in the Basatin cemetery east of Old Cairo at the beginning of the twentieth century, material which was 'openly sold'.

What sorrows Goitein is that given such a haphazard mode of 'transfer', the Geniza materials became scattered throughout the non-Oriental world, making 'scientific' study so much more difficult. Geniza documents went to libraries not only in Schechter's Cambridge but in Oxford, London, Philadelphia, Budapest, Paris, Washington, Vienna. Some material remains in private hands. The valuable collection in Frankfurt was destroyed in the Second World War. As in Greek or Arabic papyrology, pages of one and the same book, or fragments of one and the same document, can be found in St Petersburg, Cambridge, New York. Bibliographical guidance is still absent in many collections, an 'intolerable situation'.

In general, in Goitein's view, such disorderly scattering of the collection to far-flung libraries only added to the already existing 'topsy-turvy' nature of the Cairo Geniza, its 'erratic' state when found by European enquirers. The documents were not maintained as an orderly 'archive' but in a state of 'chaos', because, unfortunately for the later scholar, they were in continuous living use by the inhabitants of the Cairo congregation, who 'turned them upside down' in the search for documents relevant to their lives. As Goitein phrases it, such documents were 'constantly called upon to satisfy the needs and greed of the living', with results that were 'hardly beneficial'. Yet Goitein also observes that the haphazard character of the Geniza in its living state was also its uniqueness and glory: 'It is a true mirror of life, often cracked and blotchy, but very wide in scope and reflecting each and every aspect of the society that originated it.' In the Geniza almost every conceivable human relationship is represented, so that its jumbled documents often read, Goitein says, like local news narrated by a gifted reporter.

Published in the early 1990s, in a different intellectual climate, *In an Antique Land* writes in a spirit of anger and astonishment of the emptying and scattering of the contents of the Cairo Geniza – 'the greatest single collection of medieval documents ever discovered' – even if it later led to reconstructive study by great scholars such as Professor Goitein. For the narrator of *In an Antique Land*, the European Jewish scholars who came to Cairo and began to take more and more documents from the Geniza were all too similar to their non-Jewish European scholarly counterparts engaged in the appropriation of Oriental knowledge (especially those besotted by Egyptology) – the discursive encircling and enclosing so powerfully critiqued in Edward Said's *Orientalism*. As *In an Antique Land* points out with justifiable passion, by the First World War the Jewish community in Cairo, which had for a millennium created and sustained and added to and preserved one of the most remarkable collections of documents in history, was left with an empty storeroom by a common act of colonialism, this time by European Jews towards their non-European co-religionists. [9]

Now teaching cultural studies in New York, the Iraqi-Israeli critic Ella Shohat has written an essay in appreciation of Ghosh's *In an Antique Land* where she talks autobiographically of coming from an Iraqi Jewish community, perhaps the last generation, as she notes, to speak Judeo-Arabic, that along with other Jewish communities in the Middle East and North Africa was forced after 1948 to migrate to Israel. These Sephardi and Oriental Jews form, along with the Palestinians who remained in Israel, the majority of the population of the new state, a state whose institutions and culture are controlled by a minority of European Ashkenazi Jews, the heirs of Elkan N. Adler and Dr Schechter in their disdain for the entwined symbiotic Jewish–Arab history creatively led by Sephardi and Oriental Jews for a millennium. Ironically, Shohat writes, these Oriental and Sephardi Jews now yearn for their lost culturally syncretic diaspora life in Baghdad, Damascus, Cairo. Shohat feels that in this situation one could reverse the biblical expression: By the waters of Zion, where we sat down, and there we wept, when we remembered Babylon. [10]

Israel is referred to obliquely in *In an Antique Land*, when the narrator suggests that the emptying out of the Cairo Geniza by European Jewish scholars prefigured modern Israel's hierarchies of culture and knowledge. At the end of the novel, the narrator visits a shrine that is not far from Lataifa, a shrine to a saint called Sidi Abu-Hasira, who, so local stories went, had been born into a Jewish family in the Maghreb, had then miraculously transported himself to Egypt, where he converted to Islam, and was soon recognized by villagers in the area as blessed with wonder- and miracle-working capacities. His tomb is venerated by Muslims and Jews alike, in a carnival-like way, with sideshows; and, says the narrator, since the opening of the borders between Egypt and Israel many followers of the saint in Israel had come every year to venerate him. The narrator, however, never does get to see the sacred tomb. He is stopped by some military officials, and interrogated. They first ask him if he is Israeli. When he says, no, Indian, they are mystified. They can see no reason why an Indian would feel he had any relation to popular Middle Eastern practices of venerating sacred spirits. In any case, the military officer is contemptuous of such popular religion, seeing a belief in saints and miracles as typical of fellaheen ignorance and superstition.[11]

In another of his books, *Jews and Arabs*, S. D. Goitein notes that a favourite meeting ground for the cultures of peoples living together is popular religion, and that such applied to medieval and later Jews and Arabs, who had largely the same background as heirs of the ancient Hellenized East, including the pagan practices of worshipping at shrines. The pivot, says Goitein, of popular religious life in Muslim countries, from the Yemen to Palestine to North Africa, lay in pilgrimages to the tombs of the saints, an activity in which Jews also participated. In North Africa, it has been estimated, no less than 31 saints' tombs were claimed by Jews and Muslims simultaneously.[12]

The significance for the narrator of *In an Antique Land* of the contemporary Jewish–Muslim shrine of Sidi Abu-Hasira is that he feels sure Bomma in twelfth-century India would also most likely have participated in a similar kind of local popular religion of spirits and shrines that would also have been similarly despised by what he refers to as 'Sanskritic Hinduism'.[13]

India

In *In an Antique Land* the narrator tells us that until that fateful day in 1978 sitting in the library reading Goitein's *Letters of Medieval Jewish Traders* he himself had never heard of the Cairo Geniza. But he learnt of its history as quickly as he could, especially the traces of information concerning the Jews from North Africa, in particular Tunisia, who had migrated eastward to Egypt and were pre-eminent in the medieval Indian Ocean trade, its most important ports Aden on one side, and Mangalore on the south-western coast of India on the other, exchanging pepper, cardamom, silk, bronze. He finds himself admiring the congregation in Fustat as 'a group of people whose travels and breadth of experience and education seem astonishing even today, on a planet thought to be newly-shrunken'. The great medieval Jewish physician and philosopher Maimonides, who had close family links to the India trade, belonged to this congregation, which was remarkable for its learning and cosmopolitanism.[14]

In search of clues in the Geniza collections in libraries around the world, the narrator himself becomes like the medieval travellers and scholar-merchants he admires. He finds that Abraham Ben Yiju, born sometime around the beginning of the twelfth century in Tunisia, highly educated, a poet, calligrapher, scholar, had moved to Aden as a young man to pursue the career of merchant, an honoured profession not only in that Judeo-Islamic world, but in the contemporaneous Indian world as well, especially amongst the Gujarati sea traders. From the letters he realizes that Ben Yiju has a gift for friendship and inspiring loyalty. Still a young man, and perhaps because of a business dispute, Ben Yiju moves to the Malabar coast at some point before 1132. He becomes part of the large expatriate Middle Eastern Muslim Arab and Jewish community there, sharing its taste in fine food and gorgeous clothing, wearing turbans, speaking Arabic, leading a cosmopolitan diasporic life, both Indian and Mediterranean. His friends send him sweets (raisins, nougat, dates) and crystallized sugar (in the Middle Ages it was Egypt that had pioneered large-scale production of cane sugar) to assuage his yearning for Middle Eastern food. He regularly has delivered from the Middle East crockery, soap, goblets and glasses.[15]

From fragments of documents, it appears that Ben Yiju, soon after arriving in Mangalore, obtained Ashu, an Indian slave woman, whom he then publicly freed on 17 October 1132, and whom he also at some stage married. At least, the narrator hastens to follow Goitein's speculation that they married. Ashu (who Goitein also guesses was 'probably beautiful') was, says the narrator, 'the woman who probably bore his children', a boy and girl. The narrator is also intrigued because Ben Yiju chose a wife from the Nair people of the southern part of the Malabar coast rather than a spouse from India's ancient Jewish community of Malabar, known for its devoutness and strictness (though Ashu would 'probably' have converted to Judaism for the marriage). The reason, the narrator feels and hopes, is that Ben Yiju married for 'love' though, he admits, the documents offer 'no certain proof' for this conjecture.[16]

Here *In an Antique Land* prefigures Salman Rushdie's *The Moor's Last Sigh*, the actions of which are ignited by an inter-ethnic, inter-religious relationship in the spice-producing regions of the Malabar coast.

After spending nearly two decades in Mangalore, Ben Yiju returned in 1149 with his two now teenage children to the Middle East, finally settling in Cairo. But disappointment and tragedy shadow his return: his beloved son dies; a long-lost brother swindles him; he appears to break from his lifelong friends because he marries his daughter to another brother's son from Sicily rather than to an old friend's son: 'this child of a Nair woman from the Malabar was wedded in 1156 to her Sicilian cousin, in Fustat.' Abraham Ben Yiju's letters and papers, along with letters and papers of the merchant friends (many living in Aden) who wrote to him, made their way to the Geniza in Old Cairo.[17]

It would appear also that when Ben Yiju returned to the Middle East and, finally, Cairo, Bomma came with him.[18]

Bomma

The narrator of *In an Antique Land*, as he re-imagines and relives this past world, decides to travel to the west coast of India in search of traces of the life led there in the first part of the twelfth century by Ben Yiju and Bomma. From the Geniza documents he has learnt that, curiously for merchants at that time, Ben Yiju does not seem to have travelled back and forth between India and Aden or Egypt, but remained stationary in Mangalore. It was his slave Bomma he trusted to travel and shop for him and transact business with the merchants in the Middle East, handling very large sums of money. Certainly he appears to have become well known to Ben Yiju's friends, for in their letters they frequently append a note adding 'plentiful greetings' to Bomma; sometimes they prefix Bomma's name with the title of Shaikh. In Mangalore the narrator works out that Bomma must have been from the Malabar region, belonging to the Tulunad people, who traditionally worshipped spirit-deities known as Bhutas before and then alongside the classical Hindu mythology of 'the high Sanskritic tradition'.[19]

Here, the narrator feels, is common ground for Ben Yiju and Bomma. Ben Yiju would, he conjectures, have known something of the popular religious practices shared by medieval Arabs and Jews, not only the visiting of saints' tombs but those involving magic and exorcism, practices which are the subversive counter-image of the orthodox religions of the Middle East, as cults like those of Bhuta-shrines are in relation to canonical Hinduism.[20]

But Bomma was a slave. How can the narrator admire a life and times that assumed the natural existence and desirability of slavery?

Slavery

Goitein argues for the distinctiveness of medieval Judeo–Arab Mediterranean slavery.[21] Rulers in the medieval Middle East surrounded themselves with slaves from distant regions, who very often became rulers themselves (most famously, the Mamluks in Egypt); and slaves were recruited for armies. But generally in this world and period slavery denoted a personal service, which could, especially if the master were of high rank or wealthy, carry with it economic advantage and social prestige. Slaves in the eleventh to the thirteenth centuries were, however, expensive and had to be imported from afar, from Nubia, Europe, India. Their high value protected them, and in addition the three monotheistic religions made humanitarian laws and urged various admonitions in their favour. Goitein notes that reports in the Geniza records are few of slaves running away from their masters, perhaps because they became so much part of families. Slaves were baptized into Judaism, and the great Maimonides ruled that slaves, once they had accepted baptism, were members of the covenant of Israel. The acquisition of a male slave was, says Goitein, an affair of note, a man being congratulated almost as if a new son had been born. In general, male slaves belonged to the world of commerce and finance. The slave was deployed in a position of great trust, managing the affairs of his master, travelling with him or on his behalf; the slave who was a business agent was an important merchant in his own right, and could do business on his own account. In the India trade especially, the local agents/ slaves were indispensable. The Geniza records indicate that male slaves were often freed, the act of manumission occurring before a Jewish court; it converted the slave into someone with all the religious duties of a Jew, and he could also then marry a Jewish wife. There were no legal inhibitions or discriminations against emancipated slaves.

In every prosperous family, Goitein notes, slave girls were to be found as domestic help and nurses of children. Mothers were usually sold together with their children, and separation of mothers and children was illegal. A female slave had legal rights and according to the Geniza records made active use of them. There was often a strong attachment between the slave girl and the family. Slave girls were greeted in family letters and they sent greetings to the relatives of their masters.

In terms of eros, religious differences mattered. In medieval Islam, a female slave was at the disposal of her master, a situation which in a polygamous society had advantages for the family over marriage with free wives enjoying equal rights. For the minorities it was different. Christianity and Judaism disapproved of sexual relations outside marriage; Judaism in particular counted it a great sin, punishable even by excommunication. Yet, says Goitein, it was understandable that the habits of the majority affected Christians and Jews as well. The Middle Eastern society revealed in the Geniza documents could not rival the situation of the Jews in Spain during the thirteenth century, when slave concubinage became, Goitein sternly notes, 'a blatant social evil'. But it did occur in the Classical Geniza world to the degree that Maimonides decided in several cases that a young Jewish man could emancipate the slave girl he loved and marry her. As Goitein says, Maimonides here relied on a daring maxim of the ancient sages: 'Pay regard to God by disregarding his law.'

The narrator of *In an Antique Land* writes of master–slave relations in the practical understanding spirit of Maimonides and Goitein. Abraham Ben Yiju was to the end of his life closely attached to his trusted business agent Bomma; and, paying heed to God by disregarding his law, he purchased and manumitted and married his female slave Ashu the beautiful Nair.

European colonialism

What happened to this trading seafaring adventurous world that was so inclusive, stretching from Moorish Spain to India?

Janet Abu-Lughod, arguing against internal interpretations of the development of Europe, suggests that in medieval times Europe globalized its economy precisely by joining already existing global economies, the Geniza world evoked by Goitein, a world system that had many overlapping centres, dominated neither by the Middle East nor by India nor by China.

> Before Europe became *one* of the world-economies in the twelfth and thirteenth centuries, when it joined the long distance trade system that stretched through the Mediterranean into the Red Sea and Persian Gulf and on into the Indian Ocean and through the Strait of Malacca to reach China, there were numerous preexistent world-economies. Without them, when Europe gradually 'reached out', it would have grasped empty space rather than riches.[22]

Europe came late, very late, to the international networks of trade and exchange already long established in the Islamic world, and for a lengthy period, Abu-Lughod notes, it was but a minor player, at a 'relatively primitive level' of development, but a player that had everything to gain from the association. The Italian merchants, for example, borrowed existing mechanisms of money and credit from their Muslim counterparts in the Middle East who had been using them for centuries. Credit instruments were highly developed in the Middle East and China long before they became critical to business transactions in Western Europe. So profiting from what had already long existed, Europe would by the sixteenth century gain world hegemony in trade, commerce and industry. Europe, Abu-Lughod writes, reshaped the pre-existing multi-centred world economy to its own ends, creating the conditions for its own domination.[23]

In terms of the medieval Indian Ocean, unowned by any power, colonizing Europe, in particular Portugal, ended that historical achievement, quickly and brutally. Vasco da Gama landed on the west coast of India on 17 May 1498. Two years later a Portuguese fleet arrived on the Malabar coast, demanded that the Hindu ruler of Calicut expel all Muslims, and then bombarded the city-state for two days. Another year on and Vasco da Gama returned with a much larger fleet. *In an Antique Land* observes that in all the centuries when trade and contact between India and East Africa and southern Arabia and the Middle East flourished, no state or king or ruling power had ever tried to control the Indian Ocean by force of arms, in part because, so speculates the narrator, the influential Gujarati traders were pacifist in their beliefs and customs.[24]

In the late fifteenth/early sixteenth century, the Europeans came, saw, destroyed utterly.

My tattoo

In an Antique Land is in part a scholarly romance with the work of Shlomo Dov Goitein, acting on a desire to further Goitein's own desire to research into the Geniza world's flourishing India trade and connections.[25] *In an Antique Land* is a homage to a master of knowledge: Goitein as a contemporary Moses Maimonides.

In an Antique Land also enacts a utopian romance between the narrator, a diasporic Indian Western-trained anthropologist, writer and traveller, and the cosmopolitanism and plurality, the lack of exclusion, of Ben Yiju and Bomma's world, this lost world that is so remarkable in its multiplying differences. The narrator romances the characters he has created: he also is Ben Yiju the scholar-merchant-traveller; he too is Bomma; he too falls in love with Ashu. He is a One who makes himself Many. But his utopian wish to recover that world, to imagine it as 'in some tiny measure, still retrievable', is shadowed by the dystopian fear it has been lost to him as an Indian and Westerner forever – lost in that dismal symbolic moment when he was not permitted to visit the shrine of the Jewish–Muslim saint in Egypt.[26]

I share that romance and utopian hope and dystopian fear that has also received expression in what we might call an anti-Zionist, post-Zionist, literature, infused by passions and intensities that inspire, I think, Ella Shohat's essay on *In an Antique Land* and her other striking essays on the relation of Zionism to Sephardi and Oriental Jews.[27] Such passions and intensities also inspire the evocations in a book I treasure, Ammiel Alcalay's *After Jews and Arabs: Remaking Levantine Culture* (1993), of the rich cultural history of Oriental and Sephardi Jews in the rich cultural history of the Arab world.

One way I geniza-quest (may I turn *geniza* into a verb?) is through genealogy, to investigate my mother's stories when I was growing up that we were descended from Portuguese Jews. My dream/hope/fantasy delusion is that my ancestry may reveal Sephardi as well as Ashkenazi descent, so that I can connect myself, at least in imagination and fancy, to the long Sephardic history that goes back through English and Dutch and Portuguese history to Moorish Spain (before the 1492 expulsion of the Sephardi Jews) to the medieval Judeo–Arab–Indian Geniza world.

When I told a few people in the middle of 1997 that I was determined to acquire a tattoo, my friends were immediately concerned, mainly as to my sanity; they needed to be reassured, more than once, on the e-mail. They demanded to know reasons and were also, dare I say, oddly excited in their curiosity, their urgency of interest. I asked the tattooist (in my view, Australia's finest, a Canberra artist with the professional name of eX de Medici) to create an androgynous figure, of head and shoulders and drawn-back cloak. eX suggested that thinning the lips on the sculpted face would help it look androgynous. I also asked eX to make the tattoo appear vaguely Oriental, so that he/she might signify the phantasmal figure of my desire, a biblical ancestor, or a Sephardi–Spanish–Portuguese ancestor, or a Geniza ancestor. Sometimes I thought of Tiresias in T. S. Eliot's *The Waste Land*, the blind seer foretelling nothing in the dead land of modernity. The tattoo is the fantastical, illusory *doppelgänger* that corresponds to the patient work of my research assistant's genealogy. It is the imaginary flight and site (looking far too much like an extra in a Hollywood biblical movie) of that which is me and not me, an other on my skin; a futile attempt to connect to the Geniza world where identity, as the narrator of *In an Antique Land* found to his continual discomfort, was so much written on the body.

Of course, my fantasy's one success has been to create considerable mirth. One friend locked me in her university office and demanded I take my shirt off immediately so she could see it. I fled. Others have looked and whispered amongst themselves that it's not androgynous at all but obviously female. The implication is that, for all my fluent pro-feminism and anti-Orientalism, I had banally repeated a common or garden male Orientalist gesture.

They're probably right. The Veiled Stranger on my shoulder is my absurd doubling of *In an Antique Land*'s vision of Abraham Ben Yiju's twelfth-century Ashu.

I feel a strange affinity here with an anonymous French criminal in the nineteenth century (when in Europe the tattoo was considered a sign of the low, degenerate and pathological) who had tattooed on his body the following eloquent cry to history: 'Le passé m'a trompé, le présent me tourmente, l'avenir m'épouvante' (The past has deceived me, the present torments me, the future terrifies me). [28]

The tattooed cook

Yet another way I geniza-quest is via food. For decades now I have been an enthusiastic amateur cook, drawn to cuisines as distant as possible, so it has always turned out, from an inherited English food culture. I have absorbed myself in cooking Italian, Indian, Singaporean (my treasured copy of Wendy Hutton's *Singapore Food* has telltale food stains all over favoured pages), Malaysian, Indonesian and, more recently, Thai recipes, and searching for the spices and vegetables and condiments necessary: ground coriander, cumin, ginger, paprika, turmeric, cayenne pepper, cardamom, cloves, cinnamon sticks, whole nutmeg; fresh ginger and coriander (including roots), galangal, ginger, tamarind, blachan, lime leaves, kaffir limes, lemon grass; coconut milk, soy sauce, oyster sauce, fish sauce, yoghurt; various long-grain rices, also rice in noodle form. I love cooking with aubergine and okra.[29] At some stage I realize I have become addicted to chillis, I'm a chillihead. In reading cookbooks and working on my cooking, what I feel has become clear is that Persian food, so subtle and delicate, is a kind of ur-cuisine, that historically spread and enriched and interacted with cuisines from Moorish Spain and Morocco to Venice and the eastern Mediterranean, to India and beyond in the East. In this vast cuisinary crescent, India and South-East Asia remain connected to the Mediterranean, past and present.[30]

In the last few years I have increasingly absorbed myself in exploring the historical adventure that is Mediterranean cuisine. A great find has been Barbara Santich's *The Original Mediterranean Cuisine: Medieval Recipes for Today*, which sees the Mediterranean as an intricate continuum in space and time that connects North Africa and southern Europe, from Morocco and Spain to the Levant, an always interrelated mutually influencing cuisinary area. I turn with delight the pages of Jeanette Nance Nordio's *Taste of Venice: Traditional Venetian Cooking*, where so many recipes blend Italian and Middle Eastern ingredients and styles. I try my hand at North African food, absorbing myself in Paula Wolfert's *Good Food from Morocco*. I've added to my kitchen stores pomegranate syrup, sumac, preserved lemons, pickled turnips, rose water, orange water; I seek out high-quality oranges in order to make Moroccan orange salads.[31]

I acquire with great pleasure Claudia Roden's *The Book of Jewish Food: An Odyssey from Samarkand and Vilna to the Present Day* (1997). I begin by reading her very interesting and moving introduction, concerning her upbringing in a Sephardi family in Egypt (via Aleppo and Istanbul), their having to leave in 1956, and, in London, their diasporic nostalgic continuous re-imagining of and yearning for their lost Cairene world: 'At 16 Woodstock Road, it seemed that we had never left Cairo.... The smell of sizzling garlic and crushed coriander seeds in the kitchen, or of rose water in a pudding, and my mother's daily meals, reinforced the feeling.' In London she would share passionate memories with her parents about their life in Egypt: 'The Egypt I knew was a French-speaking cosmopolitan Mediterranean country', where the 'Jewish community had a happy and important place in the mosaic of minorities — which included Copts, Armenians, Syrian Christians, Maltese, Greeks and Italians, as well as British and French expatriates — living amongst the Muslim majority.'[32]

Yet when later in her introduction I read that the cooking of the Jewish communities in India came as a 'surprise' to her, I feel a little surprised.[33] It seems to confirm the narrator's feeling in *In an Antique Land* that India had dropped out of Middle Eastern awareness as part of its intimately connected worlds.

Then I race to the Sephardi section, finding myself drawn to those recipes that share maximum spiciness with non-Jewish Middle Eastern and North African and Indian dishes. The first dish I try is Kofta à la sauce tomate, but as I prepare it I feel that the spices recommended — cinnamon and allspice — are not piquant enough. So I look at the regional variations *The Book of Jewish Food* lists, and enthusiastically add fresh coriander and garlic (Tunisian), ground ginger, turmeric, garam masala and chilli powder (Indian Baghdadi), and also insert pine nuts into each meatball (Syrian). Roden notes that in Salonika they sometimes added honey instead of sugar to the tomato sauce, so I do this as well because it reminds me of Moroccan tagine sauces. I also hasten to the Sephardi vegetable section: 'The Sephardim have a reputation as vegetable lovers even by Mediterranean standards. . . .' I check out the aubergine and okra dishes, and come across Syrian recipes for both, cooked or dressed with pomegranate syrup and tamarind, and think: I must do these. I also make the wonderful sweet potatoes dish. Wandering around the book (which has a touch of geniza chaos in its presentation), I mark off other recipes I must soon try, like 'Shoulder of lamb with rice stuffing and sour cherry sauce', a Syrian Jewish dish that uses cherries rather than the more familiar apricots.[34]

I read with interest the section beginning 'Aleppo (Syria) was the pearl of the Jewish kitchen', where Roden says that a large proportion of the recipes in her book are Syrian, and most particularly from Aleppo. She recalls the dozen or more Syrian dishes 'we get when we visit our families in Los Angeles, Mexico and Colombia, Paris and Geneva'.[35]

It soon also turns out that my favourite fruit and vegetables shop in Canberra now sells sun-dried cherries, which I hope are similar to those that Claudia Roden mentions were used by Syrian Jews as an alternative to dried apricots, and these dried cherries, soaked and gently simmered in water and lemon juice, have become a new sensuous delight I try out as a sauce not only with lamb but with other dishes.

Lately I've been trying new combinations, for example, grilling aubergine slices and then piling on top of them a Sephardi version of the Italian *salsa verde* that Roden outlines.[36] With hubris, I dream of being the author of a dish 'Grilled aubergine with Sephardi *salsa verde*'. I'm also trying now the arranging on a plate a contrast of sauces. I will make *salsa verde* or aubergines or bell peppers with a lemon, chilli and garlic sauce. I will make a blindingly sweet sauce, like Sephardi versions of *haroset*, a Passover sauce that cooks in wine (as in an Italian recipe Roden details) apples, pears, pine nuts, ground almonds, dates, raisins, prunes, sugar or honey, cinnamon and ground ginger.[37]

The cook is an obsessed figure, suffusing practicality with dreams. As at nights I cut and slice and put in the oil and stir and add and mix and nudge ingredients about, my tattoo looks on, concealing its thoughts. Is it sceptically thinking that every utopian desire is shadowed by its dystopian double, that Utopia and Dystopia are allegorical twins spinning through space and time, clasping and clawing at each other, creating and devouring amidst history's ruins?[38]

Notes

1. S. D. Goitein, *A Mediterranean Society: The Jewish Communities of the Arab World as Portrayed in the Documents of the Cairo Geniza* (Berkeley: University of California Press), vol. I: *Economic Foundations* (1967), p. 142. Cf. Isadore Twersky (ed.), *A Maimonides Reader* (New York: Behrman, 1972), pp. 175–7.
2. Ammiel Alcalay, *After Jews and Arabs: Remaking Levantine Culture* (Minneapolis: University of Minnesota Press, 1993), pp. 130–42; James Clifford, 'Looking for Bomma', *London Review of Books* (24 March 1994), pp. 26–7 and 'Diasporas', *Cultural Anthropology*, 9 (3) (1994), pp. 302–38, reprinted in his *Routes: Travel and Translation in the Late Twentieth Century* (Cambridge, MA: Harvard University Press, 1997), ch.10; Ella Shohat, 'Taboo memories and diasporic visions: Columbus, Palestine and Arab-Jews' in May Joseph and Jennifer Natalya Fink (eds), *Performing Hybridity* (Minneapolis: University of Minnesota Press, 1999), pp. 131–56.
3. Amitav Ghosh, *In an Antique Land* (London: Granta/Penguin, 1994).
4. In *Letters of Medieval Jewish Traders* (Princeton, NJ: Princeton University Press, 1974), Goitein writes that Abraham Ben Yiju is the 'single most important figure of the India papers presented in the Geniza'; Goitein refers to Ben Yiju's Indian slave as Bama (pp. 13, 186, 191).
5. Ghosh, *In an Antique Land*, p. 19.
6. *Ibid.*, pp. 67–8.
7. *Ibid.*, pp. 47–8, 61–2, 126, 171, 203.
8. *Ibid.*, pp. 204.
9. *Ibid.*, pp. 59, 80–95.
10. Shohat, 'Taboo memories and diasporic visions'.
11. Ghosh, *In an Antique Land*, pp. 95, 329, 334, 340.

12. S. D. Goitein, *Jews and Arabs: Their Contacts Through the Ages* (New York: Schocken Books, 1974), pp. 187–89.

13. Ghosh, *In an Antique Land*, p. 263.

14. *Ibid.*, pp. 13, 18–19, 55–6, 279. On Maimonides and the India trade, cf. Goitein, *Letters of Medieval Jewish Traders*, pp. 207–12.

15. Ghosh, *In an Antique Land*, pp. 18–19, 153–8, 158, 161, 267–9, 279. In *Letters of Medieval Jewish Traders* (p. 190, n.14), Goitein notes that wheat was frequently sent to Ben Yiju for religious purposes: 'Grace was said over bread, not over rice' (in southern India the staple food was rice). Cf. Arjun Appadurai, 'How to make a national cuisine: cookbooks in contemporary India', *Comparative Studies of Society and History*, 31 (1) (1988), pp. 10–14, for a brief overview of the question of cuisine in Indian history.

16. Ghosh, *In an Antique Land*, pp. 227–30.

17. *Ibid.*, pp. 34, 54–7, 328.

18. *Ibid.*, p. 349.

19. *Ibid.*, pp. 16, 18, 159, 249–56, 266. Concerning greetings to Bomma, cf. Goitein, *Letters of Medieval Jewish Traders*, pp. 13, 191.

20. Ghosh, *In an Antique Land*, p. 263.

21. Goitein, *A Mediterranean Society*, vol. I, pp. 130–47.

22. Janet L. Abu-Lughod, *Before European Hegemony: The World System A.D. 1250–1350* (New York: Oxford University Press, 1989), p. 12; also ch. 7. Cf. James Walvin, *Fruits of Empire: Exotic Produce and British Taste, 1660–1800* (London: Macmillan, 1997), pp. 2–4.

23. Abu-Lughod, *Before European Hegemony*, pp. 6, 11–12, 15–16, 33. See also Stuart Hall, 'When was "the post-colonial"? Thinking at the limit' in Iain Chambers and Lidia Curti (eds), *The Post-Colonial Question* (London: Routledge, 1996), pp. 249–51; and Clifford, 'Diasporas' in *Routes*, p. 276.

24. Ghosh, *In an Antique Land*, p. 287.

25. *Ibid.*, p. 100.

26. *Ibid.*, p. 237. For the importance of allegory in *In an Antique Land*, see Robert Dixon, '"Travelling in the West": the writing of Amitav Ghosh', *Journal of Commonwealth Literature*, XXXI (1) (1996), pp. 15–23.

27. See Ella Shohat, 'Staging the Quincentenary: the Middle East and the Americas', *Third Text*, 21 (1992–93), pp. 95–105, and 'Sephardim in Israel: Zionism from the standpoint of its Jewish victims', *Social Text*, 19/20 (1988), pp. 1–35, reprinted in Anne McClintock, Aamir Mufti and Ella Shohat (eds), *Dangerous Liaisons: Gender, Nation, and Postcolonial Perspectives* (Minneapolis: University of Minnesota Press, 1997).

28. Jane Caplan, '"Speaking Scars": the tattoo in popular practice and medico-legal debate in nineteenth-century Europe', *History Workshop Journal*, 44 (1997), p. 132.

29. After I had finished the manuscript of this book, I learnt from an e-mail correspondent of Victor Perera's *The Cross and the Pear Tree: A Sephardic Journey* (New York: Alfred A. Knopf, 1995). The reader can imagine my feelings when I read in the opening paragraph of the introduction that Perera considers okra and eggplant to be 'detestable vegetables'. I'm afraid my interest in this autobiographical and genealogical work, in some ways similar in quest to mine, never quite recovered.

30.   Cf. Jack Goody, *Cooking, Cuisine and Class* (Cambridge, UK: Cambridge University Press, 1982), p. 127: 'The cuisine of the Middle East derives from that of Mesopotamia, of Assyria and later from that of the Persian Empire, dating from 550 B.C., the earliest empire to envelop the whole region.' I might list here some of the books that feature in my working library, my live archive, of cookbooks: Arto der Haroutunian, *The Barbecue Cookbook* (London: Pan, 1986); Wendy Hutton, *Singapore Food* (Sydney: Ure Smith, 1979); Madhur Jaffrey, *Madhur Jaffrey's Indian Cookery* (London: BBC, 1982) and *Eastern Vegetarian Cooking* (1981; London: Arrow, 1990); Sisamon Kongpan, *The Best of Thai Dishes* (Bangkok: Sangdad, 1991); Aglaia Kremezi, *Mediterranean Hot: Spicy Dishes from Southern Italy, Greece, Turkey and North Africa* (New York: Aristan, 1996).

31.   Jeannette Nance Nordio, *Taste of Venice* (London: Webb and Bower, 1988); Paula Wolfert, *Good Food from Morocco* (1973; rev. edn London: John Murray, 1989).

32.   Claudia Roden, *The Book of Jewish Food* (London: Viking, 1997), p. 3.

33.   Roden, *The Book of Jewish Food*, p. 12.

34.   *Ibid.*, pp. 336–7, 349–50, 436, 442, 446.

35.   *Ibid.*, pp. 485–90. Cf. Goody, *Cooking, Cuisine and Class*, pp. 129–32.

36.   *Ibid.*, p. 334.

37.   *Ibid.*, pp. 532–3.

38.   For an allegorical reading of history as ruins see Walter Benjamin, *The Origin of German Tragic Drama*, trans. John Osborne (1928; London: Verso, 1996), pp. 176–8. See also Beatrice Hanssen, *Walter Benjamin's Other History: Of Stones, Animals, Human Beings, and Angels* (Los Angeles: University of California Press, 1998), esp. Part I.

2

Genealogy and diasporic memory: searching my family tree

... what the historians call a 'fragment' — a weaver's diary, a collection of poems by an unknown poet (and to these we might add all those literatures of India that Macaulay condemned, creation myths and women's songs, family genealogies, and local traditions of history) — is of central importance in ... thinking other histories ...

> Gyanendra Pandey, 'In defense of the fragment ...'[1]

While writing this book, I asked my mother-in-law Barbara Curthoys, who lives in Manly in Sydney and whom I knew to be a dedicated genealogist, to embark on a genealogical adventure for me.[2] It then occurred to me, when she had provisionally completed the family tree, to ask her to write about how she came to do the genealogy and to evoke the experience of doing it.

The genealogist: Barbara Curthoys' story

My son-in-law is writing a book — it is one of many, but this time he wants to include information about his ancestors.

'Would you have time to trace my family tree?', he asks.

For a number of years now I have been an avid family researcher. Once a week I join the army of amateur genealogists invading the NSW state public library, opposite Sydney's Botanic Gardens. Gradually we are taking over the place. We spend hours gazing at microfiche until the print becomes a blur, or ploughing through rolls of microfilm until our necks ache, thrilled when we find a family connection. Some people wonder why we bother, but I explain it this way.

In exploring our family tree we immerse ourselves in history and in the process we transform it and make it personal. This is our history. This is part of our identity. We can never know how our ancestors lived, but we can imagine it and give it life. When I find my own great-grandmother's death certificate and realize that she had fourteen children, twelve of whom lived, I empathize with her and I wonder how she coped. When I see pictures of the sailing ships on which my great-great-grandparents travelled to South Australia in 1838, I marvel at their stoicism. When scanning through nineteenth-century death certificate files and I see an Aboriginal death entered as 'native' with no name, I am appalled. Starkly, the harsh lives of my ancestors are juxtaposed with the dispossession of those who were here before us. Even so, none of this has prepared me for the Jewish genealogical journey I am about to take.

'My book involves the poetics of the Jewish diaspora in the fifteenth and sixteenth centuries. It relates to Dutch and Portuguese Jewish history and particularly to Sephardi Jewry', John continues. 'My mother's family came to Australia from London's East End in the 1920s. I believe one of her ancestors may have come from Holland. If this is so, I am interested to know whether my antecedents were of Sephardi or Ashkenazi origin.'

John may have expected a knowledgeable reply, but as the only Ashkenazi I had ever heard of was Vladimir Ashkenazi the famous Russian pianist, and as I had never heard the word Sephardi, I merely nod my head and tell him I'd like to do it.

John sends me the first two draft chapters of his book in order to better understand the connection between tracing his family tree and what he is writing. The subject is Moorish Spain, which ended in 1492, and its consequences for the Jews who had been living there. These are the Sephardim.

Further reading reveals that after the expulsion of Jews from Spain, Amsterdam in the seventeenth century became significant for the Sephardi Jewish diaspora as a whole. Liberal Holland of this period also attracted numbers of German and East European Jews, the Ashkenazim. Gradually in the eighteenth century their power and influence in Amsterdam surpassed that of the Sephardim.[3] If any of John's ancestors came from Holland I suspect that John would prefer that their origins were Sephardi, but, pragmatically, I say to myself 'Sephardi or Ashkenazi? Facts are facts and I will follow where the genealogical path takes me.'

His uncles and aunts dredge their memories in order to help and I have the details of John's birth certificate. The information is meagre; so I approach the Jewish Genealogical Society. They happen to be running an all-day seminar, giving out information and help to those who wish to trace their Jewish ancestors, and they invite me to attend. Though I have never considered myself as Jewish, my mother once suggested that I may have had a great-grandmother who was Jewish, so I can join the society, and my journey begins.

At the library in Lindfield in Sydney where the Genealogical Society meets every fourth Sunday I am overwhelmed by their kindliness and desire to help. I listen to their stories. On the table in front of me is a book of names. It is several inches thick and in it are the names of thousands of Dutch Jews who were killed by the Nazis during the Second World War. Maybe some of these victims were relatives of John. There are other books with similar lists on the shelves. I am told of a List of Names in America where the names of all those who perished in the Holocaust are recorded, even if the survivors can recall only the first name. It is a cry from millions of lost souls saying 'We were here. We lived. Don't forget us.'

However, my search does not begin in Holland. It begins in London. Elsie Levy, John's mother, was born in Bow in the East End. Her parents were Philip and Rose Levy. She had two younger brothers and the family lived in Alfred Street, which was later destroyed in the London Blitz.

At Rumsey Hall, Kent Street, at the Rocks, near Sydney's beautiful harbour, where the Society of Australian Genealogists houses its overseas collection, Terry Newman from the Jewish Genealogical Society is giving a lecture on ways to trace Jewish forebears in London. From the Quay, I trudge up the hill through the Argyle Cut in order to hear it because the location of relevant sources, the translation of common Hebrew words (I learn Sepharad is Spain in Hebrew) and a brief history of the Jews in London are the contents of his talk. He believes that Levys, named after one of the twelve tribes of Israel, are predominantly Ashkenazi.

When and how did Jews arrive in London? Expelled from England in 1290, it was during the Elizabethan era that Jews trickled back. Cromwell was petitioned by the Portuguese Dutch Jews and in 1656 he permitted the Sephardic Crypto-Jews freedom of worship. In 1701 the Bevis Marks Synagogue was built by London's Sephardi community. The Sephardi community flourished, but by the end of the eighteenth century the more recent Ashkenazi immigrants from Central and Eastern Europe became more numerous and influential. [4]

I concentrate on the Levy line as I have very little information on Elsie Levy's mother Rose, at the beginning not even her single name. Through birth, death and marriage certificates and the British censuses I discover Elsie's grandparents Abraham and Elsie Levy and the names of their children. In the Ketuboth of Bevis Marks in the Lindfield Library of the Jewish Genealogical Society there is a Ketubah (marriage contract) for an Elizabeth Levy and an Isaac Anidjar Romain, which took place in the Dutch Portuguese Synagogue in London in 1891. This looks promising. She is Philip's elder sister and John's great-aunt. This is a Sephardic connection but as I trace the Levy paternal line back to the late eighteenth century, the ancestors appear to be predominantly Ashkenazi.

A centre of research which proves invaluable is the Greenwich Family Library attached to the Church of Jesus Christ of Latter-day Saints. Why here? The Church encourages research into one's ancestors because it believes that life is eternal and that as a result families will come together after death. The library has microfilm of all the British censuses from 1841 until 1891, invaluable for tracing the entire family, the street in which they lived, occupations, and country of origin. In addition the Church has microfilmed millions of names from most countries of the world and placed them in the International Genealogical Index, a wonderful tool for genealogists. Many libraries have this Index on microfiche, but in Sydney and NSW the Greenwich Family Library is one of the few to have the full British censuses.

The Internet opens up the World Wide Web of Jewry for me, a labyrinth of many diasporas. On the Jewishgen Digest, hundreds of genealogists interested in their Jewish heritage exchange information and assist each other with their family trees. Subscribers from America, England, Holland, France, Poland, Lithuania, Ukraine, Argentina, Brazil, New Zealand, Australia, South Africa, Israel, Morocco, Russia and many more participate, offering their own slice of expertise without stint. Topics cover Hebrew, Yiddish and Ladino (Judeo-Spanish language) names, Jewish occupations in past centuries, Jewish customs, obscure shtetls not readily found on maps, the addresses of synagogues and Jewish genealogical societies in many countries. Home pages proliferate: Jeffrey Maynard's London base, Dutch Jewish Genealogy, and Sephardic Genealogy among many others. A world hitherto unknown to me is available daily, whenever I connect to the Internet.

Still tracing the Levy line, it is at Mandelbaum House, Sydney, the home of the Australian Jewish Historical Society, that I really hit gold. Civil registrations began in England in 1837. For births, deaths and marriages before that time it is necessary to rely chiefly on synagogue records, which the Historical Society has on microfilm. One afternoon, on these films I find Elsie Levy's great-grandparents' marriage and also that of her great-great-grandparents, a leap of two generations. Unfortunately for me many of the records are written in Hebrew. I call on the aid of Helen Bersten, the librarian, and she can read some of the handwritten words, but not all. Finally it is Derek Wolfson, the father of my grandson's best friend, who translates the entire record. The Hebrew name of Daniel Levy, Elsie Levy's great-great-grandfather, was Gedalia ben Mordechai the Levite. In 1821 he married Hannah Davis, the daughter of Abraham Davis.

Feeling triumphant with this finding, it is time to leave the Levys and begin the search for Elsie Levy's maternal antecedents. Rose Levy's single name as shown on her death certificate is Rose Simmons. However, in tracing her birth certificate I am faced with conflicting accounts of her age. The ages given on the marriage and death certificates differ and family members believe she was born several years later than the date on either certificate. There are many Rose Simmonses recorded on the Catherine House Index in the 1890s, the decade in which she was born. So, honing my detective instincts, I approach the problem from a different angle.

I start with the fact that I know her occupation, and the name of her father, Lewis Simmons, and his occupation. In London, prior to the family's emigration to Australia, Rose Simmons was a skilled 'cigar-maker'. After further recollection, members of the family believe that it is her father, also a cigar-maker, who came from Holland. Further reading reveals that in the seventeenth and eighteenth centuries the Sephardi-owned tobacco spinning and blending workshops of Amsterdam provided work for poor Sephardi as well as Ashkenazi Jews. So cigar-making is a Dutch trade.[5]

Following this thread, the microfilm at Mandelbaum House reveals a Lewis Simmons and Esther Jacobs, married in 1878, both cigar-makers. Later I find that in 1892 their third child was Rose. It seems very likely that I have the right family and that somewhere along the line either Lewis Simmons or one of his ancestors may have emigrated from Holland. I feel sure I am on the right track.

John has finished his book and wants my story; so I leave it here. However, the search to find his antecedents as far back as I can reach will continue. Similarly, with the genealogy of my own Australian family, I will continue to follow the English, Welsh, Danish and Scottish pathways which led to my birth. With the marriage of John to my daughter Ann, all these winding criss-cross trails of all our diasporas meet. What a vast spread of history lies behind this simple fact.

The genealogy

This is the record of John's mother Elsie Levy's ancestors as traced by Barbara Curthoys on behalf of John Docker in 1997, 1998, 1999 and into 2000. Levy and Simmons relations were researched and the search continues.[6]

First generation

Elsie Levy (Philip 2, Abraham 3, Mark 4, Daniel 5, Mordechai the Levite 6), daughter of Philip Levy and Rose Simmons, was born in 23 Alfred Street, Bow, London, 25 September 1912. She married Ted Docker in Bondi, Sydney, 1941. Elsie died 4 August 1988 in Bondi.

Elsie Levy arrived in Australia from London with her parents and brothers on 26 October 1926 in the ship SS *Herminius*. Philip Levy, her father, gave his occupation as 'saddle maker'. He was 50 years of age. Rose Levy put her age (inaccurately) as 38 years, though her birthdate was 1882. Elsie was 14 and her two brothers Lewis and Jerome were 12 and 10 respectively. They were to be met by one of Philip Levy's brothers when they arrived but he failed to appear. They were in very straitened circumstances as a result and initially were forced to receive help from charity. Eventually Philip worked as a taxi driver though he was a mechanical engineer by trade. Rose's occupation was cigar-making but she had to work as a cleaner. When she was old enough Elsie took a job in the textile trade to help support the family.

Elsie Levy and Ted Docker had the following children:

Lorraine Docker, born Bondi 1941
Julie Docker, born Bondi 1944
John Edward Docker, born Bondi Junction 8 October 1945

Second generation

Philip Levy (Abraham 3, Mark 4, Daniel 5, Mordechai the Levite 6) was born in 15 Duke Street, Aldgate, 3 August 1876. Philip died 25 December 1968 in Bondi at 92 years of age.[7]

He married Rose Simmons in East London Synagogue, Mile End Old Town, London, 10 December 1911.[8] His father, Abraham Levy, was deceased. Rose Simmons's father, Lewis, was present. Occupations were listed as mechanical engineer for Philip and cigar-maker for Rose (Miss Rosa). Her father Lewis was also a cigar-maker. Philip's Hebrew name was Pinchas. One brother was mentioned, Gershon. The witnesses were E. H. Kloot and E. Staal. Joseph F. Stern was minister and secretary. On the Jewish calendar the date of marriage was Monday 19 Nisan 5672. According to the certificate obtained from the United Synagogue, London, a witness was Aron Goldman, Stepney Green.

Philip Levy and Rose Simmons had the following children:

Elsie Levy
Lewis Levy, born 23 Alfred Street, Bow, London, 1914
Jerome Abraham, born 23 Alfred Street, Bow, London, 8 January 1916

Rose Simmons (Lewis 3, Solomon 4) was born in 82 Mile End Road, London, 28 December 1882. It was difficult to trace Rose Simmons's birth certificate because there was a great deal of confusion about her birth year. The marriage certificate (1911) stated her age as 27. The death certificate (1963) stated her age as 77. A family member thought she was 72 when she died. Eventually her birthdate was found to be 28 December 1882 and her birthplace was 82 Mile End Old Town Eastern, County of Middlesex.

Rose died 15 May 1963, 42 O'Brien Street, Bondi, at 81 years of age.

Third generation

Abraham Levy (Mark 4, Daniel 5, Mordechai the Levite 6) was born in 7 Harrow Alley, Houndsditch, London, 7 March 1850.[9]

He married Elsie Marks in Zetland Hall, Mansell Street, St Mary's, Whitechapel, 21 October 1869.[10] Zetland Hall is a Jewish synagogue, later incorporated in the Federation of Synagogues. Mansell Street is one of four streets surrounding Goodman's Fields, which is heavily Jewish, including English, German and a large number of Dutch Jews. (Information from Geoffrey Maynard, compiler of London Jews Database on the Internet.)

Both Abraham and Elsie lived at 10 Harrow Alley, Houndsditch, at the time of their marriage. Abraham's father was Mark Levy (clothier) and Elsie's father was Lewis Marks (clothes dealer). The witnesses were Godfrey Levy (Abraham's elder brother) and Louis Isaacs. The rabbi conducting the service was Moses Keitner.

1881 British census: Abraham Levy's family lived at 4 Castle Street, St Botolph, County of Middlesex
Abraham Levy (head), age 31, occupation: clothier
Elsie Levy (wife), age 30
Lizey Levy (daughter), age 10
Philip (son), aged 4
Mark Isaac (son), age 1
Martha Batts (boarder), stay-maker
Two servants: Louise Grocock and Emai Termer, age 22

1891 British census: Abraham Levy's family lived at 118 Houndsditch Street, Central London (Aldgate Municipal Ward)
Abraham Levy (head), age 41, occupation: clothier
Elsie Levy (wife), age 40, occupation: clothier
Elizabeth Dawn (daughter), age 19. (On 18 August 1891 she married Isaac Anidjar Romain)
Godfrey (son), age 16, occupation: tailor's apprentice

No Philip. He must have been sleeping elsewhere that night. He would have
   been 14 at the time of the census
Mark (son), age 11
Joseph (son), age 8
Luis L. (son), age 6
Beatrice Dawn (daughter), age 3
Gertrude (daughter), age 2
There were two servants: Emma Lauer, age 30, and Ada Cox, age 24

In 1891 Abraham Levy is registered as a donor for the Society for Relieving
the Aged Needy (Geoffrey Maynard's database: 1891 annual report of the
Society).

Elsie Marks' birthdate and therefore the identity of both her parents are not
yet known; her father was Lewis Marks.

Rose Levy's father Lewis Simmons married Esther Jacobs in Bethnal Green,
St Matthews, 28 August 1878.[11] Lewis Simmons (the spelling of the name
varies from Simons to Simmons to Simmonds) was 25 at the time of his
marriage. His profession was that of gentleman, as stated on his marriage
certificate. Esther Jacobs was 22 and her father was Lewis Jacobs, commission
agent. They were married in the presence of Marcus Hart and Louis Isaacs.
Moses Keizer was the minister and secretary of the synagogue. In the 1881
census both Lewis and Esther gave their occupations as cigar-makers.

In 1891 Lewis and Esther were living at 10 Cottage Court, Old Town
Eastern, Mile End. Their family was recorded in the 1891 British census.

Lewis Simmons, head, age unclear, occupation: cigar maker; born Spitalfields
Esther Simmons, wife, age 31, born Whitechapel
Priscilla (daughter), age 11, born Mile End
Rose (daughter), age 11, born Mile End
Aaron (son), age 7, born Mile End
Solomon (son), age 5, born Mile End
Sarah (daughter), age 3, born Mile End
Abigail (daughter), age 17 months, born Mile End
Another daughter, Rachel, does not appear in the 1891 census, but had been
   listed in the 1881 census. She may have been away that night; or she may
   have died.

Esther was 22 in 1878 when she married, according to the certificate; in
1891 she was listed as 31; there is an age discrepancy here. She was born in 28
Duke Street, Aldgate, between 1855 and 1859. Her birthdate has not been
found.

Lewis Simmons died on 31 May 1922 at 2 Argyle Road, Mile End Old Town, North Eastern.

Lewis Simmons's father was Solomon Simmons. There are several Solomon Simmonses, each of which could be correct; at this stage, none of these will be entered on the family tree chart.

Fourth generation

Mark Levy (Daniel 5, Mordechai the Levite 6) was born in Aldgate approximately 1825. Mark died 11 February 1873 in Aldgate.

He married Sarah Lazarus in 3 Court Street, Whitechapel, 11 February 1846.[12] Mark Levy was a general dealer. He died of gangrene of the foot 11 February 1873. His family announced his death in the Jewish press, which was not a very common thing to do in those days. He also became a freeman of the City of London on 17 October 1856. This was the first month in which the freedom could be obtained by anyone on the City's parliamentary register of voters.

Mark Levy and Sarah Lazarus had the following children:

Godfrey Levy, died 9 January 1873 in Aldgate, at 26 years of age. (He was married to Esther Green)
Abraham Levy
Esther Levy
Isaac Levy, born Aldgate 8 February 1857. (He married Sarah Van Leer in Aldgate, 16 February 1881)
John Jacob Levy, born 20 May 1859; died 5 March 1863 in Aldgate, at 3 years of age
Elizabeth (Dolly) Levy, born in Aldgate 27 September 1860. (She would marry Solomon Ephraim Green in Aldgate)

Fifth generation

Daniel Levy (Mordechai the Levite 6) was born in Aldgate 1782. He married Hannah Davis in Aldgate, 25 November 1821.[13] The bride's name was listed as Hannah, daughter of Abraham. The bridegroom's name was Gedalia, son of Mordechai the Levite (Levy). The names of the witnesses were the Rev. David Werthheim and Mr Shlomo (Solomon) whose second name is unclear. The day of marriage is given as Monday 1 Kislev.

Daniel served in the Navy January 1805 to 31 October 1813. Daniel Levy sailed aboard several ships. He entered the Navy at the age of 23 in January 1805 on the *Circe*. He was discharged 31 October 1813. Some of this time was spent in Gibraltar. He then appears on the *Astrea* from 2 November 1813. Then he was on the *Creole* and then the *Tamar*, where he was paid off 23 March 1816. During this time he was captured. Cathy Martin, one of his descendants, has documents stating this information but they are too faded to make out more. On his discharge papers he is described as being five feet three inches, dark complexion, and 35 years of age (1816). Hannah lived to an old age and spent her widowhood with her son Mark. She was still living with her son as recorded in the 1861 census, aged 90.

Daniel Levy and Hannah Davis had a son, Mark, born approximately 1825.

Sephardi or Ashkenazi? Barbara's conclusions

Elsie Levy's family tree is far from complete. I doubt whether a family researcher is ever satisfied with the products of her research. There are always more ancestors to find, more lines to follow, and each generation expands laterally so that, if the families of each sibling were traced, the search would be endless. In addition, our ancestors — often careless with ages, names and dates as they recorded their births, deaths and marriages — heeded not the needs of modern-day genealogists. Elsie Levy's ancestors are no exception.

The family lines under search have been the Levy, Simmons, Marks, Jacobs and Lazarus families. The most successful of these has been the Levy line.

In the late eighteenth and early nineteenth century European Jews were compelled by the laws of their chosen country to adopt surnames. Before choosing a surname, Elsie Levy's ancestor Daniel Levy, born Aldgate, London, 1782, was named Gedalia ben Mordechai and his wife Hannah was Hannah bat Davis. Family names were often arbitrary. They might be given by the local rabbi, chosen perhaps from one of the tribes of Israel, even though the recipient was not descended from one of the old 'houses'. However, there were a few who were correctly assigned their new surname. In the case of Daniel Levy, 'Levy' is not by chance as his father was referred to as Mordechai Halevi (the Levite) on the Ketubah (marriage contract) of Daniel and Hannah. This indicates that he was descended from the second level of priesthood after the Cohens (Cohanim). [14]

From this evidence it seems that Elsie's lineage on the Levy side dates back to the Jews who migrated to England in the mid-eighteenth century or even earlier, and that they are most likely either of German or East European stock. Dutch origin cannot be ruled out but it appears unlikely. Before 1837, births, deaths and marriages were recorded in the synagogues, and information on

Levy ancestors is kept in the Ashkenazi United Synagogue archives, indication that the Levys were Ashkenazis.

By the middle of the nineteenth century there was an established Ashkenazi community in London living in Houndsditch and the eastern fringe of the City of London, close to Duke's Place where the Great Synagogue was situated. By 1891 Elsie's grandfather Abraham Levy was living in Houndsditch Street, Central London. He would appear to have been a well-to-do merchant, prosperous enough to have two servants and to be able to donate to the poor and needy. When in 1891 his daughter Elizabeth married Isaac Anidjar Romain in the Sephardic Synagogue, Bevis Marks, he was able to make a gift of £50 for their Ketubah, not a mean sum in those days.

The Simmonses were cigar-makers, a prevalent occupation among Dutch Jews. However, there is not enough evidence to show this family came from Holland.

I feel able to conclude that Elsie Levy is a descendant of the Ashkenazi Jews who were well established in London before the middle of the nineteenth century. Further research is necessary to discover the country of origin, prior to settling in London, for each family line. As records prior to 1880 are sketchy and sometimes non-existent this is a difficult task but may not be impossible.

Postscript

In early 1999 Barbara sent me a copy of an article (dated December 1998) written by an English genealogist, Aubrey Jacobus, on Dutch Jews in London. Aubrey Jacobus explains that while he is descended from a Polish immigrant family, his wife's family were of Dutch descent. His research into her ancestry led him into what he feels is the historically neglected world of the vanished 'Dutch' community of the latter half of the nineteenth century which existed in a particular number of streets in Spitalfields, Whitechapel. Immigrants were arriving in this area from Holland, often as young married couples. They were Ashkenazim (a common family name was Polak, indicating their pre-Dutch origin), and they were fleeing not from religious persecution but from economic hardship. By the middle of the nineteenth century the once powerful Dutch empire was in terminal decline while the British empire was expanding. Amsterdam as a financial centre had given way to London, a transition which sparked a bitter and unseemly sectarian struggle between the old Sephardim merchants in Amsterdam and the (in their eyes) upstart Ashkenazi brokers in London. Unfortunately for the new immigrants, their new home in Spitalfields was almost as depressing as the poverty they had left. The Dutch community in England, however, in spite of the expense and difficulties of travel, maintained contact with relations in Holland. This was especially so in practising traditional marriage customs, where weddings should take place in the bride's home town and the prospective bridegroom would leave for Holland and return with his bride.

Aubrey Jacobus writes that the 1871 census lists many of these Ashkenazi Dutch immigrants as 'cigar makers from Amsterdam'.

Jacobus feels that there was a long history of bad relations existing between the Ashkenazi and Sephardi communities in England stretching back before the nineteenth century; there was bitterness against wealthy Sephardim who appeared reluctant to help their poorer brethren. Marriages between Sephardim and Ashkenazim were rare.

By the later nineteenth century Jews who were established in England resented the influx of immigrants from Eastern Europe, which increased the number of Jews in England from 47,000 in 1881 to 150,000 in 1906. The Dutch Jews, as they became absorbed into the English Jewish community, felt disdain for the incoming Eastern European Jews, whom they felt would stimulate an already vigorous anti-semitism as well as increasing competition for jobs and accommodation. The Dutch Jews, says Jacobus, carried with them a tradition of acculturation in Holland (including not speaking Yiddish). They were keen to become 'English' while paradoxically jealously protecting their 'Dutchness' in terms of ancestry, some vocabulary, and cooking. They also had established their own synagogue (in Sandy's Row).

The Polish and Russian immigrants in turn were suspicious of Jews who knew no Yiddish; they suspected the Dutch Jews, whom they called 'Dotchkies', of lacking Judischkeit, an unfounded prejudice. The Eastern European immigrants had often come straight from the enclosed communities of the shtetl, and so had all manner of artisan skills, as cabinet-makers, tailors, shoemakers, and so on. By contrast, the Dutch Jews, having been denied entry to the Dutch guilds, had virtually no skilled tradesmen. They could, however, be butchers, a trade that was permitted to Jews in Holland. In London the poor Dutch immigrants were forced into 'self-employment' of sorts, largely as hawkers, costermongers, peddlers, 'general dealers' or low-grade leather workers, or they worked in the tobacco factories of the East End. Their grandchildren included a large number of taxi drivers, a means of livelihood which continued the feeling of independence given by self-employment.

Jacobus says that he has met many Jews in contemporary England who assume or hope that because their families came from Holland they must have been Sephardic, the word Sephardi still retaining an elitist cachet. He has to advise them otherwise; but he also feels it is important to remind the Anglo-Jewish community of the interesting history of the Ashkenazi Dutch Jews in Victorian London.

Barbara happily effected an e-mail connection for me with Aubrey Jacobus. In an e-mail dated 24 June 1999 he gave me his thoughts on my particular genealogy, suggesting that there seems no way of knowing from present knowledge if some of my family were or were not part of the Victorian Dutch community: 'the problem is that as I mention in my article the chances of tracing the country of origin of Ashkenazi Jews in London in the first decades of the 19c are very slim. The first census 1841 gave no information on the country – also the names in this case Levy, Marks, etc. while they all can be found in Holland belong to that group ... of surnames derived from Jewish patronymics which were found everywhere. There are secondary circumstantial inferences – trade, house location, family lore and families that they married into which strongly favour a Dutch connection – but proof is elusive. Remember too that before 1812 very few Dutch Jews had surnames of any sort.'

The mystery, the inconclusiveness, continues. But as I e-mailed back to Aubrey Jacobus, it is the genealogical journey itself which I find exciting and enchanting.

Notes

1. Gyanendra Pandey, 'In defense of the fragment: writing about Hindu–Muslim riots in India today', _Representations_, 37 (Winter 1992), p. 50.
2. Barbara Curthoys is an author and historian in her own right. See Barbara Curthoys and Audrey McDonald, _More than a Hat and Glove Brigade: The Story of the Union of Australian Women_ (Sydney: Bookpress, 1996); and Barbara Curthoys, 'The Comintern, the CPA, and the impact of Harry Wicks', _The Australian Journal of Politics and History_, 39 (1) (1993), 'The Communist Party of Australia and the Communist International (1927–1929)', _Labour History_, 64 (May 1993) and 'IWD in Newcastle in the 50s and 60s – a personal account', _Labour History_, 66 (May 1994).
3. Jonathan Israel,'The Sephardim of the Netherlands' in Elie Kedourie (ed.), _Spain and the Jews_ (London: Thames and Hudson, 1992), pp. 209–10.
4. Aubrey Newman, 'The Sephardim in England' in Kedourie (ed.), _Spain and the Jews_, pp. 214–18.
5. Israel, 'The Sephardim in the Netherlands', p. 205.
6. Barbara Curthoys created a professional genealogy with tables and numbered generations and detailed footnotes. I retain the original family tree as done by Barbara, copies of which I sent to my uncles Lew and Jock.
7. Death certificate from NSW Registry Office, Sydney, certified by Chevra Kadisha Rabbi D. Kraas.
8. Certificate: Philip was 35 and Rose's age was stated as 27, though she was born in 1882.
9. Birth certificate from London GRO, application no. R00143B; certificate no. BXBY 226819; handwritten no. 9377.

10. Marriage certificate from London GRO, certificate no. MXA 199035; written no. 9090.
11. Marriage certificate: application no. R006230/B; written no. 9748, printed no. MXA 228026.
12. Mark Levy and Sarah Lazarus married at 3 Court Street, Whitechapel, in the parish of St Mary's. This was the home of Sarah Lazarus. Mark Levy lived at 7 Harrow Alley, Aldgate. Sarah's father was Isaac Lazarus, dealer. Certificate no. 195 in the marriage records of the Great Synagogue.
13. Evidence of marriage of Daniel Levy to Hannah Davis, p. 206 of marriage records of the Great Synagogue, London, found on microfilm held at the Jewish Historical Centre, Mandelbaum House, Sydney.
14. Translation of the marriage records by Derek Wolfson.

3

The collision of two worlds: Sir Walter Scott's *Ivanhoe* and Moorish Spain

It behooves the victim for the sake of his religion to escape and flee to the desert and the wilderness, and not to consider separation from family or loss of wealth.

Moses Maimonides, 'Epistle to Yemen', 1172[1]

The Franj had taken the holy city on Friday, the twenty-second day of the month of Sha'ban, in the year of the Hegira 492, or 15 July 1099, after a forty-day siege. The exiles still trembled when they spoke of the fall of the city: they stared into space as though they could still see the fair-haired and heavily armoured warriors spilling through the streets, swords in hand, slaughtering men, women, and children, plundering houses, sacking mosques.

Two days later, when the killing stopped, not a single Muslim was left alive within the city walls. ... The fate of the Jews of Jerusalem was no less atrocious. ... Re-enacting an immemorial rite, the entire community gathered in the main synagogue to pray. The Franj barricaded all the exits and stacked all the bundles of wood they could find in a ring around the building. The temple was then put to the torch. Those who managed to escape were massacred in the neighbouring alleyways. The rest were burned alive.

Amin Maalouf, *The Crusades Through Arab Eyes*[2]

Ivanhoe, entertaining, controversial, provocative and disturbing from the moment it was published in 1819 in the midst of historical turmoil, a novel I find extremely enjoyable and endearing to read, remained throughout the nineteenth century the most popular of Scott's novels, stimulating not only literary lines of influence in England and Europe, but also paintings, dramas and operas.[3] *Ivanhoe* inspired as well a specific American literary history, where the young Jewess Rebecca goes through a series of transformations as the American Other, or Other Americans.[4] In *Ivanhoe* many literary and cultural histories cross and contest: of romance and history, medievalism and modernity, diaspora and nation, the Crusades and the home society, the idea of the European nation-state, Europe and the Orient, Eurocentrism and anti-Eurocentrism, exoticism and Orientalism; the representations in *The Merchant of Venice* of Portia, Shylock, and his daughter Jessica; images of national, ethnic and racial identity, English, European, Andalusian, Jewish, Arab, African; tensions between anti-semitism and philosemitism; Zionism and cosmopolitanism; the significance of the genre of the historical novel itself in the construction, and deconstruction, of national identity; and, not least, the odd, unsettling, deranging erotics of self and other.

The story of Rebecca might also fancifully intersect with the history of Jewish mysticism in the medieval Kabbalah.

Twice in *Ivanhoe* Rebecca the black-tressed dark-eyed daughter of Isaac of York urges flight to Moorish Spain. When she is accused of witchcraft and 'necromancy' in her possession of medical knowledge, she writes to her father in Hebrew of her imminent death: 'do not tarry, old man, in this land of bloodshed and cruelty; but betake thyself to Cordova, where thy brother liveth in safety, under the shadow of the throne, even the throne of Boabdil the Saracen; for less cruel are the cruelties of the Moors unto the race of Jacob, than the cruelties of the Nazarenes of England.' And when at novel's end she has her famous conversation with the 'fair Rowena', now married to Wilfred of Ivanhoe, she similarly tells the surprised Saxon princess that she and her father will leave England: 'I leave it, lady, ere this moon again changes. My father hath a brother high in favour with Mohammed Boabdil, King of Grenada – thither we go, secure of peace and protection, for the payment of such ransom as the Moslem exact from our people.'[5] As commentators have pointed out, here is an outrageous anachronism, for Rebecca and Isaac will have to leave in some kind of time machine to journey three centuries from late twelfth-century England to late fifteenth-century Spain.[6] Boabdil, last sultan of a Moorish Spain facing final defeat on the Iberian peninsula, gave up the keys of Granada early in 1492 to the Catholic monarchs Ferdinand and Isabella, who a few weeks later decreed that all Jews were to be expelled from Spain; the Jews had been expelled from England in 1290.

Why did Rebecca and her father make such a choice, and why does the novel perform such an exercise in fantastical temporality? I would like to explore *Ivanhoe*'s suggestions of another history besides that of England and Western Europe, that of the Judeo–Islamic Mediterranean of which medieval Moorish Spain was such a spectacular part; and to attempt to explain, rather than smile at, this and other anachronisms, especially as the Crusaders, so important in the narrative of *Ivanhoe*, had intervened in the eastern Mediterranean crescent of the Judeo–Islamic world. What I hope to do, in a diasporic reading, is wrench the text away from received and persisting Eurocentric and Anglocentric readings.

Menippean satire

Scott's *Ivanhoe*, in form a historical romance, draws on the extravagant theatricality of contemporary melodrama and Gothic. It may also be entertained as Menippean, drawing on much older novelistic traditions of the kind Mikhail Bakhtin has evoked, of the chronotopes of adventure-time, chance meetings and secret benefactors.[7] In these terms, the novel follows the philosophical idea that a nation-state's progress must be through a unified culture, one land, one religion, one people. The novel tests this idea, this mythos, in forest, castle, tournament, banquet-symposium, through scenes of masking and disguise, abduction, attempted rape, graveyard comedy, false trial. The novel is Menippean in other ways. There is no authoritative or omniscient author, but rather a narrator – purportedly an Englishman, Laurence Templeton – who is self-parodying about his research into manuscripts, especially the so-called Wardour Manuscript, which he admits are imperfect histories of what he refers to as those 'dark ages' of England at the end of the twelfth century, the time of King Richard's return to England from his Crusade and then captivity in Austria.[8] Further, Wilfred of Ivanhoe, the novel's nominal eponymous hero, is a curious hero indeed: for much of the novel he is utterly inactive. Such lack of positive intervention in events may relate to Lukács's definition of the Scott hero as a waverer, a space across which historical forces, embodied in the different characters, contend.[9] Yet the young man's level of inactivity requires, I think, further turning over.

Wilfred of Ivanhoe returns to England from Palestine, where he had been a Crusader with Richard, disguised as a palmer, a poor if holy pilgrim who is permitted a lowly place at the table of his father Cedric the Saxon and of Cedric's ward Rowena of the beautiful blue eyes; neither recognizes him. Wilfred had been banished from his home by Cedric because of the affection he and Rowena have for each other. Cedric still yearns to restore the primacy in the land of the 'manly' Saxon language, inheritance and ways; he hopes Rowena will marry his 'ally and kinsman, Athelstane of Coningsburgh', descended from the last Saxon monarchs of England, though Athelstane is comically 'inanimate in expression, dull-eyed, heavy-browed, inactive and sluggish in all his motions', flaws not usually perceived by Cedric in his pugnacious idealizing of the Saxon past. Cedric has also repudiated Wilfred because he has adopted some of the ways of the Normans, particularly chivalry and jousting at tournaments. In effect, Wilfred has also become the son of

Richard, representing a union of two worlds, the Saxons who feel oppressed by the Norman yoke, and the Normans who, except for Richard, despise the Saxons as barbarous peasant 'porkers'. In these terms, Wilfred is the first Englishman.[10]

The rough bluff tough Cedric boasts of his liberal observance of the laws of hospitality in a land where travel is perilous, so that against his evident wishes, and to the distaste of the other guests, he has to admit to his table an old man, Isaac of York, who has disguised himself as poor and penniless; Isaac wears 'a high square yellow cap of a peculiar fashion, assigned to his nation to distinguish them from Christians'. Who will give Isaac a place at the table? In this symposium-banquet scene (which for epigraph has part of the famous speech of Shylock, 'Hath not a Jew eyes?'), Cedric coldly assigns Isaac a place at the lower end of his table, but no one will make room for him except Wilfred: 'While Isaac thus stood an outcast in the present society, like his people among the nations, looking in vain for welcome or resting place, the pilgrim who sat by the chimney took compassion on him, and resigned his seat.' The palmer and Isaac (referred to by Cedric's servants as the 'unbelieving dog' and 'the child of circumcision') are also assigned to sleep near each other in lowly stalls or 'cells'.[11]

Also guests at Cedric's table are some Normans travelling to a tournament, including the Knight Templar Brian de Bois-Guilbert, who has in attendance two Saracen slaves he has brought back from Palestine. The Knight Templar expresses astonishment at Cedric permitting Isaac to be near the presence of a Crusader like himself: 'A dog Jew to approach a defender of the Holy Sepulchre?'[12]

Wilfred overhears the Knight Templar say in Arabic to his Saracen slaves that they should rob the Jew Isaac when he leaves: for Wilfred, like the other returned Crusaders, also understands and speaks Arabic. Wilfred helps Isaac escape, and Isaac in turn will fund Wilfred with horse and equipment to enter the tournament near Ashby-de-la-Zouche to which the knights are heading. Here Wilfred disguises himself as an unknown knight, 'with the Spanish word *Desdichado*, signifying Disinherited' on his shield. Wilfred defeats the fierce Knight Templar, though he is also wounded by the end of the tournament, especially as he is set upon by more than one Norman: codes of chivalry and courtesy in the novel are subject to relentless irony. Wilfred is only saved by the intervention of King Richard disguised as a black knight.[13]

The only person to tend to the injured Wilfred after the tournament is over is Rebecca, who saves his life. But for the rest of the novel's actions Wilfred is a marginal almost risible figure, ill and weak. (The reader has already heard that Wilfred had been delayed in his return from Palestine because, as Rowena tremulously puts it, of his 'impaired health'.) He is carried about in a 'horse-litter', as in the forest scenes when the group of Jews and Saxons, who had accidentally come together, are captured by the Norman knights disguised as 'Saxon outlaws' and taken to the castle of the brutal Norman of the expressive name Sir Reginald Front-de-Bœuf (actually Ivanhoe's own castle, which the invading Norman ancestors of Front-de-Bœuf had stolen by massacre and rape).[14]

Late in the novel Wilfred does recover sufficiently to ride across country to try and save Rebecca's life, when she is accused of being a sorceress who has bewitched Brian de Bois-Guilbert into abducting her to the Knight Templars' 'Castle, or Preceptory' at Templestowe; Rebecca, after a trial in which she is her own eloquent advocate, is to be burnt as a witch unless a champion appears to combat and defeat Bois-Guilbert. When Wilfred arrives, his horse is exhausted, he is still palpably poorly, and he is thrown from his mount by the Templar. Who or what can save Rebecca?

Orientalism, eros, identity

Ivanhoe is a novel intimately concerned with the effects on the Crusaders, and through the Crusaders on England and Western Europe, of their travels to the East. Such can be witnessed in both Wilfred and his enemy in other ways Bois-Guilbert. (After the taking of St John-de-Acre in the Levant, a tournament was held where Wilfred had defeated Bois-Guilbert; both are keen to renew their contest in England, a bitter contestation between the new English national identity and Norman claims to superiority.[15])

In a novel of superbly managed suspense and surprises, in its final tournament involving the fate of Rebecca, the Templar wins against Wilfred, but then dies on the spot: 'Unscathed by the lance of his enemy, he had died a victim of his own contending passions.' Bois-Guilbert's life is riven by the conflict within him between his duties as a warrior-monk in the Levant to impose Crusader rule, recover the Holy Sepulchre, and kill as many Saracens as possible (he boasts of the blood of 300), along with a political ambition to become head of his order; and his desire for Rebecca as Eastern Woman, as mysterious Other. What saves Rebecca from cruel death by slow fire is not Wilfred's heroism but the Knight Templar's Orientalism.[16]

Indeed Wilfred himself, while being cared for by one who is repeatedly referred to as the beautiful Jewess, is drawn to her as European man to Oriental female, to an exotic erotics he cannot completely control even after he learns she is a Jew and therefore to be despised. Wilfred throughout is ambivalent (as is the novel's narrator) to Isaac as if he were the Shylock of *The Merchant of Venice*.[17] When he knows Rebecca is Jewish he becomes formal and distant in his manner towards the woman who is saving his life by her medical knowledge, kindness and (hopefully concealed) affection.[18]

If Wilfred attempts (as we see at the end of the novel, not entirely successfully) to repress his attraction to Rebecca as the female Orient, Bois-Guilbert permits his open 'wild' expression. Far more than Wilfred in his horse-litter being carted ignominiously about, Bois-Guilbert the Knight Templar is prominent, increasingly so, in the novel's scenes, just as is the jousting tournament of words and perspectives between the Templar and Rebecca. Yet his cultural and ethnic identity is far from straightforward: who, indeed, is the Knight Templar? From the beginning the Templar is evoked as a haughty Norman knight, fierce, impulsive, peremptory, high-handed, arrogant, violent. In many ways he is a symbol of the fate of his order, which had begun in ascetic dedication but become corrupted by wealth and power and a sensuality that its members had particularly permitted themselves in the East they had gone ruthlessly to subdue. The Crusaders are already suspected in England of having given themselves over to voluptuousness, dissoluteness, hypocrisy and atheism. (At one point at Cedric's table all join in a Pater Noster except 'the Jew, the Mahomedans, and the Templar'.[19])

The Templar, we quickly see, has become markedly Orientalized and Africanized: 'The whole appearance of this warrior and his retinue was wild and outlandish.' A man past 40, his high features had been burnt 'almost into Negro blackness by constant exposure to the tropical sun'. Like the Oriental Isaac, he has 'keen piercing dark eyes'. On his brow is a 'deep scar', accenting his countenance with 'additional sternness' and a 'sinister expression'. With his 'thick curled hair of a raven blackness', he has an 'unusually swart appearance', a 'swarthy stranger' to the land. On one side of his gallant warhorse hangs a battle-axe richly inlaid with Damascene carving. The dress of his squires is 'gorgeous'. His two slaves, Hamet and Abdalla, by their 'dark visages, white turbans, and the Oriental form of their garments', revealed themselves to be 'natives of some distant Eastern country'. Their dress is marked by silk and embroidery, with silver collars round their throats, and silver bracelets on their 'swarthy' legs and arms; they are armed with 'Turkish daggers', and darts or javelins, 'a weapon much in use among the Saracens'. Their horses are of Arabian descent. In this portrait, the Knight Templar is very much an Oriental(ist) figure, a potentate, a despot with 'Eastern bondsmen'.[20] Does he wish, with Rebecca as perceived Eastern Woman, to possess a harem as well?

There is a cast to the 'reckless' Templar's sensibility that recalls the Byronic noble brigand, dedicated to a fatal consuming passion. Early in the novel his travelling companion the Prior Aymer of Jorvaulx jests to the Templar that when they stay that night at Cedric the Saxon's, the 'soft expression of a mild blue eye' will chase from the Knight's memory the 'black-tressed girls of

Palestine, ay, or the houris of old Mahound's paradise'. At Cedric's dinner, Bois-Guilbert does indeed stare insolently at Rowena (she draws with dignity her veil around her face), with her profuse hair of a colour between brown and flaxen and her exquisitely fair complexion.[21]

But it is his Byronic fate (as in those extraordinary poems *The Corsair* and *The Giaour*) to find himself irresistibly drawn to the East for its non-English, non-European sensuousness and erotic power. Addressing Rebecca as 'Fair flower of Palestine', Bois-Guilbert tells his captive that he has 'made a vow to prefer beauty to wealth' – and to power as well. 'I lose fame, I lose honour, I lose the prospect of such greatness as scarce emperors attain to – I sacrifice mighty ambition ... this greatness will I sacrifice ... if thou wilt say, Bois-Guilbert, I receive thee for my lover.' Even to the very end Bois-Guilbert pleads with Rebecca to flee with him to the East where, he declares, he will become a rebel Crusader, perhaps even ally himself with Saladin, and install himself and her as king and queen of Palestine, 'on Mount Carmel'.[22]

Little wonder that, with such disordered visions, Sir Brian de Bois-Guilbert dies of internal contradictions.

Arabs and Africans in England

The Muslim Arab and Oriental-African characters in *Ivanhoe* are referred to in recurrent essentializing images, both servile and barbaric, familiar from Said's evocations in *Orientalism*. Bois-Guilbert relates that his Eastern attendants Hamet and Abdalla were once fierce and intractable. But his 'master of the slaves' has made them 'humble, submissive, serviceable, and observant' of his will, though they are still keen to use poison and the dagger if given the slightest encouragement.[23]

The Crusaders have learnt from the Saracens not only voluptuousness but also pleasure in inflicting pain. We learn of Front-de-Bœuf, when he is trying to extort money from Isaac captured in the castle, that he knows Arabic, 'for he also had been in Palestine, where, perhaps, he had learnt his lesson of cruelty'. Certainly the Templars and not least Bois-Guilbert are feared for their Eastern-like cruelty.[24]

The novel creates relations between Muslims and Jews as if naturally mirroring the binary hostility of Christians – the Nazarenes, as Rebecca calls them – to Jews in England and Europe. When Cedric mockingly suggests at his dinner that perhaps Bois-Guilbert's 'turban'd strangers' might like to admit the society of Isaac at his table, Bois-Guilbert replies for them: 'my Saracen slaves are true Moslems, and scorn as much as any Christian to hold intercourse with a Jew.' When Isaac nears them where they are sitting, the Saracens 'curled up their whiskers with indignation, and laid their hands on their poignards', at the very thought of such 'contamination' of a Jew's presence.[25]

Rebecca, intent on escaping England and fleeing to Cordova (or Grenada) in Moorish Spain, is far from believing that medieval Muslims were uniformly cordial to Jews. As she makes clear to her father, while she believes 'the cruelties of the Nazarenes of England' towards Jews are great, the Muslims too can exhibit 'cruelties' to the race of Jacob.[26] Here Rebecca is in some agreement with her great (non-fictional) contemporary Moses Maimonides.

Maimonides, in his 1172 'Epistle to Yemen', expressed to his fellow Jews in Yemen his anger at the treatment of Jews by Christians, a sect that had gained power by claiming that its faith was God-given like 'our divine religion', and then proceeded to try and wipe out every trace of the 'Jewish nation and religion': 'The first one to have adopted this plan', Maimonides scathingly notes, 'was Jesus the Nazarene, may his bones be ground to dust.' In the 'Epistle to Yemen' Maimonides is also irritated by certain Muslim claims that Scripture has veiled allusions to Islam, and he refers to Muhammad as 'the Madman'. He reveals his anger at the Arab world's treatment of Jews: 'Remember, my coreligionists, that on account of the vast number of our sins, God has hurled us in the midst of this people, the Arabs, who have persecuted us severely, and passed baneful and discriminatory legislation against us. ... Never did a nation molest, degrade, debase, and hate us as much as they.' Maimonides wrote to encourage the Jewish community in the Yemen, which at that time was in a highly troubled state: since about 1165 it had been suffering religious persecution, the blandishments of a recent apostate, and the presence of a self-proclaimed messiah. Maimonides was also writing out of his personal anger and bitterness at the wandering from city to city, country to country, he had suffered since his family had been forced to flee Cordova – a great centre of Jewish learning where eight generations of the Maimon family had served as rabbis and judges – after the invasion in 1147 of Moorish Spain by the fanatical Almohades, who railed against its laxity and presented all non-Muslims with the choice of conversion or death. The Maimon family, like tens of thousands of other Jews in Spain, began to wander, including a stay in Fez in Morocco where the Almohades also ruled with the same repressive zeal. It is not known whether Maimonides was forced to convert in Morocco, though he later wrote of these years: 'Since we went into exile, the persecutions have not stopped. I have known affliction since childhood, since the womb.' In 1165 Maimonides had fled Morocco and travelled eastwards, finally settling in Cairo, where he began to practise medicine, with such knowledge and skill that he became the house physician of Saladin's vizier and one of the most respected court physicians.[27]

Rebecca, however, reverses Maimonides' verdict: understandably, given the circumstances confronting her. She feels that it is not the Muslim world but the

Christian 'nation' of England and Europe that most molests, degrades, debases and hates 'us'.

In one of *Ivanhoe*'s climactic scenes there is a swift repugnant portrait of Africans. The inquisitional fire, the 'pile of faggots', is assembled by 'four black slaves, whose colour and African features, then so little known in England, appalled the multitude'. When they talk, the African slaves 'expanded their rubber lips, and showed their white fangs'. The multitude look upon them as demons called into being by the witch (Rebecca) or her master Satan himself.[28]

Ivanhoe is so saturated with ethnicized and racialized terms and consciousness, characters and narration that it was immediately accused of anachronism, especially for the introduction early in the action of Hamet and Abdalla. In reply, Scott appealed both to history and to genre. In terms of historicity, he observed that since it was well known that the Templars 'copied closely the luxuries of the Asiatic warriors with whom they fought', it was entirely natural to expect them to have in their service 'enslaved Africans, whom the fate of war transferred to new masters'. In defence of literary fantasy, he recalled that his friend Matthew Lewis had introduced a 'set of sable functionaries' into his fiction; in any case, Scott added, the author of a 'modern antique romance' is not 'obliged to confine himself to the introduction of those manners only which can be proved to have absolutely existed in the times he is depicting'.[29]

Like other Scott fiction, *Ivanhoe* is decidedly not a positivist or empiricist historiography; drawing no firm distinction between fiction and history, it robustly issued a challenge to those deadening forms of historical writing, with their claims to history as science, that were asserting their power in and from the 1820s and thence later in the nineteenth century and into the twentieth century. In 'The historian as taxidermist', the first chapter of his *The Clothing of Clio*, Stephen Bann tells us that Ranke, appalled by Scott's historical fiction, resolved to avoid all imagination and invention and restrict himself severely to the facts, to show only what actually happened (*wie es eigentlich gewesen*).[30]

In this historiographical duel we can see *Ivanhoe* imagining in a kind of divinatory way different histories, Mediterranean and African and European, intersecting in England in the tumultuous conflicts of the twelfth century. The cultural critic Paul Gilroy has called for an ethnohistorical perspective. This would recognize that there has been a strong persistent presence of Anglo-Africans in England during and since the eighteenth century; in modernity English history has continuously intersected with a diasporic transcultural international formation he calls the Black Atlantic. Gilroy suggests, however, that an outsider to Englishness like Scott may be an exception to construction of the English nation as ethnically homogeneous and culturally pure.[31]

Certainly, I think, we can say that *Ivanhoe's* vision of England in a formative moment as ethnically differentiated and conflicting, and as including Saracens and Africans, already tries to come out and meet Gilroy's desire for an inclusive diasporic ethnohistory. Scott himself, in his defence of his placing Africans in English history, related a story from a medieval romance of how a minstrel painted himself black and 'succeeded in imposing himself ... as an Ethiopian minstrel'; 'negroes', he concluded, must therefore 'have been known in England in the dark ages'.[32] In *Ivanhoe*, these are Africans not from the European plantation-slavery Atlantic diaspora, but from a much older medieval Middle Eastern Mediterranean diaspora. It is one of the most challenging aspects of *Ivanhoe* that it establishes a connection in thought and speculation and imagination between the two diasporas; the novel's history gives Africanicity an antique lineage within English history.

Ivanhoe is decidedly not a realist novel. The explanation for its unabashed enjoyment of anachronisms lies in the affinity of its historical romance both with genres like Menippean satire and with another, Oriental, literary history, *The Thousand and One Nights*, in their common hospitality to the marvellous and fantastical. Scott may have got the names Hamet and Abdalla from Galland's early eighteenth-century translation of the *Nights*,[33] which 'Laurence Templeton' salutes in his Dedicatory Epistle. In his 1830 Introduction Scott refers the forest scenes of the disguised King Richard carousing with Friar Tuck to Haroun Al-Rashid's night-time adventures in Baghdad. The influence of the *Nights* is evident also in the narrativity of *Ivanhoe*, its proliferating stories within stories (as in the narrative of Ulrica the Saxon, who has been enslaved by the Normans in the castle).

As *Ivanhoe's* narrator says, he feels like 'old Ariosto', not obliged to maintain continuity and uniformity in the presentation of his drama.[34] *Ivanhoe* as ethnohistorical romance, both European and Oriental, feels itself free to introduce and play with different histories and temporalities, to bring them together and make them tilt and joust in the same textual tournament.

Andalusia

Ivanhoe's wandering textuality permits it to notice the impinging on Europe of other cultures, including that of a remarkable Muslim society within medieval Europe. There are interesting references to medieval Spain in the novel, suggesting a superior technological civilization. The Prior rides on stately occasions 'one of the most handsome Spanish jennets ever bred in Andalusia', horses imported 'for the use of persons of wealth and distinction'. For the dinner at Cedric's, the Prior wears sandals of the finest leather 'imported from

Spain'. On the same occasion Rowena wears a 'veil of silk, interwoven with gold', which as protection against the Norman gaze could be drawn 'over the face and bosom after the Spanish fashion'. De Bracy, leader of the mercenary Free Companions or Condottieri, one of the Norman knights who had abducted the Saxons (he has designs on Rowena) and Jews, is hit by an arrow from Locksley (Robin Hood) in the storming of the castle, but is saved by a 'shirt of Spanish mail'. Locksley is enraged: 'Curse on thy Spanish steel-coat!' He avers that had an English smith forged it, his arrows would have gone straight through.[35]

Rebecca and the Geniza world

In *Ivanhoe* Rebecca, her general expression one of 'contemplative melancholy', is created as learned, intelligent, noble, dignified, gentle, firm, commanding, just, tolerant, generous, and liberal in her faith and sympathies. She is evidently beloved by the besotted (even voyeuristic) narrator:

> ... the beautiful features, and fair form, and lustrous eyes, of the lovely Rebecca; eyes whose brilliancy was shaded, and, as it were, mellowed, by the fringe of her long silken eyelashes, and which a minstrel would have compared to the evening star darting its rays through a bower of jessamine.[36]

As Graham Tulloch argues in his *tour de force* on the novel's biblical references, Rebecca emerges in such intertextuality (her language drawing on the New Testament as well as the Old) as a Christ figure. Readers and audiences in the nineteenth century (in Thackeray's parody of the novel, as in plays and operas) wished Rebecca had converted and then married Wilfred of Ivanhoe at the close.[37]

Yet the Rebecca of Scott's novel is not the Jessica of Shakespeare's play, the Jessica who leaves the house of her fathers and father, converting to Christianity and assimilating her life to the Venetians, in a drama where at the end Shylock is also forced to convert.[38]

Isaac and Rebecca proudly yet sadly recall a history where Jews once had independence as a nation and knew military victories. Isaac says he trusts in the 'rebuilding of Zion' and a 'new Temple'. Rebecca, in discussion with Wilfred on the virtues of chivalry, tells him that 'until the God of Jacob shall raise up for his chosen people a second Gideon, or a new Maccabeus, it ill beseemeth the Jewish damsel to speak of battle or of war'. At her trial she says that 'alas! we have no country'. To the Knight Templar she feels keenly for her people 'who are no longer their own governors, and the denizens of their own free independent state'. In such moods Rebecca comes close to Maimonides' lament in 'Epistle to Yemen' for Israel's lost 'independence' as a nation and state. She also anticipates the recognizable nationalist and Zionist visions of modernity.[39]

To Wilfred, who delights in chivalry as the defence of liberty with lance and sword, Rebecca insists that the Jews of ancient times were never aggressive: 'I am, indeed ... sprung from a race whose courage was distinguished in the defence of their own land, but who warred not, even while yet a nation, save at the command of the Deity, or in defending their country from oppression.' Yet there is irony in Rebecca's mention of ancient Jewish military prowess, with its suggestions of war over land, for England's history is also created in *Ivanhoe* as always-already torn, created by successive conquests, fought over by peoples who came from elsewhere to a chosen island.[40]

Sometimes when Rebecca refers to 'my country' she appears to mean the Jews of the Diaspora, the 'dispersed children of Zion', as she puts it.[41]

In terms of diasporic multiple consciousness, we can regard Rebecca in the novel as belonging to more than one history, space, temporality, world. When the ill Wilfred wakes, he begins by speaking in Arabic to his 'kind physician', who replies: 'I am of England, Sir Knight, and speak the English tongue, although my dress and my lineage belong to another climate.' Wilfred sees standing before him a 'turban'd and caftan'd damsel' of an appearance that brings to mind his 'Eastern travels'.[42] Rebecca is 'of' a less than hospitable England. But she is also perceived to be, and creates herself as, Oriental, of Oriental 'lineage'.

The house in the village of Ashby where she and Isaac stay is 'richly furnished with decorations of an Oriental taste'. Rebecca is seated on cushions which served, 'like the estrada of the Spaniards, instead of chairs and stools'. If Gentile visitors come, Rebecca veils herself ('a screen of silver gauze which reached to her feet'). At the tournament near Ashby, Rebecca appears in 'a sort of Eastern dress, which she wore according to the fashion of the females of her nation'. Prince John vulgarly shouts to his Norman companions that she looks like an 'Eastern houri'. When Ulrica in the castle later sees the captured Rebecca, she demands to know if she be Saracen or Egyptian. Rebecca has learnt her surgical skills and knowledge of medicinal herbs and elixirs from, as her father admiringly says, 'the lessons of Miriam, daughter of the Rabbi Manasses of Byzantium' (though Miriam, charged with 'necromancy', had fallen victim to the Christian fanaticism of the times, having been burnt at the stake). Indeed, Rebecca's 'powerful mind' had enlarged the medical knowledge medieval Jews were known for 'in the course of a progress beyond her years, her sex, and even the age in which she lived', so much so that her community 'almost regarded her as one of those gifted women mentioned in the sacred history'.[43]

Rebecca, then, belongs to an international community that extends (at least) from England to Byzantium. She has clearly travelled on trading ships with her father. Isaac mentions that in a storm he had once, to save their lives, thrown overboard his merchandise including choice silks, myrrh and aloes, gold and silver work.[44] Such trading occurred in a long-established Oriental world with which Shakespeare's Venice would later interface: the medieval world of the Levant, the Judeo–Arab world of the Mediterranean and far beyond, which prized the scholar-merchant (of which Muhammad was one) and travel as necessary for education. She is (like her father) multilingual, understanding or speaking Saxon, French, Latin, Hebrew and Arabic.

Rebecca, in this portrait, in her cosmopolitanism and urbanity, is remarkably similar to aspects of the Judeo–Arab scenography evoked by S. D. Goitein in *A Mediterranean Society*, based on the Cairo Geniza documents. In terms of women's standing and power within medieval Geniza society, it is observable that Rebecca in the novel carries herself and speaks as a fully independent person and relates to her father, in speech and correspondence, as an equal.

In a section 'The world of women' in *A Mediterranean Society*, Goitein writes that one way modern observers can gain insight into women's life and consciousness in the Geniza world is through the names women chose for their daughters; what is noticeable is the complete absence of biblical and other Hebrew names among the Jewish women of Egypt. Not only did the women choose secular names, but such names frequently refer to ideas of ruling, overcoming and victory; many names are composed with the word *sitt*, meaning female ruler. Chastity and Fertility, regarded, says Goitein wryly, by men as the most praiseworthy attributes of a woman, are all but absent from female Geniza nomenclature. Such secular naming, Goitein feels, demonstrates what he refers to as the chasm between the popular local subcultures of the women and the world-wide Hebrew book culture of the men; and he also observes that in Judaism the exclusion of women from the study of the Scriptures, which was the main expression of piety, inevitably had a degrading effect. Yet Goitein also says he came across many Geniza documents indicating that women had considerable economic independence.[45]

Women, Goitein suggests, were provided with real estate as a way of creating for them enduring economic security, which could make them financially independent. In many cases women possessed a number of properties, which were regarded as investments. Goitein mentions the widow of an Indian trader who acquired one-sixth of two stores. In another case a father bought a quarter of a flour mill for his unmarried daughter. Women vigorously took charge of such properties. Women appeared in courts on their own behalf. Women, then, left the house frequently, they were not confined (there was no separate women's quarters; there was privacy, but no purdah).

They would visit their families and female friends, and in return expected to be visited by them. There was usually a weekly visit to the bathhouse, where some, Goitein fancifully speculates, might have played chess, like the beautiful wicked Jewish woman in *The Thousand and One Nights* who constantly defeats her Christian paramour until she has taken all his possessions (chess in the Geniza world being played for money): a fictional representation of the independent woman, says Goitein, of the Jewish Geniza society, a woman who might be a divorcée or widow. A married woman was expected to earn by engaging in some kind of work in addition to her household chores. Women participated in various professions, from brokers and agents to business-women. Women were midwives, textile workers, specialists in treating the body for burial, professional wailers at funerals, astrologers, bankers, merchants, teachers, doctors and oculists. Women travelled frequently, and for a variety of reasons, including visiting extended family for weekends or holidays, or visiting a holy shrine, or going to Jerusalem, and a woman who had visited Jerusalem might be called The Pilgrim. Women travelled by sea, and single women travelling by sea are mentioned in the Geniza, says Goitein, as a matter of common occurrence.[46]

We can recognize Rebecca (though her name is not secular) as confidently and assuredly belonging to just such a world.

Recall that the injured Wilfred sees Rebecca as a 'turban'd and caftan'd damsel' of an appearance that brings to mind his 'Eastern travels'. What in more detail might Rebecca have been wearing? The editor of the Edinburgh edition of *Ivanhoe* glosses that Rebecca and Jews in general in medieval England would have been wearing Christian-type clothes, except for the distinctive badge or hat which they were obliged to wear to identify themselves as Jews.[47] *Ivanhoe*, by contrast, wishes to distinguish in this regard how Oriental Rebecca appeared and wanted to appear.

In a discussion of clothes, Goitein observes that an extreme concern with clothing and outward appearance was an ancient Near East tradition that continued into Islamic times. How indeed the Prophet dressed, perfumed and dyed his hair was extensively covered in the classical biographies of Islam's Founder. The occupation of dealing with clothing was considered noble, and not unsuitable for a religious scholar. Sumptuous display was an expression of gratitude towards God (except by pietist movements like Sufism; the word for Sufism is derived from the word for wool, then the clothing of the poor). Since nakedness was considered an abomination in the Mediterranean Geniza world, the limbs of the body and its contours were hidden from the eye by numbers of wraps; consequently male and female fashions did not differ much. (Goitein speculates that in the Near East the process of disrobing, with its delight in ever more gorgeous dresses emerging, was an intrinsic part of lovemaking.) A man should demonstrate by his clothing his standing in the community. A woman should show her respect to her fellows by making herself inconspicuous, if not invisible: but Goitein doubts that this latter principle was always adhered to. Elaborate head covers were much sought after, and the bigger the turban, the more important its bearer, though the meticulous covering of the head was also performed for religious reasons. The most popular clothing material was linen, closely followed by silk (used for millennia in China), while cotton, in which in modern times Egypt became pre-eminent, was nowhere near so popular in medieval times. Spanish silk, richly represented in the Geniza, was usually referred to as 'Andalusian'. A particular textile, probably made from cotton, was imported from India to be made into a robe. There was a medieval Mediterranean passion for brilliant and variegated colours, and dyers were kept busy trying to satisfy the multifarious demands. Certain frequent dyeing materials, indigo and brazilwood, were traded from India. There was a predilection of Geniza women for subdued shades of white (their next favourite colour was blue), though white was also popular with men as well, and Goitein suggests that the great Maimonides probably wore as outer wear a white turban, a white broad shawl, a white cloak and a white scarf.[48]

Rebecca is also an accomplished physician, a profession, Goitein points out, that held a singular place in the medieval Judeo–Arab world, a unique role of spiritual leadership and honoured social position. The medieval doctors of the Mediterranean area, disciples of the Greeks and heirs to a universal tradition transcending barriers of religion, language and country, were the torchbearers of secular erudition, the professional expounders of philosophy and the sciences. Any doctor of distinction was likely to be a member of the entourage of a caliph, a sultan, a vizier, a general or governor, sharing the glory of the great of his world without, Goitein mordantly notes, being involved in their crimes and their hateful ways of oppression. Goitein feels that medieval rulers, many of them soldiers with only scant education, wished to attract physicians to their courts because an immense belief in books and deep veneration for scientific attainments were part of the spirit of the age, and it was doctors who knew the books, in particular the ancient books and ancient sciences. Such respect for medical art was not confined to the upper classes, but was widespread and popular. In the thirteenth century, however, when an orthodox reaction ousted philosophy from most of the countries of Islam, the sciences, and in time medicine as well, fell into disrepute, even total eclipse, until modern times.[49]

If, says Goitein, medicine was a prominent constituent of Islamic civilization in its creative period, it was paramount in the life of the protected communities, the Christians and Jews. Writing in Arabic, Christians and Jews were very important in the Arab literature on medicine, and the most important authors would be translated into Latin on the northern shores of the Mediterranean, in France and Italy. Renowned physicians would frequently be leaders of their communities, the most famous examples, perhaps, being Maimonides and his descendants, for families and generations of physicians were common. In the late twelfth century Maimonides became the central figure of the Jewish community in Egypt and its dependencies, and his descendants continued to be leaders for the next two centuries. A student of philosophy who had read the first part of Maimonides' just published *Guide of the Perplexed* (composed between 1185 and 1190) asked the famous doctor questions about the book as well as consulting him about dietetic problems; Maimonides devoted himself to both queries. It was not considered undignified for physicians to engage in business as a sideline. Often bibliophiles, they might dabble in the book trade. Physicians, Muslim, Christian and Jewish, wrote poems in Arabic, and Jewish doctors also wrote poems in Hebrew. Judah ha-Levi, the great poet, practised as a physician in Spain, and was also a communal leader.[50]

In her speech, skilled in the art of conversation and presentation of argument, and in her advanced medical art, Rebecca belongs to this world of veneration of books and knowledge, unlike the Saxon and Norman characters in the novel, who spend much of their time in an energetic oral culture of shouting, bellowing and boasting, of imprecations, curses, threats and oaths. Rowena the Saxon princess does not seem to have been learned in any evident way.

Rebecca, then, is in part a Levantine figure. Drawing on Goitein's great work, Ammiel Alcalay in *After Jews and Arabs* (1993) evokes a Levantine world characterized by cultural mixing, relative freedom of travel, and multi-lingualism. Alcalay suggests that the notion of the Jew as always pariah, outsider, wanderer, is a Eurocentric conception, a myth that obscures recognition of a space where the Jew *was* native, was not a stranger but an absolute inhabitant of time and place. For more than a thousand years of history in the Middle East, North Africa, Muslim Spain, Jews, like Christians, protected Peoples of the Book, did not live in ghettos, shared their lives with their Arab neighbours in intimate intricate ways, enjoyed religious and cultural autonomy and prospered in multiple occupations, as artisanal workers, scholars, medical professionals, traders, administrators.[51]

For Alcalay, the Cairo Geniza documents suggest that the historic world of Islam established an internationalization of space, a world of mobility, autonomy, diversity, translatability, fluidity, yet of deep attachment to particular cities; a world where Jewish creativity flourished, sometimes following Islamic culture, sometimes leading. Jews were not passive, were not victims, as in the Eurocentric conception. There was, for example, the historical figure of Mashallah, an eighth-century Jewish engineer and astronomer, who was one of the few chosen to determine the location of Baghdad, that 'utopian project' of Islamic ascendancy where Haroun Al-Rashid was Caliph in the eighth century. Translation, in which Jews featured, was encouraged. Schools were established to carry out the systematic transference of texts from Greek, Persian, Syriac and the Hindu languages into Arabic, the influx of so many new and conflicting ideas making Baghdad a time and place of 'intense speculation, bewilderment, and innovation', a society liberal, tolerant, secular. Alcalay talks of the carnival-like diversity of the crowds of Baghdad, the city as crowded palimpsest, as dense texture, without single origin or primary layer.[52]

In Alcalay's view, this Judeo–Islamic world enabled a circulation of cultures, ideas, discourses, languages, where cities were linked with cities, Baghdad with Beirut with Damascus with Jerusalem with Cairo – a poetics of heterogeneity.[53]

Alcalay's general argument is that Zionism as a nationalist discourse of singularity contradicts such Levantine and Geniza poetics of heterogeneity and cosmopolitanism: a conflict that can be perceived as well in Rebecca.

Oriental and Mediterranean cuisine

In the evening in the house in the village of Ashby where Rebecca and Isaac stay, silver lamps are placed upon the table, with 'the richest wines, and the most delicate refreshments', suggesting a sophisticated appreciation of fine foods that certainly did not seem abundant at the rude table of Cedric the Saxon. What might Rebecca and her father have been eating?

Goitein notes of the medieval Geniza world that the secularly minded, sophisticated courtiers and government officials, together with their company of littérateurs and philosophers, enjoyed talking about food, just as the intellectuals of Late Antiquity had done before them. There was also much serious thinking and research, and many treatises, on the subject of food and health.[54]

The great French Orientalist scholar Maxime Rodinson mentions that Maimonides wrote a book on dietetics.[55]

In *The Book of Jewish Food* Claudia Roden recalls: 'Years ago I came across an analysis by the French Orientalist Maxime Rodinson of a thirteenth-century culinary manuscript of Syrian origin. It was written in the Ayyubid period by someone close to the court, with references to the sultan and the royal kitchens. Mr Rodinson listed the names of seventy-four dishes and described them. Many are very like the recipes given to me by my aunts.'[56] Claudia Roden would appear to be thinking of an article 'Recherches sur les documents arabes relatifs à la cuisine' (1949), a legendary essay, sometimes whimsical and playful, that has interesting autobiographical touches and an eye for the curious and unusual.[57]

Rodinson's essay is largely devoted to evoking the high cuisine (*alimentation princière*) of the twelfth and thirteenth centuries, developing in the Abbasid and then the Ayyubid periods. Such high cuisine was extraordinarily sumptuous, complex and rich, often celebrated in *poèmes culinaires*. The dishes demanded a great deal of time to prepare and cook: multiple operations involving roasting, boiling and frying. Complexity was desired not only in taste but also in décor, in visual appeal. The elements deployed were abundant and varied, though foods considered common and low were largely ignored; Rodinson instances here lentils, lady's fingers (*gombo*), broad beans and figs. The courtly cooks put to use products which were costly and came from afar, in particular the spices which came variously from China, the Sunda Islands, India and Oriental Africa; such spices included pepper, ginger, cinnamon, cloves, cardamom, mace, betel, musk, nutmeg. Many foods grown in distant parts were cultivated in the Middle East, as with rice and sugar (indeed were cultivated long before the medieval epoch).

In general, Rodinson writes, such high cuisine represented a confluence of various traditions, local and exotic, traditional and contemporary, country and town, all enriched, refined and complicated. In terms of influence, the primary was Persian, to be noticed in dishes like meat with an aromatic vinegar sauce; diversely stuffed meatballs; meat cooked with aromatics and raisins ground with pomegranate; delicacies composed of almonds ground with sweetened rose water. Other recipes come from Arabia, Egypt, the Caucasus (especially Georgian), the Maghreb (for couscous), Byzantium; there were also Turkish elements, and Indian.[58]

The cosmopolitanism of this cuisine, lending itself to a strong element of conspicuous consumption (Rodinson here referring to Thorstein Veblen's famous phrase), was above all manifested in the intensive use of aromatic plants and spices: beside garlic and onion there were parsley, mint, rue, thyme, wild thyme, lavender, dill, mallow, purslane, caper, sesame, tarragon, fenugreek, laurel, dodder, lettuce, safflower, caraway, poppy, rose buds and petals, pistachio, hemp seed, sumac and mustard.

Among meats there was a predilection for chicken (if chicken were not used, 'meat' usually meant lamb or mutton), and indeed Rodinson lists in the *Wusla*, the famous cuisinary treatise by a Syrian courtier of the mid-thirteenth century (the treatise Claudia Roden was remembering), 74 chicken recipes. Chicken was cooked whole or ground. There was chicken cooked with fried aubergine; with sesame oil; with lemon; with pomegranate grains; with rhubarb; with egg and aromatics; with quinces; pistachios; hazel nuts; almonds; poppy; sumac; orange; breadcrumbs with saffron, rose water and pistachio; prune jelly; blackberries;

onion, cinnamon, dill and sesame oil; with rice seasoned with red pepper (*pimente*).

Rodinson points to the importance of spices for the writer of the *Wusla*, who has a separate recipe for a spice mixture, comprising lavender, betel, laurel leaves, nutmeg, mace, cardamom, cloves, rose-buds, beechnuts, ginger and pepper. (Reading this I instantly thought of *ras el hanout* in contemporary North African cuisine, and *garam masala* in Indian.)

Cooking meat with fruit was also clearly very important to the thirteenth-century Syrian cuisinier. There was a meat ragoût with green beans, pistachios and sometimes eggs; meat cooked with bitter oranges (*viande au jus d'orange amère*); with apricots; oranges; dates dried and fresh; even *aux bananes*. Rodinson sees part of the treatise's importance as a contribution to the history of anti-ascetic sentiment in Islam.[59]

Alcalay also suggests that a fascination with subtle delicate cuisine was characteristic of the Geniza world's culinary culture, when imported foods were considered basic staples: apricots, peaches and plums entered Egypt in a half-dried or glazed state; almonds, pistachios, walnuts, hazelnuts and olive oil came in from east and west; cheese came from Crete, Sicily and Byzantium; sugarcane was exported by Iran and southern Iraq, honey by Tunisia, Palestine and Syria. Spices came from everywhere and formed the basis for both the druggist's and perfumer's trades.[60]

Goitein reports that medieval Muslim sayings singled out the Jews for being particularly dedicated to culinary relish, a popular maxim being 'Sleep in a Christian bed and enjoy Jewish food', and Jews were also known for their infatuation with vegetables. In this Judeo–Arab society, to be a glutton and to become obese were considered odious. There were normally two meals a day, a light morning meal and a more substantial evening meal. Food of all descriptions was prepared by specialists in the bazaar and could be bought from them. Jews and Muslims alike relished 'garden mallow', the famous *mulukhiya*, a herb still widely cultivated in Egypt, Palestine and Syria, to be made into a thick soup (*mulukhiya* also had, and has, the byname of 'Jewish vegetable'). Fruits were eagerly sought after. Goitein also comes across mention of 'lemon hen', chicken cooked in lemon sauce and spices, still a delicacy in the Middle East.[61]

It's interesting to read in Claudia Roden's *The Book of Jewish Food* her belief that the Sephardim, even when deeply religious, were known to be tolerant and easygoing in the observance of Jewish dietary laws. Roden notes that European travellers to Egypt and Syria in medieval times were shocked to see local Jews buying from non-Jews in the bazaar cooked food such as harissa (a meat-and-wheat porridge enriched with cinnamon — not the peppery-hot Tunisian paste of the same name today), and pastries and sweetmeats.[62]

Did Rebecca combine her interest in medicine with interests in fine foods and sound diet? Did she read the medical treatises written by Jewish and Arab scholars that were translated into Latin and followed in Europe?[63]

Enjoyment of delicate cuisine was also characteristic of Moorish Spain, where Rebecca's uncle already lived, either in Cordova or in Granada (Rebecca, in situations of distress and peril, is a little confusing in her Spanish references), Granada of the pomegranate name. Here was the western end of the Geniza world, the Moorish Spain – Andalusia or al-Andalus – where thrived *la convivencia*, the living together of Muslim, Christian and Jewish communities: Iberia remained home to all three faiths from 711 to 1492, a remarkable multireligious, multicultural and multilingual history and society. Soon after the original Arab and Berber conquest, the Muslim invaders introduced to the Iberian peninsula the Arab civilization and sophistications of the Middle East, including profitable new crops from the east such as citrus fruits, bananas, figs, cinnamon and almonds.[64]

The food historian Barbara Santich comments on medieval Mediterranean cuisine that the

> cities of Andalusia adopted the manners and refinements of the Baghdad court, which required educated aristocrats and court officials not only to have a knowledge of law and religion, but also to appreciate poetry and music, to show a discriminating palate, and to be skilled in the art of blending spices and other aromatics. In this society pleasure was not only legitimized but discussed, debated and exalted. According to a thirteenth-century Arab book of recipes, known in English as the *Baghdad Cookery-Book*, the six classes of pleasure were food, drink, clothes, sex, scent and sound – and of these, food was said to be the noblest.[65]

Santich suggests that from Muslim Spain and Arab Sicily (conquered by the Arabs in the ninth century), Arab–Persian cuisine influenced the entire Mediterranean region, including the thickening of sauces with almonds and/or walnuts; the introduction to the medieval larder of citrus fruits and sugar (sugar refining and sugar confectionery were Arab inventions); a preference for sweet–sour combinations, where the sourness of lemon juice, vinegar, unripe grapes or pomegranates was tempered with the sweetness of sugar, or the juice of dates or sweet grapes; the development of marzipan as a sophisticated confection made out of sugar and almond paste; the scenting of food with rose water; dishes involving new ingredients like spinach, aubergines and rice. In discussing the medieval recipe for Chicken in pomegranate juice, Santich refers to the research of Maxime Rodinson in tracing the origin of the dish to an

Arab recipe, and believes that it came to Western Europe through the early translations of Arab dietetic writings; the recipe she works from is also found in a thirteenth-century Andalusian text. She notes that the Arabs were making a pomegranate syrup as early as the ninth century. In her recipes section, Santich places next to Chicken in pomegranate juice a recipe for Chicken in lemon sauce, which includes onions, ground blanched almonds, ground ginger, freshly ground pepper, lemon juice and saffron.[66]

Were these some of the refreshing delicacies of which Rebecca and Isaac might have been partaking, as they sipped rich wines?

Moorish Spain

As Jane S. Gerber evokes it in *The Jews of Spain*, Cordova boasted 700 mosques, including the famous Grand Mosque, perhaps as many as 3000 public baths, paved and illuminated streets, indoor plumbing in luxurious homes, countless villas along the banks of the Guadalquivir, and bustling markets. There were innumerable reflecting pools and fountains, and the noise of cascading water mingled with the humming of thousands of looms weaving silk and brocades. There were palaces as well as mosques, and 70 libraries; the Umayyad princes endowed hospitals and hospices, imported architects and scientists from the East and established schools to translate classical works into Arabic.[67]

Gerber evokes a Sephardi Jewish Golden Age as part of this Moorish Golden Age, especially in the tenth and eleventh centuries. Cordova was not the sole seat of Andalusian culture, which flourished in smaller centres like Seville, Granada, Malaga and Lucena. Jewish tastes, Gerber notes, mirrored those of the Muslims. The great mosque of Cordova not only set the pattern for Islamic art in Spain, it also served as a source of inspiration and imitation for synagogue architecture. There was a proliferation of new synagogues, and Jews commonly wore lavish clothing – Spanish silks dyed brilliantly in many colours were especially prized – and adopted Muslim patronyms. Jews became important in the government and bureaucracy of the Muslim courts.[68]

The Jewish courtier-intellectuals were profoundly influenced as well by a cosmopolitan culture of secular knowledge at the Moorish courts, the pursuit of philosophy, mathematics and the sciences, including the translation of the Greek classics. The Sephardic courtiers shared with their Muslim counterparts a broad humanistic education, in astronomy, astrology, geometry, optics, calligraphy, rhetoric, philology, metrics.[69]

Until the twelfth century, Gerber notes, most of the philosophic and scientific classics composed by Sephardic scholars were written in Arabic.

Gerber feels that in medieval Andalusia Jews were faced with the challenge of the novel philosophical arguments and rational discussions they heard in the exclusive salons of Islamic society. As they adopted the Arabic language, Jews were exposed to the conceptual world of classical antiquity, and, like the Muslims, they became engaged in trying to reconcile their revealed religion with the philosophies of ancient Greece, especially that of Aristotle. Rereading the Bible in the light of rationalistic philosophical formulations, the Arabized Jews of Andalusia began to question its textual contradictions as well as its numerous anthropomorphic references to God, where God should be transcendent and unknowable.[70]

For all that Maimonides in 'Epistle to Yemen' rails against the Arab world, and his family had to leave Cordova and experience many years of suffering and persecution because of the Almohad invasion, his career after he settled in Egypt was in many ways characteristic of the historical experience of educated Jews in Moorish Spain during its Golden Age: the influential courtier who becomes a leader of his community, combining the duties of rabbi, local judge, appellate judge, chief administrator and overseer of philanthropic foundations; at the same time being a versatile scholar and benevolent patron of learning, in Maimonides' case famed throughout the Mediterranean for commentaries in philosophy, law, astronomy and medicine. Gerber observes that his Muslim contemporaries mourned his death with official public ceremonies in Egypt, and Maimonides himself sensed the irony of a productive life in that particular land, for Egypt was supposed to be for Jews the ultimate symbol of exile.[71]

Andalusian tolerance, Gerber argues, in the conditions of post-Cordova instability and political and military decline of Moorish Spain, eventually withered, the prominence of Jewish courtiers becoming a target for resentment. In 1066 thousands of Jews in Granada were slaughtered, and Jewish prominence throughout the little kingdoms came to an end. By the time of the 1147 Almohad assault, which led to further massacres, the Golden Age of Moorish Spain, of *convivencia* between Muslims, Jews, Christians, with its tolerant, secular and hedonistic culture, was — except for the continuing Muslim kingdom of Granada — coming to an end.[72]

With the enormous condescension of posterity (to adapt E. P. Thompson's haunting phrase), there is sad irony in Rebecca's seeking haven for herself and her father in late fifteenth-century Granada. Yet Rebecca did not know that: Granada as alternative to an excluding England must have seemed a wise choice; Granada as an island of cosmopolitian values in an enveloping Catholic Spain; Granada in Andalusia, close to the Judeo–Arab Mediterranean; Granada/Geniza.

Rebecca and the Kabbalah

Rebecca may relate to medieval and in particular twelfth-century world histories in another, mystical, way. Recall that in *Ivanhoe* the narrator tells us that Rebecca is so skilful in medical art that her community 'almost regarded her as one of those gifted women mentioned in the sacred history'. Perhaps, in a theological flight of fancy, we might envisage Rebecca signifying a holy figure, indeed an emanation of the Shekhinah in medieval Kabbalah. Here I turn to Gershom Scholem's *Origins of the Kabbalah*: like Goitein, Scholem was another great German scholar who went to live in Palestine in the 1920s. Scholem evokes the rise of the Kabbalah, especially in the book *Bahir*, in Provence in the latter part of the twelfth century, before its spreading to Jewish communities in nearby Spain. Scholem argues that, in terms of the history of Jewish mysticism, a major new element in Kabbalah was the importance accorded to the feminine. The fragmented textuality of the book *Bahir*, important for the innovations it introduced which helped make the Kabbalah so new a movement in the history of Jewish mysticism, worked by metaphors, symbols, enigmatic parables and allegories, in particular, allegorical readings of biblical passages and later rabbinic commentaries. One such fascinating reading was to suggest that when Genesis 24:1 says 'And the Lord had blessed Abraham in all things', this means that Abraham had a daughter, who is interpreted to be the last of the divine powers (the tenth sefiroth), the Shekhinah, related to the Sophia, or divine wisdom.[73]

The Shekhinah, Scholem says, is holy bride, daughter, mother, an immanent force in the world. The Shekhinah becomes a divine quality distinct from God himself and capable of entering into dialogue with him. The Shekhinah, the feminine, becomes an autonomous entity. The feminine is the beautiful vessel where all jewels are preserved, and at the same time also the receptacle for the power of the masculine; she nevertheless possesses riches, she has within herself a positive strength.[74]

From their first appearance in medieval Provence and Spain the Kabbalists were accused of heterodoxy (which is why they often wrote in secrecy and highly allusively and felt they had to censor themselves). The Kabbalists were seen, in their mystical anthropomorphism, as reducing the divine to the corporeal, for the Kabbalists journeyed into faith as sexual desire, as sensuous unity with the godly. There was theological danger in emphasizing the different potencies of God and in particular in conceptualizing the Shekhinah as a divine quality distinct from God himself and capable of engaging in dialogue with him: critics accused the book *Bahir* of attacking foundational Jewish monotheism, of creating a multiplicity of divine forces, two supreme principles in God and Shekhinah. One prominent critic, Meir of Narbonne, wrote of the

Kabbalists: 'They are an abomination to all flesh; the worm of their folly will not perish, and the fire of their nonsense will not be extinguished. For they have chosen many gods....' The Kabbalists strongly repudiated such charges, but, says Scholem, there was a tension in medieval Judaism between the mystical conception of God and a static type of monotheism such as was taught outside the Kabbalah, and opposition to the Kabbalists has never entirely stilled in the course of Jewish history.[75]

Yet, says Scholem, the politics of the medieval Kabbalists were highly contradictory, as often on the side of rabbinical tradition and authority as open to charges of heresy themselves. The Kabbalists were divided in their attitudes to rationalist Jewish philosophy, a powerful contemporary trend, as in Maimonides and his followers after his death in 1204. Some Kabbalists did vigorously oppose such rationalism, especially in the quarrel with the adherents of Maimonides that erupted in Spain and France in 1232–35, wishing to stress the esoteric, the gnostic, the mystical, the symbolic, the irrational and inexpressible, the hidden and inaccessible. In relation to Maimonides' rationalism, the Kabbalah is a kind of return of the repressed: of allusion, parable, cosmology, cosmogony, metaphor, mythology, ritual, numbers and language mysticism.[76]

Scholem suggests that much of the imagery and mythology of the Kabbalah in praise of the Shekhinah drew on Oriental and Gnostic sources of antiquity which celebrated female power.[77] In *Adam, Eve, and the Serpent*, Elaine Pagels, contemplating the Christian Gnostic valuation of Eve, remarks that whereas orthodox Christians often blamed Eve for the Fall and pointed to women's submission as appropriate punishment, Gnostics often depicted Eve – or the feminine power she represented – as the source of spiritual awakening. The majority of the known Gnostic texts depict Adam as representing the *psyche* (the emotional and mental impulses), while Eve represents the *pneuma*, the spiritual element of our nature. In contrast to Adam, Eve is the higher principle.[78]

In *Carnal Israel* Daniel Boyarin writes scathingly of the negative view of the body in Maimonides' *Guide of the Perplexed*, a negative view that issues directly, Boyarin feels, from Maimonides' neo-Platonism and neo-Aristotelian-ism. In Boyarin's view, Maimonides interprets the story of the creation of Adam and Eve in terms of a Platonic designation that Matter is female and Form is male, leading to a virulent misogyny. Unfortunately for man, it is impossible for form to exist without matter. Man is noble in his form, indeed is the image of God, but at the same time he is bound to matter, which is earthy, turbid and dark. Everything good in man, as in his apprehension of his Creator, his mental life, his control of desire and anger, are consequent upon his form. Everything bad in man, his eating and drinking and copulation and his passionate desire for such things, is consequent on his matter. Boyarin feels that Maimonides' revulsion against bodily life and in particular his aversion to copulation rivals that of any neo-Platonist.[79]

Whatever we think of Boyarin's interpretation of Maimonides – Boyarin has made it clear that he is no friend of Platonizing tendencies in the history of Jewish thought[80] – the portrait of Rebecca in *Ivanhoe* is a reply to rationalist misogyny: Rebecca as emanation of the Shekhinah, as Abraham's daughter, as a Gnostic Eve, as Sophia, as divine wisdom immanent in the world.

Conclusions

Ivanhoe, as critics have noted, is a complex rewriting of *The Merchant of Venice*. Rebecca's father is often Shylock, cringing, timid, tentative; he is tediously over-concerned with financial calculations, though Isaac's avaricious manner is explained as the result of Christian persecution. In *The Merchant of Venice* Shylock is pathetically fearful of risk, as if Jews, enclosed in ghettos and moneylending, had never been and could never have been adventurous merchant-scholar-travellers themselves – as if only the Venetian Christian gentlemen were capable of boldness, flair and risk-taking in trading voyages across perilous seas.

Ivanhoe does, however, also suggest that Isaac belongs to another cultural history whose existence he and other Jews in England keep alive in 'the pomp and wealth' within their walls.[81] As Goitein notes, there were many great travellers in the medieval Judeo–Islamic–Indian free-trade world, Muslim and Jewish, who travelled remarkable distances, into cold Europe or as far as Ceylon and China, and certainly a common topic in the Geniza papers was 'travel and seafaring'. Shorter distances were hardly noticed in Geniza letters: 'A journey from Spain to Egypt or from Marseilles to the Levant was a humdrum experience, about which a seasoned traveller would not waste a word.' To get to the Indian Ocean, regarded as more frightening than the friendly Mediterranean, merchants had to cross deserts by caravan. Travel could be for trade, pilgrimage and knowledge, Goitein reflecting that in Judaism 'traveling for the sake of study was common even in antiquity'.[82]

The references in *Ivanhoe* to Isaac trading in choice silks, myrrh and aloes, gold and silver work, suggest that Isaac can be imagined as participating in the Mediterranean trade with India. In *Letters of Medieval Jewish Traders* Goitein observes that over half of the commodities traded on the Mediterranean market were imported from India and the Far East, though the risks were tremendous. Goitein includes a letter from Maimonides' younger brother David written while on his way to India. ('Tender love between brothers', says

Goitein, 'is one of the most attractive traits of the Geniza correspondence.')
David, however, drowned in the Indian Ocean, and Goitein quotes from what
Maimonides wrote some eight years afterwards:

> On the day I received that terrible news I fell ill and remained in bed for
> about a year, suffering from a sore boil, fever, and depression, and was
> almost given up. About eight years have passed, but I am still mourning
> and unable to accept consolation. And how should I console myself? He
> grew up on my knees, he was my brother, he was my student; he traded
> on the markets, and earned, and I could safely sit at home. He was well
> versed in the Talmud and the Bible, and knew [Hebrew] grammar well,
> and my joy in life was to look at him. Now, all joy has gone. He has
> passed away and left me disturbed in my mind in a foreign country.
> Whenever I see his handwriting or one of his letters, my heart turns
> upside down and my grief awakens again. In short, 'I shall go down to
> the nether world to my son in mourning' (Genesis 37:35).

While Goitein considers that David was rash in his travels and had in this case
disregarded his older brother's advice to stay in the Sudan and not go to India,
it's clear that Maimonides himself felt his younger brother was worthy of
being counted amongst what Goitein refers to as 'those daring, pious, and
often learned representatives of Middle Eastern civilization during the High
Middle Ages: the overseas traders'.[83]

So influential has the portrait of Shylock been in English theatrical and
literary history that these histories of Jewish travel and the names of great
travellers like the twelfth-century Spanish rabbi Benjamin of Tudela have not
become part of general Western cultural memory. Oftentimes the portrait and
inheritance of Shakespeare's Shylock threaten to overwhelm Isaac as an
independent character. Yet *Ivanhoe* also offers in the much-travelled
multilingual merchant Isaac, father of Rebecca, glimpses of such alternative
traditions, the overseas trader as daring, pious and learned.

Much more sharply, Rebecca is a clear riposte to Jessica. Her own advocate
in her trial, Rebecca is a Portia who defends Shylock, is not hostile to Moors,
and condemns the Christians of England for their exclusivity and inability to
provide the freedom of difference.

In some ways the novel is a narrative of progress of English national culture,
formed in the union of Saxon and Norman under the aegis of Richard and
embodied in Wilfred returning at last to his Ithaca. In *Ivanhoe*, Wilfred is
Ulysses (as in the epigraph from *The Odyssey* to Cedric's banquet scene), while
Gurth the swineherd is a 'second Eumæus', who, after a whispered word from
Wilfred, recognizes and then assists his young master in his difficult re-entry.[84]

In other ways *Ivanhoe* is a drama of confrontation between the cosmopolitan Judeo–Arab world of the Mediterranean and Moorish Spain and the mythos of origin of 'merry England', where the English characters, including Robin Hood who himself had been saved by Rebecca's medical art, all combine to exclude the Jew – and Saracen and African – from their constitution of a unified national culture.[85]

In *Ivanhoe* such exclusion is particularly focused on the Jews: 'Norman, Saxon, Dane, and Briton, however adverse these races were to each other, contended which should look with greatest detestation upon a people, whom it was accounted a point of religion to hate, to revile, to despise, to plunder, and to persecute.' Such exclusion is practised also by tricksters and outlaws, those who might be expected to sympathize with those shunned by the conventional and powerful. While Wamba, Cedric's licensed fool, turns his topsy-turvy carnivalesque wit on the Norman Crusaders in particular, he will not make room at Cedric's table for Isaac the Jew. Chillingly, at the climactic tournament, with the inquisitional fires burning for the witch Rebecca, Robin Hood and Friar Tuck ('gallant outlaws, whose deeds have been rendered so popular in English song') are in attendance, but do nothing to assist or defend her. Friar Tuck explains: 'it is hard that so young and beautiful a creature should perish without one blow being struck in her behalf! Were she ten times a witch, provided she were but the least bit of a Christian, my quarter-staff should ring noon on the steel cap of yonder fierce Templar.' They are prepared to watch Rebecca – a 'coarse white dress, of the simplest form, had been substituted for her Oriental garments' – die by fire before them.[86]

Yet the Normans like Brian de Bois-Guilbert the Knight Templar and Wilfred of Ivanhoe the first Saxon-Norman desire the Orient. That which they set out to conquer, conquers them as desire for the difference they abhor. In Wilfred as sick and ailing for much of the novel, and Bois-Guilbert dying of his desire, English national culture, in its violence of impossible singularity, is constructed in this remarkable text as always fatally wounded.

Two final fragments. The one: how to theorize the multiple disguises and maskings of the novel?[87] There is much veiling as well. The Norman women (as at the Ashby tournament) wear veils. The Saxon women wear them, it is said, because of the extent of Norman rape during the conquest. At her trial Rebecca is commanded to 'unveil herself'. At the end of the novel, in a remarkable moment, Rebecca asks Rowena to lift her bridal veil.[88] *Ivanhoe* perhaps suggests that at the foundational moment of English national character, identity is always concealed as well as revealed; is always performed; is theatre and drama; is the comedy, pathos, tragedy and violence of (in Clifford Geertz's enduring phrase) deep play.

The other: we might wish ourselves to enjoy a romantic fancy. Rebecca tells Rowena at the close that she will always be a maid, dedicating herself to good works.[89] Half in love with Wilfred Rebecca may be, but she is also about to embark on another life, in another time and space, in sensuous sophisticated fifteenth-century Granada, scene and city of the Alhambra.

Yet 'Rebecca', whatever her future existence in Granada, would, after 1492, be exiled again: exile within exile within exile.[90]

We can return to our initial question about anachronism, the novel's leap from late twelfth-century England to late fifteenth-century Spain. Recall Gerber in *The Jews of Spain* evoking the Sephardi Jewish Golden Age as part of the Moorish Golden Age, especially in the tenth and eleventh centuries: it would have been far more sensible (in terms of realist criteria) of *Ivanhoe* to have suggested Rebecca and her father travel from Britain to contemporary Spain in the late twelfth century itself. The Sephardi and Moorish Golden Age may have been receding, and Moorish Spain was under attack from Catholic forces in the Reconquista, but Moorish Spain was still a palpable presence on the Iberian peninsula. By the late thirteenth century, however, let alone the fifteenth, Granada was the only remnant left of Moorish Spain. It would appear that *Ivanhoe* wished to draw attention precisely to Boabdil's Granada and its imminent fall as a moment of extraordinary historical romance and pathos, when the last reminder of a multicultural and pluralist alternative to the European nation-state fatefully fell.

Notes

1. Isadore Twersky (ed.), *A Maimonides Reader* (New York: Behrman, 1972), p. 448.
2. Amin Maalouf, *The Crusades Through Arab Eyes*, trans. Jon Rothschild (London: Al Saqi Books, 1984), Prologue, p. ii.
3. Sir Walter Scott, *Ivanhoe*, ed. A. N. Wilson (London: Penguin, 1986), introduction, pp. xix, xx. I did not obtain, until after I had written the chapter, the 1998 Edinburgh edition, ed. Graham Tulloch, though I have benefited from reading its notes. Concerning the particular date of publication, see James Chandler, *England in 1819: The Politics of Literary Culture and the Case of Romantic Historicism* (Chicago: University of Chicago Press, 1998). For contemporary contexts in the 'long eighteenth century', see Michael Ragussis, *Figures of Conversion: 'The Jewish Question' and English National Identity* (Durham, NC: Duke University Press, 1995); David Simpson, *Romanticism, Nationalism, and the Revolt Against Theory* (Chicago: University of Chicago Press, 1993); Iain McCalman, 'New Jerusalems: prophecy, Dissent and radical culture in England, 1786–1830' in Knud Haakonssen (ed.), *Enlightenment and Religion: Rational Dissent in Eighteenth-Century Britain* (Cambridge: Cambridge University Press, 1996), pp. 312–35.

4.   Alide Cagidemetrio, 'A plea for fictional histories and old-time "Jewesses"' in Werner Sollers (ed.), *The Invention of Ethnicity* (New York: Oxford University Press, 1989), pp. 14–43.

5.   *Ivanhoe*, pp. 107, 201, 430–3, 499, 517.

6.   Cf. Michael Ragussis, 'The birth of a nation in Victorian culture: the Spanish Inquisition, the converted daughter, and the "secret race"', *Critical Inquiry*, 20 (1994), p. 479.

7.   Mikhail Bakhtin, *Problems of Dostoevsky's Poetics* (Manchester: Manchester University Press, 1984), pp. 111–37, and *The Dialogic Imagination* (Austin: University of Texas Press, 1981), 'Forms of time and of the chronotope in the novel', pp. 95–6.

8.   *Ivanhoe*, pp. 106, 494, 512, 514.

9.   I would like to acknowledge discussions on this point with the Crabbe scholar Gavin Edwards.

10. *Ivanhoe*, pp. 52, 84, 196. Cf. Graham Tulloch, '*Ivanhoe* and Bibles' in J. H. Alexander and David Hewitt (eds), *Scott in Carnival: Selected Papers from the Fourth International Scott Conference, 1991* (Aberdeen, 1993), p. 311; Ragussis, *Figures of Conversion*, pp. 104–5, 116.

11. *Ivanhoe*, pp. 37, 49–51, 62.

12. *Ibid.*, p. 49.

13. *Ibid.*, pp. 58, 64, 96, 139–42, 198–9, 229, 299.

14. *Ibid.*, pp. 61, 169, 191, 203, 239, 245, 293. Bakhtin, 'Forms of time and of the chronotope in the novel', writes that the 'historicity of castle time has permitted it to play a rather important role in the development of the historical novel', relating such castle historicity both to Gothic generally and to Scott in particular (pp. 245–6).

15. *Ivanhoe*, p. 55.

16. *Ibid.*, pp. 25, 216–17, 437, 506; the trial is evoked in ch. XXXVII. Apropos England as inquisitional, see Ragussis, 'The birth of a nation in Victorian culture', pp. 486, 496, and *Figures of Conversion*, p. 112.

17. Cf. Ragussis, *Figures of Conversion*, pp. 113, 118. See also Silvia Mergenthal, 'The shadow of Shylock: Scott's *Ivanhoe* and Edgeworth's *Harrington*' in Alexander and Hewitt (eds), *Scott in Carnival*, pp. 327, 330.

18. *Ivanhoe*, pp. 65, 71, 299–301.

19. *Ibid.*, pp. 38, 55, 97, 216, 325, 390, 394, 442.

20. *Ibid.*, pp. 19–22, 27–8.

21. *Ibid.*, pp. 27, 44–5, 57.

22. *Ibid.*, pp. 248, 441–2.

23. *Ibid.*, pp. 26, 28.

24. *Ibid.*, pp. 38, 229–30, 233.

25. *Ibid.*, pp. 49–51.

26. *Ibid.*, p. 433.

27. *A Maimonides Reader*, Introduction, pp. 1–5, 10; 'Epistle to Yemen', pp. 441–2, 450, 457; Jane S. Gerber, *The Jews of Spain: A History of the Sephardic Experience* (New York: The Free Press, 1992), pp. 79–89.

28. *Ivanhoe*, p. 495.

29. *Ibid.*, pp. 551–2 (endnote 5).

30. Stephen Bann, *The Clothing of Clio: A Study of the Representation of History in*

Nineteenth-century Britain and France (Cambridge: Cambridge University Press, 1984), pp. 8, 23. Cf. Lionel Gossman, *Between History and Literature* (Cambridge, MA: Harvard University Press, 1990); Ann Curthoys and John Docker, 'Time, eternity, truth, and death: history as allegory', *Humanities Research*, 1 (1999), pp. 5–26.

31. Paul Gilroy, *The Black Atlantic: Modernity and Double Consciousness* (London: Verso, 1993), pp. 1–19; the reference to Scott is on p. 11.

32. Walter Scott, *Ivanhoe*, ed. Graham Tulloch (Edinburgh: Edinburgh University Press, 1998), p. 513.

33. *Ivanhoe*, p. 552 (endnote 14).

34. *Ibid.*, p. 189. Cf. Robert Irwin, *The Arabian Nights: A Companion* (London: Allen Lane, 1994), p. 98.

35. *Ivanhoe*, pp. 18, 40, 45, 85, 322, 335.

36. *Ibid.*, p. 299.

37. *Ibid.*, Scott's Introduction, p. 544; Tulloch, '*Ivanhoe* and Bibles', pp. 316–18; Ragussis, *Figures of Conversion*, pp. 87, 116.

38. Cf. Wilmon Brewer, *Shakespeare's Influence on Sir Walter Scott* (1925; New York: AMS Press, 1974), pp. 298–302.

39. *Ivanhoe*, pp. 107, 117, 318, 422, 439; Maimonides, 'Epistle to Yemen', pp. 452–3. Cf. Ragussis, 'The birth of a nation in Victorian culture', pp. 507–8.

40. *Ivanhoe*, pp. 8–10, 121, 155, 318, 344.

41. *Ibid.*, pp. 117, 516.

42. *Ibid.*, p. 299.

43. *Ibid.*, pp. 82–3, 116–18, 245, 294, 295–6, 389, 399–400, 402.

44. *Ibid.*, p. 116.

45. S. D. Goitein, *A Mediterranean Society*, vol. III: *The Family* (Berkeley: University of California Press, 1978), pp. 312–59. See also Ammiel Alcalay, *After Jews and Arabs* (Minneapolis: University of Minnesota Press, 1993), pp. 138–9.

46. Goitein, *A Mediterranean Society*, vol. III: *The Family*, pp. 312–59. See also S. D. Goitein, *A Mediterranean Society*, vol. II: *The Community* (Berkeley: University of California Press, 1971), pp. 183–5, section on 'Education of girls, women teachers'. Goitein here mentions examples of women as teachers of embroidery and other female arts as well as in Bible teaching, as scholars, and as Hebrew calligraphers. See also S. D. Goitein, *A Mediterranean Society*, vol. I: *Economic Foundations* (Berkeley: University of California Press, 1967), pp. 127–30.

47. *Ivanhoe*, ed. Graham Tulloch, pp. 526–7.

48. S. D. Goitein, *A Mediterranean Society*, vol. IV: *Daily Life* (Berkeley: University of California Press, 1983), pp. 150–200. See also Goitein, *A Mediterranean Society*, vol. I: *Economic Foundations*, pp. 99–107.

49. Goitein, *A Mediterranean Society*, vol. II: *The Community* , pp. 240–61.

50. *Ibid.*

51. Alcalay, *After Jews and Arabs*, pp. 21, 24–5, 28, 44, 51, 213, 223–4, 253.

52. *Ibid.*, pp. 21, 116–17, 120, 122–7, 128–43, 179. See also James Clifford, 'Looking for Bomma', *London Review of Books* (24 March 1994), pp. 26–7.

53. Alcalay, *After Jews and Arabs*, pp. 61, 109–10, 120, 126, 143, 163, 231–3, 236, 244, 247–50, 256, 276–9.

54. Goitein, *A Mediterranean Society*, vol. IV: *Daily Life*, p. 229. See also the section on 'Wine and other beverages', pp. 253–61.

55. Maxime Rodinson, 'GHIDHA', entry in B. Lewis, C. Pellat and J. Schacht (eds), *The Encyclopaedia of Islam*, new edition, vol. II (Leiden: E. J. Brill, 1965), p. 1068. A great deal of this essay is devoted to Muslim laws concerning food. (I must thank Ahmad Shboul for this reference.)

56. Claudia Roden, *The Book of Jewish Food* (London: Viking, 1997), p. 490.

57. Maxime Rodinson, 'Recherches sur les documents arabes relatifs à la cuisine', *Revue des Etudes Islamiques* (1949), pp. 95–165.

58. *Ibid.*, p. 136.

59. *Ibid.*, esp. pp. 132–9, 144, 152.

60. Alcalay, *After Jews and Arabs*, p. 139. Cf. Goitein, *A Mediterranean Society*, vol. IV: *Daily Life*, p. 253.

61. Goitein, *A Mediterranean Society*, vol. IV: *Daily Life*, pp. 227, 229–31, 234, 245.

62. Roden, *The Book of Jewish Food*, pp. 19, 189. On medieval harissa cf. Rodinson, 'GHIDHA', p. 1064.

63. Cf. Rodinson, 'Recherches ...', pp. 110–11.

64. Gerber, *The Jews of Spain*, p. 30. Cf. Barbara Santich, *The Original Mediterranean Cuisine: Medieval Recipes for Today* (Adelaide: Wakefield Press, 1995), pp. 11–14.

65. Santich, *The Original Mediterranean Cuisine*, p. 11. Cf. Rodinson, 'Recherches ...', p. 102; A. J. Arberry, 'A Baghdad cookery-book', *Islamic Culture* (January and April 1939).

66. Santich, *The Original Mediterranean Cuisine*, pp. 11–14, 68–71. See also Roden, *The Book of Jewish Food*, pp. 186–90, concerning cuisine in Moorish Spain. On the order of dishes, cf. Rodinson, 'GHIDHA', pp. 1071–2.

67. Gerber, *The Jews of* Spain, pp. 28–9, 31.

68. *Ibid.*, pp. 29, 31, 36, 42, 52–3, 55.

69. *Ibid.*, pp. 44–5.

70. *Ibid.*, pp. 45, 74–6.

71. Twersky, *A Maimonides Reader*, Introduction, p. 5; Gerber, *The Jews of Spain*, pp. 79–89. For detailed consideration of Maimonides as philosopher, see Shlomo Pines and Yirmiyahu Yovel (eds), *Maimonides and Philosophy* (Dordrecht: M. Nijhoff Publishers, 1986).

72. Gerber, *The Jews of Spain*, pp. 56–7, 89. See also Angus Mackay, 'The Jews in Spain during the Middle Ages' and Eleazar Gutwirth, 'Towards expulsion: 1391–1492' in Elie Kedourie (ed.), *Spain and the Jews* (London: Thames and Hudson, 1992), chs 1 and 2.

73. Gershom Scholem, *Origins of the Kabbalah*, trans. Allan Arkush, ed. R. J. Zwi Werblowsky (Princeton, NJ: Princeton University Press, 1990), pp. 87–8.

74. *Ibid.*, pp. 163, 165, 169, 177.

75. *Ibid.*, pp. 54, 398–413. See also Daniel C. Matt, *The Essential Kabbalah* (San Francisco: HarperCollins, 1995), Introduction, p. 10.

76. Scholem, *Origins of the Kabbalah*, pp. 393–8, 403–8, 412–13.

77. *Ibid.*, pp. 86–8.

78. Elaine Pagels, *Adam, Eve, and the Serpent* (London: Weidenfeld and Nicolson, 1988), pp. 66–8. See also James M. Robinson (ed.), *The Nag Hammadi Library in English* (Leiden: E. J. Brill, 1984). My thanks to Graeme Clarke for the references to Pagel and Robinson.

79. Daniel Boyarin, *Carnal Israel: Reading Sex in Talmudic Culture* (Berkeley: University of California Press, 1993), pp. 57–60.

80.   Cf. Daniel Boyarin, 'The eye in the Torah: ocular desire in midrashic hermeneutic', *Critical Inquiry* 16 (Spring 1990), pp. 533–4, where he also critiques Maimonides as part of a neo-Platonic and Aristotelian revision of Judaism.

81.   *Ivanhoe*, p. 246.

82.   Goitein, *A Mediterranean Society*, vol. I: *Economic Foundations*, pp. 27, 42–3, 50–1, 59, 61, 66–7. Cf. Richard Hall, *Empires of the Monsoon* (London: HarperCollins, 1996), ch. 1.

83.   S. D. Goitein, *Letters of Medieval Jewish Traders* (Princeton, NJ: Princeton University Press, 1974), pp. vii, 175, 185, 207–12.

84.   *Ivanhoe*, pp. 16, 40, 66, 68, 112–15, 123, 515.

85.   *Ibid.*, pp. 7, 370.

86.   *Ibid.*, pp. 7, 23–4, 34, 42, 47, 49–50, 53, 69, 284, 499, 503–4.

87.   Cf. Ragussis, *Figures of Conversion*, pp. 103, 115.

88.   *Ivanhoe*, pp. 106, 138, 242, 305, 419, 517.

89.   *Ibid.*, p. 518.

90.   Cf. Ragussis, 'The birth of a nation in Victorian culture'. On the life of Iberian women who came to live in the Middle East after the 1492 expulsion, see Joel L. Kramer, 'Spanish ladies from the Cairo Geniza' in Alisa Meyuhas Ginio (ed.), *Jews, Christians, and Muslims in the Mediterranean World After 1492* (London: Frank Cass, 1992), esp. pp. 243–67. Kramer concludes (p. 263): 'The Spanish Jewish women who appear in our Geniza documents are vibrant and dynamic, and hardly fit the stereotype of the traditional Jewish female as esconced in her house and under the protective wings of father, husband, and brothers.'

4

Nation, race and identity in Joyce's *Ulysses*

'Three things come unawares: the Messiah, a found article, and a scorpion.'
Talmudic teacher of third century,
in Gershom Scholem, The Messianic Idea in Judaism[1]

BLOOM: I stand for the reform of municipal morals and the plain ten commandments. New worlds for old. Union of all, jew, moslem and gentile. ... General amnesty, weekly carnival, with masked licence, bonuses for all, esperanto the universal brotherhood. No more patriotism of bar spongers and dropsical imposters. Free money, free love and a free lay church in a free lay state. ... Mixed races and mixed marriage.
'Circe'[2]

In the introduction to her World's Classics edition of *Ulysses*, based on Joyce's 1922 version, Jeri Johnson suggests that, after all the accretions of criticism in the twentieth century, 'we may need to make it strange again'.[3] In this and the following chapters, I would like to wrench the world's great modernist novel from its usual provenance in English and European literature.

What struck me in reading *Ulysses* this time was just how ethnicized and racialized is its language throughout. There are continuous references not only to what we expect, Ireland and Jewishness, but also to Moorish Spain, the Orient and Africanicity. In *Ulysses* Bloom is referred to not only as Odyssean wanderer, as a figure from European literature of antiquity – 'Jewgreek is greekjew' – but also as similar to famous characters in popular Arabian literature, to Haroun Al-Rashid and Sindbad the Sailor of *The Thousand and One Nights*.[4]

In this chapter I pursue these references, so often baffling as they are, pushing on and on into intertextual relationships and cultural histories that are Oriental as well as European; involving a Levantine and Mediterranean cultural history that includes Jews as well as Arabs.

I'll begin by tugging away at constructions of identity and ethnicity, nation and race, in relation to discourses, dramas and desires surrounding nationalism, both Jewish and Irish, for the Zionist movement in its recognizable twentieth-century form had been launched by Theodor Herzl in the 1890s, not long before Mr Bloom's long day early in the new century.[5]

Jewish nationalism

Heir to a century of controversy and division concerning 'the Jewish Question' amongst Jews and non-Jews alike,[6] what might Mr Leopold Paula Bloom, age 38, tall by Dublin standards, not poor, not unhandsome, of an olive complexion, an ad canvasser for the *Freeman's Journal*,[7] of Central European Jewish ancestry, his grandfather's name Virag, Hungarian for flower, think of Jewish nationalism, specifically Zionism?

From early on 16 June 1904 Bloom is certainly acutely aware of the contemporaneous Zionist movement, yet his musings are ambivalent as well as impassioned. In 'Calypso', Mr Bloom goes to the shop of Dlugacz the 'ferreteyed porkbutcher' to purchase his favourite parts of meat to cook for breakfast. Outside he stares with pleasure at what is on offer: 'he breathed in tranquilly the lukewarm breath of cooked spicy pig's blood.' Inside at the counter Bloom sees on a newspaper a reference to Moses Montefiore, an English philanthropist who was encouraging Jewish colonization of Palestine. As he walks home with a kidney (a 'moist tender gland' in his 'sidepocket'), Bloom glances at a leaflet he'd picked up at the porkbutcher's advertising a Zionist plan to buy Palestine from the Turkish government, with individual Jews abroad purchasing a plot of land. Bloom rejects this plan, with its suggestions ('Agendath Netaim: planter's company') of English colonial practices: 'Nothing doing. Still an idea behind it.' (Much later he recalls it as a possible moneymaking scheme.) He greets someone in the street, who doesn't return his salute, and thinks again of the Zionist desire to return to Palestine. Again he rejects it ('No, not like that'). The Zionist vision of Palestine as an empty land he finds frightening, images of a barren terrain and dead sea, so barren and dead it is no longer fertile, it's dead like an old woman ('the grey sunken cunt of the world'): 'Grey horror seared his flesh.' 'Desolation.'[8]

Much, much later, in 'Ithaca', with Bloom and Stephen Daedalus together as if like Odysseus and his son Telemachus, the narrator suggests that the Jews and Irish Catholics have experienced, since the ancient times of Israel and Ireland, a history of discrimination and proscription, of 'dispersal, persecution, survival and revival'. To match the 'possibility of Irish political autonomy or devolution', Bloom begins to chant a Zionist anthem calling for 'restoration in Chanan David of Zion', but has to stop because his memory gives out. Stephen sings a song, curious in the circumstances, about the 'jew's daughter' who, dressed all in green, cuts off a little boy's head with a penknife. Bloom, father of Milly, wonders about the phrase, dressed in green, for a 'jew's daughter'.[9] Where can Bloom feel he belongs: in Ireland with a green-dressed daughter (the child of the outsider putting down roots, though in common song suspected and feared as nevertheless beneath the green still a Jew, a secret dangerous female Orient), in Zion in a restored Israel, or anywhere and nowhere (Bloom as 'Everyman or Noman')?[10]

For all its possible appeal as an alternative to estrangement and hostility, Bloom will in the end repudiate Zionism. In those ugly phrases of Palestine as dead and desolate Bloom suggests the ugliness of the Zionist vision of Palestine, that Eurocentric view which assumed the Ottoman Eastern Mediterranean to be (as the British colonists assumed of Aboriginal Australia) a *terra nullius*, unpeopled, uncultivated, deserted, a desert, awaiting those who knew.[11] In the Zionist imaginary, the Orient is not an alluring sensuous female presence, as in so much European Orientalist literature and art.[12] It is a dying disgusting arid old woman, to be swept aside so that fertility can be brought from outside: the Zionist trope of making the desert bloom.[13]

In 'Ithaca', back home at 7 Eccles Street, we see Bloom setting alight to the 'prospectus (illustrated) entitled Agendath Netaim', the advertisement for a Zionist colony he'd looked at near the beginning of his day in 'Calypso'. Now Bloom submits it, with the aid of candleflame, to 'total combustion'.[14]

Irish nationalism

To focus on Bloom's feelings towards nationalism, not only Jewish but Irish as well, is to question an apparent given in much Joyce criticism, that Bloom is a character passive and gentle, without malice, without violence, without hate.[15] Turning to the 'Cyclops' episode, where Irish nationalism appears very much akin to an exclusionary European and English – and Zionist – nationalism, I will modify this portrait by sketching in lines of anger, passion and anguish, while not forgetting all the irony, parody, comedy, vaudeville.[16]

In 'Cyclops', around 5 p.m. on 16 June, about the time Blazes Boylan is visiting Molly Bloom at 7 Eccles Street, Bloom approaches Barney Kiernan's pub, where some of the good men of Dublin are drinking, including a loudly self-proclaimed Irish nationalist, the 'citizen'. The nameless narrator, some kind of debt collector, casts a coarse, jaundiced eye over various happenings and proceedings, with scathing references to Jews throughout, including a reference to Bloom's darkness of cast. A question hangs over the conversations in the pub: is Leopold Bloom a true Irishman? Bloom clearly appears as an outsider to the men in the bar. Initially he doesn't wish to enter, since he's come to meet Martin Cunningham to help arrange some complicated insurance matters for the family of Paddy Dignam, whose funeral had been held that morning. But his staying outside annoys the citizen, who makes a snarling reference to Bloom as a 'bloody freemason'. When he does enter the bar he irritates its denizens by his caution and prudence, refusing a drink and saying he'll content himself with a cigar. The citizen also suspects Bloom is not properly masculine, is a womanly man, 'a half and half', a 'fellow that's neither fish nor flesh'. While Bloom talks to others, the citizen casts increasingly hostile scowls and comments in his direction, growling, 'We want no more strangers in our house'. Bloom finds himself in an argument about the British colonizers, the citizen loudly proclaiming that the Irish should pit 'force against force', Bloom trying to demur.[17]

A discussion about the meaning of national identity is launched. Another good citizen, John Wyse, asks Bloom if he knows what a nation means, Bloom replying, yes, that a 'nation is the same people living in the same place', a definition the others find laughably inadequate. The citizen asks Bloom what *is* his nationality, and when Bloom replies that it is Irish, for he was born there, his interlocutor spits. ('The citizen said nothing only cleared the spit out of his gullet and, gob, he spat a Red bank oyster out of him right in the corner.') A little later, Bloom becomes angry, pointing out that he belongs to a 'race' that is 'hated and persecuted'. Bloom then famously declares his utopian pacifism, that history, with its recourse to 'force', with its 'insult and hatred', is of 'no use', that it is the very reverse of what is really life, which is love, the 'opposite of hatred'. More than a little unsettled, Bloom decides to look outside the bar again for Martin Cunningham, but the citizens in the bar think his leaving is a ruse, that Bloom has had a bet on a horse, Throwaway, without sharing the tip around, and has gone to collect. The men darkly refer to Bloom's darkness; the citizen calls him a 'whiteyed kaffir'. They offer various calumnies against Bloom and his father as a fraudulent old bagman. Bloom's associate Martin Cunningham comes into the bar, and immediately agrees that Bloom is a 'perverted jew ... from a place in Hungary'. They deride Bloom for not being a true man, for once having been seen shopping for baby food before the birth of his son Rudy, for his sexual inadequacy, for not sharing his racing tip, for not shouting drinks, and for not being obvious in his religious identity, not clearly Jew or Roman or Protestant.[18]

The narrator declares that it would be an act of God to throw someone like that into the sea. The citizen declares that we shouldn't allow 'things' like

Bloom to 'contaminate' Irish shores. When Bloom returns, the mood is ugly. Martin Cunningham hurries Bloom out to a waiting carriage, with the citizen bawling Judeophobic curses after him. Bloom, also enraged, reminds the citizen of great Jews of the past like Karl Marx and Spinoza, and that in any case Christ was a Jew: 'Your God', he notes. The citizen froths: 'By Jesus ... I'll brain that bloody jewman for using the holy name. By Jesus, I'll crucify him so I will. Give us that biscuitbox here.'[19]

The scene in Barney Kiernan's pub and environs ends in farce. The citizen, amidst much laughter from the narrator and bystanders, hurls the biscuitbox after Bloom's retreating carriage, recalling and parodying the violence of the Cyclops in *The Odyssey*, the one-eyed monster who hurls a rock at Odysseus' boat as it flees across the winedark sea. Bloom meanwhile is indeed transfigured into the Messiah and prophets of old, the narrator perceiving a great brightness surrounding the carriage, now become a chariot, a voice from heaven calling out Elijah! Elijah! Bloom, in the closing words of 'Cyclops', ascends 'at an angle of fortyfive degrees over Donohoe's in Little Green Street like a shot off a shovel'.[20]

The 'Cyclops' episode is a kind of negative epiphany, of crisis, confrontation and unpleasantness mixed with burlesque. The men in the bar are hardly presented as ideal, and the narrator throughout has hardly been fully admiring of the citizen, commenting that the fellow had once grabbed the holding of an evicted tenant.[21] Their suspicions of Bloom over the horse are based on a misunderstanding they make no attempt to clarify with him.[22] Yet they and the narrator come close to uniting behind the citizen in his nationalist insistence on a single true identity, a national type, a presumed ethnic essence, as against Bloom's pluralist – we might say multicultural – stance that a nation includes everyone living in that nation. The men in the bar loudly declare their contempt for their colonizers, that the Irish are persecuted, yet they assume the colonizer's conception of a single ideal identity, share in the colonizers' violence and threats of violence, and feel no sympathy or empathy for their non-Irish (or those they see as non-Irish) fellow-persecuted and dispersed around the globe.[23]

Bloom, by contrast, appears as a redeemer for the Irish, though like all saviours and messiahs is met with incomprehension, contempt and violence. In the later 'Eumaeus' episode, at the cabman's shelter, Stephen Daedalus refers to Bloom as *Christus*. Bloom tells Stephen he resents 'violence or intolerance in any shape or form', and that it's a 'patent absurdity on the face of it to hate people because they live round the corner and speak another vernacular, so to speak'. Stephen, we know, has rejected his own father and all the patriarchal fathers of Ireland, actual and literary, meeting Bloom the Odyssean wanderer by day's end as his possible symbolic parent. By contrast to the Irish patriarchs in the pub, Bloom figures Enlightenment values of reason and debate, of cosmopolitanism and internationalism.[24]

In *The Dialogic Imagination* Mikhail Bakhtin talks of the various rights and postures of the fool. The fool can parade naïvety, an inability to understand usual conventions. Deploying masks permits the fool not only to act life as a comedy and to betray to the public a personal life, down to its most private and prurient little secrets, but also the right to rip off masks, to rage at others with a primeval, 'almost cultic', rage.[25] Bloom in 'Cyclops' is recognizable in these terms as fool and trickster, including his 'almost cultic' rage at the nationalist citizen.

Roc and auk: Bloom, Odysseus and Sindbad

In *The Odyssey*, Odysseus and his protector the goddess Pallas Athene create a world of disguise, transformation and metamorphosis, so that identity in the ancient Mediterranean world is fluid and uncertain, is rarely what it seems, is always masking and concealing so that protagonists continuously doubt what they see. Yet there are key differences between Bloom and Odysseus. Odysseus is often described as clever, wily, resourceful, a trickster; but he is also frequently evoked in repetitive recognition phrases as a sacker of cities. Odysseus – like the nationalist citizens of Barney Kiernan's pub – clearly demarcates those he considers fellow Greeks, and those he feels are barbarians. When Odysseus wakes from sleep in an unknown land, in the Nausikaa episode, he wonders with a groan if the people he'll meet will be hostile, uncivilized savages, or kindly, god-fearing people. The reference to kindliness is just a little odd, for Odysseus is wandering the seas, searching for Ithaca his home and yearning to return to Penelope his everpatient wife, after helping to sack Troy, bringing doom and slaughter to the Trojans. In the 'Cyclops' chapter Odysseus tells how in the travail of his travels he came to Ismarus, the city of the Cicones; he sacked the city, destroyed its menfolk and captured the women as well as vast plunder. Women are taken as prizes in war and for slavery. At the same time, Odysseus will frequently loudly lament for the men of his party he has lost in such murderous raids. Bloom neither shares such ethnic exclusivism nor Odysseus' desire for bloodthirsty revenge, as in the hideous violence Odysseus and Telemachus inflict on the suitors at the epic's end.

In the final moments of 'Ithaca', as Bloom is drifting towards sleep ('He rests. He has travelled'), the narrator enigmatically associates Bloom's tired thoughts not with Homer's Odysseus but with Sindbad the medieval Oriental Odyssean adventurer:

> Going to a dark bed there was a square round Sindbad the Sailor's roc's
> auk's egg in the night of the bed of all the auks of the rocs of Darkinbad
> the Brightdayler.[26]

The roc is a giant Arabian mythological bird of prey, with huge talons, which
eats serpents and feeds its young on elephants. What could the mammoth roc
and its mammoth egg signify for Leopold Paula Bloom falling asleep at the feet
of Molly Bloom?

In *The Thousand and One Nights* the Sindbad the Sailor stories are another
writing of *The Odyssey*. We first see Sindbad as a wealthy retired mariner,
living in splendour in Baghdad, the City of Peace, in the reign of the far-famed
Caliph Haroun Al-Rashid, telling his friends and kinsfolk of his remarkable
travels. Typically, Sindbad, sated by the pleasures of city life, will periodically
equip himself with merchandise, sail down the Tigris to Basrah, join a ship and
journey about trading from port to port and island to island (not raiding and
looting – though when he returns, as well as distributing large sums in charity
among the poor of the city including widows and orphans, he usually acquires
fine houses, rich farm-lands, concubines, eunuchs and slaves). As fate will have
it, however, his ship will meet with a storm, be blown off course into unknown
seas, and Sindbad will find himself washed up alone on a mysterious land or
island. In his adventures he survives great perils to acquire rare jewels that can
be traded for great wealth: there is a repeated narrative of death by
abandonment, rebirth and renewal. Sindbad encounters a roc on his second
voyage, when he has been left behind on an uninhabited island (in a primal
nightmare, he'd fallen asleep and his ship had sailed off). He experiences terror
and despair. Then he notices a huge white dome, which he realizes is an egg
when the mother bird, a roc, returns, her wings darkening the sky; mother falls
asleep on dome. Like Odysseus, Sindbad is clever and resourceful. He escapes
the Island of the Roc by tying himself to the slumbering bird's talon with his
turban, hitching a ride when it wakes to a distant hillside above a valley. He
then discovers that the valley floor is covered with glittering diamonds among
which are coiled deadly snakes and vipers. Having first secured many of the
rare jewels about his person, Sindbad, by tying himself to the underside of a
sheep carcass that a roc flies away with, guilefully hitches a ride to a hillside
summit on these Diamond Mountains.[27]

On his fifth voyage, Sindbad's ship comes to a desert island. From the deck
Sindbad and his merchant companions see the white dome of a roc's egg. In a
scene recalling an episode in *The Odyssey* (where Odysseus' men refuse to heed
his warning not to eat the sacred cattle, symbol of fertility, on Thrinacia, island
of the sun-god), the other merchants go ashore, foolishly break open the egg
with stones and dismember the unborn bird for a feast. Sindbad is horrified.

That which he fears happens: the parent rocs bombard and sink the fleeing ship with rocks. Sindbad holds on to some wreckage and finally reaches an island, where, however, he is enslaved by the Old Man of the Sea, whom he has to carry about on his shoulders (the bestial old man 'discharging his natural filth upon me').[28] For Sindbad, then, and perhaps also for Bloom, the roc and roc's egg signify rescue *and* disaster: escape from the nightmare of being left behind, death-by-aloneness in a hostile land; yet humiliation on a Ship of Fools heading for death by drowning, death brought on by the insensitive, thoughtless, violent actions of his male companions.

One more thing about Sindbad. He marries. On his last voyage, which occupies some 27 years. From Basrah he sets sail, with a fair wind and rich cargo, in the company of some eminent merchants; they voyage to the China Sea, when a violent tempest drives them into the world's farthermost ocean, where a giant whale seizes the ship in its mouth. Only Sindbad saves himself, clinging to a piece of timber, at length to be cast on a bountiful island; he makes a raft from an exotic tree, pushes off down a river, to be finally rescued by a venerable old man who takes him to his city. Sindbad prospers in the new land. His raft, made of sandalwood, earns him a fortune, and the old man prevails upon him to marry his daughter; they grow to love each other dearly, living together in happiness and contentment. But, it turns out, the land is stranger than he thinks, turns unexpectedly hostile. Every year the men grow wings and for a whole day fly high in the air, leaving their wives and children behind. If, however, the word Allah is uttered, the men fall directly to the earth. Sindbad finds this out all too rudely, having hitched a ride with a man he thought was a friend; he is cursed when, as they fly about, he praises Allah, King of the Universe. Hearing of this misadventure and his being cursed by a supposed friend, Sindbad's wife enjoins that they must leave these people, for they are the brothers of Satan and know not the True God; her father, who has died, was, she explains, of an alien race, who shared none of their creeds and did not lead their life. Sindbad and his wife sell their possessions, and sail away to Baghdad.

In his final dreamy moments before sleep, does Bloom too feel that he and Molly should leave a land and society where hostility, insult and pain they face? But if Sindbad can return to his own people, his true friends and kinsfolk, in Baghdad, City of Peace, where can Bloom and Molly go? Is such flight and return impossible, like a 'square round'? An extinct species of hope, like the subarctic auk? Or are these smiling thoughts, jokes Bloom is enjoying as consciousness fades, given the previous passage where Bloom plays with Sindbad's name in apparent reference to the popular 1890s pantomime *Sindbad the Sailor*?[29]

In any case, Bloom, unlike Odysseus or Sindbad, has, except in his thoughts, hardly travelled anywhere; he's a 'landlubber'. To leave a land of false friendship where he has been cursed and insulted, where can Bloom go, if only in dream and nightmare (the 'dark bed' of 'Darkinbad the Brightdayler')? The narrator similarly wonders, adding to Bloom's final thought a hanging, unanswered 'Where?'[30]

In 'Ithaca', Bloom doesn't think of the Orient in Zionist fashion as deserted or unpeopled: it is at the very least inhabited for him by figures like Haroun Al-Rashid and Sindbad. Jerusalem, the 'holy city', calls to his mind images of the 'mosque of Omar and gate of Damascus'.[31]

In his final sleepy, dreamy, nightmarish thoughts, it is an Arab Oriental scene, of Sindbad and the mythical roc, entwined with the extinct auk of cold northern seas, that Bloom invokes.

Perhaps, too, as he nestles into bed, Bloom associates Molly with the powerful female figures of *The Thousand and One Nights*, stories where women work and travel and are important in their own right. Women can be resourceful, rich, daring, out-tricking men of power, men who wish to abuse their power ('The Young Woman and Her Five Lovers'). As *jinneyah* they work magical transformations ('The Porter and the Three Girls of Baghdad'). Frequently they are disdainful or contemptuous of the men who wish to control them.[32]

In her soliloquy, Molly, for all that she has just entertained Blazes Boylan that afternoon as lover, has as little time as her eccentric Poldy for the good men of Ireland and all the conventional patriarchal men of all the world ('itd be much better for the world to be governed by the women in it'), men who spend so much of history gambling and getting drunk, killing and slaughtering, men who show no empathy for the gender that has brought them into existence. Mentions of the exotic abound in Molly's final thoughts, indeed gather pace, accompanied by those enigmatic scatterings of 'yes'. We note a stream of nostalgic dreaming references to her girlhood in Gibraltar, where she was a Flower of the mountain, when she would put a rose in her hair 'like the Andalusian girls used to'; and beyond Gibraltar to the towns of Moorish Spain, with their 'queer little streets and pink and blue and yellow houses'. She thinks of the 'figtrees in the Alameda gardens', and 'those handsome Moors all in white and turbans like kings'. Molly invokes in Moorish Spain a cosmopolitanism ('the Greeks and the jews and the Arabs and the devil knows who else from all ends of the earth') characteristic of the traditional Islamic world, and close to Bloom's invocation (that we saw in our epigraph) of a desired union of all, 'jew, moslem and gentile'.[33]

It is a cosmopolitanism, an anti-monoculturalism, that, like her Leopold, she sees as clearly other to contemporary Dublin and Irish society.

Postnationalism, post-Orientalism, post-Zionism

The Thousand and One Nights is part of a long tradition of Arab influence on, and interactions with, European literary and intellectual history, not least in the impact of the brilliant literature and philosophy of al-Andalus, Moorish Spain, which introduced to medieval Europe poetry and music that would be taken up by the troubadours, as well as the medical and scientific knowledge of the Greeks (Galen, Ptolemy, Aristotle). The works of Ibn Rushd (Averroes), Ibn Sina (Avicenna) and Maimonides were studied by the doctors of the Church, reappearing in the philosophy of St Thomas Aquinas (that not inconsiderable figure in Joyce's intellectual formation). The framing story and the wandering textuality of medieval Arab narratology were influential in Chaucer's *Canterbury's Tales* and Boccaccio's *Decameron*.[34]

Early in the eighteenth century, Galland's French translation of *The Thousand and One Nights* became almost immediately immensely popular and influential, helping establish the Oriental Tale,[35] accompanied by parodies and burlesques, farces and pantomimes, as a major generic field in English literature and theatre. The Oriental Tale – in Montesquieu's *Persian Letters*, Voltaire's *Zadig*, Beckford's *Vathek*, Bage's *The Fair Syrian* – was a constant source of inventive stories, of high romance and adventure, exotic and marvellous, magical and fantastical: a range of possible narratives, frequently deploying the epistolary form, from the moral to the philosophic to the satiric, that were continuously Europeanized and transformed, crossed with philosophical speculation, Gothic, romance and romanticism, erotica and pornography. The story of Sindbad was particularly popular as model, the life and adventures of a picaresque hero as he travels through various strange lands learning the ways of humanity and seeking his fortune, with stories being constantly told of the people and creatures, wonders and perils, he observes and survives. I mentioned *The Thousand and One Nights* in the preceding chapter in relation to the fantasticality of *Ivanhoe*. Here I will press their relevance much more strongly as an always thriving fissiparous alternative to stable literary canons and aesthetic homogeneity, even, or especially, in the Enlightenment. The 'long eighteenth century' did not have to wait for Gothic to introduce textual heterogeneity, the unnerving and uncanny.[36] In his essay 'Raymond Schwab and the romance of ideas' Edward Said suggests we should notice the degree of 'derangement' stimulated by the Orient in Europe in the pre-Romantics and Romantics.[37]

In his introduction to *The* Arabian Nights *in English Literature* (1988), Peter Caracciolo observes that the *Nights* in the eighteenth century existed and persisted as an alternative repertory of writing to neoclassical demands for unity and continuity. Other essays in the book point to how much English writing in the nineteenth century and later, as in Dickens and Wilkie Collins, or

Conrad, Wells and Joyce, was influenced by the *Nights* in terms of narrativity and complexity, an other to realism, even though Oriental Tales themselves had gone out of fashion.[38] In *The Arabian Nights: A Companion* Robert Irwin writes that in the twentieth century the *Nights* influenced not only *Ulysses* but the arabesques and magical realism of Borges, and that in general twentieth-century modernism drew on the *Nights* for framing, self-reflexivity, embedded references, hidden patterns, recursiveness and intertextuality, playfulness, *doppelgängers*, and labyrinthine structuring.[39]

If modernism wished to rebel against what it saw as a previous dominance of a nineteenth-century monologic novel controlled by an all-powerful narrator, it could return for inspiration to the enemy of its enemy, to the Oriental Tales, to stories ever begetting more stories, moving sideways rather than resolutely forward, denying and defying any aesthetic and cosmology of unicity: *Ulysses* as dialogic and polyphonic. In which case the allusions to Haroun Al-Rashid and Sindbad the Sailor in *Ulysses* refer not only to Bloom as trickster and wanderer but also to the form of the novel itself.

Often in the *Nights*, in terms of chronotopes, it is random chance rather than the characters' own inner strivings and choices that propel incidents in the narratives.

The operation of chance can perhaps (violently adapting Lyotard) be seen as 'postmodern' in its cosmology, a refusal of any tyrannical demand for coherence, cohesion, order, pattern. Rather the world is constructed as the effect of unpredictable accidents, as the calamities, brutalities, reversals and strokes of good fortune of fate and mischance, a world where misfortune can strike at any moment from anywhere – and in *Ulysses*, we recall, it was only that morning, back from the pork butcher, with kidney in sidepocket, that Bloom, perusing the letters that had just come, realized that Molly would be entertaining Blazes Boylan that afternoon.

The eighteenth-century literature of the Oriental Tales might strike us now as 'postmodern' in another way, in allowing for disagreement, differing views, difference, without an omniscient narrator directing and judging. Indeed, this kind of narrative method continued strongly into the nineteenth century in mystery novels, not least in Wilkie Collins's *The Woman in White* and *The Moonstone*: the alleged dominance in the nineteenth century of the classic realist novel is a curious twentieth-century modernist myth.[40] There is talk of Wilkie Collins in *Ulysses*. In 'Wandering Rocks' the typist Miss Dunne wonders if there is too much mystery for her liking in *The Woman in White*. Molly, a great reader of popular romance-melodramas as well as mystery novels, talks of her fondness for Wilkie Collins, in particular *The Moonstone*.[41] In Collins's immensely popular novels the author appears usually as no more than a detached editor of a body of letters, a collector, redactor, arranger.

Joyce criticism has applied the notion of an Arranger to *Ulysses*, a presence in the episodes in addition to the various narrators.⁴² Bakhtin had already implied such a notion in *Problems of Dostoevsky's Poetics* when he argues that in Dostoevsky's texts the author acts as organizer and participant in the dialogues, the clashes of conflicting positions and voices, but without retaining for himself the final word. The author tends to recede from view, while taunting and provoking the characters, caught in crisis and threshold states, to expand in their consciousness and self-consciousness. Characters remain unfinalized and with strong rights as autonomous subjects in the narrative, as if 'author-thinkers' themselves. Everywhere in Dostoevsky's novels we partici-pate as readers in the unresolved clash of heterogeneous, contradictory aesthetic modes and ideological values.⁴³

If *Ulysses* is now discussed as postmodern in its textuality of excess, pastiche, heterogeneous fragments, incommensurable discourses,⁴⁴ we might also see it as prefiguring postmodernity in another sense, as post-Orientalist and post-Zionist. It destabilizes a key trope of modernity, that which Said's *Orientalism* protested against, the West constructing the Orient as different in essence and being; Said sees Zionism as Orientalist in these terms as well.⁴⁵

In *After Jews and Arabs* Alcalay argues that Zionism was and is a Eurocentric discourse and colonial practice that in the establishment of Israel effected a disastrous tragic double transfer of peoples, of the Arabs out of Palestine and the Jews out of the Arab world. Hundreds of thousands of the Arabs of Palestine were forcibly expelled, those remaining being reduced to subordinate status in a society insisting on a purity of nation and race, European nationalist concepts alien to the pre-colonial history of the Levant. The Oriental Jews, the Sephardic, Levantine, Ottoman, Arab and Persian Jewish communities, were forced in the 1950s to uproot themselves from their home societies to join transit camps in Israel, there to be despised in racist terms by the European Ashkenazi Jews as inferior, primitive, backward, premodern, and condescend-ingly expected to assimilate to a new, Eurocentric, Jewish identity.⁴⁶

Alcalay suggests that the Zionist intervention in the Levant was a cruel disruption of more than a thousand years of history in the Middle East, North Africa, Muslim Spain.⁴⁷

In Alcalay's view, Jews participated in the Levantine poetics of heterogeneity up to the Second World War, until the Zionist coupure. Alcalay feels, nevertheless, that in recent cultural production by Palestinians and Oriental Jews the lineaments can be perceived of a 'postmodern' pluralistic New Levant, a reprise, in new forms, of the traditional Levant where there was an 'almost anarchic lack of purity and exclusivity, the inexhaustible knack of being in many places in many times at once'. In this New Levant, Oriental Jewish playwrights, film-makers, writers, poets, intellectuals share a sense of belonging to a common world with Arab playwrights, film-makers, writers, poets, intellectuals. Palestine/Israel will become 'the country of the people living in it, rather than some ever-expanding "home" for all Jews', a land where the Jews of European origin, those enforcing the Zionist master narrative of nationalism and European superiority, will find themselves more and more challenged.[48]

In *Ulysses* the thoughts and consciousness of Leopold Bloom, rejecting Zionism, invoking Jerusalem as Levantine, and calling in a utopian way for 'Union of all, jew, moslem and gentile. . . . esperanto the universal brotherhood', prefigure such post-Orientalist, post-Zionist and postnationalist discourse and desire, the recognition of the history of Jewish identities as indeed a poetics of heterogeneity, as Oriental, Levantine, Mediterranean, as well and as much as European.

Bloom and race

Is Bloom, however, a complete outsider to Irish and more generally Western discourses of race, to European superiority?[49]

Throughout *Ulysses* I came across a language of race that I found disturbing, especially references to 'coon', 'nigger' and 'niggers', even if opaquely ironic and parodic. In 'Lotus-Eaters', Bloom thinks of the Catholic Church's attempts to convert 'blacks' in its African mission: 'Like to see them sitting round in a ring with blub lips, entranced, listening.' And refers to them as 'cannibals'. In 'Hades' a good citizen, John Henry Menton, exclaims over Molly, or Marion Tweedy as was, marrying 'a coon' like Bloom. In 'Scylla and Charybdis' Stephen enunciates his theory of Shakespeare (a theory he immediately disavows) to the librarian John Eglinton in the National Library, at one point joking about death as 'the place where the bad niggers go', a curiously casual racial reference, parodying an old minstrel song, to reverberate in such a locale. In 'Wandering Rocks', while the very reverend John Conmee is on a tram, the narrator observes: 'From the hoardings Mr Eugene Stratton grinned with thick niggerlips at Father Conmee.' Father Conmee thinks of the Church's African mission and all the millions of lost, wasted black and brown and yellow souls. In 'Nausikaa', Gerty MacDowell is wearing a 'coquettish little love of a hat of wideleaved nigger straw contrast trimmed with an underbrim of eggblue chenille and at the side a butterfly bow to tone'. After he has masturbated, Bloom spots Gerty watching the fireworks with one of the children she is looking after, the one with 'the mop head and the nigger mouth'. In the fantasia of 'Circe' Bloom suspects that Molly has a taste for 'slumming', for the 'exotic' – 'Negro servants too in livery if she had money. Othello black brute.'

This vision gets Bloom thinking of a (white) minstrel group with black masks, 'coloured coons in white duck suits', with 'paler smaller negroid hands', 'white Kaffir eyes', singing with 'smackfatclacking nigger lips'. (Recall that in 'Cyclops' the nationalist citizen refers to Bloom as a 'whiteyed kaffir'.) Molly in her soliloquy, perhaps masturbating, does indeed bring forward in her mind's eye the mythical phallus of 'a black man Id like to try a beauty'. Molly also thinks of one of Mina Purefoy's many children as 'like a nigger with a shock of hair on it Jesusjack the child is a black'.[50]

In 'Eumaeus' Bloom and Stephen, having left the vaudevillean brothel, come across a group of Italians having a heated discussion. Bloom thinks their language is so 'vivacious', so 'animated', so 'beautiful', poetic, melodious, full. Stephen has to drily explain that the Italians are enraged over money matters, deflating Bloom's essentializing and idealizing of Italian speech. In the nearby cabman's shelter a nationalistic redbearded sailor, W. B. Murphy, strikes up a conversation, telling them in a kind of stage sailorese of his travels to distant parts and the strange sights he's witnessed. He shows Stephen and Bloom and the cabmen at the shelter a picture postcard he claims is a scene in Bolivia, a 'group of savage women in striped loincloths' squatting with a swarm of infants outside some 'primitive shanties', 'stark ballocknaked' eating 'dead horse's liver raw'. The sailor seeks to impress his audience with more arcane exotic knowledge, that in Trieste he saw an Italian stab a man in the back with a knife, and that Chinese cook rats in their soup, leading to a general muttering in the shelter about 'foreigners', knives, and murder. The sailor particularly objects to 'them black lads ... I hate those buggers. Sucks your blood dry, they does.'[51]

In this scene, Bloom and Stephen exchange glances of detachment from the curious sight of the Irish, victims of the racism of an imperial power, being so unselfconsciously casually racist themselves. Yet Bloom can position himself as a superior European. In Barney Kiernan's pub in 'Cyclops' Bloom objects to Irish nationalist essentializing of Irish identity. In 'Eumaeus' he notices the 'wholesale whoppers' other fellows coin, not least those directed at Bloom himself. Yet in 'Eumaeus' Bloom goes on, at least speculatively, to agree with the sailor, that Italians perhaps do like to stab people in the back, and capture cats for eating with garlic; and, Bloom continues, Spaniards might have 'passionate temperaments', like that of his wife, because 'climate accounts for character'. Here Bloom, rather to Stephen's bemusement, is talking conventional northern European mythology ('wholesale whoppers') about southern Europeans. Then he tells Stephen of a visit to a museum where he saw antique statues of women of splendid proportions of hip and bosom, women not to be seen 'here' – an interesting touch in Bloom of late nineteenth-century *fin de siècle* primitivism. Yet, again, not long after, Bloom tells Stephen of how offensive the nationalist citizen had been to him in Kiernan's bar, that he's just as good an Irishman as 'that rude person', and that he resents 'violence or intolerance in any shape or form'.[52]

No, Bloom as other, as trickster, as anti-nationalist, as anti-Zionist Jew does not inhabit a pure outside, beyond Irish, European and Western essentializing fantasies, casual prejudices, erotic myths, white mythologies, racist nonsense. And perhaps that is one reason why their friendship appears to fade into inconsequentiality, and why Stephen does not stay the night at 7 Eccles Street, though he is immensely tired and has nowhere to go. In this aspect does Bloom fail Stephen as all the other fathers of Ireland have failed him? For Stephen is not like Telemachus, unquestioning of the values of his father Odysseus, King of Ithaca (he who is so contemptuous of those he constitutes as barbarian others).

Perhaps. Stephen, after all, also deployed racial language in the National Library and intoned that childhood anti-semitic song in Bloom's kitchen.

Is there, in its references to Africans particularly, a heart of darkness in *Ulysses*?

Notes

1. Gershom Scholem, *The Messianic Idea in Judaism* (New York: Schocken, 1978), p. 11.
2. James Joyce, *Ulysses* (1922), intro. and notes by Declan Kiberd (London: Penguin, 1992), pp. 610–11. All page references will be to this edition.
3. Jeri Johnson, introduction to James Joyce, *Ulysses* (1922; Oxford: Oxford University Press, 1993), p.x.
4. *Ulysses*, pp. 59, 622, 685, 871. Cf. Richard Brown, *James Joyce and Sexuality* (Cambridge: Cambridge University Press, 1988), p. 28; Robert G. Hampson, 'The genie out of the bottle: Conrad, Wells and Joyce' in Peter L. Caracciolo (ed.), *The Arabian Nights in English Literature* (Basingstoke: Macmillan, 1988).
5. Cf. Bryan Cheyette, *Constructions of 'the Jew' in English Literature and Society* (Cambridge: Cambridge University Press, 1993), ch. 6.
6. Cf. Michael Ragussis, *Figures of Conversion: 'The Jewish Question' and English National Identity* (Durham, NC, and London: Duke University Press, 1995); Reina Lewis, *Gendering Orientalism: Race, Femininity, and Representation* (London and New York: Routledge, 1996), pp. 191–217; Sander Gilman, ' "I'm down on whores": race and gender in Victorian London' in David Theo Goldberg (ed.), *Anatomy of Racism* (Minneapolis: University of Minnesota Press, 1990).
7. For references to Bloom's middle name Paula see *Ulysses*, pp. 842, 852. See also Hugh Kenner, *Ulysses*, rev. edn (Baltimore: Johns Hopkins University Press, 1987), pp. 28, 30, 44.
8. *Ulysses*, pp. 70–3, 845. Kenner (p. 47) passingly refers, in relation to the horror here, to Bloom's 'bad scare', but shows no interest in telling the reader what the

horror and desolation are about – odd, given his insistence on Bloom's mildness and evenness of temperament. For allusions here see Don Gifford and Robert J. Seidman, *Notes for Joyce: An Annotation of Joyce's Ulysses* (New York: E. P. Dutton, 1974), pp. 54–5.

9. *Ulysses*, pp. 806–7, 809–10.
10. *Ibid.*, p. 858.
11. Cf. my analyis of Leon Uris's *Exodus*, 'Orientalism and Zionism', *Arena*, 75 (1986), pp. 58–95, and my 'Jews in Australia', *Arena*, 96 (1991), pp. 145–57.
12. See Lynne Thornton, *Les orientalistes, peintres voyageurs 1828–1908* (Paris: ACR Edition, 1983); Joanna de Groot, '"Sex" and "Race": the construction of language and image in the nineteenth century' in Susan Mendus and Jane Rendall (eds), *Sexuality and Subordination* (London: Routledge, 1989). I'm not assuming that Europe to Orient is as male to female is the only Western mode; see Billie Melman, *Women's Orients: English Women and the Middle East, 1718–1918* (Basingstoke: Macmillan, 1992); Lewis, *Gendering Orientalism*; and John Docker and Iain McCalman, *Sheer Folly and Derangement: The Exotic in British Culture 1700–2000* (forthcoming).
13. Cf. the critique of Israeli films which deploy this trope in Ella Shohat, *Israeli Cinema: East/West and the Politics of Representation* (Austin: University of Texas Press, 1989), p. 9 and *passim*. See also Shohat, 'Staging the Quincentenary: the Middle East and the Americas', *Third Text*, 21 (1992–93), p. 102.
14. *Ulysses*, p. 830; Gifford and Seidman, *Notes for Joyce*, pp. 54, 485.
15. Cf. Constance V. Tagopoulos, 'Joyce and Homer: return, disguise, and recognition in "Ithaca"' in Vincent J. Cheng and Timothy Martin (eds), *Joyce in Context* (Cambridge: Cambridge University Press, 1992), pp. 188, 193; Kenner, p. 1. Later, nevertheless, Kenner notes that Bloom 'lost his head' during 'Cyclops' (p. 127).
16. The following analysis of 'Cyclops' was written before I read Vincent J. Cheng's fine study *Joyce, Race, and Empire* (Cambridge: Cambridge University Press, 1995), in particular pp. 191–218, section on '"What is a nation?": nationalism, Ireland, and "Cyclops"'. I appreciate that our analyses are quite close. I enjoyed Cheng's witty use of the term 'cycloptic' (p. 198); he is especially illuminating on the parodies in 'Cyclops' of the contemporaneous 'Celticist agenda and dynamics' (p. 204).
17. *Ulysses*, pp. 387, 405, 416, 420, 427, 430. For Bloom as womanly, cf. Richard Ellmann, *James Joyce* (Oxford: Oxford University Press, 1982), pp. 342, 373, 395, 450–1, 463–4, 515; Ellmann suggests that Joyce was attracted to a theory in Otto Weininger's *Sex and Character* (1903) that Jews are by nature womanly men. See also Sander L. Gilman, *Freud, Race, and Gender* (Princeton, NJ: Princeton University Press, 1993), pp. 77–9. Apropos Weininger, cf. John M. Hoberman, 'Otto Weininger and the critique of Jewish masculinity' in Nancy A. Harrowitz and Barbara Hyams (eds), *Jews and Gender: Responses to Otto Weininger* (Philadelphia: Temple University Press, 1995), pp. 141–53; David Glover, *Vampires, Mummies, and Liberals: Bram Stoker and the Politics of Popular Fiction* (Durham, NC, and London: Duke University Press, 1996), pp. 124–8; Ritchie Robertson, 'Historicizing Weininger: the nineteenth-century German image of the Feminized Jew' in Bryan Cheyette and Laura Marcus (eds), *Modernity, Culture and 'the Jew'* (Cambridge: Polity, 1998), pp. 23–39.

18. *Ulysses*, pp. 430, 432, 435–6, 438–9. Kenner (p. 103) feels that Cunningham is only using Bloom, whom he regards as a kind of Shylock, adept at money matters.

19. *Ulysses*, pp. 439, 444–5.

20. *Ibid.*, p. 449.

21. *Ibid.*, p. 426.

22. In the introduction to her World's Classics edition, Jeri Johnson explains the misunderstanding over Throwaway (pp. xxviii–xxix). See the conversation with Bantam Lyons, *Ulysses*, p. 106.

23. Kenner's view (p. 103) of this scene is rather genial; he thinks the citizen is not so much anti-semitic as, like the Irish in general, rejecting of outsiders of any category. He notes that Bloom 'is rather frequently disregarded and snubbed, though with no special malice. The Irish can be great overlookers of any non-Celts' (p. 43). Kenner appears to share the perception of the citizen in 'Calypso' that Bloom is not truly Irish.

24. *Ulysses*, pp. 496, 745, 718; also 821.

25. Mikhail Bakhtin, *The Dialogic Imagination* (Austin: University of Texas Press, 1981), p. 163. Apropos Joyce and Bakhtin more generally, see M. Keith Booker, *Joyce, Bakhtin, and the Literary Tradition* (Ann Arbor: University of Michigan Press, 1997), though – except for an occasional reference, for example, to *The Voyages of Sindbad* (p. 27) – this work tends to construct the 'literary tradition' to which Joyce relates as European only.

26. *Ulysses*, pp. 870–1.

27. *Tales from the Thousand and One Nights*, trans. and intro. N. J. Dawood (London: Penguin Classics, 1973), pp. 121, 124, 127, 135, 151, 155.

28. *Ibid.*, p. 148.

29. Gifford and Seidman, *Notes for Joyce*, p. 494.

30. *Ulysses*, pp. 722, 871.

31. *Ibid.*, p. 857; Gifford and Seidman, p. 490. Ammiel Alcalay, *After Jews and Arabs: Remaking Levantine Culture* (Minneapolis: University of Minnesota Press, 1993), p. 115, refers to the brilliant engineering of the Dome of the Rock that 'squares the circle and hovers along the divide between earth and heaven'.

32. *Tales from the Thousand and One Nights*, pp. 290, 293, 295, 301, 314–17. Cf. Docker and McCalman, *Sheer Folly and Derangement* (forthcoming) for a discussion of powerful female figures in *The Thousand and One Nights*. For female trickster figures in contemporary Arab storytelling, see Inea Bushnaq (ed.), *Arab Folktales* (Harmondsworth: Penguin, 1987), section on 'Wily women and clever men'.

33. *Ulysses*, pp. 610, 926, 932.

34. Maria Rosa Menacol, *The Arabic Role in Medieval Literary History: A Forgotten Heritage* (Philadelphia: University of Pennsylvania Press, 1987), p. 139; Alcalay, *After Jews and Arabs*, p. 6. See also Elizabeth Disney, 'Al-Andalus – remembering Islamic Spain', *Journal of Arabic Islamic and Middle Eastern Studies*, 1 (1993).

35. See e.g. Robert L. Mack (ed.), *Oriental Tales* (Oxford: Oxford University Press, 1992), introduction, and Robert Irwin, *The Arabian Nights: A Companion* (London: Allen Lane, 1994).

36. Vijay Mishra, in his otherwise excellent *The Gothic Sublime* (Albany: State University of New York Press, 1994), introduction, p. 5, appears to suggest a

continuous Enlightenment tradition of homogeneous textuality finally disrupted by Gothic.

37. Edward Said, *The World, the Text, and the Critic* (1983; London: Vintage, 1991), p. 253.
38. See Caracciolo (ed.), *The Arabian Nights in English Literature*, introduction, p. 4, and the following chapters: Michael Slater, 'Dickens in Wonderland'; Peter L. Caracciolo, 'Wilkie Collins and the ladies of Baghdad, or the sleeper awakened'; Hampson, 'The genie out of the bottle: Conrad, Wells and Joyce'.
39. Irwin, *The Arabian Nights: A Companion*, pp. 272, 278.
40. Cf. John Docker, *Postmodernism and Popular Culture: A Cultural History* (Melbourne: Cambridge University Press, 1994), ch. 6.
41. *Ulysses*, pp. 293–4, 896. Kenner (p. 80) notes that *Ulysses* resembles nineteenth-century detective stories like *The Moonstone*; interestingly, Kenner here suggests that the detective story is the 'paradigm of the nineteenth-century novel'.
42. Cf. Kenner, ch. 7.
43. Mikhail Bakhtin, *Problems of Dostoevsky's Poetics* (Manchester: Manchester University Press, 1984), pp. 47–75.
44. Brian McHale, *Constructing Postmodernism* (London: Routledge, 1992), pp. 42–58; cf. Booker, *Joyce, Bakhtin, and the Literary Tradition*, pp. 4, 16, 202.
45. Edward Said, *Orientalism* (London: Routledge and Kegan Paul, 1980), pp. 286, 306–7, 318–20.
46. Alcalay, *After Jews and Arabs*, pp. 21, 24–5, 28, 44, 51, 213, 223–4, 253. See also Ella Shohat, 'Sephardim in Israel: Zionism from the standpoint of its Jewish victims', *Social Text*, 19/20 (1988), pp. 1–35, and 'Antinomies of exile: Said at the frontier of national narrations' in Michael Sprinker (ed.), *Edward Said: A Critical Reader* (Cambridge, MA: Blackwell, 1992), pp. 121–43.
47. *After Jews and Arabs*, pp. 21, 116–17, 120, 122–7, 128–43, 179.
48. *Ibid.*, pp. 61, 109–10, 120, 126, 143, 163, 231–3, 236, 244, 247–50, 256, 276–9. In relation to the notion of the postnationalist more generally, cf. William E. Connolly, *The Ethos of Pluralization* (Minneapolis: University of Minnesota Press, 1995), pp. 135–49.
49. As noted before in relation to 'Cyclops', I wrote the following analysis before I read Cheng, *Joyce, Race, and Empire*, in particular pp. 169–84, section on 'Seeing ourselves: Orientals, Negroes, and Jews', which has an acute analysis of Bloom's ambivalence, his participating in racist and Orientalist images and thinking yet also his detachment from such.
50. *Ulysses*, pp. 98–9, 134, 273, 285, 435, 455, 484, 573, 877, 890. Gifford and Seidman, *Notes for Joyce*, p. 203, note that 'where the bad niggers go' refers to the chorus of Stephen Foster's (1826–64) song 'Old Uncle Ned', where the chorus' final line tells us that Ned has 'gone whar de good niggers go'.
51. *Ulysses*, pp. 716–17, 721, 729.
52. *Ibid.*, pp. 735, 736–7, 744–6. Kenner (pp. 130–1), except for a footnote reference to the sailor as untrustworthy, glides in one easy movement over these conversations.

5

Strangers amongst the nations: Mr Bloom and Spinoza

He [Spinoza] was of a middle size, he had good features in his Face, the Skin somewhat black, black curl'd Hair, long Eye-brows, and of the same Colour, so that one might easily know by his Looks that he was descended from Portuguese Jews.

Colerus, biographer of Spinoza, 1705[1]

To what lengths will the folly of the multitude not carry them?

Spinoza, Tractatus Theologico-Politicus[2]

Mr Bloom's Jewishness has always been an intriguing question. In this chapter I explore a diasporic reading of how Bloom's own self-presentations in *Ulysses* create his ethnic and cultural identity. A diasporic reading – by invoking other cultural histories apparently far in time and space from the up-close texture of the world of early twentieth-century Dublin and Ireland – might help us make sense of the supreme puzzle that is Leopold Paula Bloom, as in his notorious eating of pork, his diverse religious affiliations, and the frequent disjunctions between his outer behaviour and inner thoughts. I will also cross a diasporic with an allegorical reading.

In *The Origin of German Tragic Drama*, Walter Benjamin suggests that in allegorical figures in the Baroque theatre and art of the seventeenth century, there is always a teasing tension between mimesis and fantasticality, between an apparent simplicity of moral meaning and the accumulation and multiplying of accompanying representations, personifications, ideas, symbols, text. Benjamin drew attention to the riddle and enigma of allegorical pictorial signs, as in Cesare Ripa's famous *Iconologia*, first published in Rome in 1593, illustrated from 1603, widely translated and popular throughout Europe for some two centuries as a handbook of emblematic figures intended for artists, writers, poets, sculptors, theatrical designers and builders of wedding and funeral decorations. For its sources the *Iconologia* variously drew on classical literature, biblical episodes, medieval bestiaries and encyclopedias, and Renaissance speculations concerning (undeciphered) Egyptian hieroglyphics. In the *Iconologia* we observe and ponder fragments of meaning in a dispersed state, laying about close or next to each other, yet not relating or necessarily relating; the fragments often offer alternative allegorical suggestions. Benjamin argues that in baroque allegory the multiplicity, even chaos, of examples, in fragments, overwhelms any clarity and certainty of interpretation.[3]

Bloom appears to be a simple, straightforward man, not given to ontological doubt or philosophical perplexity: more *shlemiel* than Hamlet, a bumbling zaddik, a good man trying to do good things in a world that sometimes baffles him when it doesn't reciprocate or acknowledge his small quiet good acts.[4] Yet with Bloom we also know that one is always joyfully drawn to the plural and porous, to coming across yet another example that seems to modify or contradict an earlier illustration of his character. Bloom as allegorical figure – of Jewishness, of modernity, of the outsider, of stranger amongst the nations, of the marrano and converso, of Levantine sensibility, of Habsburg liminality – could well have been one of Ripa's more developed and complex iconological portraits, one of his more rococo creations.

As we know from his *monologue intérieur*, Bloom's consciousness is constituted in extreme ambivalence, oddities, stray thoughts, trivia, ludic nonsense, pleasures, sadnesses, disappointments, whimsies, fancies, idiosyncrasy, secret desires, erotic and romantic and masturbatory fantasies, heretical observations, scatological reflections, anger and anguish; an unrespectable inner life as inchoate and curious perhaps as much to Bloom as to generations of *Ulysses*' readers, connoisseurs, flâneurs and habitués.

Mr Bloom's vagaries are indeed multiple. Throughout *Ulysses* we note that he goes to the pork butcher (Dlugacz, himself a Jew) to buy a kidney to cook for breakfast, that he and Molly sleep head to toe, that he fetishizes his wife's buttocks, that he hasn't fully (as it were) made love to Molly since the death of their baby son Rudy over a decade before, that he might be bringing Stephen home to 7 Eccles Street in 'Ithaca' as an offering to Molly in order to dislodge her liking for Blazes Boylan (and in her soliloquy Molly certainly entertains sexual fantasies about the youthful Stephen), that he's attracted to Molly because he envisages her as dark, Spanish, Moorish, Oriental (he dreams of her in Turkish costume, in red slippers, wearing breeches, in 'superior position', just as she is attracted to him as dark, a foreigner, and womanly), and that he has intense masochistic and inversionary fantasies, as we see in the carnivalesque World Upside-down brothel scenes involving Bella Cohen the madam.[5]

Bloom's religious affiliations are exceedingly uncertain. Is Bloom Jew or

Catholic or Protestant? Is he a Mason? In 'Eumaeus' Bloom tells Stephen that 'in reality' he's not a Jew. In the hallucinatory scenes of 'Circe' his dead father Rudolph accuses Bloom of leaving the house and the god of his fathers, though the accusation is shadowed by an irony we will soon explore.[6]

In the funeral scenes of 'Hades' Bloom at one points thinks: 'If we were all suddenly somebody else'. In 'Ithaca' we can ponder the following:

> What, reduced to their simplest reciprocal form, were Bloom's thoughts about Stephen's thoughts about Bloom and Bloom's thoughts about Stephen's thoughts about Bloom's thoughts about Stephen?
> He thought that he thought that he was a jew whereas he knew that he knew that he knew that he was not.[7]

As in Baroque allegory, definite meaning in *Ulysses* is like sand coursing through fingers – if graspable, not for very long, and when looked at again, gone, perhaps never there.

The stranger

Bloom is recognizable in the sociologist Georg Simmel's essay 'The stranger', a figure who, simultaneously and disturbingly, fuses features of both wandering and fixity. The stranger, says Simmel, is the wanderer who comes today and stays tomorrow. While he belongs to a spatially defined group, he always remains a potential wanderer. His position in the group is determined by the fact that he has not belonged to it from the beginning, that he imports qualities into it which do not and cannot stem from the group itself, and that he is always considered as not an owner of soil. In terms of their relationship to him, distance means that he who is close by is far and he who is far is near. The stranger is like the poor and inner enemies. He is an element of the group itself, in his interactions with it both a full-fledged member yet outside it and confronting it. His relations with it are contingent, exhibiting a kind of abstraction. Towards the group the stranger feels a certain kind of objectivity, a particular structure of feeling composed of nearness and distance, involvement and indifference, though such is not to be confused with passivity. Such objectivity gives him a kind of freedom, in terms of perception, understanding and evaluation of what others in the group take as given, qualities which he also brings to his close and intimate relationships.[8]

Simmel suggests that throughout the history of economics the stranger everywhere appears as the trader, or the trader as stranger, for trade permits unlimited combinations. Given his mobility in intermediary trade, the stranger comes into contact with every individual in the group, but he is not organically connected, through estabished ties of kinship, locality and occupation, with any single one. Simmel cites as classical example European Jews.[9] But he could well have been thinking of Mr Bloom, who as a wandering ad canvasser mobilely interacts with Dublin as a defined space in combinations unlimited.

As the stranger whose father Rudolph Bloom wandered across Europe, entered the house of Ireland and stayed, Bloom is not quite the image of the Jew that Hegel dismissively conceived. In his youthful writings Hegel argued that Abraham's departure from Chaldea and nomadic journey through the desert signified the Jews' fundamental alienation from earth, family, love and beauty, in contrast to Greek culture.[10] Simmel's evocation of the advantages of being a stranger could well stand as a reply to the young Hegel's admonitory reflections on the Jew as wanderer. In her book on Walter Benjamin's ideas of history and nature, Beatrice Hanssen questions Judaism's supposed hostile relationship to Nature and the natural, suggesting that Abraham's departure was a refusal to be determined by one's place of birth.[11] It is one of Bloom's most engaging traits that he can so frequently be so detached about Irish – and English, European, Western – society in ways that the Irish men he encounters in Dublin and especially in Barney Kiernan's bar, consumed by a nationalist passion of authentic identity and suspected betrayals, can never be. The Irish patriarchs live inside the circumstances of their history, almost as if in a trance of self-absorption. At the end of a fatiguing day and night, Bloom reflects on the violence of the self-appointed Irish 'citizen' towards him in the pub as emblematic in more general terms of the historical relations between European nationalism and Jews: 'the altercation with a truculent troglodyte in Bernard Kiernan's premises (holocaust).'[12]

Hanssen also suggests that the Jew is not necessarily divorced from or hostile to the natural, drawing attention to the way Benjamin notes in Kafka's writings an acute attentiveness (*Aufmerksamkeit*) to the creaturely. Benjamin's highly metaphoric writing also displays just such attentiveness in exploring images of stones, animals and angels. In Hanssen's view, Benjamin foregrounds the divergent tendencies suggested in the term *Kreatur*, which could signify human depravity, monstrosity, the lowliest form of animality, as well as possibly signifying an ethical call for an all-inclusive turn towards nature.[13]

Aufmerksamkeit in relation to the creaturely is also characteristic of Mr Bloom,[14] attentive (notoriously so, in the history of attempted censorship of the novel) to the graininess of the urban and seaside scenes through which he moves as well as to the world of his own body: defecating with quiet satisfaction in the morning (while reading an old number of *Titbits*); masturbating in the evening; urinating, together with Stephen, late at night back at 7 Eccles Street. 'The trajectories of their, first sequent, then simultaneous, urinations were dissimilar', Bloom's 'longer', Stephen's 'higher, more sibilant'. With Stephen gone, Bloom, just before enfolded by sleep, turns his attentiveness to his wife's creaturely form: 'He kissed the plump mellow yellow smellow melons of her rump, on each plump melonous hemisphere, in their mellow yellow furrow, with obscure prolonged provocative melon-smellonous osculation.'[15]

Spinoza the heretic

If and when Bloom does think of himself as Jewish, what kind of Jewishness can we discern?

In arguing in 'Cyclops' with the nationalist citizen in Barney Kiernan's bar, Bloom identifies the Jewish tradition he admires, that of emancipated Enlightenment Jewry, of Marx and Spinoza. (He also throws in the face of the enraged citizen that Jesus was a Jew.) He knows that such an identification marks him off as a particular kind of modern Jew, a non-Jewish Jew, atheistic, secularist and sceptical. His admiration for Spinoza reprises a further aspect of entwined Oriental–European cultural histories, in the continuing story of the Sephardi diaspora in Portugal and Holland that so influenced Spinoza's thought. In pursuing Spinoza, we may understand Bloom.

When the Jews of Spain were expelled early in 1492, the majority journeyed into a welcoming Ottoman Empire, while some moved into Europe, usually initially to Portugal. They couldn't find asylum in England or France, which had banished their Jewish communities in the thirteenth and fourteenth centuries. In Portugal, however, they were within a few years forcibly mass-baptized, becoming part of the conversos or New Christians, who were frequently also marranos or secret Jews.[16] Further, the Inquisition was instituted in Portugal in 1536, and pursued even more enthusiastically there than in Spain. For the next few generations the crypto-Judaic practices of the Portuguese marranos had to be ever more subterranean; and as in Spain, there were distinctions based on supposed blood lines between New and Old Christians.[17] Over the centuries the New Christians entered Western European countries as Portuguese merchants and physicians (medicine was one of the few professions in Portugal not barred by blood purity regulations). What distinguished the conversos and marranos who went north in the succeeding centuries was that they now knew very little of their religion.[18]

The Portuguese Jewish diaspora, which during the seventeenth century stretched from the Ottoman Empire to Goa in India,[19] from Denmark and northern Germany to Brazil and the Caribbean, took on its own special characteristics. The Portuguese Jews regarded themselves as citizens of a nation with a uniquely heroic and tragic past. As they moved north into Europe and tried to return to Judaism, they often revealed a scepticism towards both Judaism and Christianity, many going so far as to deny the central Jewish doctrine of the unique election of Israel and indeed to reject all religious particularism. Such scepticism especially found voice in the greater religious freedom of Holland in the seventeenth century, where the ex-New Christians, now re-Judaizing, still retained a characteristic Sephardic affection for all things Spanish.[20]

The philosopher Benedict (Baruch) Spinoza (1632–77) was among the Sephardic sceptics of Portuguese descent who set the elders of the Amsterdam Jewish community on edge. Born of marrano parents in Amsterdam, he was educated within the Portuguese Jewish community there. For Spinoza, many traditional Jewish tenets appeared to conflict with reason and the laws of nature. He must have made his doubts known, for in 1656, when only 23, Spinoza found himself excommunicated (though excommunication was not uncommon in Spinoza's day, amongst the Dutch Calvinists as well as the Sephardim). What was unusual was that Spinoza chose to remain outside the Jewish community after the *herem* (ban), in a world where the unattached and unaffiliated were not yet a common phenomenon.[21]

The attempted banning of unconventional ideas, and the attempted disciplining of those who entertain such ideas, is usually in history productive precisely of those ideas. It would appear that the expulsion and exiling of a young man in his twenty-fourth year from his family's community lent a bitter edge to Spinoza's subsequent reflections on the proper relations in history between theology (Jewish and Christian), philosophy and good government. Spinoza lived in Amsterdam for a few years after his excommunication, but journeyed into further exile to other parts of the Netherlands, near to and then in The Hague. He took up the grinding of lenses as a means of making a living. He changed his name to Benedict (latinizing the Hebrew Baruch), was reportedly a sociable person and had good friends, and became part of a European-wide circle of philosophers in a century where scepticism and rationalism and the natural sciences became prominent yet which was still obsessed with alchemy, religion and religious disputation. Spinoza felt the clarifying of the relationship between religion and the state was so historically important and urgent that he interrupted the writing of his most famous philosophical work the *Ethics* to write the *Tractatus Theologico-Politicus*, which was published in late 1669 or 1670.[22]

Spinoza wrote the *Tractatus* in Latin, in part because he wished a work which contained controversial readings of the Bible, a body of writings central not only to Judaism but to Catholicism and Protestantism, to be read only by those of liberal religious sentiments. He didn't want it to be read by the ordinary run of theologians and preachers — priests, pastors, rabbis — who he felt were prejudiced to the point of superstition; and certainly not by the mass of people in Holland, in a time when religious hatreds and mob violence in political conflicts were all too common. The heterodoxy of the *Tractatus*, however, quickly became known not only in Holland but across Europe. The *Tractatus* provoked some of the most violent responses to any published work in the seventeenth century. It was widely perceived and denounced as blasphemous, abhorrent, subversive, atheistic, infamous and pestilential. The Reformed Synod of North Holland called for an official ban on the work. In England Spinoza was compared to Hobbes and denounced as a doubtless close associate of Satan, Richard Blackmore penning a poem that was the reverse of a panegyric:

> Spinoza next, to hide his black design
> And to his side the unwary to incline,
> For heaven his ensigns treacherous displays;
> Declares for God, while he that God betrays;
> For whom he's pleased such evidence to bring,
> As saves the name, while it subverts the thing.

In Germany a critic referred to the 'abominable doctrines and hideous errors which this shallow Jewish philosopher has (if I may say so) shit into the world'. A French opponent felt moved to describe the *Tractatus* as 'un livre dangereux et plein de méchantes maximes qui ruinent la religion'. His early biographer Colerus observed that Spinoza's readings of the Bible made it into a kind of wax nose to be shaped at will, a fool's cap which may be worn howsoever one pleased. [23]

Colerus here suggests images of the carnivalesque fool and trickster, and it may be under such a heading that Bloom senses an affinity with Spinoza. At first sight, Bloom's admiration for Spinoza may seem odd, given Spinoza's reputation for a relentless rationalism, the advancing *more geometrico* of universal axioms leading to a strict logic of deductions and inferences; whereas Bloom's wandering mind is always on the edge of chaos. Yet Spinoza's texts are more turbulent than his reputation for severe reason might suggest. Deleuze suggests of the *Ethics*, for example, that the book is written twice simultaneously, once in the flow of definitions, propositions and demonstrations above the line, and again in the footnotes, often bitter, angry and passionate, forming another, subterranean, text. [24]

In the *Tractatus*, the two textual forces meet and compete. Before embarking on this book I'd never read Spinoza myself, I always felt what I'd heard of Spinoza's rationalism was rather frightening. But as soon as I started reading the *Tractatus* I realized it was a text in turmoil, written with a kind of Voltairean or Swiftean satirical scorn that tips crazily over into a relishing of the absurdities, contradictions, illogicalities and inconsistencies being high-lighted. There is an unresolved tension between the rationalist security of the truth of certain universal postulates, and a recognition of the irreducible uncertainty of interpretation, because interpretation is always trying to explain and reconcile 'diverse narratives', as in the 'historical narratives' of the Bible with their 'glaring contradictions'.[25] I was reminded of what Benjamin wrote about the medieval treatises that he admired, that such may be didactic in tone, but they lack the conclusiveness of an instruction, they dispense with the coercive proof of mathematics, their method becomes one more like digression.[26] Spinoza's *Tractatus* has something of a novelistic quality, with a fierce narrator.

The *Tractatus* argues for the complete separation of both the state and philosophy from theology.[27] It tries to suggest what, ideally, the spheres of state, philosophy and theology should be and do in their separate activities.

The ideal state is a democracy where freedom of judgement is fully granted to the individual citizen and where nothing is esteemed dearer and more precious than freedom; not only can this freedom be granted without endangering piety and the peace of the commonwealth, but the peace of the commonwealth and piety depend on this freedom. In such a commonweath all aim to live in security and in safety free from fear, and in good health. Sovereignty is vested in all citizens, and laws are sanctioned by common consent. The citizen is thereby a subject, not a slave. All citizens resolve to live only by the dictates of reason. Citizens will reason and judge in their own individual ways, they will have different and conflicting views, but they agree to abide by common decisions; they agree that a proposal supported by a majority of votes shall have the force of a decree, meanwhile retaining the authority to repeal the same when they see a better alternative. The right of the sovereign, in both religious and secular spheres, should be restricted to men's actions, with everyone being allowed to think what he will and to say what he thinks.[28]

The 'good commonwealth', then, Spinoza avers in utopian spirit, grants to everyone the freedom to philosophize. Spinoza concedes that there may sometimes be disadvantages in allowing such freedom. But what institution, he asks, was ever so wisely planned that no disadvantage could arise therefrom?

He who seeks to regulate everything by law will aggravate vices rather than correct them. What cannot be prohibited must necessarily be allowed, even if harm often ensues. How many are the evils that arise from dissipation, envy, avarice, drunkenness and the like? Yet we tolerate these, because although they are in reality vices they cannot be prohibited by legal enactment. Much more, then, should we allow freedom of judgment, which is assuredly a virtue, and cannot be suppressed.[29]

Furthermore, such freedom is in Spinoza's view of the first importance in fostering the sciences and the arts. We can see why Spinoza's thought is recognized as harbinger of the modern, secular, democratic state.[30]

At one point Spinoza suggests that his 'main purpose' is to secure the 'differentiation of philosophy from theology'. Spinoza spares no feeling of sympathy for past thinkers, in particular Maimonides the medieval Aristotelian, who tried to mix philosophy with religion, especially in their readings of the Bible. Supposedly rationalist philosophers like Maimonides and others are, says Spinoza, 'concerned only to extort from Scripture some Aristotelian nonsense and some fabrications of their own; and this I regard as the height of absurdity'. Maimonides undermines philosophy in maintaining that those who are guided by reason alone thereby cannot be dwellers among the pious nor be among the wise of nations, because they ignore prophetic inspiration and divine revelation, the commandments revealed to Moses. Maimonides, says Spinoza, assumes that the 'prophets were in agreement in all matters, and that they were outstanding philosophers and theologians; for he holds that they based their conclusions on scientific truth'. Not so, says Spinoza: scientific truth is not established in Scripture, which does not engage in demonstrations and does not validate its teaching by appealing to definitions and first causes. Spinoza condemns Maimonides as a Pharisee, indeed as the first among the Pharisees who openly held that Scripture must be made to conform with reason. What Maimonides did not understand was that theology does not have to be subordinated to reason nor does reason have to be subordinated to theology, for each has its own domain. The domain of reason is truth and wisdom, that of theology is piety and obedience.[31]

Philosophy in its highest form represents the intellectual love of God, since God is Nature: 'the power of Nature in its entirety is nothing other than the power of God through which all things happen and are determined.' Spinoza does believe in a divine law, which is concerned with the supreme good, that is, the true knowledge and love of God. We love God in 'true freedom', and such means freedom to live within the natural light of reason, which is universal. The freedom of reason does not derive goodness from 'authority and tradition', which are mere shadows; nor does reason 'demand belief in historical narratives of any kind whatsoever', and certainly not the biblical historical narratives. Philosophers, those who endeavour to understand things from 'clear conceptions', are necessarily and unfortunately few in the world. Philosophers realize that the humanity of which they are a superior segment is not the centre of the world, for God takes account of the whole of Nature, and not of the human race alone: 'God directs Nature in accordance with the requirements of her universal laws, and not in accordance with the requirements of the particular laws of human nature.' Spinoza is an avowed rationalist, but he does not believe in the hubris of reason, that it can master or control the world. We should not, Spinoza felt, imagine Nature is so limited that 'man' is its chief part.[32]

Spinoza writes also in the terms of a modern sceptical historical consciousness when he turns his attention to the Bible. Spinoza does express belief in a 'true religion', but such ideal religion is not to be identified with Scripture, or at least not much of Scripture: indeed, very little of Scripture. There is a revealed Word of God, and such is a simple conception of the divine mind as revealed to the ancient prophets; this is to obey God with all one's heart by practising justice and charity, which are to be held in universal esteem. He who is blessed abounds in charity, joy, peace, patience, kindness, goodness, faithfulness, gentleness and self-control; and one should love one's neighbour as oneself. The moral value of a man's creed should be judged only from his deeds. Beyond practising such fundamental principles of practical faith, everyone should be allowed the freedom and right to interpret the basic tenets of faith as he thinks fit. The supreme authority to explain religion and to make judgement concerning it is vested in each individual. Religion does not pertain to the sphere of public law and authority, but to the sphere of individual right.[33]

God's eternal word is lodged within men's hearts, within men's minds. It follows that public ceremonial rites — Jewish, as in all those specified in the Old Testament and indeed the whole Mosaic Law; or Christian, as in baptism, the Lord's Supper, festivals, public prayers and all the other ceremonies that are and always have been common to all Christendom — are not necessary to blessedness or intrinsic holiness. A person living in solitude is therefore not bound by them. Also a person living under a government where the Christian religion is forbidden can nevertheless live a blessed life. Spinoza cites as an instance the case of Japan. The Dutch living there were required by the East India Company to refrain from practising any external rites.[34]

In Spinoza's view, the only useful purpose these public ceremonies serve is the unification of a particular society.[35] Mr Bloom's reflections, when he slips into All Hallows church in Dublin in June of 1904 and watches those partaking of the Eucharist, are in tune with Spinoza here: the ceremonies allow the religious to be unified in their belief and to practise piety in a quiet, restrained, sustaining way, if absurd in the light of reason.

The words of the Bible are not the Word of God, and here we have to observe Spinoza's remarkable elitism – an elitism I would have disdained during the writing of my *Postmodernism and Popular Culture: A Cultural History*, but to which, as a kind of selfconscious millennial Dyspeptic Dystopian, I am now strangely drawn. For Spinoza, it is clear that Scripture 'teaches only piety, not philosophy, and that all its contents were adapted to the understanding and preconceived beliefs of the common people'. Philosophy is concerned with reason, not imagination. This is why philosophy is separate from the biblical writings, especially those of the prophets, whose works were in Spinoza's scornful opinion clearly written for the level of their audience, the common people believing in imagination and fantasy rather than reason. Accordingly, to please and reach and persuade that audience, the prophets 'perceived God's revelations with the aid of the imaginative faculty alone' rather than through 'assured rational principles'. We can now see why, says Spinoza, the perceptions and teachings of the prophets were nearly all in the form of vivid parables and allegories and signs, for these are more appropriate to the imaginative faculty, as is the expression of spiritual matters in corporeal form. Because of the 'common imagination of God and Spirits', the prophets anthropomorphized God: this is why God was seen by Micaiah as seated, by Daniel as an old man clothed in white garments, by Ezekiel as fire; why the Holy Spirit was seen by those with Christ as a dove descending, by the Apostles as tongues of flame, and by Paul at his conversion as a great light.[36]

In Spinoza's view, the prophecies or revelations proclaimed varied in accordance with the ingrained prejudices of the prophets, who held diverse, even contrary, beliefs and prejudices. The gift of prophecy did not render the prophets more learned, but left them with the assumptions and beliefs they previously held, however absurd. It therefore follows that to understand the mind of the prophets and so of Scripture is by no means the same thing as to understand the mind of God. Above all we should understand that Scripture is 'adapted to the intellectual level not only of the prophets but of the unstable and fickle Jewish multitude'.[37]

Performing a historical and 'temporal' reading of the Scriptures, Spinoza openly questioned the view that the Jews are a Chosen People. Spinoza argued that this usual designation was for no other reason than that God chose them for a certain territory where they could live in security and wellbeing, material success and prosperity. The Hebrew nation was chosen by God before all others not by reason of its understanding, for the Hebrews' ideas of God and Nature were quite commonplace; nor by reason of its spiritual qualities, for, in respect of virtue and the true life, here again they were on the same footing as other nations, 'very few of them being chosen'. The Jews were deluded in thinking that they excelled others in true human perfection. The Hebrew nation was chosen by reason of its social organization and the good fortune whereby it achieved supremacy and retained it for so many years. Chiefly by God's external help alone, the Jews overcame great dangers and achieved security for themselves: 'In other respects they were no different from other nations, and God was equally gracious to all.' God did not choose the Hebrew nation absolutely, nor unto eternity. God had earlier chosen the Canaanites, but had abandoned them because of their dissolute living, their folly, and their corrupt worship. If the Hebrews, however, prove to be disobedient and break the Covenant, then they too will experience the downfall of their state, suffer the severest hardships, and be destroyed by God. In any case, other nations had their own state and their own special laws by God's external guidance.[38]

Since God is equally merciful and gracious to all, the individual Jew possesses no gift of God above other men, and there is no difference between him and a Gentile. Since, also, the function of the prophet was to teach true virtue rather than the special laws of his country, then there can be no doubt that all nations possessed prophets and that the gift of prophecy was not peculiar to the Jews. Other nations had prophets, who prophesied to them and to the Jews. In the Old Testament we find that Gentiles and the uncircumcised, such as Noah, Enoch, Abimelech and Balaam, did in fact prophesy, and also that Hebrew prophets were sent by God not only to their own nation but to many others. Thus Ezekiel prophesied for all the nations that were then known. Isaiah bewails and foretells the calamities, and prophesies the restoration, not only of the Jews but of other nations, including the Egyptians. Jeremiah is called the prophet not only of the Hebrew nation but of all nations absolutely; Jeremiah bemoans the coming calamities of the Moabites and also prophesies their eventual restoration, as also the restoration of the Egyptians, the Ammonites and the Elamites.[39]

Famously, Spinoza was scornful of the very idea and possibility of miracles, a conception he again laid at the door of the multitude, who, ignorant of natural causes, always suppose that God's power and providence are most clearly displayed when some unusual event occurs in Nature, 'particularly if such an event is to their profit or advantage'. Such events are termed miracles, or works of God, by the 'common people'. Spinoza suggests that this idea seems to have originated with the early Jews, who boasted of miracles in order to refute the Gentiles of their times who worshipped visible Gods; the Jews wished to prove to the Gentiles that their gods were weak and inconstant. The Jews' miracles visibly proved to their own satisfaction that the whole of Nature was directed for their sole benefit by command of the God whom they worshipped; an idea, Spinoza sardonically observes, enthusiastically taken up by other peoples in the course of history till the present day. There are many passages in Scripture to the effect that God wrought wonders, as in Exodus; but it only follows that the beliefs of the Jews were such that they could be readily convinced by these miracles. In any case, Scripture did not try to explain events through natural causes, but to strike the imagination and excite the wonder and engage the fantasy of the masses in order to instil piety in their minds. In these terms, we can think of such events as merely symbolical and imaginary; for example, that God came down from heaven and that Mount Sinai smoked because God descended upon it surrounded by fire, or that Elijah ascended to heaven in a chariot of fire. Yet, says Spinoza, 'all who have any smattering of education know that God does not have a right hand or a left hand, that he neither moves nor is at rest, nor is he in any particular place, but is absolutely infinite, and contains within himself all perfections'.[40]

In Spinoza's view, a miracle, either contrary to Nature or above Nature, is 'mere absurdity'. For, whatever is 'contrary to Nature is contrary to reason, and whatever is contrary to reason is absurd, and should therefore be rejected'.[41]

Spinoza, nevertheless, did praise Scripture and the prophets in particular for the way they commended above all 'justice and charity', even if such belief cannot be demonstrated with exactitude.

> It would be folly to refuse to accept, merely on the grounds that it cannot be proved with mathematical certainty, that which is abundantly confirmed by the testimony of the prophets, that which is the source of so much comfort to those less gifted with intelligence, and of considerable advantage to the state, and which we can believe without incurring any peril or hurt. Could we live our lives wisely if we were to accept as true nothing that could conceivably be called into doubt on any principle of scepticism? Are not most of our actions in any case fraught with uncertainty and hazard?[42]

In the *Tractatus* Spinoza's historical method and his philology also explore uncertainty and the hazards of interpretation. The *Tractatus*, it is well known, helped establish modern biblical exegesis.[43] It also seems to me to have established much of what we take to be modern critical method in the interpretation of literary texts in its stress on establishing the inner relationships of texts, their world as a world in itself, not a reflection of an exterior world.

For Spinoza, the interpretation of texts like Scripture does not observe any proclaimed external authority, certainly not that of the Pharisees who believe they are in possession of a sure tradition or true explanation transmitted from the prophets themselves; nor that of a pontiff whose interpretation is supposedly infallible, as the Roman Catholics boast.[44]

Spinoza described his own method as one of immanence, of internal textual criticism, based on 'the principle that knowledge of Scripture must be sought only from Scripture'; such is 'the only true method'. Scripture has to be studied 'closely', in particular paying attention to the 'nature and properties of the language in which the Bible was written and which its authors were accustomed to speak', that is, a thorough knowledge of the Hebrew language is required. The Hebrew nation, however, has 'lost all its arts and embellishments (little wonder, in view of the disasters and persecutions it has suffered)', retaining only a few remnants of its language and few of its books. The meanings of many nouns and verbs occurring in the Bible are either completely unknown or subject to dispute; the idiom and modes of speech peculiar to the Hebrew nation have been consigned to oblivion by the ravages of time. It is therefore difficult to discover all the possible meanings which a particular passage can yield from linguistic usage; and there are many passages where the sense is obscure and indeed incomprehensible. The Hebrew language itself gives rise to so many ambiguities as to render it impossible to devise a sure method that can tell us with certainty how to discover the true meaning of all scriptural passages. In Hebrew, conjunctions and adverbs can have multiple meanings; there is a disregard for tenses; there are no letters for vowels; nor was it the custom of the ancient writers to punctuate their texts. The ancient writers indeed did not employ points (that is, vowels and accents); men of later ages added both of these in accordance with their own interpretation of the Bible: 'Therefore the accents and points that we now have are merely contemporary interpretations, and deserve no more credibility and authority than other commentaries.'[45] Spinoza's critical method, then, recognizes textuality as palimpsestial, to deploy a term become common in our poststructuralist times.

Scripture has also to be submitted to 'historical study', above all avoiding 'confusing the minds of the prophets and historians with the mind of the Holy Spirit and with factual truth'. Historical study should set forth the circumstances relevant to all the extant books of the prophets, giving the life, character and pursuits of the author of every book, detailing who he was, on what occasion and at what time and for whom and in what language he wrote. Historical study should relate what happened to each book, how it was first received, into whose hands it fell, how many variant versions there were, by whose decision it was received into the canon, and how all the books now universally regarded as sacred were united into a single whole. It is important to discover whether or not Scripture may have been contaminated by spurious insertions, whether errors have crept in, and whether these have been corrected by experienced and trustworthy scholars. These difficulties are so 'grave', says Spinoza, that it means in many instances either we do not know the true meaning of Scripture or we can do no more than make conjecture.[46]

Yet, Spinoza recognizes, such historical knowledge is very difficult to accomplish, because scholars have either no knowledge at all or only doubtful knowledge of the 'authors' or 'writers' of many of the books, and do not even know on what occasion or at what time these books of unknown authorship were written. Spinoza's perhaps most controversial adventure of thought was to question the authorship of the Sacred Books, the Pentateuch: 'The author is almost universally believed to be Moses, a view so obstinately defended by the Pharisees that they have regarded any other view as heresy.' Spinoza argues that it was not Moses who wrote the Pentateuch (that is, the first five books, of Genesis, Exodus, Leviticus, Numbers and Deuteronomy, in Jewish tradition the Torah). From a close textual reading of Joshua, Genesis, and especially Deuteronomy, Spinoza concludes that 'it is clear beyond a shadow of a doubt that the Pentateuch was not written by Moses, but by someone who lived many generations after Moses'.[47]

The *Tractatus Theologico-Politicus* is I think one of the great books of world literature: exuberant, witty, wise, mordant, sceptical, cynical, proud.

Certainly Spinoza was egregiously elitist, believing the mass of people are credulous and so limited in intelligence that they cannot understand philosophy. He also defined philosophy as the superiority of reason, where philosophy deploys a language of pure concepts. Here Spinoza participates in and brilliantly helps further philosophy as the hubris of epistemology, a method positing a conceptual language that is held to be completely above or separate from imagination, fantasy, image and metaphor: the kind of Western philosophical project that would be protested against by the Jena Romantics, Walter Benjamin, and poststructuralists like Paul de Man and Derrida. Spinoza also evidently regarded the realm of concepts as a masculine sphere; in his preface to the *Tractatus* he makes a derisory reference to men who, as victims of superstition of all kinds, 'implore God's help with prayers and womanish tears'.[48]

We might make contrast here with Benjamin's prologue to *The Origin of German Tragic Drama*, which suggests that truth is always historical, it does not exist in a pure realm of ideas and concepts; historical truth cannot be directly apprehended in terms of epistemology, since the language of philosophy always involves representation (*Darstellung*). The search for truth is consequently always indirect, as it becomes aware of the intervening presence and workings of its own language, its own representations and figures, metaphors and rhetoric, stories and allegories — there is no realm of pure concepts that can be absolutely separated from imagination and fantasy.[49]

Yet Spinoza's elitism and hubris can be sympathetically qualified. Spinoza may appear inordinately arrogant in his belief in the superiority of philosophy, but he was also historically fighting for a public space for philosophy and knowledge to work and breathe in. His plea for recognition of individual thought and judgement anticipates Voltaire and the wisdom of the Enlightenment in attempting to establish a public sphere of debate and discussion, a historically sanctioned space for the freedom of intellectuals and the liberty of ideas. His libertarian arguments against legal repression are also of great contemporary relevance in the new millennium (one has only to think of the disastrous insistence by most societies around the contemporary world, under the aegis of the American imperium, that drugs be illegal). Further, Spinoza had every reason to fear the multitude and regard them as potentially or actually hostile to those who practise 'speculative thought'. He feared their political and religious violence. He feared the violence involved in religious prejudice provoked by preachers and theologians, in particular the persecutions incited under the cloak of religion, when beliefs are put on trial and condemned as crimes. In such situations, the 'adherents and followers of these beliefs are sacrificed, not to the public weal, but to the hatred and savagery of their opponents'. Spinoza felt that those who valued reason rather than prejudice were becoming fewer and fewer and more and more threatened.[50]

In terms of political violence, it is well to recall that in 1672, not long after the publication of the *Tractatus*, a mob attacked, killed and mutilated two republican political leaders, Cornelius and Johan de Witt. Spinoza was so angry he wanted to post a placard denouncing those responsible; his landlord, however, dissuaded him from doing so, fearful of subsequent violence. A year later Spinoza did indeed have to confront a mob outside his residence, but was successful in dispelling the crowd.[51]

Spinoza wryly writes in the *Tractatus* that study of the biblical historical narratives can be very profitable in the matter of social relations: 'For the more we observe and the better we are acquainted with the ways and manners of men – and it is their actions that best provide this knowledge – the more prudently we can live among them.'[52]

Spinoza is one of history's great heretics, perhaps reminiscent (while philosophically exceedingly different) of the Cathars of Provence in the late twelfth and early thirteenth centuries; until brutally suppressed by the Inquisition, the Cathars preached against the corruption of the Catholic clergy, against its social privileges and hierarchy and authority, and against many dogmas of the Church.[53] That same Inquisition would in Portugal some centuries later decisively affect the lives of Spinoza's immediate ancestors.

Spinoza as converso and marrano

The marranos had for generations in Portugal, in their secret consciousness, in perilous circumstances, developed what Yirmiyahu Yovel refers to as a dauntless and even proud attitude that was not merely a form of vanity. Their pride was not conceit but the philosophical demand for personal conviction and consent. Since in hostile dangerous inquisitional Portugal the marranos had lost the support of Jewish religious tradition and authority, all they could rely on was their own reasoning.[54]

In the seventeenth century many marranos able to reach Holland did indeed rediscover Judaism and become solid members of the Amsterdam community.[55] But for some intellectuals their marrano heritage of secular rationalism and distinctive consciousness proved precisely that which they wished to continue, even with difficulty and anguish, as with Uriel da Costa and Juan de Prado, who desired to remain within the Jewish community while openly espousing a kind of deism; or with anger, as with Spinoza, who nevertheless accepted excommunication as his fate.[56]

In *The Marrano of Reason* Yirmiyahu Yovel fascinatingly evokes and analyses the converso and marrano milieu of sixteenth- and seventeenth-century Portugal. Yovel does not equate conversos with marranos; marranos were those conversos who were secret or crypto-Jews. The conversos were the former Jews in Spain and Portugal who had voluntarily converted to, or been forcibly baptized into, Christianity, becoming the New Christians. Many conversos transferred a messianic enthusiasm that was a Judaic form of consciousness into an enthusiastic Christianity, sometimes engaging in virulent anti-Jewish polemics, some even becoming officers of the Inquisition. (Torquemada himself appears to have been a converso.) Many, especially early on before later waves of hostility to the New Christians, rose to high positions in the society, including clergy and nobility. It was the visible success of the New Christians as part of the new Iberian urban bourgeoisie that created resentment, a success that inspired the Statutes of the Purity of Blood which could be used to bar New Christians from public and ecclesiastical offices and honours. As Yovel observes, the Statutes spread 'their rule over other races as well (black Africans, Chinese, and Moors) and into the Iberian colonies'.[57]

Yovel argues that the Portuguese marranos developed a special culture, their own phenomenological category, in response to their situation and daily dangers; a culture that produced many dualities, especially an opposition between inner and outer life and a mixture of the two religions that might lead to a radical questioning of both Christian and Jewish beliefs. Such a culture also emphasized disguise, a play of masks, a multiplicity of personas, a distance, an ironic self-consciousness, the leading of a double life in a language and aesthetics of duality and equivocation; the marranos developed special linguistic sensibilities.[58]

There could also be elitism amongst the marranos, an outward social conformity accompanied by a sense of superior inner knowledge, and a rationalist mythos, as in Spinoza, that the multitude, amongst whom the philosopher must live, is capable of *imaginatio* but not *ratio*. Left to itself, the *imaginatio* of the multitude breeds superstition, intolerance, fanaticism, violence, war. But such elitism must be concealed, must be attended by the rule of prudence of accommodating to the society one is in. The philosopher engages in public discourse in order to persuade others to a life of reason, often by provoking perplexity; but prudently, with caution. Spinoza, Yovel notes, wore a ring inscribed *Caute*.[59]

Further, Yovel points out, it was not simply a question for the marranos in Portugal of an outer surface or husk of Christian belief and a secure, defined, inner core of persisting Jewish faith. The marranos were profoundly versed in Christian symbolism and learning (often attending universities), and their Christianity influenced the ways they tried to continue their Judaism, which was in any case remembered in only fragmentary ways: their inner consciousness was multicontradictory, was confused, dissonant, ambivalent, paradoxical, incomplete, doubting, self-doubting, potentially or actually heretical. Marranos developed hybrid Catholic–Jewish beliefs, for example, in individual salvation (a Christian view, where Judaism rather emphasizes collective redemption). There was the development of secret cults, as in a devotion to St Esther (Queen Esther in biblical narrative had saved the Jews when the king her husband had threatened to kill them). There was a (Christian) notion of having lapsed from a true state of faith, and an associated guilt.[60]

In Yovel's view, there was surprising liking for visual representation. Yovel takes us on a tour of a Portuguese Jewish cemetery in Ouderkerk, near Amsterdam, where many gravestones are fashioned as exquisite art with representations of human and animal figures, including representation of God himself, beams of light gleaming about his head. Yovel notes that here in this elegant cemetery the inner consciousness of the marranos was given an extraordinary plastic and visual expression in the Baroque mode of the Catholic states of southern Europe, yet in violation of the second commandment forbidding graven images.[61]

Marranos also tended to become this-worldly, believing in neither Christian nor Jewish eschatologies of transcendence, and impatient with any religious establishment: the kind of secularism, rationalism and sceptical independence emphasizing the freedom and dignity of the person and toleration of different beliefs which would influence Spinoza and was a harbinger of the culture of modernity. The marranos prefigured modernity in other ways. Marrano lives could be marked by sharply different phases, for example, as New Christian in Portugal, New Jew in Amsterdam, so that there is constant rupture with their past, their present, their future: 'The unassimilated Marrano is the true wandering Jew, roaming between Christianity and Judaism and drifting between the two and universalism.' In always having to regard themselves as New, the marranos, Yovel feels, were proto-modernist outsider figures, both inside and outside of any cultural context.[62]

The marranos also helped establish a new relationship between ethnic ancestry and identity. People came to be defined as of Hebrew extraction, Yovel suggests, whether their religion be Judaism, Christianity or deism; or, as with Spinoza, whether they devoted their life to secular reason and the intellectual love of God as deified nature. While Spinoza had rejected Judaism and had been rejected by his community, and become notorious in Calvinist-dominated Holland as an alleged atheist, he was still regarded by his fellow citizens, who might be Calvinist, Catholic, Lutheran, as a Jew: but now a new phenomenological concept, a secular Jew, a non-Jewish Jew. Spinoza, says Yovel, remained locked in a paradox, unable either to live positively as a Jew or to shed his basic Jewish identification.[63]

Identity remained entwined with ethnic ancestry, mind with body, not as an expression but as a tortuous unresolved relationship, all the more interesting given Spinoza's own controversial, anti-Cartesian view that the mind is the 'idea' of the body.[64]

Bloom as converso, marrano, heretic

Can we see here a proleptic embodiment of Bloom in *Ulysses*? Is Bloom a marrano doubled in Dublin?

Clearly Bloom is not created as an intellectual giant like Spinoza (it is Stephen who regards himself as a brilliant mind, ignored and disregarded), nor as a rationalist constructing sustained systematic philosophical argumentation. Bloom does not believe that he belongs to an elite of philosophers in history. Nor does he wish to separate out supposedly pure concepts from fantasy and imagination. Nor does he assume thought is masculine or that men cannot also be (as it were) feminine.

Nor does he share Spinoza's contempt for mass or popular interest in the visual and pictorial, as if – in a view that anticipates conventional aesthetic modernism – the visual must yield only intellectual simplicity or uncomplicated belief. Both Mr Bloom and Walter Benjamin are opposed to Spinoza here.[65]

Yet Bloom shares similarities of situation and features of personality and sensibility with the sixteenth- and seventeenth-century conversos and marranos who influenced Spinoza, not least a kind of baroque visuality in his gaze on the world of Catholic Ireland he finds himself in.

Mr Bloom's demeanour in the public sphere of colonial Dublin early in the new century is observably one of watchful caution and prudence, a desire inoffensively to observe normative behaviour, a plea to be considered inconspicuously normal, an ordinary Irish citizen amongst ordinary Irish citizens, neither harming nor provoking anyone, always willing to assist, as in helping tidy up the just buried Paddy Dignam's financial affairs, and always hoping that he is at least appearing to listen in any conversation. After the bitter argument in the pub over Bloom's identity, Bloom feels that he is as good an Irishman as the 'rude' citizen, and he is also pleased that as a Jew he was not passive, that he answered the citizen back. Yet Bloom also wishes to retreat from such open conflict, forgiving the citizen in his own mind: 'Perhaps not to hurt he meant.'[66]

Even when Bloom finally gets into bed (having first 'removed a pillow from the head to the foot of the bed' and 'prepared the bedlinen accordingly'), he exercises caution. How does he enter the bed, the narrator asks.

> With circumspection, as invariably when entering an abode (his own or not his own): with solicitude, the snakespiral springs of the mattress being old, the brass quoits and pendent viper radii loose and tremulous under stress and strain: prudently, as entering a lair or ambush of lust or adder: lightly, the less to disturb: reverently, the bed of conception and of birth, of consummation of marriage and of breach of marriage, of sleep and of death.[67]

It may also be part of Bloom's habits of outwardly conforming – another part is that he clearly enjoys such parts – that he eats the inner organs of pigs. In any case, in terms of pork-eating, Bloom follows the conversos and marranos in this practice, though in inquisitional Spain and Portugal they had no choice.[68]

What is also immediately observable about Mr Bloom is that he can never get the modalities of ordinariness and normality (as he conceives them) of model Dublin men quite right, as in his choosing not to drink in Barney Kiernan's pub, or, once drawn inside, his lack of attention there to the interest of the regulars in horse racing, as in the misunderstanding over Throwaway.

Whatever his desire to outwardly conform in every situation, the good men of Dublin don't think of Bloom as like themselves, they're always quick to be suspicious of and with him, to imply a distance that he always detects, a shadowing hostility and uneasiness. Bloom has the marrano's sense of life-unease, of never fully belonging, of fear of being perceived as never fully belonging, of living under the shadow of suspicion and vulnerability, disaster and cruelty.

In terms of Yovel's evocation of the marranos, we can say that Bloom is proud of his own inner independence, his sense of his own personal convictions, his distance from and critiquing of the society around him, his self-reliance, his striking his own path, however confused and fantastical, rather than receiving meaning from institutional authority or patriarchal power. Like Spinoza with his ring marked *Caute*, Bloom is wary of the *imaginatio* of the multitude, irrational, violent and intolerant, believing also with Spinoza that a lay state, secular and tolerant, can be a civilizing agent (in Bloom's utopia, 'a free lay church in a free lay state').[69]

Politically, Bloom thinks towards his own independent position. He is a utopian pacifist and sexual libertarian: 'Free money, free love and a free lay church in a free lay state.' He believes in the reverse of a fixity of identity, indeed in inversion, transformation, metamorphosis: 'weekly carnival, with masked licence', sharing the marrano interest in masking and play of personae. Like the marranos his sense of Jewishness is fragmentary, and like them his inner consciousness is multicontradictory, dissonant, ambivalent, paradoxical, incomplete, doubting, self-doubting, potentially or actually heretical. Like the marranos he is very this-worldly, and like them he is inside and outside his surrounding society at the same time: his existence is one of double consciousness, managing and negotiating duality, as perhaps in diaspora consciousness in general.

Like the marranos, Bloom emphasizes the freedom and dignity of the person and toleration of different beliefs. Like Spinoza, whatever his religious affiliations or secularist thought, Bloom is considered Jewish.

In *The Jews of Spain* Gerber mentions that some marranos in seventeenth-century Holland, in the intellectual ferment and free and open atmosphere of the Dutch metropolis, saw lineage as passing through the father, in contradiction of Jewish law, which is matrilineal.[70]

In terms of descent, Bloom sees his Jewishness as stemming from his father.

> Bloom, only born transubstantial heir of Rudolf Virag (subsequently Rudolf Bloom) of Szombathely, Vienna, Budapest, Milan, London and Dublin and of Ellen Higgins, second daughter of Julius Higgins (born Karoly) and Fanny Higgins (born Hegarty) ...
>
> 'Ithaca'[71]

Bloom's ancestry is mixed indeed, both Jewish and Christian. It would appear that Bloom's mother and her mother are not Jewish – though his mother's father 'Julius Higgins (born Karoly)' might be Jewish. Furthermore, as Michael Ragussis reminds us, Bloom's father had in 1865 been converted to Protestantism by the predatory London Society for the Promotion of Christianity Amongst the Jews when he got to London from Central Europe; Bloom would subsequently in 1880 break from his father's Protestantism, then in 1888 convert to Catholicism with a view to matrimony with Marion Tweedy.[72]

Bloom, then, is part of an Irish converso family, with his father (before his suicide in 1886) even after his conversion possibly also a marrano, a secret Jew, surrounded by an intensely Christian society. While Bloom tries outwardly to conform to that society, because born and growing up there he feels part of it, because he is married to a Christian, and because he fears its hostility and othering, he also maintains an inner sense of difference and Jewishness. But, like the sixteenth-century Portuguese marranos, his Judaism is residual, so that he is often ignorant of it – or, rather, we often cannot tell if he doesn't know the received meanings of Judaism or he is playing with them.[73]

Bloom and Central Europe

Spinoza was excommunicated by the Jewish community in mid-seventeenth-century Holland. Bloom, variously Jewish, Protestant and Catholic, was in 'Cyclops' in effect excommunicated by the nationalist citizens of Barney Kiernan's pub, reviling him as not-Irish, leading to his then seeking the company of the marginal and liminal, in Bella Cohen's brothel, along with the selfconscious outsider-intellectual Stephen Daedalus. Bloom's family experiences on his father's side would have prepared him for such liminality, his father 'Rudolf Virag (subsequently Rudolf Bloom) of Szombathely, Vienna, Budapest, Milan, London and Dublin', having come from the Austro-Hungarian Habsburg empire.

> What first reminiscence had he of Rudolph Bloom (deceased)?
> Rudolph Bloom (deceased) narrated to his son Leopold Bloom (aged 6) a retrospective arrangement of migrations and settlements in and between Dublin, London, Florence, Milan, Vienna, Budapest, Szombathely, with statements of satisfaction (his grandfather having seen Maria Theresa, empress of Austria, queen of Hungary), with commercial advice (having taken care of pence, the pounds having taken care of themselves). Leopold Bloom (aged 6) had accompanied these narrations by constant consultation of a geographical map of Europe (political) and by suggestions for the establishment of affiliated business premises in the various centres mentioned.[74]

It was, perhaps, such Central European movement between city and city, inducing scepticism and mobility of mind and observation, that Bloom inherited and that made him so receptive, in Catholic and Protestant Ireland, to the heritage of Enlightenment Jews like Spinoza and to Sephardi Jewish traditions of converso and marrano-like multiple consciousness that prefigured modernity.

Rudolph Bloom also imparts to his son a Central European love of theatre, concert and opera that Bloom cultivates in Dublin, though L. Bloom's tastes are perhaps more popular than would have been held to be respectable or sufficiently serious in nineteenth-century Vienna and Budapest.[75]

Whatever Bloom's troubled feelings towards his father, he learns from Rudolph Bloom a depth of diasporic consciousness, an attentiveness to other and previous histories, a worldly ease of reference and multiple habitation, a lack of fear of the elsewhere.

Bloom, we might say, is by descent a kind of Hungarian-Irish marrano, adding fragments of contradictory diasporic consciousness to other fragments of contradictory diasporic consciousness. Bloom's sensibility and sensitivities are like an archipelago. My *Shorter Oxford English Dictionary* tells me that no such word as 'archipelago' appears in ancient or modern Greek; it is an Italian formation signifying in one meaning the Aegean Sea, between Greece and Asia Minor, a sea studded with many islands.

I hope I have shown that a diasporic and allegorical reading permits observant journeys around the many islands of Bloom's mind even while they shimmer unto distance endless; islands that gaze many ways, to Asia Minor and the Levant and the Orient as well as to Greece and Western Europe and Central Europe.

Notes

1. Quoted in Genevieve Lloyd, *Spinoza and the* Ethics (London: Routledge, 1996), p. 2.
2. Baruch Spinoza, *Tractatus Theologico-Politicus*, trans. Samuel Shirley, intro. Brad S. Gregory (Leiden: E. J. Brill, 1989), p. 125.
3. Walter Benjamin, *The Origin of German Tragic Drama*, trans. John Osborne (London: Verso, 1996), section on 'Allegory and Trauerspiel'; Edward A. Maser (ed.), *Cesare Ripa: Baroque and Rococo Imagery. The 1758–60 Hertel Edition* (New York: Dover Publications, 1971), Introduction. See also Ann Curthoys and John Docker, 'Time, eternity, truth, and death: history as allegory', *Humanities Research*, 1 (1999), pp. 5–26.
4. Cf. Samuel H. Dresner, *The Zaddik: The Doctrine of the Zaddik According to the Writings of Rabbi Yaakov Yosef of Polnoy* (New York: Schocken Books, 1974). The zaddik was associated with the Hasidic movement which developed in Eastern Europe in the eighteenth century.
5. James Joyce, *Ulysses* (1922), intro. and notes by Declan Kiberd (London: Penguin, 1992), pp. 104, 350, 495, 497, 519, 566, 570, 797–8, 836, 843, 850, 869, 932–3.

All page references are to this edition. Cf. Natalie Davis, *Society and Culture in Early Modern France* (Stanford, CA: Stanford University Press, 1975), ch. 5, 'Women on Top'.

6. *Ulysses*, pp. 465, 496, 569, 745–6.
7. *Ibid.*, pp. 139, 797.
8. *The Sociology of Georg Simmel*, ed. and trans. Kurt H. Wolff (Glencoe, IL:The Free Press, 1950), pp. 402–8. My thanks to Igor Primoratz for drawing my attention to Simmel's brilliant essay.
9. *Ibid.*, p. 403.
10. See Yirmiyahu Yovel, *Dark Riddle: Hegel, Nietzsche, and the Jews* (Cambridge: Polity Press, 1998), pp. 35–8.
11. Beatrice Hanssen, *Walter Benjamin's Other History: Of Stones, Animals, Human Beings, and Angels* (Berkeley, Los Angeles and London: University of California Press, 1998), pp. 128–9, 144.
12. *Ulysses*, p. 859.
13. Hanssen, *Walter Benjamin's Other History*, pp. 5–6, 104–7, 127–8, 140–5, 152–6, 162–5. Cf. Jane Bennett, *Thoreau's Nature: Ethics, Politics, and the Wild* (Los Angeles and London: Sage, 1994), esp. chs 2 and 3.
14. I'm grateful to Ned Curthoys for this point.
15. *Ulysses*, pp. 82, 825, 867.
16. Jane S. Gerber, *The Jews of Spain: A History of the Sephardic Experience* (New York: The Free Press, 1992), pp. xii–xv and ch. 7; Haim Beinart, 'The conversos and their fate' in Elie Kedourie (ed.), *Spain and the Jews: The Sephardi Experience, 1492 and After* (London: Thames and Hudson, 1992), pp. 92–122. See also Raymond B. Waddington and Arthur H. Williamson (eds), *The Expulsion of the Jews: 1492 and After* (New York and London: Garland, 1994). For an older historiography see Cecil Roth, *A History of the Marranos* (New York: Hermon Press, 1974) and *Gleanings: Essays in Jewish History, Letters and Art* (New York: Hermon Press, 1967), 'The religion of the marranos', pp. 119–51.
17. For the Catholic Spanish doctrine of blood purity, *limpieza de sangre*, formulated in the fifteenth century, see Marc Shell, 'Marranos (pigs), or from coexistence to toleration', *Critical Inquiry*, 17 (1991), pp. 306–35. See also Henry Kamen, *Inquisition and Society in Spain in the Sixteenth and Seventeenth Centuries* (London: Weidenfeld and Nicolson, 1985). Kamen (p. 8) says that the word *marranos* is of obscure origin. The Inquisition followed the Sephardi marranos to Venice in the sixteenth and seventeenth centuries: see Brian Pullan, *The Jews of Europe and the Inquisition of Venice, 1550–1670* (Oxford: Basil Blackwell, 1983).
18. Gerber, *The Jews of* Spain, pp. xxiii, 138–9, 143, 146, 186–7, 189, 193.
19. For the Inquisition in Goa, directed at both Portuguese New Christians and Hindus who had converted to Christianity, see Anant Kakba Priolkar, *The Goa Inquisition* (New Delhi: Voice of India, 1991).
20. Gerber, pp. 189–91, 195, 197, 199.
21. *Ibid.*, pp. 200–2. While doing the final revising of this book, I had the good fortune to be able to read Steven Nadler, *Spinoza: A Life* (Cambridge and New York: Cambridge University Press, 1999); see ch. 6, 'Cherem', pp. 116–54.
22. See the introduction by Gregory to Baruch Spinoza, *Tractatus Theologico-Politicus*, pp. 5, 18.
23. Gregory, introduction to *Tractatus*, pp. 27–32. See also Pierre-François Moreau,

'Spinoza's reception and influence' in Don Garrett (ed.), *The Cambridge Companion to Spinoza* (Cambridge: Cambridge University Press, 1996), ch. 10, and Nadler, *Spinoza: A Life*, ch. 11, 'Calm and turmoil in The Hague', esp. pp. 295–319.

24. Gilles Deleuze, *Spinoza: Practical Philosophy*, trans. Robert Hurley (San Francisco: City Lights Books, 1988), pp. 28–9. See also Warren Montag and Ted Stolze (eds), *The New Spinoza* (Minneapolis: University of Minnesota Press, 1997).

25. Spinoza, *Tractatus*, pp. 121, 231.

26. Benjamin, *The Origin of German Tragic Drama*, p. 28.

27. Spinoza, *Tractatus*, pp. 87, 221–6, 275, 280, 284.

28. *Ibid.*, pp. 51, 90, 117, 239, 241, 243, 282, 297, 299.

29. *Ibid.*, p. 295.

30. *Ibid.*, p. 295. See also Steven B. Smith, *Spinoza, Liberalism, and the Question of Jewish Identity* (New Haven and London: Yale University Press, 1997).

31. *Ibid.*, pp. 63, 87, 122–3, 158, 232.

32. *Ibid.*, pp. 89, 103–5, 125, 131.

33. *Ibid.*, pp. 55, 103, 123, 159, 211, 281.

34. *Ibid.*, pp. 119, 205.

35. *Ibid.*, p. 119.

36. *Ibid.*, pp. 70–2, 228, 233.

37. *Ibid.*, pp. 78, 131, 145, 210, 220.

38. *Ibid.*, pp. 54, 91–2, 98–100, 131.

39. *Ibid.*, pp. 94, 96.

40. *Ibid.*, pp. 124–5, 131–6.

41. *Ibid.*, pp. 130, 134.

42. *Ibid.*, p. 234.

43. Gregory, introduction to Spinoza, *Tractatus*, p. 42.

44. Spinoza, *Tractatus*, p. 148. In Nadler, *Spinoza: A Life*, pp. 336–40, we read that Spinoza, in controversy with an ex-friend turned Catholic, gave his scornful opinion of the Roman Catholic Church: while Jesus is to be found wherever there is 'justice and charity', the Catholic Church is mere 'institutionalized superstition'; his ex-friend, Spinoza continues in this letter, should acquaint himself with the histories of the Church, and especially 'with what craft the Pope of Rome finally gained supremacy over the Church six hundred years after the birth of Christ'.

45. Spinoza, *Tractatus*, pp. 141–3, 149–51.

46. *Ibid.*, pp. 141, 144–7, 153.

47. *Ibid.*, pp. 152, 161–6. For a rather disdainful appraisal of Spinoza in his historical context, see Richard H. Popkin, 'Spinoza and Bible scholarship' in Garrett (ed.), *The Cambridge Companion to Spinoza*, ch. 9.

48. Spinoza, *Tractatus*, p. 49. I owe a great deal to discussions with Ned Curthoys concerning the Jena Romantics and Walter Benjamin. Concerning 'womanish tears' and the lure of superstition, Spinoza employs metaphors of the witch and the siren who call men away from reason and philosophy; Spinoza also thought women were naturally unsuitable to hold political power: see Nadler, *Spinoza: A Life*, pp. 339, 344, 348.

49. Benjamin, *The Origin of German Tragic Drama*, pp. 29–31. See also Jacques Derrida, *Margins of Philosophy*, trans. Alan Bass (Chicago: University of Chicago

Press, 1986), 'White mythology: metaphor in the text of philosophy', pp. 209–29, and Paul de Man, 'The epistemology of metaphor' in Sheldon Sacks (ed.), *On Metaphor* (Chicago and London: The University of Chicago Press, 1979), pp. 11–28. While doing the final revising, I began reading Moira Gatens and Genevieve Lloyd, *Collective Imaginings: Spinoza, Past and Present* (London and New York: Routledge, 1999), who highlight in Spinoza's philosophy 'the positive role of the imagination in even the highest forms of intellectual life', that imagination has complex relations with emotion, desire and intellect (pp. 4–5).

50. Spinoza, *Tractatus*, pp. 51–2, 56, 78, 161, 262.

51. Gregory, introduction to Spinoza, *Tractatus*, p. 8. For the gruesome murder of the De Witt brothers, see Nadler, *Spinoza: A Life*, pp. 305–6.

52. Spinoza, *Tractatus*, p. 105.

53. Gershom Scholem, *Origins of the Kabbalah*, trans. Allan Arkush, ed. R. J. Zwi Werblowsky (Princeton, NJ: Princeton University Press, 1990), pp. 14–16.

54. Yirmiyahu Yovel, *Spinoza and Other Heretics*, vol. I: *The Marrano of Reason* (Princeton, NJ: Princeton University Press, 1989), pp. 12, 64–5, 67, 71.

55. Isaac Orobio de Castro, for example, became the champion of traditional Judaism against sceptics like Juan de Prado (an old friend of Orobio) and Spinoza. See Yovel, *The Marrano of Reason*, pp. 51–4, 57–80. See also Yosef Kaplan, *From Christianity to Judaism: The Story of Isaac Orobio de Castro*, trans. Raphael Loewe (Oxford: Oxford University Press, 1989), pp. 122–78, 263–9.

56. Yovel, *The Marrano of Reason*, pp. 3, 6, 42–50, 57–80, 178. For the tortured life in Amsterdam of Uriel da Costa who committed suicide, see Nadler, *Spinoza: A Life*, pp. 66–72.

57. Yovel, *The Marrano of Reason*, pp. ix, 7, 15–17, 24–5, 54, 91, 189. Cf. Ella Shohat, 'Staging the Quincentenary: the Middle East and the Americas', *Third Text*, 21 (Winter 1992–93), pp. 95–105.

58. Yovel, *The Marrano of Reason*, pp. ix, 23, 26, 29–30, 63, 69, 91, 96, 108, 111, 136.

59. *Ibid.*, pp. 78, 92, 129–36, 141–5, 150, 153, 175–6, 196; the reference to *Caute* as the inscription on Spinoza's ring is on p. 141.

60. *Ibid.*, pp. 19–22, 28, 41, 65, 83–4, 98. Apropos Queen Esther, cf. Eve Kosofsky Sedgwick, *The Epistemology of the Closet* (Berkeley: University of California Press, 1990), pp. 75–6.

61. Yovel, *The Marrano of Reason*, pp. 54–6.

62. *Ibid.*, pp. x–xi, 13, 26–7, 34–5, 49, 91, 95. Apropos the marranos prefiguring modernity, see Ammiel Alcalay, 'Exploding identities: notes on ethnicity and literary history' in Jonathan Boyarin and Daniel Boyarin (eds), *Jews and Other Differences: The New Jewish Cultural Studies* (Minneapolis: University of Minnesota Press, 1997), p. 339. See also Elaine Marks, *Marrano as Metaphor: The Jewish Presence in French Writing* (New York: Columbia University Press, 1996). In his essay 'Circumfession', Derrida says he regards himself as 'a sort of *marrane* of French Catholic culture': 'I am one of those *marranes* who no longer say they are Jews even in the secret of their own hearts'; see Geoffrey Bennington and Jacques Derrida, *Jacques Derrida*, trans. Geoffrey Bennington (Chicago and London: University of Chicago Press, 1993), p. 170.

63. Yovel, pp. 32–4, 68, 70, 76, 99, 127, 137, 148, 172, 184, 200. Cf. Isaac Deutscher, *The Non-Jewish Jew* (London: Oxford University Press, 1968).

64. Cf. Lloyd, *Spinoza and the* Ethics, pp. 6–9, 23–4, 48–55.
65. Cf. John Docker, *Postmodernism and Popular Culture: A Cultural History* (Melbourne: Cambridge University Press, 1994), esp. chs. 3 and 4.
66. *Ulysses*, p. 496.
67. *Ibid.*, p. 862.
68. Roth, *Gleanings*, p. 137.
69. *Ulysses*, p. 610.
70. Gerber, *The Jews of Spain*, p. 200.
71. *Ulysses*, pp. 797–8.
72. Michael Ragussis, *Figures of Conversion: 'The Jewish Question' and English National Identity* (Durham, NC and London: Duke University Press, 1995), pp. 9–10.
73. A point made by Neil R. Davison, *James Joyce, Ulysses, and the Construction of Jewish Identity* (Cambridge: Cambridge University Press, 1996), p. 221.
74. *Ulysses*, p. 854.
75. *Ibid.*, p. 93. Cf. John Felstiner, *Paul Celan: Poet, Survivor, Jew* (New Haven, CT and London: Yale University Press, 1995), p. 6. Cf. also Andrew Riemer, *The Habsburg Café* (Sydney: Angus and Robertson, 1993). See my analysis of and rejoinder to *The Habsburg Café* in John Docker, 'Rethinking postcolonialism and multiculturalism in the *fin de siècle*', *Cultural Studies*, 9(3) (1995), pp. 418–22.

6

Mr Bloom's penis

And I will make thee exceeding fruitful, and I will make nations of thee, and kings shall come out of thee.

And I will establish my covenant between me and thee and thy seed after thee in their generation for an everlasting covenant, to be a God unto thee, and to thy seed after thee.

And I will give unto thee, and to thy seed after thee, the land wherein thou art a stranger, all the land of Canaan, for an everlasting possession; and I will be their God.

And God said unto Abraham, Thou shalt keep my covenant therefore, thou, and thy seed after thee in their generations.

This *is* my covenant, which ye shall keep, between me and you and thy seed after thee; Every man child among you shall be circumcised.

And ye shall circumcise the flesh of your foreskin; and it shall be a token of the covenant betwixt me and you.

And he that is eight days old shall be circumcised....

(Genesis 17:6–12)

Sexual union is holy and pure, when performed in the right way, at the right time, with the right intention. ... The right kind of union is called *knowing*. ... This matter is not as Rabbi Moses Maimonides, of blessed memory, imagined and thought in his *Guide of the Perplexed*, where he praises Aristotle for stating that the sense of touch is shameful. God forbid! This matter is not as that Greek said; what he said smacks of subtle heresy. If that Greek scoundrel believed that the world was created with divine intention, he would not have said what he said. But we, who possess the holy Torah, believe that God created everything as divine wisdom decreed. God created nothing shameful or ugly. If sexual union is shameful, then the genitals are too. Yet God created them! How could God create something blemished, disgraceful, or deficient. ... When sexual union is for the sake of heaven, there is nothing as holy or pure. The union of

man and woman, when it is right, is the secret of civilization. Thereby, one
becomes a partner with God in the act of Creation.

'Sexual holiness', the Kabbalah[1]

Dear John

Have I told you 'my' circumcision story? I went to my nephew's
circumcision which, despite the presence of a number of medical doctors,
was carried out by a rabbi (who looked about 12) at my brother's home.
My mother and I along with my sister in law, her mother and one of her
sisters went to the bedroom at the other end of the house so we wouldn't
hear the screams. The other sister (as godmother and very orthodox)
remained with my nephew. He was very tiny. Meanwhile in the bedroom
my sister in law presented me with my belated birthday present, an
umbrella (which I still have some 8 or 9 years later, it's the only thing I
have not been able to lose). The moment I took hold of the handle it
came off coinciding with muffled cries elsewhere in the house. I found out
later that my nephew suffered an infection as a result and later had the
job tidied up under anaesthetic.

Rifka (e-mail, 12 November 1998)

Mr Bloom's Jewishness is teasingly intriguing. In this chapter I explore the
implications of whether or not he is circumcised: no small matter. I'll begin my
journey into this area (as it were) once more through the Enlightenment
philosophy of Benedict Spinoza, philosophy which at times Bloom comes close
to, at times turns sharply away from. Spinoza's thoughts and Mr Bloom's
thoughts come together and part and merge again as in an arabesque.

In *Tractatus Theologico-Politicus*, Spinoza was certainly interested in the
historical consequences for the Jews of circumcision. His statements here have
proved highly controversial. Contemplating the continued existence of the
Jews for so many years while scattered and stateless, Spinoza mordantly
remarks that such is not surprising, since 'they have separated themselves from
other nations to such a degree as to incur the hatred of all, and this not only
through external rites alien to the rites of other nations but also through the
mark of circumcision, which they most religiously observe'. Spinoza then
expands on his reference to circumcision in the following remarkable passage:

The mark of circumcision, too, I consider to be such an important factor
in this matter that I am convinced that this by itself will preserve their
nation for ever. Indeed, were it not that the fundamental principles of
their religion discourage manliness, I would not hesitate to believe that
they will one day, given the opportunity – such is the mutability of

human affairs – establish once more their independent state, and that God will again choose them. The Chinese afford us an outstanding example of such a possibility. They, too, religiously observe the custom of the pigtail which sets them apart from all other people, and they have preserved themselves as a separate people for so many thousands of years that they far surpass all other nations in antiquity. They have not always maintained their independence, but they did regain it after losing it, and will no doubt recover it again when the spirit of the Tartars becomes enfeebled by reason of luxurious living and sloth.[2]

These comments have been rejoiced over by generations of Zionists to mean not only that Spinoza was foretelling and anticipating the rebirth of the Jewish nation but that he was a Zionist, and therefore a national hero of modern Israel. Indeed, such was the enthusiasm amongst the founders of Zionism that Levinas was moved to protest against the project put forward by Ben Gurion that the 1656 excommunication be lifted in Israel. Levinas remarked with severity of his fellow philosopher that 'we cannot ignore the harmful role Spinoza played in the decomposition of the Jewish intelligentsia', in particular the acceptance of Jesus as exemplary historical figure and the consequent triumph of Christianity in modern Western Jewish thought. Levinas concludes that Ben Gurion's lifting of the ban would be harmful to Judaism, 'which ultimately, for Ben Gurion himself, preserved a nation to love and the opportunity to build a state'.[3]

Yet, as Yirmiyahu Yovel notes, Spinoza was not recommending or advocating a reborn Jewish state, he was simply saying it was a temporal possibility in history.[4]

Spinoza's reference to the Chinese and the Tartars is interesting, revealing how much, in international and cosmopolitan spirit, he wished to bring into conversation diverse world histories. Mr Bloom does not believe in Zionism, and he is also very aware of non-European histories and contexts. He is close to Spinoza in another way. In terms of Spinoza's anti-Cartesian suggestion that appetite and reason come together in the mind conceived as idea of the body, Bloom famously is always registering his every thought on or in or with or through his body and in observations of the bodies of others, in a wide range of situations, including religious.[5]

Spinoza in this famous passage remarks that the fundamental principles of Jewish religion 'discourage manliness', by which he meant that, given the primacy of external authority in their religion, Jews were not free to think for themselves as men ideally should in a secular society; they could not be manly, freethinking, philosophers. Bloom certainly does think for himself in a protracted, arduous and tormented day in June 1904. But the question of 'manliness' might reveal a difference concerning conceptions of the body between Mr Bloom and the seventeenth-century philosopher he so admired; a difference in which Mr Bloom perhaps emerges as surprisingly Kabbalistic.

Representation and absence

The freethinking self-taught philosopher Mr Leopold Paula Bloom has no respect for any purity of concept or category. While nominally or possibly a Catholic, Mr Bloom's eyes when in the (very funny) 'Lotus Eaters' episode he slips into All Hallows church by the back door are those of a detached, mildly astonished observer, looking with wonder on the Eucharist as a kind of 'theatre' he feels is absurd, risible, grotesque. Bloom finds much of the action odd and mysterious; he appears not to know what's going on; his mind strays to erotic thoughts: 'Nice discreet place to be next some girl. Who is my neighbour. Jammed by the hour to slow music. That woman at midnight mass. Seventh heaven.' Then he quizzically regards the action of the priest putting communion bread into the mouths of the women present: 'The next one. Shut your eyes and open your mouth. What? *Corpus*. Body. Corpse. ... They don't seem to chew it; only swallow it down. Rum idea: eating bits of a corpse why the cannibals cotton on to it.' Bloom, a little later, having left the church at the end of the performance ('All over'), recollects Molly as Mediterranean ('the darkness of her eyes. Looking at me, the sheet up to her eyes, Spanish') and looks forward to masturbatory pleasure in a Turkish bathhouse ('Enjoy a bath now: clean trough of water, cool enamel, the gentle tepid stream. This is my body'), an anticipated experience, parodying baptism, that he associates with 'mosque', 'minarets', the 'Fleshpots of Egypt'.[6]

Bloom sees Catholicism as intensely corporeal. In Bloom's view, in All Hallows church, Dublin, 1904, eating of Christ's body ('They don't seem to chew it; only swallow it down') is not only cannibalistic but necrophilic, oral eros, with hint of fellatio ('Shut your eyes and open your mouth'). Bloom's sensuality in the church, his onanistic voyeurism, is in one way the blasphemy of the amused outsider. In another way, like Bakhtin's innocent fool figure who exposes conventions by his incomprehension of them, Mr Bloom's sensuality is part of Catholicism's own sensuality, the corporeality associated with the fetishizing of Christ's body.

In *The Mystic Fable*, Michel de Certeau offers an explanation for such fetishizing, linking it to the development of medieval Christian mysticism. Christianity, de Certeau feels, was founded upon a double loss of sacred bodies. Christianity chose to distinguish itself from Judaism, where the Jews were held to be anchored in biological and social difference, separate by virtue of being chosen, and distinct by virtue of circumcision. Christianity would make itself catholic, that is universal, and pentecostal, that is spiritual, by uniting its community in the word rather than in a particular ethnic body and ancestry. In its foundational narratives, however, Christianity lost more than the body of Israel, a particular people and nation. It also lost the body of Jesus Christ. Before the empty tomb stood Mary Magdalene, not knowing where they have put him; she questions a passer-by, to the effect that if you are the one who carried him away, tell me where you have laid him. For century after century Christians hauntingly cried and cry out to history, repeating Mary Magdalene's anguished question, her impossible mourning, searching the historical places where Jesus had been but is no longer, seeking for the unknowable place where he might yet be. They anxiously interrogate the passing of time, desiring a *kairos*, a single unique time-event that might restore Christ's historical body. They hope the body can be made from the word, flesh from logos. They create institutions and discourses (ecclesiastical bodies, doctrinal bodies) that attempt to be surrogates for the absence of the divine body, to meet the pain of the originary disappearance. The consecrated bread and wine of the Eucharist is held to be the visible signifier of that which is always sought. Mystical discourse, too, joins in the quest, searching for the *corpus mysticum* (where *mysticus* means hidden), likewise obsessed by Mary Magdalene's question – indeed, Mary Magdalene becomes the figure of the mystic. As de Certeau says, the mystical body is the intended goal of a journey that moves, like all pilgrimages, towards the site of a disappearance. Mystics offer their bodies to the spirit, they attempt to incarnate an ideal union with the lost divine presence, to be reborn in his body of which there are only images: 'Mystical literature', de Certeau writes, 'composes scripts of the body ... it is cinematographic.'[7]

Many Christians, as Marc Shell points out, historically desired to possess or see remnants of Jesus' body, in relics of blood, sweat, tears, baby teeth, hair, umbilical cord, fingernails, urine, faeces; many churches claimed to have vials of the Virgin Mary's breast milk. Above all, there was an obsession with supposed remnants of the Holy Foreskin, apparently removed from Jesus' body eight days after his birth. Paradoxically, such desires were intensified by Paul's attempts to transcend the purported materialism of Judaism; theologians took to investigating whether the divine body into which the Eucharist wafer is transformed, in the throat of the celebrant, is circumcised. Literalizing the figurative, the veneration of the Eucharist became an adoration of the treasured foreskin. Yet traditionally Christians, refusing to recognize such odd veneration in such a place, have projected it onto supposed barbaric or cannibalistic peoples who reportedly eat the foreskins and testicles of their enemies; or onto Jewish ritual circumcision as ground of anti-semitism.[8]

The theologian Roland Boer suggests that there is a logic of absence in Judeo-Christianity: the disappearance of Christ's body follows on from the ban on images of God in the Hebrew Bible. Representation and absence or lack become linked. God insists on circumcision for his people, but circumcision then becomes a signifier of the absence of the divine body itself.[9]

We might argue that Judeo-Christianity sees history as a wound, to be messianically healed.

Mr Bloom and the Kabbalah

In the history of mysticism, faith and eros curiously entwine. In terms of de Certeau's argument concerning the mystical search for the lost body, there may here be a link with Mr Bloom's desire to value the feminine in the world and recognize the feminine within himself. Contrary to Spinoza's prizing of manliness and despising that which is womanish, Mr Bloom in Dublin in 1904 imagines impersonating various girls or women he sees or thinks of as he strolls about and along. He dislikes the rigid rituals and prescriptive culture of masculinity in Dublin's patriarchs, and doesn't appear to have a male friend. He doesn't want to enter Barney Kiernan's bar because he doesn't want to go through the effort of conforming to their conformist culture. He feels contempt towards the men of Dublin: 'Ought to go home and laugh at themselves. Always want to be swilling in company. Afraid to be alone like a child of two.' He feels sorry for the children: 'Waiting outside pubs to bring da home. Come home to ma, da.' Thinking about his conversation with Bantam Lyons, he feels disdain towards their constant gambling. ('Silly lips of that chap. Betting.') He feels they're incapable of playing tranquil sports as the English play cricket, instead 'Donnybrook fair more in their line. And the skulls were acracking ...'. In contrast to Irish masculine externality and violence, Bloom conceives himself in terms of a feminine sympathy and empathy. He sees himself as androgynous, experiencing male monthlies, his body female as well as male as in his (tender yet lascivious) reflections on his daughter Milly's budding maturity: 'Loved to count my waistcoat buttons. Her first stays I remember. Made me laugh to see. Little paps to begin with. Left one is more sensitive, I think. Mine too. Nearer the heart.'[10]

In Chapter 3 I fancifully speculated, in terms of Scholem's *Origins of the Kabbalah*, on the possibility that Rebecca in Scott's *Ivanhoe* might be an emanation of the Shekhinah, the feminine aspect of God so prominent in Kabbalistic mysticism when it appeared in the twelfth and thirteenth centuries in Provence and Spain.[11]

Here I would like to brush in a fancy about the possible mystical implications of Mr Bloom's androgyny, or desire to be androgynous, related perhaps to his desire, as revealed in the phantasmagoric brothel scenes with Bella Cohen, that he not be on top in sexual union. I'm not forgetting that Mr Bloom is perceived in other scenes as a possible Messiah, a prophet, an Elijah, a redeemer, a figure from the mystical visions of approaching the Throne of God in Ezekiel, his carriage become a divine chariot as he escapes from Barney Kiernan's bar. Scholem tells us that redemption in the book *Bahir* results from the union of the masculine and the feminine, which mystically operate as principles of the divine world. Scholem deploys the term 'syzygy' for this union, a copulation and pairing and joining which is both sexual and celestial; a notion drawn from deep within the Gnostic tradition. In this mystical conjunction the feminine is created in an array of images, as the bride and king's daughter, as symbolic of the earth which conceives, as the moon which receives its light from the sun, as the fruit of beautiful trees (drawn from Leviticus 23:40), and as the date (or rather the stone of the date), considered to be an image of the vagina. The masculine is figured in an image, prominent in the Gnostics, of the palm tree and in particular the date palm. Scholem also very interestingly refers to 'the bisexual character of the palm tree. ... This would bring us back again to the Orient, where the cultivation of the date palm occupies so prominent a place.' In these terms, the androgynous Mr Bloom is like the bisexual date palm, which incorporates both vagina and phallus. The moon and sun are contained within the palm. The syzygy of masculine and feminine represents a union of East and West (the Shekhinah dwells in the West).[12]

Recall that Scholem says the Shekhinah is holy bride, daughter, mother, an immanent force in the world, a potency distinct from God himself and capable of entering into dialogue with him.[13] Mr Bloom recognizes the Shekinhah within himself and also wishes to interact with it in its immanent terrestial manifestations – he seeks the female in the Dublin world he inhabits (and conversely avoids if he can the aggressive masculinity of the Dublin patriarchs). Does Mr Bloom obscurely respond to Molly Bloom in these mystical terms – Molly whose luminous spheres (her behind) at night in his curious head-to-toe sleeping position he reveres? Molly, who resides in spirit in the West, in Spain? Is Molly Bloom, for all her worldliness and earthiness, also a mystical figure, the Shekhinah, the Sophia, a universal and cosmic positive force, who at the end of the novel actively enters into dialogue with the unfair male God of the universe? Who, famously, in the cinematographic script that is *Ulysses*, has the last word even if God has the first?

We might also wonder if Mr Bloom recognizes the patriarch Abraham not as the source of a male line through circumcision, but as the father of a daughter, just as he, Mr Bloom, is father of a daughter, his daughter who is absent, and for whom he everywhere seeks.

The heretical Mr Bloom, while like the Kabbalists he keeps his thoughts hidden and secret, questions monotheism as a principle of the universe. In the inner world of his thought, he everywhere, including in his ideas of his own body, introduces unresolved plurality and multiplicity. In the prologue to *The Origin of German Tragic Drama*, Benjamin calls on Leibniz's notion of the monad, where every single monad contains, in an indistinct way, all the others; the idea is a monad, and, says Benjamin, the representation of an idea in philosophical history cannot be considered successful unless the whole range of possible extremes it contains has been virtually explored.[14] In these terms we can say that the structure of Mr Bloom's being is monadological, it includes a whole range of extremes and possibilities, female and male, Western and Oriental, sacred and profane, idealistic and obscene, rationalist and mystical.

In possessing a Kabbalistic side, Mr Bloom's thinking rejoins an Egyptian and post-Egyptian stream of mysticism (in Gnosticism, Hermeticism, neo-Platonism, neo-Pythagoreanism).[15]

Circumcision, identity, ancestry

To say that in Judeo-Christianity there is a logic of absence requires some qualification. God is not missing in the mystical anthropomorphism of the Kabbalists. And in the biblical narratives God, as Spinoza remarks, is on occasion described or does indeed choose to reveal himself, as he does to Moses in Exodus. Spinoza comments on this highly curious sighting:

> ... it is the indisputable meaning of Scripture that God himself spoke (for which purpose he descended from Heaven to Mount Sinai) and that not only did the Jews hear him speaking but their chief men even beheld him (Exodus ch. 24). Nor did the Law revealed to Moses ... ever require us to believe that God is incorporeal or that he has no form or figure, but only that he is God, in whom the Jews must believe and whom alone they must worship. And to dissuade them from forsaking his worship, it forbade them to assign any image to him or to make any; for, as they had not seen God's image, any image they could make would not resemble God but must necessarily resemble some created thing which they had seen. So when they worshipped God through that image, their thoughts would not be of God but of that which the image resembled, and so in the end they would attach to that thing the glory and worship of God. But indeed, Scripture does clearly indicate that God has a form, and that

when Moses heard God speaking, it befell him to see God, but to behold only his back parts. So I have no doubt here lies some mystery. ....[16]

To reveal one's behind is an ancient primary carnivalesque gesture. God revealing his back parts – perhaps his genitalia, as Jonathan Kirsch suggests in *The Harlot by the Side of the Road*[17] – introduces a mysterious note of comedy at such a sacred moment, even carnivalesque parody and self-parody. Is God mocking himself, or mocking the desire of the Israelites to see him, or mocking Moses' reverence and fear of the fearsome father-god? Is God suggesting that faith is made more philosophically complex by being able to mock and relativize itself? Mr Bloom's levity in All Hallows' church is perhaps, then, well within God's own spirit of levity and parody and relativizing.

It is also perhaps precisely such a surprising note of comedy in Scripture that informs Bloom and Stephen's thoughts about the other's member when they urinate together late in the evening of 16 June 1904, outside Mr Bloom's house.

While contiguously micturating in 'Ithaca' (though their 'organs of micturation' are 'reciprocally rendered invisible by manual circumposition'), Bloom and Stephen ponder 'different problems'. Bloom, interested in the immanent, ponders the 'problems of irritability, tumescence, rigidity, reactivity, dimension, sanitariness, pelosity'. Stephen, with a characteristic interest in the transcendental, reflects on the problems of his friend's unseen member as if Mr Bloom's penis is a sacred organ, Christ's problematic phallus reincarnated:

... the problem of the sacerdotal integrity of Jesus circumcised ... and the problem as to whether the divine prepuce, the carnal bridal ring of the holy Roman catholic apostolic church, conserved in Calcata, were deserving of simple hyperduly or of the fourth degree of latria accorded to the abscission of such excrescences as hair and toenails.[18]

Like Bloom himself in All Hallows church hours earlier, Stephen plays with the thought that the worship of the 'divine prepuce' may involve a remarkable degree of veneration ('hyperduly'). Both Bloom and Stephen in their separate meditations (one in church, the other in spray) contemplate the thought that the Christian notion of Christ as both man (with foreskin, hair, toenails) and God is one of the more bizarre and ludic not to say ludicrous ideas in human history.

Again, there are continuities here with Spinoza and his circle in the seventeenth century. In a new biography, *Spinoza: A Life*, Steven Nadler points out that while Spinoza admired Jesus' teachings, he certainly did not believe that Jesus was the son of God in the literal sense demanded by Christianity.

Spinoza didn't believe there was anything miraculous about Jesus' birth, nor did he consider anything like a resurrection took place when Jesus died. In correspondence with Henry Oldenburg, secretary of the English Royal Society, Spinoza wrote: 'The passion, death and burial of Christ I accept literally, but his resurrection I understand in an allegorical sense'; 'by his life and death he provided an example of surpassing holiness'. Spinoza felt that to say 'God took upon himself human nature' is to speak 'absurdly'.[19]

Public expression of such scepticism revealed that tolerance and secularism were still highly endangered species of thought in seventeenth-century Holland, as can be noticed in the fate of Spinoza's friend Adriaan Koerbagh, related by Nadler in *Spinoza: A Life*. In 1668 Koerbagh with great lack of caution published a work with the intention of mocking nearly all organized religions, his tone frequently one of sarcasm and contempt. In particular, Koerbagh derided the superstitions of Catholicism in a passage that anticipates Bloom and Stephen's amused scepticism:

> Altar: a place where one slaughters. Among those of the Roman Catholic faith, they are even holy places, where priests daily celebrate the divine service. But it no longer consists in the slaughter of animals, as among the Jews or pagans, but in a more marvellous affair, that is, in the creation of a human being. For they can do what even God cannot do, at any hour of the day: make a human creature from a small piece of wheatcake. This piece of cake remains what it was beforehand, and they give it to someone to eat while saying it is a man – not simply a man, but the God-Man. What an absurdity!

Inviting the charge of Socinianism, Koerbagh denied that Jesus was divine and he rejected all trinitarian doctrines (that is, denied God's tripartite nature as Father, Son and Holy Ghost). Koerbagh was arrested, brought to the authorities chained in an open cart, interrogated by the magistrates and the Dutch Reformed Church authorities in a dangerous collusion of the secular and sectarian (under questioning he revealed that he also denied Mary's virginity), and sentenced to ten years in prison, followed by ten years in exile. In confinement Koerbagh's health deteriorated rapidly, and just over a year after being sentenced he was dead. When Spinoza's *Tractatus Theologico-Politicus* was published only a little while afterwards, it too was accused by the religious authorities of committing the Socinian heresy.[20]

If Christ's Holy Foreskin were apparently removed from Jesus' body eight days after his birth, what of Mr Bloom's 'prepuce'?

Bloom's problematic Jewishness is additionally controversial in that, as we learn with some surprise from the 'Nausikaa' episode that follows 'Cyclops', he has indeed not been circumcised.[21] Such becomes clear from the rhythm of his lonely reflections while he watches Gerty MacDowell (who sees him as a 'foreigner', with his dark eyes like a matinée idol, in 'deep mourning', a 'haunting sorrow' written on his 'pale intellectual face'). Bloom masturbates, amidst much sexual fantasy, including a voyeuristic vision of Molly and Blazes Boylan – 'O, he did. Into her. She did. Done.... Ah!' (Perhaps another reason he masturbates while observing Gerty MacDowell is that he might be incestuously attracted to his daughter Milly.) Afterwards he rearranges himself, discomforted: 'Mr Bloom with careful hand recomposed his wet shirt. O Lord, that little limping devil. Begins to feel cold and clammy. Aftereffect not pleasant. Still you have to get rid of it someway.' After some more interior monologue, Bloom reflects again on his bodily state: 'This wet is very unpleasant. Well the foreskin is not back. Better detach. ... Ow!'[22]

Bloom's unholy foreskin is intact, whole. In Judaism it is held that Jewishness for men and women is passed down through the mother. A boy born of a Jewish mother is automatically Jewish, whether or not he has been circumcised. The rite of circumcision is an initiation into the covenant with God, not into membership of Judaism, which is established by birth (or by conversion, which necessitates circumcision).[23] Circumcision is held to reprise a common ancestry with Abraham, the first Jew to be circumcised by God's command, in an unbroken line: circumcision goes back and forth from Abraham to the present and future, to 'thy seed after thee in their generations', as God tells Abraham (Gen 17:9). In Genesis 17:24 we learn that Abraham was 'ninety years and nine, when he was circumcised in the flesh of his foreskin'; and God had just warned Abraham (17:14) that the 'uncircumcised man child whose flesh of his foreskin is not circumcised, that soul shall be cut off from his people; he hath broken my covenant'.

Such would appear a very firm commandment indeed, though it is not immediately taken seriously by Abraham, since the old man smiles (Gen 17:17) at another of God's instructions delivered at the same time, that he and Sarah will beget a child: 'Then Abraham fell upon his face, and laughed, and said in his heart, Shall *a child* be born unto him that is an hundred years old? and shall Sarah, that is ninety years old, bear?'

Circumcision is not an immutable historical given in Jewish history, it remains a matter of controversy and uncertainty. It is not even clear, as Jonathan Kirsch suggests in *The Harlot by the Side of the Road*, that major figures in the Bible have been circumcised, not only Adam and Noah and Jacob but also Moses, the liberator and lawgiver of the Israelites, God's chosen prophet, and role model of the Messiah.[24] In times of crisis and persecution, circumcision can be forgone, as Cecil Roth suggests occurred with the marranos in Portugal:

The fundamental rite of circumcision was obviously an impossibility: its discovery was tantamount to a sentence of death ... the generality dispensed with it. They found, indeed, some justification in the Bible. God did not account it a sin that the children of Israel born in the Wilderness were not circumcised until they reached the Promised Land, by reason of the inconvenience of their situation.[25]

In the nineteenth century, in the early days of the Reform movement, some Jews were opposed to circumcision, one of its prominent figures, Abraham Geiger, referring to the rite as a 'barbaric, bloody act, which fills the father with fear'.[26]

Traditionally in Judaism a drop or two of wine is placed in the infant's mouth (at eight days of age, as God instructed Abraham in Genesis) and the father also drinks some of the wine, sending the rest to the mother, who is not normally in the room when the rite is performed by the man appointed to do it, the mohel. According to the Talmud three separate acts are involved: the actual removal of the foreskin with a knife reserved for the purpose; the tearing off and folding back of the mucous membrane to expose the glans; and *metzitzah*, the suction of the blood from the wound.[27]

In the Old Testament circumcision is by no means a straightforward story of identity and belonging.

In Genesis we read that Abraham lost his own son, first product of his seed, forever, and even though that son was circumcised, he was not permitted a covenant with God. I'm referring of course to the story of Ishmael.

Abraham took Sarah for his wife, but Sarah 'was barren; she had no child' (Gen 11:29–30). When Abraham was 75 years old, he and Sarah went into the land of Canaan, though 'the Canaanite was then in the land'. God appears and tells Abraham that he will give this land unto Abraham's seed. A grievous famine, however, breaks out in the land of Canaan, so Abraham and Sarah travel to Egypt, where they sojourn for a while. Afraid of the Egyptians, Abraham pretends that Sarah, 'a fair woman to look upon', is his sister, and she is taken into Pharaoh's house. Because of Sarah, Abraham is treated well in Egypt: 'he had sheep, and oxen, and he asses, and menservants, and maidservants, and she asses, and camels.' But God sends great plagues to Pharaoh's house until Pharaoh releases Sarah. Pharaoh reproaches Abraham for not telling him she was his wife, not his sister; he sends Abraham on his way, with all that he had accumulated in his stay in Egypt (Genesis 12).

In chapter 15 God repeats to Abraham that he will make a covenant with him and his 'seed' to possess land 'from the river of Egypt unto the great river, the river Euphrates', that is to say, the land of the Kenites, Kenizzites, Kadmonites, Hittites, Perizzites, Rephaims, Amorites, Canaanites, Girgashites and Jebusites (Gen 15:18–21). In chapters 16 and 17 we learn that Sarah, thinking she will never conceive, persuades her husband to lie with Hagar her Egyptian maid, and by this union a son Ishmael is conceived and born. Ishmael, when 13 years old, is, along with Abraham, then 99 years old, circumcised on the very same day on God's instructions (Gen 17: 24–6). In chapter 21 we read that on Sarah's orders – because Ishmael mocked Isaac, the son she finally has with Abraham[28] – Ishmael and his mother Hagar are banished to the wilderness, though God promises to make for Ishmael 'a great nation' (Gen 21:18). The Ishmaelites, however, will become enemies of the Israelites.

So, although circumcised, and although Abraham's son, Ishmael is not, like Abraham and his son Isaac, permitted a covenant with God, though God had promised such a covenant to all the seed of Abraham: 'I will establish my covenant between me and thee and thy seed after thee in their generations for an everlasting covenant' (Gen 17:7). Ishmael's half-brother Isaac is permitted the covenant with God; which means that Ishmael is refused what that covenant promises, a promised land, the present land of the Kenites, Kenizzites, Kadmonites, Hittites, Perizzites, Rephaims, Amorites, Canaanites, Girgashites, Jebusites.

Circumcision and kinship are deeply troubled categories. In *The Curse of Cain* (1997) Regina M. Schwartz evokes biblical narratives that suggest that kinship, as a process of forming a collective Israelite identity traceable back to Abraham, is often fictional, torn, puzzling, messy, contradictory, violent, bitter and exclusionary. Kinship is an artificial construct, involving incest, rape and harsh rejection, often inexplicably favouring one brother over another brother or half-brother. Occasionally kinship involves impersonation, as in Genesis 27 when Jacob impersonates his older brother Esau in order to be blessed by Isaac; Esau is then cursed, becoming the ancestor of the Edomites; twin brothers become the ancestors of two different and rival peoples. Why, Schwartz asks in relation to Esau's agonized exclusion by his father, cannot Esau also be blessed? Similarly, Schwartz points out that in the story of Cain and Abel identity becomes a deadly contest when the Lord accepts Abel's offering but not Cain's, leading to murder and Cain's exclusion and isolation. [29]

Schwartz argues that in the biblical narratives the categories of foreigner and Israelite continually dissolve, and some narratives make a foreigner the key link in ancestral Israelite lineages.[30]

Married to Molly who is both Irish Christian yet has elective affinities with Moorish Spain, Mr Bloom (reprising Israelites in the Bible who marry non-Israelites, like Moses who married Zipporah the Midianite or King Solomon marrying an Egyptian) opposes traditional Jewish endogamy, believing in 'Mixed races and mixed marriage'.[31]

Mr Bloom's family history involves a braiding of Hungarian Jews and Irish Catholics, and Bloom in his turn continues that braiding, the very kind of intermarriage between Israelites and strangers excoriated by Jacob's sons Simeon and Levi in the story of Dinah, a gruesome narrative of great ambiguity. Told in Genesis 34, it begins by suggesting that Dinah, daughter of Leah and Jacob, adventurously chose to go forth and 'see the daughters of the land' (Gen 34:1), that is, it would appear, to mix and possibly seek acquaintance with and the friendship of the Canaanite women of her age. Dinah is noticed, says Genesis 34, by Shechem the son of Hamor the Hivite and a prince of the land; he 'saw her, he took her, and lay with her, and defiled her'. Yet in the very next line we read that 'his soul clave unto Dinah the daughter of Jacob, and he loved the damsel, and spake kindly unto the damsel' (Gen 34:2–3). Shechem asks his father Hamor to ask Jacob for Dinah's hand in marriage, and during this visit Hamor also suggests to Jacob that there be general intermarriage between his own people the Hivites and the Israelites who have settled amongst them (this story is set long before the Israelites journey to live for many centuries in Egypt). Simeon and Levi the sons of Jacob agree to 'become one people', as long as the Hivites are all circumcised. Believing in the pact they have made with the sons of Jacob, Hamor and Shechem enter their city and inform their fellow Hivites:

> These men *are* peaceable with us; therefore let them dwell in the land, and trade therein; for the land, behold, *it is* large enough for them; let us take their daughters to us for wives, and let us give them our daughters. (Gen 34:21)

On the third day after their mass circumcision, 'when they were sore', the Hivites are slaughtered and their city sacked, and 'all their wealth, and all their little ones, and their wives' taken captive (Gen 34:25, 29) by the sons of Jacob led by Simeon and Levi. At the beginning of Genesis 35 God, who had not intervened, prudently advises Jacob to betake his household to Bethel, far from the scene of deceit and treachery, death and ruin.[32]

As Schwartz notes, in this story circumcision as the very mark of Israel's corporeal identity becomes a weapon against the Other.[33] In such stories, kinship, generation and circumcision afford no guarantee of assured grounded collective identity. In the story of (apparent) love of Dinah and Shechem – its familiar lineaments anticipating other such doomed romances, of Romeo and Juliet or *West Side Story* – circumcision is deployed against curiosity, desire, passion, intermarriage, mixing, amity, *convivencia* of different peoples in the one land; a land (as Shechem the Hivite says) 'large enough' for all of them, Hivites and non-Hivites, Israelites and non-Israelites. That which is to secure the identity of the Israelites is used to exclude and destroy even their hosts.

Yet, contradictorily, as Kirsch points out in *The Harlot by the Side of the Road*,

Jacob on his deathbed curses his sons Simeon and Levi: 'Cursed *be* their anger, for *it was* fierce; and their wrath, for it was cruel' (Gen 49:7).[34]

Bloom and the covenant

Perhaps we can think of Bloom's non-circumcision not as a lack but as a positive productive sign, that his uncircumcised penis is a daily reassuring reminder to him of the benefits of *not* having the dubious burden of a covenant with the God of Abraham.

Recall in Genesis that because of the covenant between God and Abraham effected by circumcision, God will 'give unto thee, and to thy seed after thee, the land wherein thou art a stranger, all the land of Canaan, for an everlasting possession; and I will be their God' (Gen 17:8). In being uncircumcised, Bloom can exercise a kind of trickster-freedom from the violent project of colonial conquest that God here enjoins on Abraham and his descendants. In Simmel's terms in 'The Stranger', Bloom enjoys here the freedom of detachment and objectivity towards the conforming demands of group identity and unproblematized tradition.

Let us substitute 'Europe since 1492' for 'Abraham ... and thy seed after thee'. In these terms, the Judeo-Christian God says to Europe-since-1492 (read, for example, Spain, Portugal, Holland, Britain, France, Italy, Germany) that he will give a land wherein Europe-since-1492 is a stranger (read the Americas, Africa, India, South-East Asia, Australia and New Zealand and the islands of the Pacific) for an everlasting possession, and will sanctify by his presence such conquest and dispossession (of the present inhabitants of those lands, the equivalents of the Kenites, Kenizzites, Kadmonites, Hittites, Perizzites, Rephaims, Amorites, Canaanites, Girgashites and Jebusites).

Bloom's mind and uncircumcised body can dance free not only from this parable – circumcision as a contract with colonialism – but from what God also offers to Abraham and his descendants, when he says he will 'make nations of thee, and kings shall come out of thee' (Gen 17:6). Bloom is not bound in his body and his mind as idea of his body to any abiding belief that the Jews should have a nation-state and a king, a form of centralized state authority.

Because of such trickster-freedom, Bloom could resist the lure of colonialism in the Zionist project, seeing it as like British colonialism; and the lure of the nation-state as defining citizenship and being, as in his rejection of Jewish and Irish nationalism.

Because of such trickster-freedom, Bloom also can resist an associated injunction of the covenant with Abraham, that, as narrated in Deuteronomy (12:10), when the Israelites 'go over Jordan, and dwell in the land which the

LORD your God giveth you to inherit', they should destroy all places and signs of the Canaanites' pagan worship not only of gods but also of goddesses. As Kirsch reminds us in *The Harlot by the Side of the Road* (while discussing the story of Tamar and Judah in Genesis 38), the Canaanites venerated Astarte, the goddess of fertility.[35]

> Ye shall utterly destroy all the places, wherein the nations which ye shall possess served their gods, upon the high mountains, and upon the hills, and under every green tree.
> And ye shall overthrow their altars, and break their pillars, and burn their groves with fire; and ye shall hew down the graven images of their gods, and destroy the names of them out of that place. (Deut 12:2–3)

Bloom, however, evinces no desire to engage in any blanket rejection of the pagan world and its gods and goddesses. After all, he frequently sees himself, as we all know, as Odysseus the wanderer who was assisted in times of peril by the goddess Pallas Athene. Mr Bloom, rejecting the patriarchs of Ireland (especially those in 'Bernard Kiernan's premises'), is hardly likely to bow to the authority of the supreme patriarch, the Israelite God, and even less likely when God wishes to banish the ancient Mediterranean and Near Eastern worship of female divinities and associated veneration of fertility and sexuality; a perceived worship of sensuousness and sensuality that Bloom feels continues in Mediterranean Islam and Moorish Spain unto (Turkish and Moorish) Molly Bloom herself. In any case, such ancient Mediterranean traditions of powerful female cultural figures live irrepressibly on in Judaism itself, as in the importance of the Shekhinah as female principle in the Kabbalah.[36]

Because of such trickster-freedom, Bloom does not accept the commandment not to worship graven images (even though to God's great displeasure the Israelites repeatedly remained attracted to pagan imagery); the commandment that in Deuteronomy emerges as the fierce injunction to 'hew down the graven images of their gods', the divinities revered by the Canaanites. Not only does Bloom evince a remarkable interest in the visual throughout his long day and night, but his work as an ad man prefigures the explosion of visuality in modernity, not least in advertising and film and television and video, and the presence of Jews in such unrestrained extravagant flamboyant visual culture throughout the twentieth century, showing no sign of receding in the new millennium: a remarkable return of the repressed. Here perhaps Bloom is far more Canaanite than Israelite. Or, he is like the Israelites who became attracted to the Canaanite gods and goddesses and associated visuality and, despite God's injunction, refused to surrender that attraction: Mr Bloom, lover of theatre and opera and the popular stage, as well as the theatricality and surprising imagery of the urban.

Because of such trickster-freedom, Mr Bloom in the most general terms does not support one of the great disasters of European and world history, a disaster strongly urged by God in Deuteronomy and certainly continued in official Christianity: the attempted total destruction of paganism and its associated polytheism; the paganism and polytheism that in European history was a resource of myth as always tantalizingly ambivalent and puzzling and undecidable and inexhaustible in meaning.[37]

. Because of such trickster-freedom, Mr Bloom wishes to inhabit a history of layered meanings, palimpsestial. He is at liberty not to observe God's instruction to the Israelites that in Canaan they 'destroy the names of them out of that place' (Deut 12:3). In this injunction, the Canaanites are to be destroyed as history, as memory, as heritage. God directs the Israelites to render history into a single new layer (the name of the Canaanites having been destroyed) that has an absolute new existence and authority.

With such trickster-freedom, holding on (as it were) to his foreskin as a kind of periscope, looking up and around and beyond, offering the privilege of historical understanding, of not being bound and beholden to the nightmare of monotheistic history and Judeo-Christianity, Bloom is also ready to question the parables and paradigms of the biblical story of Exodus.

A further journey through the islands now beckons, to Exodus, Egypt and Canaan; to God, Moses and my mother's namesakes the Levites; namesakes who in my view commit in the story of Exodus an appalling crime.

Dear John,
    Thanks for sending me the stuff about Bloom's foreskin as a periscope.
I can't help thinking this is a rather male perspective.

                                            Rifka (e-mail, 19 November 1998)

Notes

1. Daniel C. Matt, *The Essential Kabbalah: The Heart of Jewish Mysticism* (San Francisco: HarperCollins, 1995), p. 155.
2. Baruch Spinoza, *Tractatus Theologico-Politicus*, trans. Samuel Shirley, intro. Brad S. Gregory (Leiden: E. J. Brill, 1989), pp. 99–100.
3. Emmanuel Levinas, *Difficult Freedom: Essays on Judaism*, trans. Seán Hand (Baltimore: Johns Hopkins University Press, 1990), pp. 106–10, essay on 'The Spinoza case'. For critique of Levinas in relation to Israel and the Palestinians, see Michael J. Shapiro, *Violent Cartographies: Mapping Cultures of War* (Minneapolis: University of Minnesota Press, 1997), p. 185.

4. Yirmiyahu Yovel, *Spinoza and Other Heretics*, vol. I: *The Marrano of Reason* (Princeton, NJ: Princeton University Press, 1989), pp. 190–3. Cf. Steven B. Smith, *Spinoza, Liberalism, and the Question of Jewish Identity* (New Haven, CT and London: Yale University Press, 1997), p. 204.

5. Cf. Genevieve Lloyd, *Spinoza and the Ethics* (London and New York: Routledge, 1996), p. 9.

6. James Joyce, *Ulysses* (1922), with intro. and notes by Declan Kiberd (London: Penguin, 1992), pp. 97–9, 103–7.

7. Michel de Certeau, *The Mystic Fable*, vol. I, trans. Michael B. Smith (Chicago and London: University of Chicago Press, 1992), pp. 79–83. Cf. Roland Boer, 'The resurrection engine of Michel de Certeau', *Paragraph*, 22(2) (July 1999), pp. 199–212.

8. Marc Shell, 'The Holy Foreskin; or, Money, relics, and Judeo-Christianity' in Jonathan Boyarin and Daniel Boyarin (eds), *Jews and Other Differences: The New Jewish Cultural Studies* (Minneapolis: University of Minnesota Press, 1997), pp. 345–51, 354.

9. Roland Boer, 'Significant cuts: body building, circumcision and the phallic signifier' in William Cowling, Maurice Hamilton, Terrance MacMullan and Nancy Tuana (eds), *Returning the Gaze* (Bloomington: Indiana University Press, 2001).

10. *Ulysses*, pp. 86, 106–7, 495–6, 610. The phrase 'tender yet lascivious' I have borrowed from Dacia Maraini, *Bagheria* (London: Peter Owen, 1994), p. 8: 'a father's love, at the same time so tender and so lascivious, so overbearing and so gentle.'

11. Gershom Scholem, *Origins of the Kabbalah*, ed. R. J. Zwi Werblowsky, trans. Allan Arkush (Princeton, NJ: Princeton University Press, 1990), pp. 87–8.

12. *Ibid.*, pp. 142, 151, 163, 172–3, 176. See also David Biale, *Eros and the Jews: From Biblical Israel to Contemporary America* (New York: Basic Books, 1992), pp. 104–5.

13. Scholem, *Origins of the Kabbalah*, pp. 163, 165, 169, 177.

14. Walter Benjamin, *The Origin of German Tragic Drama*, trans. John Osborne (London: Verso, 1996), p. 47.

15. Cf. Martin Bernal, *Black Athena: The Afroasiatic Roots of Classical Civilization*, vol. I (London: Free Association Books, 1987), pp. 146–50.

16. Spinoza, *Tractatus Theologico-Politicus*, p. 63. Cf. Daniel Boyarin, 'The eye in the Torah: ocular desire in midrashic hermeneutic', *Critical Inquiry*, 16 (Spring 1990), pp. 534–43, who argues that God most certainly can be seen in the Old Testament and in early rabbinic Judaism, especially in two moments in Exodus: the crossing of the Red Sea and the giving of the Torah. (My thanks to Deborah Bird Rose for this reference.)

17. Jonathan Kirsch, *The Harlot by the Side of the Road* (London: Rider, 1997), p. 8.

18. *Ulysses*, p. 825.

19. Steven Nadler, *Spinoza: A Life* (Cambridge and New York: Cambridge University Press, 1999), pp. 184–5, 290–1.

20. *Ibid.*, pp. 140, 264–9, 296.

21. Cf. Hugh Kenner, *Ulysses*, rev. edn (Baltimore: Johns Hopkins University Press, 1987), pp. 43, 70, 76, 125, 141.

22. *Ulysses* (1922), pp. 465, 482, 487. Cf. Neil R. Davison, *James Joyce, Ulysses, and the Construction of Jewish Identity* (Cambridge: Cambridge University Press, 1996), p. 221.

23. Louis Jacobs, *The Jewish Religion: A Companion* (Oxford: Oxford University Press, 1995), entry 'Circumcision', p. 81. Cf. Shaye J. D. Cohen, 'Why aren't Jewish women circumcised?', *Gender and History*, 9(3) (1997), pp. 560–78.

24. Kirsch, *The Harlot by the Side of the Road*, pp. 160–3.

25. Cecil Roth, *Gleanings: Essays in Jewish History, Letters and Art* (New York: Hermon Press, 1967), p. 129. Cf. Jane S. Gerber, *The Jews of Spain: A History of the Sephardic Experience* (New York: The Free Press, 1992), p. 163: 'circumcision, a particularly audacious act given the vigilance of the Inquisition'.

26. Michael A. Meyer, *Response to Modernity: A History of the Reform Movement in Judaism* (New York: Oxford University Press, 1988), p. 96.

27. Jacobs, *The Jewish Religion*, 'Circumcision', pp. 82–3.

28. Kirsch, *The Harlot by the Side of the Road*, pp. 48–51, speculates that during the festivities to celebrate the weaning of Isaac, Sarah sees Ishmael, then 15, not so much merely mocking as sexually molesting in some way his 5-year-old half-brother Isaac. It's not clear to me why Kirsch takes Sarah's side in an interpretation he acknowledges as highly speculative. Why not give the benefit of doubt to Ishmael? What could Ishmael have done to Isaac in such a public space?

29. Regina M. Schwartz, *The Curse of Cain: The Violent Legacy of Monotheism* (Chicago and London: University of Chicago Press, 1997), pp. 6, 78–83.

30. *Ibid.*, pp. 84–5, 87, 95, 99.

31. *Ulysses*, p. 610.

32. See Kirsch, *The Harlot by the Side of the Road*, ch. 5, for a pointed analysis of the political implications of the actions of Simeon and Levi for present-day Israel and the Middle East.

33. Schwartz, *The Curse of Cain*, p. 95.

34. Kirsch, *The Harlot by the Side of the Road*, pp. 94, 246.

35. *Ibid.*, pp. 131–3, 217.

36. Cf. *Ibid.*, pp. 215–25.

37. See my critique of Roland Barthes's notion of mythology as always delivering univocality, moral certainty and cosmological intelligibility, in John Docker, *Postmodernism and Popular Culture: A Cultural History* (Melbourne: Cambridge University Press, 1994), pp. 52–5, 72. See also Vassilis Lambropoulos, *The Rise of Eurocentrism: Anatomy of Interpretation* (Princeton, NJ: Princeton University Press, 1992). My thanks to the many e-mail exchanges I've had with Ned Curthoys concerning modernist critiques of mythology. Cf. John Docker, 'Softening monotheism, exploring polytheism: Moses, Spinoza and Freud' in Jane Bennett and Michael J. Shapiro (eds), *Demoralizing Theory!* (New York University Press, forthcoming).

7

'Do fish ever get seasick?' Spinoza and Mr Bloom interpret Exodus

No people is saintly. No people is intrinsically good or bad eternally and by their essence. No people is destined always to be victims. All peoples have been victims and executioners by turns, and all peoples count among their number both victims and executioners.

Maxime Rodinson[1]

... cultural treasures ... a historical materialist views them with cautious detachment. For without exception the cultural treasures he surveys have an origin which he cannot contemplate without horror. They owe their existence not only to the efforts of the great minds and talents who have created them, but also to the anonymous toil of their contemporaries. There is no document of civilization which is not at the same time a document of barbarism. And just as such a document is not free of barbarism, barbarism taints also the manner in which it was transmitted from one owner to another. A historical materialist therefore dissociates himself from it as far as possible. He regards it as his task to brush history against the grain.

Walter Benjamin, Seventh Thesis on the Philosophy of History[2]

The biblical story of Exodus is a cultural treasure of Western literature, ethics and political morality. A guide to action, a resource of hope in the most desperate situations, a repertory of the highest human ideals, a beacon of liberation from bondage and oppression, a promise of freedom in a new land for the formerly persecuted or enslaved; a story of daring, suspense, revelation, prophecy, vision, wise leadership, wavering of purpose, near failure, and beckoning possibility of a future forging at last one's own destiny in one's own way in one's own country – Exodus has proven profoundly influential in world history, not only in the formation in the last few centuries of European settler-colonies around the globe, but also amongst the victims of European settler-colonialism.

Is Exodus, nonetheless, in terms of Benjamin's great insight into the complicities of culture in history, a document of civilization that is at the same time a document of barbarism?

In this chapter I will focus on three moments of reception of Exodus. I'll check out what Mr Bloom thinks of the story. I'll visit Spinoza's reading; then I'll move forward to contemporary times to Edward Said's analysis, which has launched an interesting theological strand in postcolonial and diaspora theory.

For Spinoza and the Enlightenment rationalism he formatively shaped, Exodus had to be severely critiqued in order that a public sphere of freedom of ideas could be historically established: such might be the ideal future of Western liberal democracy. For postcolonial and diaspora theory, Exodus is felt to be so deeply part of the Western colonizing project that it cannot be disowned by the West; it has become foundationally part of Western mythos and being.

I should make it clear that my approach to Exodus as a text concerns its power as a narrative in world history. I am not concerned with its possible reflections of traces of ancient Eastern Mediterranean history.[3]

The Irish and the Israelites

In *Ulysses* the Irish patriarchs anchor themselves in history's swirl in terms of the Exodus story, as in 'Aeolus', the episode set at noon in the offices of the Catholic *Freeman's Journal*. Here Stephen Daedalus and Mr Bloom nearly meet. Mr Bloom is hovering about, trying to place an ad, while young Stephen has come to talk with the journalists there, who might wish to anoint him as their successor as Irish writer, intellectual, orator; but successor in their image, as Stephen is well aware.

In the newspaper office some famous oratory by John F. Taylor is recalled for Stephen's benefit. Taylor had imagined a proud haughty high priest of imperial Egypt addressing 'the youthful Moses':

> Why will you jews not accept our culture, our religion, and our language? You are a tribe of nomad herdsmen; we are a mighty people. You have no cities nor no wealth: our cities are hives of humanity and our galleys ... furrow the waters of the known globe. You have but emerged from primitive conditions: we have a literature, a priesthood, an agelong history and a polity.[4]

Taylor the orator concludes his speech by admiring the defiance and rebelliousness of Moses:

> – But, ladies and gentlemen, had the youthful Moses listened to and accepted that view of life, had he bowed his head and bowed his will and bowed his spirit before that arrogant admonition he would never have brought the chosen people out of their house of bondage nor followed the pillar of the cloud by day. He would never have spoken with the Eternal amid lightnings on Sinai's mountaintop nor ever have come down with the light of inspiration shining in his countenance and bearing in his arms the tables of the law, graven in the language of the outlaw.[5]

The present-day Irish are to regard themselves as victims of the arrogant British Pharaoh, awaiting a true Moses who will lead them to independence and freedom.

Mr Bloom reveals no interest in compliantly accepting this conventional comparison of the colonized Irish and the ancient Israelites equally oppressed by an imperial Pharaoh. He daily observes imperial-Pharaonic qualities in the Irish patriarchs: their self-admiration as 'outlaws' while he has continually to be wary of their insensitive haughty arrogance towards him as despised 'jew'; he recognizes that they have a city, a literature, and a language they share with the English; he observes their pride in their oratory in that tongue; he could not but be aware of the Irish having a priesthood that self-importantly parades itself as powerful in the land; and in Barney Kiernan's pub he is more than irritated that the Irish patriarchs' notion of a polity is modelled on Britain, a nation-state that is composed of a citizenry that defines itself by claimed ethnic purity.

The Irish patriarchs choose a victimological narrative, disregarding how much they themselves can be victimizers.

An outlaw in his own thoughts and mode of thinking, Mr Bloom does not receive any traditions as given, neither the Irish–Israelite coupling nor the accepted liberatory meanings of the Exodus story itself – certainly not that Moses is necessarily admirable and right in his leadership and provision of the 'tables of the law'. Just a little earlier we see Mr Bloom pausing in his walk through the newspaper office to watch and admire a typesetter reading type backwards, reminding him of his father reading Hebrew.

> Poor papa with his hagadah book, reading backwards with his finger to me. Pessach. Next year in Jerusalem. Dear, O dear! All that long business about that brought us out of the land of Egypt and into the house of bondage *alleluia. Shema Israel Adonai Elohenu.* No, that's the other. Then

the twelve brothers, Jacob's sons. And then the lamb and the cat and the dog and the stick and the water and the butcher and then the angel of death kills the butcher and he kills the ox and the dog kills the cat. Sounds a bit silly till you come to look into it well. Justice it means but it's everybody eating everyone else. That's what life is after all . . .[6]

Bloom's run of observations here reveals a kind of baroque allegorical mode of critical thought, ranging quickly from sadness to parody, probing, turning words and images around and about. He thinks (as he had thought not long before) of his 'Poor papa', who had suicided over his wife's death. He recalls his father reading the 'hagadah book' during Passover, the occasion for the Jews to remember and commemorate and be thankful for the Exodus out of Egypt, led by the prophet Moses. (Much later we learn that in a drawer in Bloom and Molly's home there is kept 'an ancient hagadah book in which a pair of hornrimmed convex spectacles inserted marked the passage of thanksgiving in the ritual prayers for Pessach', a book apparently handed down in the male line from grandfather Leopold Virag to father Rudolph Virag to Bloom.) Bloom finds 'silly' the contest of plagues involving various creatures engaged in by Pharaoh and God in Exodus, then thinks 'it's everybody eating everyone else', a vision of violence, retribution and more violence: that is, Bloom doesn't perceive God and the Israelites as superior to Pharaoh and the Egyptians in concepts of 'justice'. Furthermore, he appears to refer to God in the contest with Pharaoh as 'the angel of death'.[7]

In these ruminations on the Passover ritual Mr Bloom reverses the meaning of Exodus when he says to himself: 'All that long business about that brought us out of the land of Egypt and into the house of bondage.' In 'Nausikaa' at the sea shore, Bloom repeats this reversal while thinking of the 'Dreadful life sailors have':

. . . The anchor's weighed. Off he sails with a scapular or a medal on him for luck. Well? And the tephilim no what's this they call it poor papa's father had on his door to touch. That brought us out of the land of Egypt and into the house of bondage. Something in all those superstitions because when you go out never know what dangers. Hanging on to a plank or astride of a beam for grim life, lifebelt round round him, gulping salt water, and that's the last of his nibs till the sharks catch hold of him. Do fish ever get seasick?[8]

Bloom's provocative witty mischievous aphorism 'out of the land of Egypt and into the house of bondage' rejects the fixity of the Promised Land. In the metaphoric movement of the passage Bloom's mind drifts towards sea and wandering. But he chooses such diasporic wandering, even if inevitably attended by vertigo, danger and death, over the Promised Land as 'the house of bondage', implying a harsh judgement on Moses' plans and vision for the Israelites to be assembled in a specific nation and state with tablets of law for their guidance and a priesthood and a polity.

Of course Mr Bloom in such moments of contemplation does not offer a detailed analysis of Exodus; yet his feelings and thoughts while listening to his papa during Passover are potent with suggestion. His heretical reversal of Exodus again links him to the non-Jewish Jewish philosopher he feels so close to.

Spinoza on Moses

In *Tractatus Theologico-Politicus*, Spinoza suggests, let us take Exodus as a historical narrative as it is supposed to be (it is not supposed to be) myth), and examine the consequences of its alleged historicity. Exodus tells us that when the Hebrews were led from Egypt by Moses they were in a degraded, superstitious, exhausted, dependent state, the result of their slavery and oppression by Pharaoh. Yet, says Spinoza in language that uncannily anticipates Mr Bloom, the flight from bondage in Egypt delivered the Hebrews into another kind of 'bondage', where Moses, seeing what an obstinate and stiffnecked people they were, 'commanded' them to love God and keep his Law. Moses taught the Hebrews how to think and act and behave in the same way as parents teach children who have not reached the age of reason. 'Moses' aim', Spinoza writes, 'was not to convince the Israelites by reasoned argument, but to bind them by a covenant, by oaths, and by benefits received; he induced the people to obey the Law under threat of punishment, while exhorting them thereto by promise of rewards. These are all means to promote obedience, not to impart knowledge.'[9]

In their reduced condition the Hebrews were incapable of true freedom, the freedom to reason for themselves and accept God in their own individual ways, from their own independent mind and spirit, as occurs, or should occur, with the philosopher and democratic citizen.

Because of their frailty, the Hebrews accepted Moses' project, which was to create a state religion with himself as sovereign, as absolute judge and lawgiver, where the people followed his commandments because Moses alone had the right to consult God and give God's answers and interpret God's decrees. As Spinoza sardonically observes, the Hebrews 'could not even eat, dress, cut their hair, shave, make merry or do anything whatsoever except in accordance with commands and instructions laid down by the law'.[10]

It is clear, however, Spinoza argues, that the laws, decrees and ordinances Moses induced the Hebrews to follow belonged only to that specific historical situation, the time of the coming out of Egypt and state of abjection in the wilderness. It followed that the Hebrews did not necessarily have to follow such commandments and perform the prescribed rituals after that specific historical period, and indeed he felt they should not do so, because thereby the Hebrew nation became a theocracy, and theocracy was and is a historical disaster, both for the internal relations of the Israelites and their relationships with other nations and peoples.

> It was God alone, then, who held sovereignty over the Hebrews, and so this state alone, by virtue of the covenant, was rightly called the kingdom of God, and God was also called the king of the Hebrews. Consequently, the enemies of this state were the enemies of God; citizens who aimed to seize the sovereignty were guilty of treason against God, and the laws of the state were the laws and commands of God. So in this state civil law and religion ... were one and the same thing; the tenets of religion were not just teachings but laws and commands; piety was looked upon as justice, impiety as crime and injustice. He who forsook his religion ceased to be a citizen and by that alone became an enemy, and he who died for his religion was regarded as having died for his country. In short, there was considered to be no difference whatsoever between civil law and religion.[11]

Spinoza devoted considerable space to critiquing the Exodus story because he wished to distinguish its political features from ideal democracy, which was secular and plural, not theocratic and unified.

Spinoza, nonetheless, it should be noted, did admire Moses' political legacy to the Hebrews in certain ways. Moses left plans for a state whose structure could potentially have been 'quite sound'.[12] But turned out not to be so.

Moses did not wish to see instituted after his death the kind of absolute power he felt that he had had to exercise in the special circumstances of wandering in the wilderness. Moses bequeathed to the Hebrews a political system that, while still a theocracy, in certain features looks forward to modern democracies with their divisions of powers, institutional separations, and checks and balances. The people were commanded to build a dwelling to serve as the palace of God, the state's supreme sovereign. The Levites were chosen to be the courtiers and administrators of this palace of God, with Aaron, Moses' brother, as their head, to be succeeded as of hereditary right by his sons. However, Aaron was not permitted to issue commands: the position of absolute monarch was denied to him. And indeed, Spinoza points out, in the post-Mosaic dispensation the whole tribe of Levi was so completely divested of civil rights that they did not even have a legal share of territory like the other tribes so that they could provide for their own livelihood. Moses decreed that the Levites should be maintained by the rest of the people as the only tribe dedicated to God. Next, a military force was formed from the remaining twelve tribes, who were then ordered to 'invade the land of Canaan and to divide it into twelve parts which would be allocated to the tribes by lot'. For this task twelve captains were chosen, with Joshua as commander-in-chief. Joshua had the right in emergencies to consult God; but not alone, like Moses, in his tent or in the tabernacle. Joshua had to work through the mediation of a high priest, to whom God's answers were given. All men between the ages of 20 and 60 were ordered to bear arms. But the armies they formed swore allegiance not to the commander-in-chief but to their religion and God, and were thus called the armies and hosts of God, and God was called by the Hebrews the Lord of Hosts.[13]

As Spinoza says, Moses did not give to any one future minister or functionary of the state amongst his successors the sole authority which he had possessed, to make and repeal laws, decide on war or peace, and choose men for religious and secular office. On the death of Joshua, the high priest did not choose a new commander-in-chief; rather, each captain retained command of the military force of his own tribe; in this way the different tribes can be regarded as confederated states rather than as fellow-citizens (except with regard to God and religion). Each captain, commanding his own forces, could found and fortify cities and appoint judges in these cities, and make war on the enemies of his own particular state. Each tribe, Spinoza observed, in waging war separately, imposed 'terms of submission and alliance on whom it would, though they had been commanded to spare no one on any terms and to destroy them utterly. For this sin they were no doubt reproved, but nobody was in a position to call them into account.'[14]

The perfidious tribe of Benjamin was indeed held to account, but for what it did to its fellow Israelites, not for its conduct towards the enemies of the Israelites.

> The tribe of Benjamin, which had wronged other tribes and had so violated the bond of peace that none of the confederates could lodge there safely among them, was attacked as an enemy, and after three battles the victors slaughtered them all indiscriminately, guilty and innocent alike, by right of war, a deed which they later bewailed with a repentance that came too late.[15]

Spinoza concludes this part of his analysis by noting that after the death of Moses, the Israelite state was 'left neither as a monarchy nor an aristocracy nor a democracy'. Though no one person exercised all the functions of a sovereign, the state was still a theocracy: the royal seat of government was the temple; all the citizens had to swear allegiance to God, the supreme judge, to whom alone they had promised absolute obedience in all things; and when a commander-in-chief was on occasion needed, he was chosen only by God (as in the choosing of Gideon, Samson and Samuel).[16]

Did the post-Mosaic constitution work, Spinoza asks. Could it so restrain both rulers and ruled that neither would the latter rebel nor the former become tyrants?[17]

In the *Tractatus* Spinoza develops an astute farseeing sociology of power. Those who govern a state, Spinoza observes, always try to cloak with a show of legality the wrongs they commit, and they can easily achieve this when the interpretation of the law is entirely in their hands. In the post-Mosaic constitution, however, the power of the captains of the Hebrews was severely curtailed, because the entire right to interpret the laws had been assigned to the Levites, while the Levites themselves had no share in the administration of the state or its territory. In this situation, the captains had to take great care to govern entirely in accordance with the laws as laid down to all the Hebrews and with which the Hebrews were all familiar: 'If they acted otherwise they must have inevitably encountered the bitterest hatred – such as religious hatred is wont to be – on the part of their subjects.' Further, the captains were not permitted to hire foreign mercenaries, a common way for rulers to subjugate a people; rather, the captains had to respect (and fear) the independence of a citizen soldiery. Furthermore, the captains had no superiority over others by nobility of descent or right of birth.[18]

What restraints were there on the ruled, the people? The Hebrews, Spinoza argues, were absolutely committed to living in and loyalty to their state. The subjects of the state had an equal share with the captains in land and fields, and were each the owners of their share in perpetuity. No man served his equal, but only God. Charity to one's neighbour was a duty to be practised with the utmost piety in order to gain the favour of God, their king. The Hebrew citizens considered they could enjoy a good life only in their own country; abroad, they could only expect hurt and humiliation. So much was this felt to be so, that no citizen was condemned to exile as punishment for wrongdoing, for exile would be too much of an outrage. The citizens of the state were committed to such an ardent patriotism that they would have suffered death rather than foreign yoke. It was regarded as a disgrace even to emigrate, for the religious rites which it was their constant duty to perform could be enacted only on their native soil; it alone was held to be holy ground, the rest of the world being unclean and profane. The citizens believed their kingdom was God's kingdom and they alone were God's children; it followed that other nations were God's enemies for whom they felt an implacable hatred, indeed such hatred was a mark of piety, a religious duty – 'the bitterest and most persistent of all kinds of hatred'. Such hatred became continuous, for it was reinforced by reciprocation, since the 'other nations inevitably held them in bitter hatred in return'. The result was that the Hebrews would endure all things for their country with unexampled steadfastness and valour: 'Never while their city stood could they long endure foreign domination, and that is why Jerusalem was wont to be called the rebellious city.'[19]

In sum, says Spinoza, the life of the Hebrews was 'one long schooling in obedience', and to people so habituated 'obedience must have appeared no longer as bondage, but freedom', if 'without any resort to reason'. Why, then, Spinoza asks, did the Hebrews so frequently forsake the Law, and what happened to the Hebrew state, why in the end was it utterly destroyed? What internal factors made such ruin come about?[20]

For one major thing, Spinoza suggests, there was the nature of God himself and the irksome laws he promulgated. God framed laws not for the honour, welfare and security of the people, but out of anger, with the intention of avenging himself and punishing the people. The result was that their laws appeared to be not so much laws as penalties and punishments. Furthermore, the people began to find themselves irritated by the Levite priests who alone were privileged to perform the sacred rites and to whom they were required to make constant gifts, which constantly reminded the people of their defilement and rejection. The Levites were continually finding occasion to rebuke them. In turn, the people were keen to keep watch over the Levites, and to accuse them all for the misdeeds of one. The people resented having to maintain in idleness the Levites, men who were unpopular and unrelated to their kinsfolk, their specific tribe, especially when food was dear. There was a continual murmuring, and in any case the people had never fully accepted that the priests should only have come from the Levites; the people had always felt that Moses had chosen his own tribe above all others and had wrongly bestowed on his own brother Aaron the office of high priest in perpetuity. The people's morale began to fail through discontent, resentment and greed. Eventually, the people looked for change, forsaking a worship which, although worship of God, involved their humiliation and was also the subject of suspicion.[21]

The people, Spinoza points out, chose to rebel, effecting an open rupture with divine rule and seeking a mortal king, making the seat of government a court rather than a temple. The tribes no longer retained a common citizenship on the basis of the divine rule and the priesthood, but by allegiance to a king. But here was ample material for fresh sedition, which ultimately, Spinoza feels, led to the downfall of the entire state. The kings themselves constantly sought extensive changes so as to hold absolute sovereignty. The kings resented any continuing independence by the tribes; and also resented the Levites, who could debar kings just as much as their subjects from administering the sacred rites. The kings also had to be afraid of any prophet who might become too powerful. The kings permitted other temples to be built in order to avoid consulting the Levites, and they also sought out other men who might be regarded as prophets in order to counter those who were held to be the true prophets. In turn, the prophets sought to appoint as by divine right kings who would recognize them as the true prophets. Neither kings nor priests nor prophets could fully check each other's power, and the result was that there was no end to discord and civil wars.[22]

While, in Spinoza's view, 'it may perhaps be quite profitable to imitate' the separation of various powers in the post-Mosaic state, he also felt such imitation was not advisable:

> ... this form of state might possibly meet the needs of those who intend to live for themselves alone with no external ties, shutting themselves away within their own boundaries and cutting themselves off from the rest of the world; but it would not suit those who have to have dealings with the outside world.[23]

In general, Spinoza disliked the messianic cast of Exodus, the story of the Jews in the wilderness when a powerful ruler speaks on behalf of a supreme truth and of the destiny of a people, who themselves are submissive and obedient, or are made submissive and obedient (though never fully), thus opposing what should be the purpose of the state, which is freedom, the freedom that is associated with the natural right to exercise and enjoy reason.[24]

Spinoza preferred Jesus to Moses as exemplar for humanity. Moses, in Spinoza's view, did not justify his precepts by reasoning, but made them into commands with attached penalties and rewards and promises; rewards and promises, as is clear in the first five books of the Old Testament commonly attributed to Moses, that refer only to worldly success specific to the Hebrew nation (honours, fame, victory, riches, life's pleasures and health). Jesus, by contrast, was concerned with the peace of mind and true blessedness of the individual, and for this reason taught only universal precepts. Jesus' chief purpose was to teach moral doctrines, keeping them distinct from the laws of any particular commonwealth – something not understood by the Pharisees, who thought that the blessed life was his who observed the laws of the nation, that is, the law of Moses, whose aim was to coerce the Hebrews rather than instruct them. In contrast to Moses the lawgiver, Jesus was a teacher who was intent on improving people's minds and spirit rather than their external actions.[25]

Spinoza's critique of Jewish religion would influence later European Enlightenment thinking, as in Kant and the young Hegel in European philosophy or Matthew Arnold in English cultural history, that Judaism was primarily a political religion.[26]

In post-Second World War political theory, Lewis Feuer, in *Ideology and the Ideologists* (1975), looked on with dismay at the resurgence of ideology in the 1960s; for Feuer, ideology is contrary to the scientific rationalism that constitutes the only hope for the progress of civilization. Feuer argues that ideology, in a spectrum ranging from Marxism and nationalism to African Negritude to European fascism, possesses an invariant mythic structure, which can be traced back to the seductive figure of Moses liberating the Hebrews from Egypt; a drama which proves particularly attractive to young radical intellectuals who wish to revolt against the established order, the Pharaoh. The Mosaic myth, Feuer says, can be sketched as a series of situations and incidents. A people is oppressed. A young man, not himself of the oppressed, appears on history's stage. Moved by sympathy, he intervenes, striking down an oppressor's henchman. He flees, or goes into exile. He experiences the call to redeem the oppressed people. He returns to demand their freedom. He is spurned by the tyrannical ruler. He leads the actions which, after initial defeats, overwhelm the oppressor. He liberates the people. He imparts a new sacred doctrine, a new law of life, to them. The newly liberated people, however, unfortunately relapse from loyalty to their historic mission. Almost disillusioned, their leader imposes a collective discipline on the people to re-educate them morally for their new life. A false prophet arises who rebels against the leader's authoritarian rule, but is destroyed. The leader, now a revered lawgiver, dies, as he glimpses from afar the new life.[27]

For Feuer as for Spinoza, what humanity and civilization need is secular reason, not mythology – and certainly not the far, far too influential story of Exodus, one of the West's key creation stories.[28]

Exodus in postcolonial and diaspora theory

I was alerted to Lewis Feuer's interesting argument by a reference in Edward Said's 'Michael Walzer's *Exodus and Revolution*: a Canaanite reading', a wonderfully iconoclastic essay, Spinozist in its heretical spirit.

Said suggests that the dangerous seductiveness of the Exodus story, promising liberation to the suffering and oppressed, should be resisted. Said points out that the narrative of Exodus provides history with the model of a messianic and millenarial politics of redemption that can be disturbingly extreme, constituted in zealotry and violence. The narrative of Exodus identifies an imperial power that unequivocally oppresses and persecutes, a power that it iconically names in history as Pharaonic Egypt or simply Egypt. The narrative of Exodus has an inspiring vision of freedom for one people that is yet premised on defeat and even extermination for another, the Canaanites, those who already inhabit the Promised Land, a land which by divine injunction and sanction is to be conquered and occupied. During conquest and upon victory, the Canaanites are to be considered as excluded from the world of moral concern. Said sees the displaced and dispossessed Palestinians as the present-day Canaanites of the Middle East, part of a world history where Exodus has unfortunately proven all too exemplary, inspiring Puritans in New England slaying Native Americans or South African Boers laying claim to and moving in on huge areas of formerly African-held lands.[29]

Taking up Said's Canaanite reading, Ella Shohat suggests that Americans historically have been more receptive to the claims on understanding and sympathy of Israel and Zionism than to the plight of the Palestinians, victims of victims. Americans stress their similarity with Israelis in relation to British colonialism, the British Pharaoh, against which both Americans and Israelis fought. Americans admire the image of the *sabra* pioneer, the new Israeli-born Jewish man, just as they admire in themselves the true American as Adam charged with a civilizing mission in a New Canaan, the Promised Land of the New World, in a virgin state until the American Adam's redemptive arrival. Both New Jewish Man in Israel and New American Man could free themselves from the baggage of the Old World of Europe. Each is blessed with the divine prerogative of naming the elements and features of the new world they encounter. And, Shohat notes, in each case the presence and civilizations of the indigenous inhabitants, the Palestinians and Sephardi and Oriental Jews in Israel and the Native Americans in North America, are ignored or held to be of no account.[30]

The influence of the story of Exodus in settler-colonies like Israel, the United States and Australia is being increasingly discussed in terms of Said and Shohat's readings: the indigenous peoples as Canaanites. Deborah Bird Rose feels that while Exodus is a foundational narrative for the way the Puritans identified New England as the New Canaan, the white settler-colony of Australia drew and draws more on a myth of expulsion from the British Eden conceived as the mother land. Ann Curthoys suggests that white Australian history reveals the uneasy workings of both the story of the fall and expulsion from Eden (a primal wound in the white Australian psyche, of rejection by the mother) and the story of the exodus from the British Pharaoh and settlement in a promised land far from British Pharaoh's shores, where a new society and national narrative and sensibility can be created. For Rose and Curthoys, white Australians see themselves in originary ways as victims, aware always of their own suffering and hardship and defeats, and so cannot view themselves as victimizers – as responsible for the suffering and hardship and tragedies they inflict on others, those they displace and dispossess and persecute.[31]

Regina M. Schwartz in *The Curse of Cain: The Violent Legacy of Monotheism* (1997) has also commented on the influence of the Exodus story in authorizing a victimological narrative, the belief in world history that earlier bondage and persecution and suffering justifies later conquest and destruction; that earlier victimhood warrants later violence and justifies present exclusionary or discriminatory policies. Schwartz suggests that the Exodus myth has been so influential because it is capable of such contradictory readings.[32]

In 'The lie of the land: the text beyond Canaan', his remarkable reading of Genesis and Exodus, Harry Berger Jnr suggests that when the Israelites fled Egypt, after a successful contest between Yahweh's magical powers and the magical powers of the Pharaoh's priests, they nevertheless brought Egyptian (so to say) conceptions of social, state and religious organization with them on the way to and into the Promised Land, the Land of Canaan. In Canaan, the Israelites instituted a kingdom that was bureaucratic, hierarchical and authoritarian, ending in destructive self-division.[33] Berger sees 'instituted judgeship' and the instituting of a kingdom and a settled state as a 'symbolic return to Egypt'. In Berger's view, whether as a unified state society, the Davidic kingdom, or in a post-exile priesthood wandering with tabernacle and tent that is yet too 'monumental' and rule-bound, such political and religious modes legitimated restoration 'of the very world from which Exodus relates the exodus': 'To build the sanctuary is to return to Egypt. To build the temple is to return to Egypt. To rebuild the temple is to return to Egypt.' Indeed for Berger the Yahweh of Exodus is a phantom double of the Pharaoh, a superpharaoh. Further, in conquering the Land of Canaan, the Israelites went from fugitives to 'captors and victors themselves'.[34]

In Berger's argument, the Israelites placed themselves in bondage to what he calls 'possessive nomadism', the species of wandering nomadic group who invade and take over a settled agricultural society (Canaan). The inevitable corollary of such a conception of the nomadic is a notion of exile as separation from a land claimed to be one's own, exile as loss and failed conquest; a mythos sustained by an Egyptian-style 'strong priesthood'. Berger contrasts possessive nomadism to mobile pastoral nomadism, to customary wanderers who wish to keep wandering. Yet Berger also feels that while the text of Exodus presents 'the flight *from* Egypt as a return *to* Egypt', the possibility of an alternative customary nomadism also lies in the text, and in the textuality of the Old Testament generally, in the ways it both represents ideas and desires yet subjects them to 'continuous critique'. In these terms, Berger finds that the biblical narratives do not yield an originary single unified Jewish identity, for

Old Testament textuality remains unresolved, setting the 'tent against the house, nomadism against agriculture, the wilderness against Canaan, wandering and exile against settlement, diaspora against the political integrity of a settled state'. Berger concludes by suggesting that the metaphoricity and self-criticality of Genesis and Exodus can be viewed as a kind of travelling ark of interpretation, where for the People of the Book the promised land becomes the text itself, 'the circumference of which is nowhere', interpreted and reinterpreted in diaspora. Such an ark permits – and here Berger is very close to Spinoza – the possible development of an 'ideal of autonomous internalized ethical art'.[35]

Just what Mr Bloom is doing, in his internalized autonomous ethical art, his care of self; Mr Bloom, who questions, and is hurt by, the Irish victimological narrative.

Egypt

In *The Curse of Cain* Schwartz argues that the Old Testament narratives have been and continue to be vastly influential not only in Christianity and Islam, but in secularized forms in modern European history in the phenomenon of collective identities like nationalism. Agreeing, we might say, with Mr Bloom's dislike of the threatening character of Irish collective identity, Schwartz identifies many moments in the Hebrew Bible narratives where ethnic, religious and national identities are defined negatively, over and against others. Monotheism stimulates such violent identity formation, with its anxious exclusive allegiance (always afraid of betrayal) accompanied by hostile othering and exclusion of the foreigner. Schwartz sees Zionism and the modern nation-state of Israel as part of this history.[36]

Schwartz suggests, however, as does Berger, that the biblical narratives are nonetheless richly heterogeneous, always offering grounds for counter-movement, doubt and critique, unseating apparently authorized institutions and covenant codes like monotheism, conquest of a promised land, judgeship, priesthood, monarchy, prophecy, kinship, endogamy. The relationships, for example, between 'Israel' and 'Egypt' are complex and contradictory, sometimes figured as opposition, at other times curiously blurred. In a way that recalls Benjamin's conception of Baroque allegory in *The Origin of German Tragic Drama* as unresolved unresolvable tension between the one and the many, Schwartz distinguishes between two broad understandings of identity in the Bible. One is grounded in negation or scarcity. In these terms, Israel is decisively not-Egypt, for the Egyptians, like other peoples who whore after false gods – Moabite, Ammonite, Canaanite, Perizzite, Hittite, Hurrian – are to be abhorred, perhaps obliterated, for they are foreign, abject and impure. The other principle is one of multiplicity or plenitude, sustaining contraries, multiplying difference, foregrounding identity as provisional, where Israel sees itself as one people not hostile to but amongst other peoples. In these terms, Israel and Egypt interact. Israel, for example, is perceived as deriving from the part-Egyptian Moses. Joseph, the son of Jacob/Israel, saves the Israelites by means of his high status (a vizier) in Egypt where he has prospered, and indeed in the Joseph story the Egyptians are more hospitable to him than are his own murderous brothers. Then there is King Solomon, who marries a daughter of Pharaoh.[37]

In terms of Schwartz's argument, Mr Bloom opposes a notion of identity grounded in negation and scarcity (as in Zionist and Irish nationalism), supporting rather the principle of multiplicity and plenitude. He expresses preference for a pre-1492 Levantine Judeo–Islamic world of plurality and co-existence of different religions: 'New worlds for old. Union of all, jew, moslem and gentile. . . . Mixed races and mixed marriage.'[38] His old/new world is one in which he could be both European, as Odysseus, and Oriental, as Haroun Al-Rashid and Sindbad. In Mr Bloom's diasporic mind and imagination, he lives amongst many places, spaces, times, histories, figures, fantasies, at once; he chooses the Many over the One.

Conclusions: the metaphysics of history

Said's Canaanite reading of Exodus as promising liberation for one people yet dispossession for another continues to prove extraordinarily productive, challenging the secularist cast of Western cultural theory.

My own reading of Exodus has been piqued for a personal reason. My mother was a Levy, and when re-reading Exodus I observe with considerable dismay a remarkable act of violence the Levites visit on their own people. Recall that Moses and his brother Aaron are Levites, who become the permanent priestly caste. In Exodus, chapter 32 Moses rebukes God for wishing to destroy his people when they have relapsed into pagan worship of the golden calf. Moses rejects God's threat of total violence, instead asking all the sons of Levi to gather about him. Moses tells them:

> . . . Thus saith the LORD God of Israel, Put every man his sword by his side, and go in and out from gate to gate throughout the camp, and slay every man his brother, and every man his companion, and every man his neighbour.
> And the children of Levi did according to the word of Moses: and there fell of the people that day about three thousand men. (Exod 32:27–8)

In the Mosaic conception, history is to create nations which have a single purpose, and those who relapse from this single purpose are to be disciplined, possibly slain, as the sons of Levi in an act of selective violence slay their fellow Israelites. What Moses most likes is when the Israelites speak with 'one voice' (Exod 24:3).

The biblical stories are certainly heterogeneous and multivalent, yet in these concluding comments I would like to point out features of Exodus which I think have influenced Western and world history very much for the worse.

Exodus creates a representation of history as like an arrow, moving away from the past, which has no value except to be seen as bondage and oppression – the demonizing of Egypt in Judeo-Christian thought. Spinoza points out that as evoked in the first chapter of Exodus the Egyptians turn against the Israelites for quite 'natural', that is to say historical, reasons; while the children of Israel in the time of Joseph had multiplied and waxed exceedingly mighty and the land was filled with them, a later Pharaoh came along many centuries afterwards who knew not Joseph; the new Pharaoh distrusted the Israelites because there were now more Israelites than Egyptians in the land and they were mightier than the Egyptians, and because in war it might be that the Israelites could not be trusted, they might side with the enemies of the Egyptians. Said, in the wake of Spinoza here, similarly points out that Genesis 47:27 tells us that in the time of Joseph the children of Israel 'had possessions therein, and grew, and multiplied exceedingly'; it was only many centuries later, in the time of a Pharaoh who had forgotten what Joseph had done for the Egyptians, that the Jews were oppressed. [39]

Such historical explanations as these of Spinoza and Said (drawing on the biblical historical narratives themselves) attempt to counter the figure of Egypt in Judeo-Christian history as a primal source of evil; even Harry Berger Jnr's argument is I think not free of such demonizing of 'Egypt'.

Exodus creates a representation of history as the desire for and ever restless pursuit of the new, for a future that will be as completely different from the past (Egypt) as possible; a hunger for perpetual change and innovation and transformation.

Exodus creates a representation of history which presumes that the past (Egypt) could not possess greater wisdom than the present or future. The past is always suspect, it has to be transcended, and those who wish to return to the past or aspects of the past are to be excoriated, are to be identified as traitors to the future and perhaps disciplined or destroyed.

Exodus creates a representation of history where the space and time that lie between an excoriated past and an always better or millenarial future is wilderness: the present is never to be valued for and in itself.

Exodus creates a representation of history which helped destroy the pagan and classical world, with its respect for the past wisdom of the Egyptians and its polytheism and visuality and myth, where the visual and many gods and the mythic offer difference and choice, performance and theatricality whose meanings are multiple and unending, ever elusive and ambiguous.[40]

Exodus creates a representation of history where history should move away from paganism and polytheism, not only in Egypt but amongst the other Semitic peoples with whom the Israelites come into contact. In Genesis and again in Exodus God again and again affirms his covenant with Abraham; God says he will send an angel ahead to drive out the Amorites, Hittites, Perizzites and Canaanites, enjoining 'thou shalt utterly overthrow them, and quite break down their images' (Exod 24:23–4).

Exodus creates a representation of history where representation itself is always under suspicion, since it is the pagan and idolatrous who create the images that God enjoins the Israelites to destroy. The creation of images is associated with fear and danger, with betrayal. Exodus enjoins a messianic aesthetic: true knowledge will forbid or at least attempt to transcend representation and images; it will call humanity's attention to observe one and only one principle of being (God). The messianic desire to sweep away all previous images (which as with the Canaanites celebrate female power) and imagery as such is, perhaps surprisingly, most evident in twentieth-century modernist and avant-garde art, which proclaimed its absolute newness in history and its spurning of given authority. Messianically, twentieth-century modernist and avant-garde art would sweep away all previous images, especially the 'female' realm of popular and mass culture.[41] Twentieth-century modernist and avant-garde art was the art that would destroy art, or that would find itself in the unrepresentability of the sublime (Lyotard).

Exodus creates a representation of history which authorizes the pathos and desirability for individuals, nations and peoples to regard themselves as victims and to be regarded as victims. The status of victim perhaps becomes the Western world's most desired subject-position, even for those who set out to conquer abroad. Those who conquer in history are always afraid of that being visited upon them (death, disease, persecution, dispossession, massacre, war) which they are visiting upon others: in the very act of conquering they somehow remain victims. When those in history who conquer are themselves conquered, they see themselves as always having been victims.

Exodus creates a representation of history where (this is an important point made by Schwartz in *The Curse of Cain*) to exact revenge and perpetuate later violence on others somehow does not alter one's status as victim and desire to be recognized as victim.

Exodus creates a representation of history that justifies the violence of revenge, indeed authorizes the maximizing of revenge-violence. Exodus opens with a new Pharaoh making the lives of the Israelites 'bitter with hard bondage', and instructing the Hebrew midwives to kill the Israelite firstborn: 'if it be a son, then ye shall kill him: but if it be a daughter then she shall live' (Exod 1:14–16). God sends Moses to tell Pharaoh to 'let my people go' (Exod 10:3). Curiously, however, God repeatedly insists that he will 'harden' Pharaoh's heart so that Pharaoh will not let the people go until after the land of Egypt has been visited by a fearsome multitude of punishments. These punishments include not only the final matching revenge of destroying the Egyptian firstborn, but also the utter spoliation of the Egyptians, God saying to Moses: 'ye shall spoil the Egyptians' (Exod 3:22, 12:35–6). The maximizing of revenge demands that 'Pharaoh' and 'Egypt', those who are constituted as the enemy, have to be brought low, totally humiliated.

Exodus creates a representation of history where prior persecution and dispossession justifies the dispossessing and persecuting of others who are unrelated to those who enacted the original persecuting and dispossessing: the Egyptians enslave the Israelites, but it is the Canaanites and other inhabitants of the land of Canaan who are to be dispossessed and persecuted by the Israelites.

Exodus creates a representation of history where the stranger can never be fully accepted. In Exodus God tells the Israelites: 'Thou should neither vex a stranger, nor oppress him: for ye were strangers in the land of Egypt' (Exod 22:21). As is his way, God soon repeats the injunction with a variation: 'thou shalt not oppress a stranger: for ye know the heart of a stranger, seeing ye were strangers in the land of Egypt' (Exod 23:9). Yet elsewhere in Exodus the stranger is excluded from the life of the Hebrews, especially their sacred life. God tells the Israelites that while Aaron and his sons for ever can eat the flesh of the consecrated ram, 'a stranger shall not eat thereof' (Exod 29:32–3). Also the 'holy anointing oil' is reserved for the priests: 'whosoever putteth *any* of it upon a stranger, shall even be cut off from his people' (Exodus 30:33). To associate too closely with a stranger is to be perceived, and cut off, as a stranger. While God instructs the Israelites neither to vex nor to oppress the stranger, God does not in Exodus positively or directly enjoin the Israelites to welcome the stranger and become interested in the life, thoughts and consciousness of the stranger. Yet, the textuality of Exodus is indeed contradictory, bizarrely so; such textuality always exceeds God's specific commands.

Near the beginning of Exodus is the strange story of Moses and Zipporah, his Midianite wife. We read that God encounters Zipporah and Moses as Moses journeyed back to Egypt to redeem the Israelites: 'it came to pass by the way in the inn, that the L ORD met him, and sought to kill him.' Moses is only saved by the quick thinking of Zipporah, who cuts off the foreskin of their baby son, an action which appeases an angry God (Exod 4:24–6).[42] Some time later in Exodus, in the wilderness, Jethro, Moses' Midianite father-in-law, appears, and offers Moses some sage political advice concerning the necessity of devolving power (Exodus 18), advice which Moses later adopts for his legacy to the Israelites after his death; a legacy which Spinoza found very interesting as a way of reflecting on how a modern liberal democracy might work in terms of separation of powers.

Exodus never quite knows what to think of the stranger. Neither do Judeo-Christian and Western history, metaphysics, narrative and poetics: such in any case is the experience of Mr Leopold Paula Bloom on 16 June 1904, in Dublin, which is part of both imperial Britain and Ireland, which are part of Europe, which is part of the West, whose every document of civilization is at the very same time a document of barbarism.

> The Veiled Stranger: Are you now dismissing Mr Bloom? You've been writing about Bloom for four chapters – are you now going to coldly forget about him, the companion of your travels?

> No, I won't be forgetting Mr Bloom: he will be the third that walks beside us.

Notes

1. Maxime Rodinson, *Cult, Ghetto, and State: The Persistence of the Jewish Question* (London: Al Saqi Books, 1983), p. 182.
2. Walter Benjamin, *Illuminations*, trans. Harry Zohn, ed. and intro. Hannah Arendt (London: Fontana, 1992), p. 248.
3. For an approach seeking to relate Exodus to ancient history and prehistory, see Sigmund Freud, *Moses and Monotheism* (1939; New York: Vintage, 1967); for commentary by an Egyptologist, see Jan Assman, *Moses the Egyptian: The Memory of Egypt in Western Monotheism* (Cambridge, MA: Harvard University Press, 1997). Cf. John Docker, 'In Praise of Polytheism', *Semeia*, special issue on 'A vanishing mediator? The absence/presence of the Bible in postcolonial criticism', ed. Roland Boer (forthcoming).
4. James Joyce, *Ulysses*, intro. Declan Kiberd (London: Penguin, 1992), p. 180.
5. *Ibid.*, p. 181.
6. *Ibid.*, p. 155.
7. *Ibid.*, pp. 145, 852–3.
8. *Ibid.*, pp. 493–4.
9. Baruch Spinoza, *Tractatus Theologico-Politicus*, trans. Samuel Shirley, intro. Brad S. Gregory (Leiden: E. J. Brill, 1989), pp. 84, 96–7, 118, 221.
10. *Ibid.*, pp. 118–23, 256.

11. *Ibid.,* p. 255.
12. *Ibid.,* p. 268.
13. *Ibid.,* pp. 257–8, 286.
14. *Ibid.,* pp. 258–60.
15. *Ibid.,* p. 260. Cf. Jonathan Kirsch, *The Harlot by the Side of the Road* (London: Rider, 1997), chs. 12 and 13.
16. Spinoza, *Tractatus,* p. 261.
17. *Ibid.*
18. *Ibid.,* pp. 261–3.
19. *Ibid.,* pp. 264–5.
20. *Ibid.,* pp. 266–7.
21. *Ibid.,* pp. 267–9, 286, 291.
22. *Ibid.,* pp. 269–70.
23. *Ibid.,* p. 272.
24. *Ibid.,* pp. 101, 293.
25. *Ibid.,* pp. 113, 122, 146, 223, 225. Cf. Steven Nadler, *Spinoza: A Life* (Cambridge and New York: Cambridge University Press, 1999), p. 290.
26. Cf. Yirmiyahu Yovel, *Dark Riddle: Hegel, Nietzsche, and the Jews* (Cambridge: Polity Press, 1998), pp. 7–10, 12, 15–17; Matthew Arnold, *On the Study of Celtic Literature and On Translating Homer* (1867; London: Macmillan, 1903), pp. 13–19, and *Culture and Anarchy* (1869; Cambridge: Cambridge University Press, 1963), ch. 4.
27. Lewis S. Feuer, *Ideology and the Ideologists* (Oxford: Basil Blackwell, 1975), pp. 1–16.
28. Cf. Keith W. Whitelam, *The Invention of Ancient Israel: The Silencing of Palestinian History* (London and New York: Routledge, 1996); Thomas L. Thompson, *The Bible in History: How Writers Create a Past* (London: Jonathan Cape, 1999).
29. Edward Said, 'Michael Walzer's *Exodus and Revolution*: a Canaanite reading' in Edward Said and Christopher Hitchens (eds), *Blaming the Victims: Spurious Scholarship and the Palestinian Question* (London: Verso, 1988), pp. 161–78.
30. Ella Shohat, 'Antinomies of exile: Said at the frontiers of national narrations' in Michael Sprinker (ed.), *Edward Said: A Critical Reader* (Oxford: Blackwell, 1992), pp. 140–1. See also Graham Hoskin, 'An analysis of Christian Zionism', *Journal of Arabic Islamic and Middle Eastern Studies,* 3(2) (1997), pp. 1–27; Sacvan Berkovitch, *The American Jeremiad* (Madison: University of Wisconsin Press, 1978).
31. Deborah Bird Rose, 'Rupture and the ethics of care in colonized space' in Tim Bonyhady and Tom Griffiths (eds), *Prehistory to Politics: John Mulvaney, the Humanities and the Public Intellectual* (Melbourne: Melbourne University Press, 1996), pp. 199–200, 203–5; Ann Curthoys, 'Expulsion, Exodus, and Exile in white Australian historical mythology' in Richard Nile and Michael Williams (eds), *Imaginary Homelands: The Dubious Cartographies of Australian Identity* (St Lucia: University of Queensland Press, 1999), pp. 1–18. Cf. John Docker and Gerhard Fischer (eds), *Race, Colour and Identity in Australia and New Zealand* (Sydney: University of New South Wales Press, 2000), introduction, pp. 8–9. See also Roland Boer, *Last Stop Before Antarctica* (Sheffield: Sheffield Academic Press, 2001), esp. ch. 3, 'Home is always elsewhere: exodus, exile, and the howling wilderness waste'.
32. Regina M. Schwartz, *The Curse of Cain: The Violent Legacy of Monotheism* (Chicago: University of Chicago Press, 1997), pp. 55–62. In 'Reading Exodus

into history', *New Literary History*, 23(3) (1992), pp. 523–54, his commentary on the Walzer–Said debate, Jonathan Boyarin also suggests that the Exodus story is susceptible to both colonizing and liberationist readings that frequently mingle in the minds of its readers. For further commentary on the Walzer–Said debate, see William E. Connolly, *The Ethos of Pluralization* (Minneapolis: University of Minnesota Press, 1995), pp. 225–6, n. 16; Michael J. Shapiro, *Violent Cartographies: Mapping Cultures of War* (Minneapolis: University of Minnesota Press, 1997), pp. 190–3.

33.   Harry Berger Jnr, 'The lie of the land: the text beyond Canaan', *Representations*, 25 (1989), pp. 125–6.

34.   *Ibid.*, pp. 126–7, 129, 134. Schwartz, *The Curse of Cain* (p. 134) comments that King David set a captured population to work as slave labourers (doing brickmaking) like the 'Israelites in Egyptian bondage'.

35.   Berger, 'The lie of the land ...', pp. 123, 135–6, 138 n. 12.

36.   Schwartz, *The Curse of Cain*, pp. x–xi, 6, 8, 10, 16–17, 95, 121–2, 140–1, 158–9.

37.   *Ibid.*, pp. 9, 18–20, 69, 101, 134, 165–6, 169. Berger, 'The lie of the land ...' (pp. 124–5) suggests that Solomon's 'weakness for foreign women' might be explained by the state necessity of forging economic and political alliances; cf. Shapiro, *Violent Cartographies*, pp. 188–9, referring to Edmund Leach's essay, 'The legitimacy of Solomon' in Michael Lane (ed.), *Structuralism: A Reader* (London: Jonathan Cape, 1970), pp. 248–92. Apropos the complexity of biblical narratives like Genesis and the book of Job, cf. William E. Connolly, *The Augustinian Imperative: A Reflection on the Politics of Morality* (London: Sage, 1993), pp. 2–30, 94–101.

38.   *Ulysses*, pp. 610–11.

39.   Spinoza, *Tractatus*, p. 132; Said, 'Michael Walzer's *Exodus and Revolution*: a Canaanite reading', p. 165.

40.   Cf. Connolly, *The Augustinian Imperative*, p. 94 (taking the biblical stories as mythic): 'the enigmatic character of the mythic registers darkly a plenitude of being that exceeds the grasp of any single interpretation. Perhaps this is part of the wisdom that emerges out of the mythic.'

41.   Cf. the classic essay by Andreas Huyssen, 'Mass culture as woman: modernism's Other' in Tania Modleski (ed.), *Studies in Entertainment: Critical Approaches to Mass Culture* (Bloomington: Indiana University Press, 1986).

42.   Cf. Kirsch, *The Harlot by the Side of the Road*, chs 8 and 9.

8

More family stories: London, Sydney, Melbourne

While writing this book, I sent copies of the family genealogy prepared by my genealogist Barbara Curthoys to my uncles Lew and Jock Levy (my mother's brothers, both younger than her), who then contacted me and said they would get together and tape a discussion on their pre-migration childhood experiences in London, and send it to me.

Arriving in 1926, my grandparents and their three children were a young family who appear to have migrated with the help of the Assisted Passage Scheme, jointly arranged by the Australian and British governments as part of general Empire settlement. Posters were placed in the London Underground and throughout English cities advertising Australia as a land of opportunity. Young family groups, mostly from English cities and provincial and industrial centres rather than rural areas, predominated on the migrant ships that brought the new settlers to Australia. Most ended up in the cities or towns, but whether in rural areas or in cities many had a very hard time in the first period of settlement. The Assisted Passage Scheme was suspended in 1929, and revived briefly in 1938–39.[1]

Between 1921 and 1929 Australia received 323,000 British migrants, 212,000 assisted.[2]

As the example of my mother's family shows, the categories 'British migrant' or 'English migrant' were general terms that could include surprising ethnic and cultural diversity.

My mother would reminisce that as a young teenager (at 14) she was the first in the family to get a job in Australia, in a Sydney clothing factory; she said she later became a tailoress. When I talked to one of my uncles and my aunt after my mother died, they stressed how important it was to the precarious fate of the family that she began that employment.

I found my uncles' taped reminiscences fascinating, funny, intriguing, touching, and asked if the tape, once I had transcribed it, could be included in my book, after I had shown it to them. This was readily agreed – 'as long, John', said my uncle Jock, 'as you think anyone would be possibly interested'. I think the poetics of memory, and here the poetics of diasporic memory, are always interesting. Lew also sent to me an essay he'd written reflecting on his mother's life and his early migration experiences in Sydney and Melbourne during the 1930s Depression, and I saw how well it would 'go' if I placed it after the taped memories.

In terms of structuring, and hopefully decentring, my narrative, I got the idea for quoting these stories and reminiscences from Wilkie Collins's delectable nineteenth-century mystery and thriller novel *The Woman in White*, a text of multiple narrators and testimonies that builds on a fused Oriental–European tradition of fiction established in the early eighteenth century by translations of *The Thousand and One Nights*, where stories beget stories that lead to more stories. In this tradition, now inherited by an interested postmodernism, the power of the single omniscient narrator – here, your author – is open to challenge and dispersal.[3]

Childhood memories: reminiscences of my uncles Lew and Jock

JOCK: John, in response to your request for our reminiscences we've decided that we would record it, so this then is what you're going to get. Now I suppose this is our contribution to oral history à la Studs Terkel, so we'll make an effort for you and see what comes out of it. Lew, would you like to contribute to your early memory?

LEW: John, my early memories of growing up in London in a working-class suburb called Whitechapel were, to quote my wife, if I had to paint or nominate a colour which tinged and stayed with me all my life, my memory is of a drab grey. We grew up in a landscape of tenement houses, poorly designed – typical working-class England.

JOCK: Yes, to give you just a little more of that, I'd like to give you some detail of the house that we lived in. I can remember that we had no bathroom. I can remember that the furniture was very primitive – sufficient chairs to go round the table but nothing elaborate in the way of lounge or any of the various things that go to make up what I think is a cultured home. The old man was a taxi driver as I remember it and during our period in England he had two taxis, one was a Unic and the other was a Fiat. The old man used to go out in the winter weather wrapped up in a rather large blanket that he would put round his middle, and I think he suffered quite a lot with the weather over there. One of the reasons I think that possibly we came to Australia was the fact that he had been in South Africa for a number of years and got the sunshine into his bones in Johannesburg. I don't know whether he had relatives there but he certainly had friends because when we came over in the boat and stopped at Cape Town I remember that he took us up to Johannesburg to meet certain people. Now, would you take over, Lew, and add something on the early life and the house?

LEW: Speaking of my father, my memory of him was that he lived in a kind of fantasy land. I think maybe staying in Johannesburg led him to believe that the streets were paved with gold. He loomed largely in our lives but not from anything he did but for what he didn't do. I have visions of him as doling out a few shillings to my mother, who struggled to provide us with some sort of quality of life ... but what stays in my mind is that these two people, my mother and father, were just barely literate. Words seemed to overwhelm them and that had quite a significant effect on my later adult life. But the vision of my father is one in which he guided us nowhere. The only attribute I can lay at his door was that he took us away from what had seemed to us to be a dour and drab England.

JOCK: I'll butt in there, Lew, and add just a few things. Now we weren't exactly poverty-stricken in England, I mean on a Day of Atonement, that is Yom Kippur, they were able to pay a servant to come in and lay the fire and do certain manual things that Jewish people weren't supposed to do on that day. Although they weren't highly religious in any sense they sort of were conformist and it's interesting in saying that because there were levels, social levels, of Jewish people in London. For instance, the Anglicized Jews were top of the ladder and then down below that there was possibly the Russians, the Poles, and ... kind of a Spanish ... Portuguese, that's the word I'm looking for. The Portuguese were possibly the lowest on the ladder. And we were taken to synagogue on certain holidays, not regularly on a Friday night or Saturday, but mainly on the holidays. Now we used to go, Lew and I, to a Chader, that is, a religious school where they taught you Hebrew and Lew even remembers some. I certainly do ... *baruch ato adinoy alo heinu melech h'olam* (blessed art thou, O lord our God, king of the world), which is the first part of the blessing for cutting the bread, drinking the wine, something like that. And at this particular Chader, a very dingy morbid sort of a joint, the teacher was shall I say a typical Jewish Russian who had come out into England, couldn't speak English very well, black coat, black hat, pince-nez and food stains all over his waistcoat, and he was a bearded man and if you didn't get the alphabet right (*alaf, bet, gimmal*) you got a rap over your knuckles and Lew and I decided, I think Lew did more than I did, I just followed, we decided rather than go along to the Chader we would experiment and go along and see where the barges went, and if we could, get a lift on the barges. Lew, you take over from there.

LEW: I don't think we really had any Homeric Odyssey, we never actually made the barges, but we knew an awful lot about trains because we lived in our street and at one end was a very small narrow dingy railway tunnel called Tom Thumb's Arch. My memories centre around this Dickensian teacher, as Jock described him, Jewish teacher, who ... really his inability to transmit knowledge in a civilized way led us to becoming what I think could be called religious fringe dwellers. We ... he drove us crazy and our retaliation of course was to totally desert the Chader.

JOCK: And I think possibly we were pretty street-wise in those days, Lew couldn't have been any more than eight or nine, I couldn't have been any more than five or six and yet we wandered around I should imagine Clapham area and Stepney area so we were always on our own. Maybe the fact that there weren't very many motor cars on the road, very few taxi cabs and things like that. The horse-drawn vehicles I suppose would be in the majority, so the dangers weren't so great in those days.

Now I would like to move on to the food that we had on special days. I remember that on a special day, that is on a Friday night, there were no candles lit. I remember no prayers spoken. But I do remember that Rose would always have fried fish on the table, possibly plaice which is a kind of a fish somewhat larger than a sole, and on very special occasions we might have chicken but these were special occasions. Plus the fact that the old man at times would bring home fruit of the season, wonderful whiteheart cherries I remember very vividly. I loved them, plus the fact that he would go sometimes down to the fish market and bring home a box. This was a box that would be about three times bigger than a cigar box, it was made of wood and inside it would be chitlings. Now chitlings are the soft liver of the cod and Rose would cook that up and we would have it cold with vinegar, just a little vinegar, and pepper. I still remember it and obviously this was where the cod liver oil came from. Other occasions I remember Mother had a friend ... where they made wonderful Dutch pastry – Monicadams – that is absolutely right, Lew. And the old lady would take over fried fish, plaice again, give it to this lady and the lady in response, because they were very very friendly, had known each other for years, would give her a quantity of pastry – Bollars, you're so right – and this was absolutely delicious.

Now, I remember, talking of food and enterprise, that the old man must have been talked into it, I don't know who did it, but we had a copper which we boiled up the clothes in, put the fire underneath it, and on this occasion they decided to make hokey pokey. Now hokey pokey was an icecream confection based on milk and when you refrigerated it you sliced it in oblong blocks and you wrapped it in white paper and people would go out on tricycles and sell it in the street and I remember tasting this one day and – the milk had slightly burnt. I remember two very distinctive flavours, vanilla and strawberry. That didn't last very long. Christ alone knows what would happen if the health department had got onto them, you know, boiling your clothes one day and making bloody icecream the next day. Well that's what happened. Your reminiscence on that.

LEW: My memories of things gastronomic began and ended with those marvellous Dutch confections that my mother got by trading for fried fish and as Jock said she was an artist with the frying of fish. My other memory of food goes back to the days when we set forth from England to discover Australia. It was on some sort of a rust bucket called SS *Herminius*. We were third-class steerage with all the connotations that go with that. I think Jock has a memory of on the voyage we were befriended by one of the stokers, it was a coal-fired vessel obviously, who was Jewish and somehow it made him temporarily kith and kin and we perhaps did a little better than the other ten pound immigrants, so that persists in my memory.

The other thing, leaving food to one side, was that Anne and I some years ago went back to London and I thought I would show her my birthplace, my origins, my streetscape, and I'd already built up a picture of the school we went to called Malmsbury Road School and in my mind's eye it was derelict, run-down, poverty-stricken. We got to London, we found the street which we had lived in and it had been bombed flat from German Stukas, but what was still standing was Malmsbury Road School. It was a solid well-built school building and what particularly endears it to my memory was the fact that at the age I think of 11 before we left I'd won a prize at that school, so ego has etched its ugly influence on me.

JOCK: There's also a grim side of it. I remember Lew and myself playing in the street outside our home and along the avenue were horse chestnut trees and these had what we called conkers on them and if you could get four or five of these conkers, hold them on the stem, they were a pretty decent sort of a weapon and I remember some louts coming along and hitting Lew on the head and drawing blood and calling out bloody Jews, Jew bastards, and Rose came out, of course when Lew told her what happened, and she sprinted up that road and if she had caught them she'd have killed them. This is just a little grimmer side of what our childhood was.

Now, having told you about the food situation there I think one of our greatest pleasures was that Rose would take us, I remember she took me once or twice, to Woolfs, in Whitechapel, who specialized in beef, that is, salt beef on a sandwich with a pickled cucumber. It was absolutely heaven and going back in 1976 we went to Woolfs it's still there and the salt beef is almost as good as it was in those days.

LEW: Yes and I can echo that sentiment. Anne and I made the acquaintance of Woolfs and it was up to the standard we'd speculated about, so some things endure in this society.

JOCK: Now from a cultural point of view and possibly this could have influenced us in some way or another the old man, that is Phil, that is Father, was very fond of the theatre and I remember him taking Lew and I to see a ... a Rhinegold? no, Reinhardt, a Max Reinhardt production of a German mime play, no words, some music, but everything was mimed. Wonderful play, wonderful production. Also I remember taking us I think it was to the Palace, I'm not quite sure on that one or the Palladium, to see *Chu Chin Chow* ... had a wonderful effect on us. So the old man was quite good about that and I remember him taking us to Wembley stadium where they had an exhibition of a sea battle. I think it was at Zeebrugge and all the models were there and it showed you the warships, how they manoeuvred, and the consequence, how of course Great Britain, that the British Navy was triumphant. I remember that very vividly.

LEW: Not only did we have memories of Max Reinhardt and his superb production of a mime but both Jock and I remember vividly the music hall songs that went back to Victorian England, songs that were peculiar to and unique to the English working class because vaudeville essentially as you would know was a working-class contribution, or ... no I think I'll leave it at that.

JOCK: I'm going now to talk about the Southend-on-Sea. ... I'd like to recount when we went on holidays, which weren't all that frequent. I remember we went to Southend-on-Sea one time. Now this is just at the head of the Thames river where it meets the North Sea and for kilometres practically it is mud, mud and more mud, kilometres of mud. You sort of walked out to the tide and then having walked out there, picked up all the crabs and the shells and the various other things that were there, you would beat a hasty retreat trying to beat the tide coming in. I remember Rose always loved the cockles and the jellied eels and along the sea front there, the walk, they had these stalls and on the stalls there would be small saucers that would contain three or four cockles and then if you wanted you could also have a larger saucer of jellied eels with vinegar, just a little vinegar, and some pepper. I'll now sing a little song that they used to sing when advertising them.

> (*sings*)   mussels and cockles
>   all alive O!
>   winkles and mussels and cockles all alive O!

That sort of stays in my memory somehow I don't know why. Now, I also remember that one day the old man took us to a place called Luton and amongst the fields and the gardens there the old lady came back with an armful of dahlias and flowers of the season and this was unusual because I don't ever remember seeing any flowers at home at any time, can you, Lew?

LEW: No, I can't, no.

JOCK: John, in tracing the family tree I noticed that Rose had some sisters and particularly I think one was named Sarah, definitely, and another named Abby for Abigail and I think another was named Prissy. I got somehow the feeling that there were more in the family than the tree reveals, because I remember Mother at one time saying that one of the sons – her brothers in other words, one of her brothers – had died of TB and another had been killed in the Great War. So it must have been a fairly large family. Now, I can't confirm the name of the brother who was killed in the Great War but I think it was Harry. Also the fact that Lew was getting into trouble with Sarah, when she used to come to the place and sit down there and they would converse and Lew would get a pin and stick it in Sarah's arse and this of course created all sorts of problems. Another thing we noted, people didn't come to the house very often if hardly at all and we didn't go to anyone else's house. I can remember once being taken to our grandparents on Phil's side at the White Swan, a pub, and meeting his parents but only once. I can't remember any other people coming to the house or us going visiting.

I also remember that at the back of the street there was a factory. I think it was an engineering factory called Perry's and also just a little distance away from that was Bryant and May's. Bryant and May's made the matches and if you remember this was the first strike by women in England because of the phossy jaw ... because of the yellow phosphorus that was used in the manufacture of the matches and they touched their jaws, touched their mouths, and then of course they developed a cancer which developed to such an extent I think that probably led to a very early death. I remember ... later on ... this was strange ... directing a play at the New Theatre called *The Matchgirls* which depicted this strike, the very first strike of women in England, and I remember that George Bernard Shaw supported it.

LEW: What comes to mind, John, is my response, I would imagine it would also correspond to Jock's memory, to winter in working-class London. What used to rile me was that people would talk quite lyrically about the soft snow falling. To both of us what it meant was bitter cold and inadequate clothing and to this day I can never look at snow with any kind of benign appreciation of its aesthetics. It was its thermal properties that worried us or our lack of shall I say defence. ... Just in case, John, you may get the wrong impression, we both saw our mother as a caring loving tender woman ... our father was more distant from us ... and, looking back, we virtually had no social life but that to two children seemed to be normal. We thought that everybody in the world had the same pattern of living that we had.

JOCK: Yes, I'd like to recount a memory that the old man always had an imperial badge that he pinned onto his lapel which I suppose is the equivalent of a returned soldier's badge here and I understand that he drove an ambulance or a truck in the First World War. I don't know whether he had the hernia before or after but he certainly had a bad hernia which he wore with a very large truss and this possibly saved him from going to the front. Also I remember that the old man was always a good whisky drinker, loved a cigar and a whisky, possibly a stout on the side, but was a very small eater.

LEW: One memory which needs to be stressed and underlined is that you will have noted that we haven't made any reference to Elsie. But that is not because of any particular reason except this, that she was several years older than Jock and I and being a woman or rather shall I say being a girl she was more or less put to the back of our minds, because Jock and I specifically sought refuge in our own company.

John, I would want to underline the fact that the past is a foreign country, recreating it sometimes brings impressions which on closer examination are not quite justified. But however that is, what we've told you is to the best of our ability our memories of a critical time in one's growing up.

JOCK: John, you've got the reminiscences of Lew and myself. Lew goes back just about 80 years, I don't go back quite as far as that but nevertheless we hope that this can assist you in some way in your new book.

All the best, from Jock and Lew.

Lew Levy: his story

I shall never forget the first time as an adult man that I cried. I know that I shall never forget it. That day I received an urgent call to go to Sydney's St Vincent's Hospital where my mother was being treated for diabetes. I knew something was profoundly wrong because I was met at the entrance to the ward by a Sister of Mercy, who, with a compassion and a tenderness for which I never found the words to thank her, told me that my mother had died a few hours earlier.

I don't remember now how the rest of that day passed, except to say that it was with my wife and children and my brother and sister and their families. We were a close-knit group, we shared our joys and sorrows. We didn't say that much, as I remember. Handkerchiefs appeared regularly and noses were blown rather harder than usual, but as I say, not a lot was said. We never got round just then to talking about the funeral.

But I do remember so vividly, because it is seared deeply into my memory, going to bed and letting my head fall onto Anne's shoulder and feeling the tears flooding out and trying to stop the wrenching sobs which hurt me and embarrassed me. I know now that there was more to my grief than the realization that my mother's life had come to an end. I cried because of my mother's life, for what she endured in order to survive in a land halfway round the world from where she was born. The tears I shed were compounded of rage and hatred — rage that life had given her so little, and hatred of the poverty that forced these circumstances on her.

My parents were born and bred in London's East End, within the sound of Bow Bells, and they took a cockney pride in their origins. My younger brother, my older sister (me in the middle) shared that distinction, if distinction it be. My father had soldiered through the 1914–18 war unscathed (he was 92 when he died). The only skill he acquired from his army service was driving (he was in Army Transport), and in civvy street he eked out a precarious living driving a London taxi.

I don't know precisely why he decided to uproot himself and take his wife and three children to Australia. It could have been that he imagined that being poor in Sydney was preferable to being poor in London or that his children would have greater opportunities than London offered, or it could have been the blandishments of one of his brothers. I think it was the last, because he was supposed to meet us on our arrival as assisted immigrants on the battered and much-travelled SS *Herminius* which, the voyage long, was pervaded by the mixed odour of sandsoap and carbolic, the institutional perfume of the poor.

In the event there was no uncle with home and furnishings and a job for my father when we arrived. There was nobody. In the end the Salvation Army took pity on us and installed us in the People's Palace. I am not sure how long we enjoyed our Pitt Street address. It was probably a week, two weeks at most. But I am sure that I shall always be grateful for the practical Christianity of the Army.

We naturally gravitated to a tenement in the working-class suburb of Paddington. At the beginning of the 1930s refurbishing had not been invented and even now I can't go into a done-up and done-over inner-city semi-detached, complete with cast-iron lace and chipped-away sandstone, without thinking of bed bugs and missed meals. In my growing-up material prosperity never came our way.

My earliest memories of our family lifestyle until my father qualified to become a taxi driver involve the acquisition of a hessian sugar bag which I carried when I accompanied Father to where we collected a dole of seven shillings and sixpence for a week and a handout of bread and golden syrup (cockies' 'delight') which went into the hessian bag. The Great Depression was indeed depressing.

Although my father had no skills, my mother had. She was an expert cigar-maker. But she might just as well have been a space explorer for all the demand there was for that luxury in the desperate days of the early thirties. So she was denied the dignity of following her trade and went out in the early mornings and scrubbed floors and washed dishes.

My first school was Paddington Junior Technical School (still there in Oxford Street) and my most vivid memory, which seems to have blotted out any other remembrance, was of fighting. My brother a year and a half younger than me went to the same school, but in a lower class, and I seemed to be constantly involved in playground fights. I am not sure now what provoked me to battle in his defence, or, for that matter, my own. Why we were singled out I have forgotten – whether we looked different or spoke differently I do not know now. But I do remember how I made an aching way home, sometimes with a puffed eye or skinned knuckles, for I was vanquished as often as I was victorious.

I stayed at Paddo until sixth class, which was as far as their syllabus could go. To take my education further, I sat for and won a scholarship to Sydney Technical High School, then situated in Albion Street, Darlinghurst. The principal reason why that school was selected was because it was within walking distance, not that close, mind you, but I could save the penny fare each way.

Again, my memory of S.T.H.S. is hazy, but I do remember the interminable playground fights, and the reasons for them. They were twofold, I was identified as a Jew and I wore the wrong clothes. The mystery of Jewishness still intrigues me, for we weren't practising Jews, whatever our surname implied.

It was some years after I left S.T.H.S. that I came to understand the problem with my school clothes. I had reached the age for long pants but the family finances couldn't be stretched to produce the standard grey serge trousers and maroon school blazer. To help out I delivered newspapers in the mornings around Rushcutters Bay and Darling Point and after school I worked in a garage dispensing petrol. For both jobs I earned a total of seven shillings and sixpence and that became part of the family income and paid for books.

My father owned one good suit and my mother cut it down and took it in so that I didn't trip over the lower part or flop about in the top part. I saw the butchered suit as a perfectly logical response to my needs, and, as I say, I could not undersand the ridicule of my peers. Economics being what they were, I had to leave school at the end of three years at high school, but in my last year I had managed to buy a school blazer. For some reason the interminable playground fighting came to an end and, if I was not accepted, at least I had merged into the background.

I left school in 1932 during the depths of the Depression. With my mother as support I went from one interview to another in search of an apprenticeship – anything would have done – always with the inevitable result. Returned from the job-hunt, the rest of the day was spent surfing at Bondi Beach, a few minutes' walk from where we then lived. There was an endless attraction about the surf, not only because it was free.

To swim out to just the right line of breakers, pick the exact split second to launch yourself with all your might in front of the descending wave front and feel the wave pick you up and thrust you at dizzying speed towards the distant beach, was an exhilarating experience indeed, particularly if you had got the utmost from the wave's energy and rode it to the limit of its travel up the sand. To slowly (deliberately of course) raise yourself upright, imagining yourself the centre of attraction of surfing neophytes, was balm to an ego bruised by the constant rejection of employers. But Bondi was much, much more than a physical experience. It was my (and my brother's) university. It changed our lives.

After our swim we would make our way into the municipal dressing sheds to shower and change and it was there that we met a group of men who opened doors for us onto another world. As I remember there was six or seven of them. They sat in deckchairs in a group talking of politics and music and books and Aboriginal rock art and Marx – and we were spellbound. One of the group, a boot-maker, invited us to his flat and it was there that our discovery of music began. He revered Beethoven and he had the gift of transmitting his enthusiasm to us. As our acquaintanceship developed our listening focused on a special programme, the Prometheus and Coriolanus overtures, the Emperor Concerto (Schnabel the pianist) and the Symphony No. 7 (Stokowski and the Philadelphia Orchestra). We would stretch out on the floor (furniture was sparse) after bread and honey (rations were short), each taking it in turn to wind the spring-driven turntable with its large and heavy 78 rpm record. To me it was a revelation. The combination of the mastery of the pianist, the quality of the orchestra and the thrust and dynamics of the music were more than spellbinding, they were also a challenge, a challenge to change the world. Even now the passage of the years has not blunted that response.

That social change was the frequent subject of discussion seemed perfectly natural in a period of profound economic depression, and this interest was accentuated by the rise of fascism in Germany and Italy, but particularly the German experience. One of the group, as I remember, was an out-of-work shipwright, Tom Jones, who generally led the group discussion around to the existence of a new form of social organization, socialism, in the USSR.

Books weren't just read, they were devoured. But they weren't just any books. One element was essential, they had to embody a social critique, either explicit or implicit. Of all the books I read in the 1930s I still remember vividly John Reed's *Ten Days That Shook the World*, Michael Gold (of *New Masses*)'s *Jews Without Money*, Upton Sinclair's *Oil*, *The Jungle* and later *Boston, the Trial of Sacco and Vanzetti*. Maxwell Anderson in *Winterset* brilliantly dramatized the story of the crucifixion of the two immigrant Italians, and it was this play which deeply impressed me with the power of the 'theatre'. There were, of course, other playwrights, Irwin Shaw (*Bury the Dead*), John Steinbeck (*Of Mice and Men*), Albert Maltz (*Private Hicks*, *Merry Go-Round*), and Clifford Odets' *Waiting for Lefty*, *Till the Day I Die* and *Awake and Sing*. These were some of the plays so powerful in their social comment that my brother and I helped to form a theatre group which would perform and popularize plays which we thought commented on our day and age.

As I said, books were devoured. Dreiser, Dos Passos, Jack London, Lillian Hellman, Langston Hughes, Liam O'Flaherty helped convince me that the working class were heirs to a great tradition and that power and exploitation were synonymous.

The books came from two sources, the Sydney Municipal Library, then on the first floor of Queen Victoria Building above Penfolds Wine Cellars, from whence a boozy aroma perfumed the whole building. The other and by far the richer source of my reading came from Dymocks Library, located at the rear of the bookshop still located in George Street. The joining fee the library charged was beyond me, so I would settle back in their comfortable armchair and read as long as I could. It was well stocked by a discerning librarian and it was there that I took my first step down that slippery path to crime, for often I borrowed a book and 'forgot to return it'.

In the pre-dawn light of a February morning (it was nearly 3am) the dimly lit mile-long platforms at Albury railway station seemed to stretch to infinity. I climbed down from the Melbourne Express, which terminated at Albury because of the change of gauge, and found a seat in a Victorian Railways carriage to continue the journey to Melbourne. I felt like an exile in my own country. I left Sydney because I was unemployed and I was convinced that I would not be offered employment. The Depression was at its deepest and I had become an economic burden that the family could no longer sustain.

I wanted to become an apprentice, preferably in a trade associated with engineering, but that proved to be impossible. My mother and I would scan the *Sydney Morning Herald* and then seek interviews. Nothing came from our efforts. My first job came from the efforts of my sister, two years my senior, who worked as a machinist in a clothing factory. I graduated from general rouseabout, climbing under sewing machines to repair broken leather belts and flick them back onto the whirling shafts without stopping the machines; to seam presser, wielding a fifteen-pound electric flat iron; to, finally, learning the trade of tailor's cutter.

My sister, my brother and I joined the Communist Party and my sister and I became members of the Clothing Trades Union, an organization unbelievably conservative. Though we strived mightily, our most militant achievement over some few years was to force the union into marching in the annual May Day Procession.

Although I was a conscientious worker I lost my job and I was dismayed to find that no one in the clothing trade would employ me.

I was not able to get a job in Melbourne in my trade, but I do not think that I was such a notorious radical that employers feared me. What was most probable was that my unemployment was the product of the depressed economy of 1939. I had made contact with Ralph Gibson, then the CP State Secretary, who suggested that I could work for the Party and this I did with alacrity. I felt honoured to be involved so directly in the class struggle even though all the Party could offer me was 30 shillings a week. I had a general brief to raise funds for the Party from Jewish left and liberal supporters, speak at factory gate meetings and, generally, do whatever I could to encourage the Jewish community to participate in the anti-fascist struggle. This latter I did by becoming involved in a Jewish cultural organization, the Kadimah, located in Carlton, liberal-leftist in its political orientation, in which I formed a theatre group. The Kadimah enjoyed a very wide support particularly among those Jews who had not moved from the wrong side of the tracks to St Kilda, the goal of the upwardly mobile. I remember two plays which enjoyed a wide audience, both of which I had been associated with in Sydney, Zangwill's *The Melting Pot* and *Israel in the Kitchen*.

My social life was nothing if not precarious. Of my 30 shillings allowance, twenty shillings went to pay for a room in Carlton with a Polish couple whose English was limited. Thus for the week I had ten shillings for food, fares and other necessities of life. I devised a simple answer to the problem. Every day I spent one shilling on a bag of bruised fruit from the local fruiterer. The other three shillings was spent on tram fares. When that ran out, I walked. Melbourne, I regret to say, saw my second venture into crime. Often when I came home late from a meeting, and particularly when whatever fruit I had left had passed the edible stage, I would wait until my landlord and his wife had gone to bed and then I would carefully and silently make my way into the kitchen. I would then cut one slice of bread, not too thick in case it was noticeable, and quickly get back to my room to enjoy its crisp crunchiness. It was ambrosial.

My depredations must have been more noticeable than I thought, for one night I was caught in the act of stealing the slice of bread and I was asked to leave. What still lingers in my memory is the embarrassment of discovery (for it was a dishonourable act for a Communist), how sustaining fruit could be, but especially the flavours, the subtleties, the sheer joy of crunchy bread. I did regret that my income did not run to a whole loaf.

Somehow I think providence kept half an eye on my dietary needs, for they took a turn for the better when I met Rochel Holcer. She was a talented professional Polish actress who, with her husband, had fled Poland to join relatives in Melbourne. She gave readings, mainly in Yiddish, to enthusiastic audiences at the Kadimah, but she wanted to extend her audience by learning and ultimately performing in English. I was asked to be her teacher, probably because it was the only language I knew. Her first request was to learn Rudyard Kipling's 'Boots' which, to my surprise, transformed into a powerful anti-war statement. To hear her beautifully modulated voice declaim

> ... Boots – boots – boots – boots – movin' up an' down again
> An' there's no discharge in the war. ...

was a profoundly moving emotional experience.

Each week I regularly presented myself at the Holcers' flat. Whilst I was flattered by the association with one so talented, the real attraction was lunch, for that was the only payment they could offer. I remember the sliced ham, crunchy bread with butter, coffee and cake. Far be it for me to disparage fruit, bruised or unbruised, but lunch at the Holcers' was an unforgettable experience.

There were too many people whose friendship I acquired in my late teens to whom I shall remain eternally grateful. One was Syd Mostyn, a gentle man, a boot-maker. He made elegant shoes with the simplest of machinery, but the bulk of his income, such as it was, came from repairing. As I said, he taught us a love of classical music, especially Beethoven, and to this day I cannot hear a major Beethoven work without experiencing the smell of leather, eating brown bread and butter with honey and winding the clockwork gramophone which played the 78 rpm records. We all developed two special skills. One was to know when the steel needle in the tone-arm needed replacement, and the other was to react instantaneously to the moment when the first musical distortion occurred because the clockwork motor needed rewinding.

Mostyn had left England early in his youth, but I never knew very much about his origins. He not only read widely but deeply. He had an analytical mind, able to cut through the extraneous layers to the heart of the matter. He was a Marxist and he gave to us all a sense of class and a belief that we were heirs to a rich culture that recognized the need for change, and that culture had to be constantly fought for. What I took from him was the need to criticize ignorance, not the ignorant, and to search for the social roots of the former to change the latter.

Mostyn's gentleness was in stark contrast to the woman who he lived with. Bella Weiner was (and still is) the most remarkable woman I have ever known. She was not just dynamic, she was of its very concentrated, triple-distilled essence. She had fled Poland because of that country's anti-semitism. There she had been a member of the Bund, a Jewish Social Democratic Party, but when I met her she was a Communist.

If she was not exactly knee-high to a grasshopper, anybody of average height towered over her. The only other physical characteristics I remember are her great mop of dark brown hair and eyes that pierced you through horn-rimmed spectacles. Not only was she fluent in her native tongue, but in Yiddish and English also, and she could (and did) hold an audience spellbound in any of those languages.

It seemed to me that she never had the depth of knowledge of socialist theory as did Mostyn, for she usually deferred to his view in matters of theory, but she was a political creature *par excellence*. She knew everybody in the Sydney Jewish community, their political views and their likely contribution to any particular cause.

If Bella did not see herself as the Lenin of the Australian revolution she most certainly considered herself its Krupskaya. I saw her not only in that role but as our Rosa Luxemburg and La Pasionaria. She enveloped us in her fervency. The fire did not just burn in her belly, it raged. She seemed to glow with a special kind of incandescence. Weiner was irresistible.

Mostyn and Weiner were instrumental in forming a Jewish branch of the Communist Party which included my sister Elsie, my brother Jock and the two Hyman brothers, Bizzy and Buzzy, and me. It was from this group that there emerged the idea that we should form a Jewish Youth Theatre.

We wanted to destroy the stereotype of the Jew as wealthy, a merchant, entombed in the Old Testament and the Synagogue, and show them as working people, struggling for a livelihood, whose circumstances tied them to the working class, and whose emancipation was inextricably linked with a radical and militant political party. We sought to be a rallying point, a meeting ground for those whose interest in theatre could be extended to a critical examination of the social and political ideas of the playwright.

One of the problems was the paucity of translated Jewish dramatic literature. We played and read Sholem Aleichem, Peretz and Israel Zangwill, but there just was not enough to exclusively occupy a theatre group determined to perform at least four plays every year. We were thus driven to widen our choices and this we did by selecting plays which could inspire an audience to the adoption of a socially critical view.

Our first theatre was rented on the first floor in Macquarie Place and there enthusiasm, like faith, moved mountains. Timber was scrounged and under the guidance of a carpenter with a touch of genius, we built a stage, sewed curtains and even made our own spotlights.

Somehow Bella had conjured up some chairs, this trade union gave us some paper, that trade union the use of a Gestetner, and the Jewish Youth Theatre was born. For some reason (I think because I was more studious, or, more probably, because no one else was willing) I became the producer. Unlike Lawrence of Arabia I had but two pillars of wisdom, Stanislavsky's *An Actor Prepares* and Nemirovich-Danchenko's *My Life in Art*, and between us we produced Maxim Gorky's *Lower Depths*, Chekhov's *The Cherry Orchard*, Green's *Hymn to the Rising Sun* and a host of interesting and provocative plays.

If I acquired the glimmerings of a producer the real glory belongs to my brother Jock. Most of the members became passing good at acting, but Jock was brilliant. He was tall, handsome, he moved easily and his voice was beautifully modulated. He brought an enormous inner strength and conviction to everything he did.

I know that applause is an actor's meat and drink, but there is one response which is much more difficult to achieve, that is that intense, magical silence, just for a second or two, which can come at the end of an actor's performance. It is testimony and tribute to the actor's skill and it was not an infrequent response to my brother's prowess. When Peter Finch left Australia for Hollywood and fame and fortune he wanted Jock to go with him. My brother did not want to commercialize his talents. He gave them freely to those whose causes he approved. Finch, of course, did go on to fame and fortune, but I do not think my brother ever regretted his decision.

We created a sizeable audience, both Jewish and non-Jewish, and a group of enthusiastic participants who took the aim and objects of the Jewish Youth Theatre seriously. The sharing of a common purpose seemed to forge personal links of uncommon strength. For those members who married, the relationship endured. I met Anne through the theatre, Jock met Jeannette, Bob met Annette, Les met Judy, Buzzy met Eve. And there were others. To this day I can recall but one divorce, and the friendships formed endure to this day.

It was not, however, one long saga of success. One of the aims we had set ourselves was to create a knowledgeable, that is, a critical audience, one able to analyse what was offered. To this end, after each performance either the director or the cast would dissect the play, separate theme from story, make bare the dramatic structure, expound on the ideas and their development. We tried hard and persistently, but we were never able to generate that much enthusiasm or audience participation for the analytic process, and in the end we abandoned the idea.

The Jewish Youth Theatre years were exciting and stimulating. There was the constant challenge of creating a performance. There was always the stimulation of ideas, the discussions, the friendships, the music with Syd Mostyn. But like so much else, the theatre became a victim of Hitlerism. In 1940 the men (and I was one) were called up for military service, and the women into essential industries or into military support auxiliaries. The audience dwindled.

The only thing the army ever contributed to my development, apart from a monumental contempt for bureaucracies, was a sense of vocation. I wanted to become an engineer. I saw engineering as essential and creative. Nature was waiting to be dominated and transformed to provide plenty for all. Rivers would be tamed, deserts would blossom and I would be the master of the rivers and the gardener of the Gobi. All this would I do for the poorer countries (the euphemism 'Third World' had not yet been coined and the concept of 'environmental studies' had not yet been popularized).

I was discharged in 1941 and Anne and I were married the following year. It was then that I started that long hard slog whereby I worked during the day as a fitter in an oil refinery and studied at night to finally qualify as a professional engineer. I never did hear from the Third World.

I do not now buy bruised fruit. I have not done so since my Melbourne days, neither have I stolen slices of bread since then and the books I want I can buy. But I still rage for the death of my mother. Now, though, the anger has changed not abated. It is about her living, or rather her not living. I rage because she, whom I knew, and the many I never will know, were denied their inalienable right, their potential, by poverty. Surely, poverty is the final obscenity.

(Sydney, *c.* 1988)

Jock Levy: man of theatre and film

In April of 1998 I went to see my uncle and aunt, Jock and Jeannette, in Sydney to discuss minor corrections to the taped Lew–Jock interview that I had transcribed and sent to them. Jock also had written some notes to queries I'd sent by mail, including how he, Abraham Jerome Levy, became known as Jock. To this query he replied that it was a nickname given him by a friend in Sydney who 'couldn't tell the difference between a Scottish and an English accent'. Jock then gave me a list of his activities as an actor, director and technician in theatre and film, in a long and remarkable career, in the Jewish Youth Theatre, the New

Theatre in Sydney (of which he became a life member), other radical theatre, the Waterside Workers Film Unit and mainstream film production.

Theatre work

1937–40: acted in a number of plays at the Jewish Youth Theatre:
The Ghost Sonata
The Melting Pot
The Petrified Forest

As director in the Sydney New Theatre:
1941 *Awake and Sing* by Clifford Odets
1944 *Lawson* adapted by Oriel Gray
1944 *A Physician in Spite of Himself* by Molière
1944 Repeat of *A Physician in Spite of Himself*
1945 *Tartuffe* by Molière
1945 *Sons of the Morning* by Catherine Duncan
1945 *Le Bourgeois Gentilhomme* by Molière (as part of the first Molière season in Australia)
1945 Repeat of *A Physician in Spite of Himself*
1946 Repeat of *Tartuffe*
1946 *God Bless the Guvnor* by Ted Willis
1947 *The Shepherd and the Hunter* by David Martin
1947 *Sons of the South* by George Farwell
1947 *Deep Are the Roots* by Gow and D'Usseau
1948 *The Matchgirls* by Robert Mitchell
1948 *The Star Turns Red* by Sean O'Casey
1948 *The Alchemist* by Ben Jonson
1949 *Pot of Message* by Pat and Cedric Flower (a political revue)
1950 *We the People* by Elmer Rice
1950 *Press the Point* by New Theatre Writers
1950 *Lysistrata* by Aristophanes
1951 *How I Wonder* by Donald Agder Stewart
1952 *Sky Without Birds* by Oriel Gray

1977 (for the 45th anniversary of New Theatre) *The Captain of Kopenick* by Carl Zuckmeyer
1980 *We Can't Pay? We Won't Pay* by Dario Fo
1982 (for the 50th anniversary of New Theatre) *The Alchemist* by Ben Jonson

1946 directed *The Front Page* by Ben Hecht and Charles MacArthur at Bryant's Playhouse

1949 directed *Love Me Sailor* by Robert Close for Spiers Production

1953 directed *The Travellers* by Ewan McColl at the Maritime Industry Theatre

Acted in the following New Theatre plays:

1939 *Red Sky at Morning* by Dymphna Cusack

1940 *New Way Wins* by Montagu Slater

1942 *Eve of St Mark* by Maxwell Anderson

1943 *Decision* by Edward Chodorov

1945 *All Change Here* by Ted Willis

1946 *Moony's Kid Don't Cry* by Tennessee Williams

1946 *Of Mice and Men* by John Steinbeck

1947 *Deep Are the Roots* by Gow and D'Usseau

1948 *The Star Turns Red* by Sean O'Casey

1948 acted in Peter Finch's production of Lope de Vega's *The Pastry Baker* at the Mercury Theatre

Film work

With Keith Gow and Norma Disher, Jock began the Waterside Workers Film Unit

Made thirteen documentary films for the trade unions, including *Hungry Mile*, winner of a Gold Medal

1960–61 Chief cinematographer on two documentaries and several commercials for television at Ampol Petroleum Limited

Other film work:

Long John Silver: property department

Smiley Gets a Gun: props and effects

Whiplash: prop buyer and master

Siege of Pinchgut: master of explosives

Three Goldsworthy films as prop master

On the Beach: standby prop master

Three in One: acted the part of Darkie in Frank Hardy's story *The Load of Wood*, directed by Cec Holmes

Wattle Films: acted in and co-produced a series of animated and dramatized short films based on Australian folksongs

Worked for three years at Visatone Film Studios

Worked for seven years at Supreme Sound Studios
Acted in *Dead Men Don't Lie*, based on a Henry Lawson story

Notes

1. Geoffrey Sherington, 'Assisted English settlement 1918–1939' in James Jupp
    (ed.), *The Australian People* (Sydney: Angus and Robertson, 1988), pp. 417–19.
    For a remarkable essay on post-Second World War British migration, mixing
    analysis with personal reminiscence, see Paul Turnbull, 'Jogging memories',
    Voices, VI(3) (1996), pp. 9–17.
2. Alfred Benedict Kuen, 'The disowned revolution: the reconstruction of
    Australian immigration 1945–1952', doctoral thesis, Monash University
    (1997), ch. 2. See also W. K. Hancock, *Survey of British Commonwealth Affairs*,
    vol. III: *Problems of Economic Policy 1918–1939*, Part I (Oxford: Oxford University
    Press, 1942), pp. 94–110; H. Burton, 'Australia's migration policy since the War'
    in W. G. K. Duncan and C. V. James (eds), *The Future of Immigration to Australia
    and New Zealand* (Sydney: Angus and Robertson and AIPS, 1937), esp. p. 122;
    W. D. Forsyth, *The Myth of Open Spaces: Australian, British and World Trends of
    Population and Migration* (Melbourne: Melbourne University Press, 1942);
    Stephen Constantine, 'Empire migration and imperial harmony' in Stephen
    Constantine (ed.), *Emigrants and Empire Settlement in the Dominions Between the
    Wars* (Manchester: Manchester University Press, 1990).
3. See Peter L. Caracciolo, 'Wilkie Collins and the ladies of Baghdad, or the sleeper
    awakened' in Peter L. Caracciolo (ed.), *The Arabian Nights in English Literature*
    (Basingstoke: Macmillan, 1988), pp. 143–77. Cf. John Docker, *Postmodernism and
    Popular Culture: A Cultural History* (Melbourne: Cambridge University Press,
    1994), pp. 69–70.

9

'Sheer perversity': Zionism and anti-Zionism in the 1940s

Now the children of Judah had fought against Jerusalem, and had taken it, and smitten it with the edge of the sword, and set the city on fire.

And afterward the children of Judah went down to fight against the Canaanites, that dwelt in the mountain, and in the south, and in the valley.

And Judah went against the Canaanites that dwelt in Hebron....

(Judges 1:8–10)

And I have given you a land for which ye did not labour, and cities which ye built not, and ye dwell in them; of the vineyards and olive-yards which ye planted not do ye eat.

(Joshua 24:13)[1]

The idea for writing this chapter actually occurred to me quite a few years ago, when I was reviewing for the *Weekend Australian* in 1991 the 1200 or so pages of the two-volume history *The Jews in Australia* by Hilary L. Rubinstein and W. D. Rubinstein, a tome whose historiography I found objectionable on almost every conceivable ground, not least as it affected my own family history. The Rubinsteins present, without any selfconsciousness or self-reflexivity, the history of Jews in Australia in terms of what I would call 'ethnic history', migration as a narrative of progress, achievement, triumph. A group comes to a new land, its pioneers experience difficult times, but after heroic effort they put down roots, establish their own communal religious and institutional life, many of their members make notable contributions to the wider society, and they flower as a community.[2]

The Rubinsteins' history innocently pursues such a narrative. We read that a handful of Jews came to Australia in 1788 as convicts, but in the decades following they, like other convicts and free immigrants, began to consolidate in the European colony. Jewish settlers saw Australia just as non-Jewish settlers did, as ripe for colonial settlement. Jewish colonists established themselves not only in Australia's cities, but in country towns and as squatters and pastoralists. It is interesting to observe, from Hilary L. Rubinstein's account, how much the Jewish settlers of colonial Australia, just like non-Jewish settlers, assumed and saw the land as a 'hitherto uncolonized' 'untamed' continent. Jewish settlers, it seems, had come to the 'virtually empty southern continent' that was full of 'myriad virgin acres'. If Jewish settlers were permitted to settle *en masse* in the Northern Territory, they would 'doubtless soon convert those barren acres into fields flowing with the proverbial milk and honey'. In the 1930s Jewish settlers saw the settlement of an apparently empty Australia – the Aboriginal peoples are nowhere in sight – in the same terms as the settling of Palestine. Jewish settlers urged each other to 'penetrate the wastes in Northern Australia, turning them into rich, fruitful and luxuriant districts', in the same way that the Jews have turned the 'arid deserts and wastelands of Palestine' – the Palestinian Arabs are nowhere in sight – into 'small fertile farms and homesteads'. In this account, migration history as a narrative of success is happily recounted as part of the larger story of triumphant white invasion of a *terra nullius*.[3]

According to the Rubinsteins – and, I soon realized, according to contemporary Jewish historiography in general[4] – because there has not been a history of deeply rooted anti-semitism in Australia, the major obstacles to the progress of the Jewish community have been internal. In particular in this historiography, Anglo-Australian Jews, my own descent group – my mother's family having arrived in Sydney from London's East End in 1926[5] as I relate in previous chapters – are to be derided and excoriated. The Anglo-Jews are almost invariably referred to as patrician, aristocratic, elite and wealthy. They controlled the Jewish community's organizational structures well into the twentieth century, adopting a policy of group inconspicuousness, slavish support for the British Empire, and a stress on Jews as being different in religion only. Consequently, Anglo-Jews left the community open to the dangers of assimilation, apathy, intermarriage and the disappearance of Jewish distinctiveness.[6]

The 'supercilious Anglo-Jewish patricians' – in W. D. Rubinstein's phrase – were also unwelcoming of, hostile to and snobbish towards the Polish and other Eastern European Yiddish-speaking Jews who increasingly arrived in the new century, especially in the 1920s and 1930s. Fortunately, however, the Anglo-Jews were dislodged from the community's 'roof bodies', and the refugee immigrants from the late 1930s took Australian Jewry in drastically new directions, which became gloriously clear after the Second World War: a new stress on Jewish distinctiveness in terms of separate schooling; and a desire that the Jewish community become non-universalistic and inward-looking, except for its overriding devotion to Zionism and Israel, considered central to Jewish consciousness.[7]

A key moment in this shift was a debate in the early years of the Second World War engendered by Sir Isaac Isaacs, the first Australian-born Governor General and a former Chief Justice of the High Court, who wrote a series of essays in the Sydney weekly newspaper *The Hebrew Standard* and also in the mainstream press urging his fellow Jews not to follow what he called Political Zionism. He was answered by another eminent jurist, Julius Stone, newly appointed as Professor of jurisprudence and international law at the University of Sydney, in articles in *The Hebrew Standard* which were then collected and reworked into a pamphlet entitled '*Stand Up and Be Counted!*', published in early 1944. Overwhelmingly, the Jewish community during the war and after it agreed with Stone's pro-Zionism rather than Isaacs's anti-Zionism, as did Herbert Vere Evatt, in the late 1940s Minister for foreign affairs in the Federal Labor Government and also (in 1947) Chairman of the United Nations Ad Hoc Committee on Palestine. Through Evatt, Australia in 1948–49 played a key role in the creation of the state of Israel and its recognition by the United Nations. Stone's pamphlet was sent in 1944 to key politicians, and, according to the biographies, Stone felt that he had indeed decisively influenced Dr Evatt.[8]

Two aspects particularly piqued me in this official history, this teleological and triumphalist historiography of the victors in a dispute, not least as presented in W. D. Rubinstein's rebarbative volume covering 1945 to the present. The suggestion of general Anglo-Jewish wealth would have surprised my grandparents, living in lifelong poverty like many other Anglo-Jews in Bondi. As for the claim that Anglo-Jews were universally hostile to Eastern European Jews, my two uncles both married migrants from Russia, two young women who were first cousins. During the 1930s my uncles and my mother joined the Communist Party, and it is interesting to read in W. D. Rubinstein's volume that after the Second World War left-wing elements were, in Rubinstein's words, systematically marginalized, purged and eliminated from the now Eastern European-dominated 'roof bodies', who mercifully moved the Jewish community towards a proper conservatism in thought and action.[9]

I was also startled by the violence of W. D. Rubinstein's contempt for Sir Isaac Isaacs in relation to the Isaacs versus Stone debate. Isaacs's anti-Zionism, Rubinstein declares, was a compound of British Empire loyalty, legalism, and a strictly religious definition of Jewishness, which Rubinstein felt was ironic because Isaacs was never a religiously observant Jew. Isaacs was purely negative in that he offered no solutions for the situation of beleaguered Jewry during the war years. Isaacs's anti-Zionism, Rubinstein felt it necessary to add, included a very large measure of 'sheer perversity'.[10]

The more dismissive Rubinstein's language became, the more I perversely thought that I rather liked the sound of old Sir Isaac Isaacs the anti-Zionist, especially as from the mid-1980s I had made my own anti-Zionism clear in essays and reviews.[11] I mentioned my interest to friends, who said: You can't defend Isaacs, he was pro-imperial, an anglophile, an old fashioned pro-British Empire man; that doesn't sound like you, John. A few years went by, but I've never forgotten the interest in Isaacs the Rubinstein volumes stirred in me, and it gives me great pleasure here to try to stage that perhaps difficult and tricky defence of the ex-Governor General, or if not a defence at least an evocation of what I find so attractive in his thinking in the controversy, and how it relates to recent cultural theory concerning diasporic identity and sensibility.

Stone: argument and rhetoric

I betook myself off to the archives to read the files of the controversy firsthand. I'll begin by reading afresh the positions and argumentative style of Julius Stone, the apparent victor in the early 1940s dispute. In 1942 Stone, long a Zionist, had only recently arrived in Australia, a little over a year, when he was, according to his biographer Leonie Star, approached by local Zionists to attempt to rebut Isaacs.[12] Apart from a report of a Stone speech at the Maccabean Hall under the auspices of the Union of Sydney Zionists (16 July 1942), Stone's letters to *The Hebrew Standard*, as well as the 1944 pamphlet *'Stand Up and Be Counted!'*, were directly addressed to Sir Isaac, then in his late eighties. Along with his name, Stone always appended his academic title and accumulated degrees: 'Professor Julius Stone B.A. (Oxford), LL.M (Leeds), S.J.D. (Harvard), D.C.L. (Oxford)'.

In the first chapter of the pamphlet, Stone summarized his objections, presumably for easy perusing by politicians.

Isaacs, says Stone, by his acceptance of the British White Paper of 1939, wishes to relegate Jews to permanent minority status in Palestine, indeed as a minority of one in three, when he should be supporting open Jewish immigration in this time of peril and agony for Jews in Hitler's Europe. Isaacs is really against the 'entire concept of a Jewish National Home', even though 'a main purpose' of the British Mandate and the Balfour Declaration is that Palestine become a Jewish Commonwealth. Isaacs was also making groundless accusations that in such a Jewish state Arabs and Christians would be excluded from citizenship and equality. This could not happen, said Stone, because of the 'repeated official pronouncements of authoritative Jewish bodies, some of them very recent, that absolute equality between all inhabitants, Jewish and non-Jewish, is at the very centre of the Zionist ideal'. When Isaacs in like manner charges that a Jewish state would endanger the Holy Places, he is 'grossly ignoring the official and unquestioned Zionist policy that their inviolability should be guaranteed'. When Isaacs suggests that the formation of a Jewish state would antagonize the Muslim world and so provoke strategic difficulties for the Empire, such is an untenable last resort of a misguided argument: 'Grievances against the Western Powers there may well be in the "Moslem World"', says Stone, 'but the Jewish National Home ... would be the last and least well based among them.' For there are 'no Arab claims, moral or otherwise', against Palestine becoming the Jewish National Home, which, Stone is sure, was guaranteed by the Balfour Declaration's 'letter and spirit'. Furthermore, it is clear, Stone avers, 'that in terms of material or cultural welfare nothing but good has come to the Palestine Arabs from Jewish rehabilitation and achievement in the National Home'.[13]

In terms of political theory, Stone charges that Isaacs in effect has no conception of 'group life'. Isaacs, Stone says, seems to believe that 'any bond, other than the purely religious, between an Australian citizen and any outside community is inconsistent with good citizenship'. Isaacs is 'apparently not aware of the elementary point made early in every standard course on political theory', that nationality has two distinct meanings, referring to citizenship as legal and political status, and to aspects non-legal and non-political, in particular, a form of intense corporate consciousness related to a home country. Stone instances the Irish, Czechs and Poles in the United States and Australia as possessing this kind of consciousness, and he cannot see how Isaacs can reasonably object to applying the notion to any nationality, including, obviously, Jews. Such group life and consciousness, not hemmed in by political frontiers, is, says Stone, essential to true democracy, and in opposing such a conception Isaacs reveals himself to be characteristically 'anti-democratic and anti-semitic'.[14]

It will be clear from these last quoted sentences that Stone's pamphlet wishes to be as wounding as possible to Isaacs's public, intellectual, and personal standing. Indeed, the rhetorical strategy of '*Stand Up and Be Counted!*' is announced in its prefatory section, called 'Background', which begins sermon-like with an invocation of the great name of the late Mr Justice Brandeis, the first Jew to be appointed to the American Supreme Court: a far greater luminary, the implication is, than a mere Australian judge, whose small light of distinction must surely fade in the comparison. In 1915, a few months before taking up his high office, Brandeis issued *The Jewish Problem — How to Solve It*, a challenge to the world to accept Zionism as the 'solution'. Stone quotes Brandeis saying that Zionism seeks in Palestine a legally secured home where Jews may ultimately expect to constitute a majority of the population and can look forward to 'home rule'. Brandeis exhorts every Jew in America to 'stand up and be counted – counted with us – or prove himself, wittingly or unwittingly, of the few who are against their own people'.[15]

Nothing in this statement troubled Stone: neither its settler-colonialist assumption that Palestine was a *terra nullius*, whose present inhabitants could not have any say in whatever was to happen to their country; nor its nationalist binary, that those who oppose the Zionists, presumed to represent all Jewry, are traitors, are 'the few who are against their own people'. Indeed, Stone adopts that chilling last phrase with relish, applying it to Isaacs in these opening seven pages of *ad hominem* insult, vituperation, slander, contempt and character assassination: setting the tone for postwar Australian Jewish historiography in the belittling, occlusion and obloquy directed at Isaacs as a historical figure.[16]

In these prefatory pages we read that Isaacs is a leader in 'injustice and reaction', an enemy of his own people, complicit with and encouraging of the forces of anti-semitism, who invariably writes in a way that is 'dogmatic and unrestrained', yet skilled in 'devices'. What Isaacs writes is opposed to logic, modern sociological and political theory, the accepted views of objective scholarship, the lessons of history, and the basic principles on which democratic progress depends. Isaacs, because of his high office, showed little interest in the lives and problems of his fellow Jews and indeed had no 'human relations with ordinary Jews'. Stone swipes that Isaacs belongs to a 'minute but vocal minority' who because of 'their positions of prestige, and in some cases, wealth or privilege or power', are isolated from any 'real understanding' of their fellow Jews. By contrast, Stone assures us of his perfect knowledge of his fellows; he knows that they consider Isaacs and his kind are a 'small sample' of a 'species' of assimilationist or escapist or anti-national Jews, whose views are regarded as 'distasteful and selfish by the vast mass of ordinary Jews'.[17]

How Stone, who had been in Australia only a short time, to become a professor at Sydney University, by many throughout its history considered a rather remote institution, could possess such intimate knowledge of Australian Jewry, is quite remarkable. Remarkable too, for its insight into Zionist modes of disputation, is that Stone could present so many pages of *ad hominem* assault, before saying a word about his opponent's arguments.

Isaac Isaacs

Yet I don't wish to present Isaacs in this controversy as by contrast wholly admirable. Isaacs, too, is frequently acerbic, given to accusing those he disagreed with of disloyalty and betrayal.

Reading Isaacs's long letters through 1942, 1943, 1944 to *The Hebrew*

Standard, it's clear that, as an admirer of Britain and the British Empire, he hoped he could use his prestige and standing to stop the Australian Jewish community – as he saw it, led, or misled, by Zionism – becoming hostile to the British government. Hostile, because of the provisions of the 1939 MacDonald White Paper, which assured the Palestinian Arabs that the Jewish population of Palestine would never exceed 40 per cent of the total; after a five-year period, during which immigration would be held to 75,000, any future Jewish immigration would be subject to Arab acquiescence. And hostile, more immediately, because of the *Struma* tragedy in 1942: a ship which sank while carrying illegal immigrants from Rumania to Palestine; refused entry into Palestine by the British, the boat, unseaworthy and designed to carry no more than 100 passengers, sank in the Black Sea with the loss of 767 Jewish refugees. Britain, which since the Balfour Declaration of 1917 had always seemed to be Zionism's friend, now appeared to be its treacherous enemy. [18]

Isaacs was dismayed by a mass meeting called to protest against the British government's refusal to admit the *Struma* and its immigrants. Isaacs wrote in *The Hebrew Standard* (2 July 1942) that the course taken by the British government was indeed 'morally indefensible', and in any case the number of intending immigrants on the *Struma* was, he noted, 'within the prescribed quota for the period' according to the MacDonald White Paper. But he also considered that the *Struma* tragedy was the joint result of Nazism and of the illegal policies of what he called the Extreme or Political Zionists. Here he quoted from a *Zionist Bulletin* issued in Melbourne which provocatively insisted that 'Jews will continue immigration, land redemption, and colonisation in all circumstances'. Isaacs voiced his suspicion that the Political Zionists were attempting to 'exploit the *Struma* disaster' in order to swell their own numbers and to strengthen the Zionist campaign to make Palestine a Jewish state, contrary to the Balfour Declaration, which called for a National Home for Jews *in* Palestine. (Isaacs also suspected that the Zionist call for open immigration was for political not humanitarian reasons, the apparent humanitarianism a mask: 4 November 1943.) Isaacs insisted, as he would continue to do in the following years, that Political Zionism is 'one of the greatest dangers to Judaism today', and a 'peril' to 'our Empire in harassing and weakening the British Government in its supreme hour of trial', given military losses in the Far East and with the Middle East under attack. Zionism, he said, was doing a 'great wrong to the British Government and the Empire, our best Friend', indeed 'the most powerful and constant Friend Jewry has ever had'. Zionism was encouraging Australian Jews to be unpatriotic and disloyal both to the Empire and to Australia.

In this (2 July 1942) and later articles (as in 30 December 1943) Isaacs agreed with the British government's refusal to constitute Palestine as a Jewish state. If that Zionist demand were to be met, it would, he argued, be 'unjust' and would antagonize the Arab population in Palestine. It would exasperate the whole Muslim world, in India as well as in Egypt, Turkey and the Arabias, who oppose the subjection of their Arab brethren in Palestine to Jewish rule, either by law or by a Jewish immigration sufficient to 'swamp' them. It would be contrary to the desire of the Christian world to preserve intact the objects and places which it holds sacred.

A feature of the dispute is the contrast in attitude by Stone and Isaacs to the Palestinian Arabs. In his speech at the Maccabean Hall under the auspices of the Union of Sydney Zionists (16 July 1942), Stone in classic Orientalist manner is contemptuous of those he refers to as the 'million sullen fence-sitting Arabs' in Palestine. Stone asserted that it was 'the Jews alone', in numbers half a million, who breathed defiance against the Axis powers, and he called for a separate Jewish army in Palestine to 'defend their new refuge and their ancient home in Palestine'.

Isaacs was concerned to understand Arab viewpoints, feelings and desires. In his reply in the next week's issue of *The Hebrew Standard* (23 July 1942), Isaacs stressed that it was important to know how the MacDonald White Paper historically came about, something, he pointed out, Stone never talked about.[19] The White Paper's call for restrictions on Jewish immigration was, Isaacs said, the outcome of the terrible events of the latter years of the 1930s, especially 1938, when civil war raged in Palestine, with the Arabs in nationalist rebellion, to the degree that the British Forces had to be reinforced with battalions and cavalry regiments from Egypt and India. To regain Arab support, the 1939 White Paper insisted that Britain would not create Palestine as a Jewish state in which the Arabs would be under Jewish political domination. It would continue to safeguard Arab political rights as guaranteed by the Mandate. Given that there were a million Arabs in Palestine, as against the 550,000 Jews (4 November 1943), including the 350,000 Jews the British government had in his view generously permitted to migrate in the previous twenty years, Isaacs felt it was obvious that Palestine could not become a Jewish state. Isaacs did, however, protest against the White Paper's provision for total stoppage of immigration after five years. In reply to Stone's implying that only the Jews of Palestine performed war service against the Axis powers, Isaacs replied: 'One would suppose that the Arabs were doing nothing to help in the war.' Isaacs pointed out that there were both Arabs and Jews in the British Army, a British government report in November 1941 recording 7985 Jews, 3383 Arabs, in Middle Eastern units.

Isaacs was moved in this reply to Stone to decry the Political Zionists' 'utter disregard of the Moslem world'. He pointed to the 'rights of Arabs that have grown up during 1400 years' (23 July 1942). In response to the Political Zionist claim that only Jews had a moral and spiritual claim to Palestine historically, Isaacs pointed out that the Arabs would especially oppose the inclusion of Jerusalem in a Jewish state: 'They have had the Mosque of Omar, which is on the site of Solomon's Temple, for a longer period than Jerusalem was in Jewish hands. Their associations with the Mosque and its site are sacred to them in a very special degree, and these they as custodians for all Islam jealously guard' (4 November 1943). Isaacs also suggested that to make Palestine a Jewish state and Jerusalem a part of it would be an injustice and moral wrong to the Christian faith as well as the Muslim: 'It would mean ignoring the great World events of Christianity and Islam and all that these mean to the millions that are faithful to those religions.' It would, indeed, be an attempt to take up Jewish history at the point where pagan Rome destroyed Jerusalem and ended Jewish hopes of nationhood in Palestine 2000 years ago, and then ignoring all religious history, all temporal and spiritual rights, after that (4 November 1943).

In response to the Political Zionist view that only Jews had a moral and spiritual claim to Palestine in the present, Isaacs proposed a vision of Palestine as a plurality, composed of the three great religions, Muslim, Christian and Jewish. He suggested that to make an autonomous state for one of these religions would create turmoil and strife between it and the other two (9 September 1943). He opposed what he saw as the Zionist vision that the places sacred to all three faiths be handed over to the political care of the Jews (9 September 1943). He said if this were to occur it would arouse the antagonism of the Arabs and the Muslim world, and in the disorders that would result there would be great danger to places and shrines sacred to the Jewish, Muslim and Christian faiths alike (9 September 1943), 'whatever the desire of the combatants to avoid injuring the Holy Places' (20 January 1944). The Zionist call for a Jewish state would also cause difficulties for Jews in other parts of the Arab world (7 October 1943). To avert such dangers and consequences, Isaacs called for the development of an autonomous Palestinian state, where Jew, Muslim and Christian alike have equal rights (9 September 1943).

Isaacs argued that to make Palestine a Jewish state would be to 'make one particular religious faith the test of citizenship', which would necessarily mean there could not be political and legal equality of citizenship rights between Jews, Arabs and Christians (30 December 1943). Isaacs suggested that a Jewish Commonwealth, with immigration exclusively in the hands of the Jewish Agency, 'connotes "Jewish citizenship" or it is meaningless'. Further, Isaacs asked, if the Jews control immigration in the new Jewish Commonwealth, 'how can it be called democratic?' Why not make citizenship Palestinian, that is, neither Arab nor Jewish (16 December 1943; 11 November 1943)? To create a Jewish state, he argued, would necessarily mean the domination of a single nationality over the other nationalities, of one race or religion over the other races and religions. A Christian or Muslim could not become a 'full citizen' of the new state (20 January 1944).

What a disaster it would be, Isaacs felt, if there were to be a Protestant Ulster: 'What would the Catholic citizens of Ulster say?' (10 February 1944).

Controversially, Isaacs saw in Zionism an argument that a citizen in one nation-state could recognize another society as a homeland. He objected to what he considered was the Zionist vision that the Jews of the world are homeless, are exiles and wanderers, and that their life except in Palestine is abnormal and unhealthy (16 December 1943). He felt that Zionism, as a form of nationalism, was advocating the segregation of Jews from Gentiles, and that such advocacy was not only a provocation to anti-semitism but also similar to Hitler's slanderous doctrines that Jews were always an alien element in whatever country they might be (9 December 1943; 16 December 1943). In Isaacs's view, the call to see Palestine as the homeland of the world's Jews necessarily implied the rejection of Australia as the homeland of Australian Jews. Such espousal and thinking was, Isaacs thought, *politically* dangerous for Australian Jews, or Jews wherever they were, in suggesting a dual *political* allegiance (30 December 1943). Such divided allegiances raised the possibility of heightened anti-semitism (20 January 1944).

Isaacs was ironic towards Zionists in Australia who demand mass Jewish immigration to Palestine, yet have no intention of going there themselves. It was as if Moses said to his followers, 'You cross the Red Sea, and plunge into the Wilderness, while I remain behind at the comfortable Court of Pharaoh' (10 February 1944).

The ark of interpretation

After a while Isaacs lost interest in Stone's open letters addressed to him, telling his readers that Stone had stooped to personal attacks that were beneath notice, and that his methods of argument were disingenuous and sophistical, constituted by what he called Omissionitis, a characteristic Zionist malady featuring 'garbled extracts' and the omitting of vital words or expressions when a quotation is made, so that the meaning is reversed (7 October 1943; 21 October 1943; 30 December 1943; 13 January 1944). He became a little tired of Stone always putting his degrees after his name (something I also found rather vulgar and meretricious, absurd and embarrassing). 'Why', he asked, 'all this unusual blazonry of decorations. ... That is quite out of the course of an ordinary newspaper letter, whose facts are left to speak for themselves.' Isaacs suggested that Stone was highlighting his degrees as part of a Zionist strategy: 'Stone is the victim of men behind the scenes stronger than himself' (9 December 1943; 6 January 1944). He felt that Stone was part of a world Zionist movement that clearly wished to monopolize Jewish opinion in the world, meeting any non-Zionist view with an immediate shower of insults (11 November 1943) and accusations of being traitorous (13 January 1944). In *The Hebrew Standard* of 20 January 1944 he said in response to a Stone letter: 'henceforth I must try to forget its author.' His contempt had become complete.

Free of Stone, Isaacs's thinking became increasingly wide-ranging, speculative and theological, probing the relationship between identity, history and place. Isaacs reminded his readers that Zionism was 'opposed to the Messianic hope and expectation which for over 1800 years rested on Scripture and on Rabbinical teaching as embodied in our Prayers' (20 January 1944). Zionism displaced the Messiah and the messianic hope of his looked-for coming (10 February 1944).

Isaacs suggested that the idea of an exclusive Jewish state, based on one nationality and religion, is a return to the medieval Christian states of Europe where only one who professed Christianity could have all the rights of citizenship. In these terms, he thought, Zionism is a giant historical step backwards, away from a modern democratic notion of a national unit formed by various nationalities (20 January 1944).

Zionism, Isaacs thought, was in another way an attempt to reverse the 'wonderful progressive step taken by Judaism after the Captivity', when it became a universal and personal religion rather than a tribal and local faith bound to a particular land; a step that Christianity followed Judaism in taking. Despite their disclaimers that religion would not be a test of citizenship (how, Isaacs asked, could it not be if the new nation is to be called the Jewish state?), the Zionists were now reverting to that older world-discarded group local religion by tying it to Palestine as the desired Jewish state (10 February 1944). Zionism was anachronistically attempting to return to antiquity where religion, nationality and citizenship formed a triple wall separating a political group from a neighbouring one. Such a notion is 'hateful to all modern thought' (10 February 1944).

He began to think Jewish history in innovative and critical ways, especially dwelling on the implications of the story of Exodus and the book of Judges. He felt that Moses had inaugurated the first Zionistic movement (10 February 1944). He challenged the historical metaphysics of Zionism in relation to Palestine, that Jewish immigration to Palestine is a matter of right because physically as well as spiritually the Jews have been continuously in Palestine from of old, whereas the Christians and the Muslims have been there as of yesterday. Yet we know from Scripture in various places, Isaacs observed, not least chapter 1 of Judges, that

for centuries the Canaanites could not be driven out of their land. And
we know that Jerusalem was not Jewish until David took it in about 1000
B.C. So that it belonged to the Jewish people only much less than 1000
years, in fact about 500 years. ... The 2000 years of [Christian]
unchallengeable and uninterrupted connection with Palestine and the
Moslem habitation for 1400 years are, by the Political Zionists, brushed
aside as conferring no 'spiritual claims', they must both give way to the
Jewish right of free immigration as the superior consideration. And the
extraordinary situation is that they 'demand' of the Christian people of
the earth assistance to execute that claim. (23 March 1944)

Isaacs then repeats what he had suggested before, that Moses was 'the first
Zionist', the clear implication being that, while it was right to flee racial
persecution and anti-semitism of the kind suffered in the later Egyptian dynastic
period long after Joseph was forgotten, and in Nazi-controlled Europe in the
present, it was not right that ancient Moses and modern Zionism should lead the
Jewish people to dominate a land that was already inhabited by other peoples, the
Canaanites then and the Palestinian Muslims and Christians now (23 March 1944).

Readers who accepted Isaacs's invitation to renew acquaintance with
chapter 1 of the book of Judges could there read that the Lord advised the
children of Israel that, with the death of Joshua, it was Judah who would fight
the inhabitants of the land of Canaan, not only the Canaanites but the
Perizzites, 10,000 being slain. The children of Israel took Jerusalem and other
cities, destroying the cities they conquered and killing their inhabitants. They
drove out the inhabitants of the coasts and also the mountain areas, though
some inhabitants of valley areas could not be driven out because they had
chariots of iron. The Israelites then shared out the land amongst themselves as
the spoils of war, with Achsah the daughter of Caleb asking for and being
granted choice land with water springs. When the Israelites were strong in the
new land, they did not utterly drive out those Canaanites who had not yet
been slain, but made them into tributaries, along with the Amorites.

In the same remarkable essay recalling the fate of the Canaanites – an essay
that pre-dates by decades Edward Said's similarly remarkable essay stressing
the repeated statements in the Exodus story that the Canaanites were already
in the Promised Land [20] – Isaacs found himself disagreeing with a certain
Zionist rabbi who had proclaimed that Palestine stands revealed as the
background of the Torah, the matrix of the Jewish spirit, the home of the
Jewish people, and the central fact and symbol of Jewish unity.

Isaacs declared that every Jew, 'conscious of his origin, of his history and of
the Faith as revealed by Scripture', was as competent to form an opinion as any
ordained minister.

Palestine is not in any essential sense the background of the Torah. Scripture tells us that the Mosaic revelation was delivered before the death of the great Leader, and therefore before Palestine was reached. Sinai is the true background of the Torah. Even the most trusted Talmud is called the Babylonian. The living picture, the Torah itself is the eternal bond, the 'background' is only of secondary importance. The Torah, like the Shechinah, knows no earthly limitation. (23 March 1944)

Palestine was the promised refuge from Egyptian bondage. But Palestine is not, Isaacs continued, the matrix of the Jewish spirit: 'Judaism, of which the core is our Religion, is its matrix.' The matrix is the Torah, which is 'written in the hearts of the Jewish people and is independent of Palestine or any locality' (23 March 1944).

In such writing Isaacs was opposing the Zionist attack on the Diaspora, that it must be secondary to the desired Jewish homeland in Palestine (11 November 1943), and that Jews outside of Palestine are mere 'sojourners' leading an 'abnormal life' (13 January 1944). He also expressed doubts about the new Jewish life in Palestine that was supposed to displace diasporic Jewish life, admirable as the Pioneers' work of transformation was. Isaacs noted that the new Jewish culture apparently blooming in Palestine, which is supposed to be Hebrew in both content and form, in literature, drama, music, painting and sculpture, is 'accompanied by a narrow nationalistic hardness, where the cultural Hebraists seek to destroy the cultural Yiddishists' (24 February 1944).

Against the Zionist insistence that Jewish identity was tied to political and military possession of a particular land, Isaacs evoked Judaism as, in the beautiful phrasing of Harry Berger Jnr, an ark of interpretation the circumference of which is nowhere. Isaacs's insistence on the right of every Jew to make her or his own interpretations, his open disagreement with the rabbi, his exploratory evocative 'poetic' writing and his view that 'Sinai is the true background of the Torah' also recall Derrida's essay on Edmond Jabès. Here Derrida contrasts the stultifying official thought of rabbis pursuing a final truth with a certain Judaic and poetic activity of seeking the restless play of interpretation and reinterpretation. Commenting on Jabès' *Livre des questions* (1963), Derrida writes in diasporic spirit of Jewish tradition as a Site that is not a site: 'The site is not the empirical and national Here of a territory. It is immemorial, and thus also a future. Better: it is tradition as adventure.' The site, the Land, 'always keeps itself beyond any proximity', for it lies in 'the Desert of the Promise'.[21]

Isaacs was an avowed positivist in intellectual method, believing in 'facts' and 'proofs' (20 January 1944). Yet towards the end of the controversy his writing on Jewish tradition became increasingly adventurous, metaphoric and lyrical.

Conclusions

Sir Isaac Isaacs was indeed an anglophile; as just one example, he admires *The Hebrew Standard* for its adherence to the 'best traditions of British journalism ... open to every side of opinion' (16 December 1943). He was pro-imperial, and in particular an admirer of Winston Churchill. Isaacs notes that one thing 'of which we can be sure is, Mr Churchill and his colleagues can be fully trusted to do at the right time what is just to all' (6 January 1944). Of Churchill he wrote that he was one of the 'bravest, noblest and most honourable men in the annals of our Empire's history' (20 January 1944).

Isaacs never questioned the imperial and settler-colonial presumption embodied in the Balfour Declaration that British politicians in London had the right to determine the demographic character of Palestine. He did not oppose Jewish immigration to Palestine under the supervision of the British Administration, whose provision of law and order enabled, he said, the 'Jewish Colonists' and 'Pioneers' to make 'wonderful progress' and do 'splendid work'; he joined 'unreservedly in the admiration that is due to them' (4 November 1943).

In terms of population, Isaacs argued that 'Jewish immigration should not be at such a rate as to SWAMP the Arabs'. He seemed to envisage an ideal state where Arabs and Jews, through immigration and as refugees, would become equal in numbers, so that neither would be in a minority: 'neither Jews nor Arabs should be condemned to that state' (23 December 1943).

Certainly, then, Isaacs was an admirer of the British Empire, its necessity and usually wise administration, its apparent unity and coherence, and its economic resources. He considered that Zionist pressures, in creating a 'Moslem disaffection throughout the Islamic world', enjoined the 'danger of disrupting our Empire' (9 December 1943). Isaacs feared that Palestine would become lost to the Empire and its strategic interests: 'Palestine was, as it is now, an essential link in the chain of Empire communications' (4 November 1943). Muslim societies in the region, Egypt with its Suez Canal, Saudi Arabia the country of Mecca, and Iraq with its indispensable oil wells, would be perturbed by the fear that their fellow Muslims might be overwhelmed by Jewish immigration; the possible consequences could severely threaten Britain's war effort (18 November 1943).

Perhaps we can perversely defend empires in some respects.

Isaacs certainly saw the Empire as valuable in imperial terms for Britain. Yet he more than once pointed out that the Muslim world that objected to Arabs being dominated in Palestine by a possible Jewish state included 'some 90,000,000 of our Indian fellow subjects' (23 July 1942), whose representatives had met to express their opposition to the Zionist project of statehood and to control of immigration and population being in Jewish hands (9 September). For Isaacs, the British Empire was an inclusive supranational, multiracial and multi-religious entity.

At one point in the controversy with Julius Stone, Isaacs drew attention to a statement by an American Zionist that a Jewish state in Palestine should be independent of all other nations, including being independent of the British Commonwealth (18 November 1943). In Isaacs's view, membership of the British Empire or Commonwealth was valuable because a larger collectivity offered the mixing of diverse peoples, so that the Muslims of India were part of the same entity, fellow subjects along with Australians and every other nationality and ethnicity. In these terms, Isaacs's thinking about the value of empires recalls the pluralistic character of previous great empires, like the Hellenistic Roman or the Arab or the Ottoman, where different communities retained rights to autonomous religious and cultural life, at the same time as mixing in multiple multifarious ways in daily life.[22] In a similar spirit, Isaacs's call that Palestine become a plural state composed of Muslims, Christians and Jews recalls the *convivencia* of medieval Moorish Spain, and indeed of the medieval Judeo–Islamic trading, social and cultural world that extended from Moorish Spain to India: I'm thinking here of S. D. Goitein's great history, based on the Cairo Geniza records, referred to in earlier chapters. Recall, too, the argument of Ammiel Alcalay's *After Jews and Arabs* that Zionist nationalism, brought to Palestine by European Ashkenazi Jews, represents a massive assault on Levantine history, its mixing, plurality, mobility; its poetics of heterogeneity. In Isaacs's emphatic terms, the 'central VICE of Political Zionism is in making the land of Palestine wholly "JEWISH" ' (10 February 1944).

Reading the files of the controversy, I was struck by Isaacs's worldliness and cosmopolitanism, as in his intimate and extensive knowledge of British Parliamentary debates and newspapers like the London *Observer*, *The New Statesman and Nation*, *The Economist* and *The New York Times* (21 October 1943).

What of Isaacs's predictions and prophecies? Isaacs suggested that the Zionist demand for a Jewish state would cause difficulties for Jews in other parts of the Arab world (7 October 1943). Such prophecy came true all too quickly after the establishment of Israel, leading to the destruction of ancient Jewish communities in North Africa and the Middle East, the destruction of a Levantine world that is lamented and mourned in the writings of Ella Shohat and Ammiel Alcalay.[23]

Isaacs felt that the Zionist goal of a Jewish state was 'impossible of attainment' (11 November 1943). From the perspective of 1948–49, such a view looks foolish. But from the perspective of the new millennium, such a view, broadly defined, is prescient. Since the 1970s, Israel has steadily lost support in the world community; it has been increasingly perceived as a conqueror not a victim, as a nation that militarily dominates its region (often ruthlessly), as a colonizer dispossessing the Palestinians in the occupied territories, as identifiable in television and newspaper reports as a Goliath with gun and bullets, not a David with stones, as harsh in its occupier's practices of deprivation of rights, confiscation of property, collective punishments, administrative detention, beatings and even state-justified use of torture.[24]

Israel is now increasingly isolated amongst the nations, its friends and allies, albeit extremely powerful, as with the United States, few. It is interesting in this regard that Isaacs suggested that if Political Zionism succeeded, a Jewish state would become a vast ghetto hemmed in on three sides by unrelenting enemies, Muslim Egypt, Trans-Jordan, Iraq and Syria. Isaacs referred to this geographic isolation as a 'dreadful possibility' (17 February 1944).

When he launched himself into the controversy Isaacs clearly felt that Zionism would fail to attract widespread support: 'I do not doubt that Australian Jewry will never accept it' (25 November 1943). He also felt that the wartime Labor Goverment in Australia (6 January 1944) and also left-liberal intellectuals (like the well-known public figure Jessie Street) would never accept the idea of a Jewish state that so prejudiced the democratic rights of Palestine's Arabs and Christians (9 September 1943; 4 November 1943).

Here, sadly, Isaacs was mistaken indeed.[25] The wartime and postwar Australian Jewish community, and the Australian polity mainstream and left-liberal, encouraged the Zionists who came to Palestine to make the Palestinian inhabitants strangers in their own land, ultimately endangering the moral reputation of Jewry in the latter part of the twentieth century and into the twenty-first.[26]

Notes

1. Cf. Jonathan Kirsch, *The Harlot by the Side of the Road* (London: Rider, 1997), pp. 126–7.
2. Hilary L. Rubinstein and W. D. Rubinstein, *The Jews in Australia: A Thematic History* (Melbourne: William Heinemann, 1991). My review appeared in *Weekend Australian* (22–23 June 1991). See also John Docker, 'Jews in Australia', *Arena*, 96 (1991), pp. 145–57.
3. Hilary L. Rubinstein, *The Jews in Australia*, vol. I, pp. 2, 4, 22, 75, 77, 81–2, 85–6, 89, 95, 112, 116, 125, 161, 163, 181–2. There was indeed a plan for mass Jewish colonization in the Kimberleys in Western Australia: see I. N. Steinberg, *Australia – The Unpromised Land* (London: Victor Gollancz, 1948); Leon Gettler, *An Unpromised Land* (Perth: Fremantle Arts Centre Press, 1993), esp. pp. 143–4.

4. See the entries by S. D. Rutland, W. D. Rubinstein and L. Glezer in James Jupp (ed.), *The Australian People: An Encyclopedia of the Nation, Its People and Their Origins* (Sydney: Angus and Robertson, 1988).

5. See also John Docker, 'Growing up a Communist-Irish-Anglophilic-Jew in Bondi', *Independent Monthly* (December 1992/January 1993).

6. Hilary L. Rubinstein, *The Jews in Australia*, vol. I, pp. 25–33, 39–45, 55.

7. W. D. Rubinstein, *The Jews in Australia*, vol. II, pp. xii, 62.

8. Leonie Star, *Julius Stone: An Intellectual Life* (Melbourne: Oxford University Press/Sydney University Press, 1992), pp. 193, 197–8; and Zelman Cowan, *Isaac Isaacs*, rev. edn (St Lucia: University of Queensland Press, 1993), p. 243. See also Suzanne D. Rutland, *Edge of the Diaspora*, 2nd rev. edn (Sydney: Brandl and Schlesinger, 1997), pp. 310–12.

9. W. D. Rubinstein, *The Jews in Australia*, pp. 11, 14, 266, 274.

10. *Ibid.*, pp. 513–14.

11. Cf. John Docker, 'Orientalism and Zionism', *Arena*, 75 (1986), pp. 58–95, and 'Blanche D'Alpuget's *Robert J. Hawke* and *Winter in Jerusalem*', *Hecate*, XIII(1) (1987), pp. 51–65.

12. Star, *Julius Stone*, p. 191.

13. Julius Stone, '*Stand Up and Be Counted!*' An Open Letter to the Rt. Hon. Sir Isaac Isaacs (Sydney: Ponsford, Newman and Benson, 1944), pp. 12–14, 17–19.

14. *Ibid.*, pp. 15–16.

15. *Ibid.*, pp. 6–7.

16. See, for example, Rutland, *Edge of the Diaspora*, pp. 298–301.

17. Stone, '*Stand Up and Be Counted!*', pp. 8–11.

18. Cf. Cowan, *Isaac Isaacs*, p. 233; Brian Lapping, *End of Empire* (London: Granada Publishing Ltd, 1985), pp. 114–16.

19. See also Isaacs, *The Age* (Melbourne) (13 November 1943).

20. Edward Said, 'Michael Walzer's *Exodus and Revolution*: a Canaanite reading' in Edward Said and Christopher Hitchens (eds), *Blaming the Victims* (London: Verso, 1988), pp. 161–78.

21. Harry Berger Jnr, 'The lie of the land: the text beyond Canaan', *Representations*, 25 (1989), p. 136; Jacques Derrida, *Writing and Difference*, trans. and intro. Alan Bass (Chicago: University of Chicago Press, 1978), ch. 3, 'Edmond Jabès and the question of the book', pp. 66–7, 74; Edmond Jabès, *The Book of Questions*, vols I and II, trans. Rosmarie Waldrop (Hanover and London: Wesleyan University Press, 1991).

22. Cf. Maxime Rodinson, *Cult, Ghetto, and State: The Persistence of the Jewish Question*, trans. Jon Rothschild (London: Al Saqi Books, 1983), ch. 3, 'From the Jewish nation to the Jewish problem', pp. 80–109.

23. Cf. Ella Shohat, 'Sephardim in Israel: Zionism from the standpoint of its Jewish victims' in Anne McClintock, Aamir Mufti and Ella Shohat (eds), *Dangerous Liaisons: Gender, Nation, and Postcolonial Perspectives* (Minneapolis: University of Minnesota Press, 1997), pp. 40–55; Ammiel Alcalay, *After Jews and Arabs: Remaking Levantine Culture* (Minneapolis: University of Minnesota Press, 1993), pp. 220–1.

24. Cf. Amnon Raz, 'National colonial theology', *Tikkun*, 14(3) (May/June 1999), pp. 11–16.

25. For a pro-Zionist interpretation of Jessie Street, see Suzanne D. Rutland, 'The

Jewish connection' in Heather Radi (ed.), *Jessie Street: Documents and Essays* (Sydney: Women's Redress Press Inc., 1990), pp. 147–53; Rutland mentions that Herbert Vere Evatt was 'Jessie's close friend and confidant' (p. 147).

26. For a rare argument supporting Isaacs' views and predictions, see the work by the late Irwin M. Herrman, *The Arab–Israeli Conflict: Sir Isaac Isaacs and Australian Politics Today* (Annual Beanland Lecture; Melbourne: Footscray Institute of Technology, 1979), pp. 1–28.

10

The disaster of 1492 in world history

[In Constantinople] in the best-stocked shops in the bazaar are seen mostly Armenians, Greeks, Italians and Jews, some of the latter having come from Andalus after the fall of Granada. There are not less than forty thousand of them and they are united in their praise for the equity of the Grand Turk. In the suqs, the turbans of the Turks and the skull caps of the Christians and Jews mingle without hatred or resentment.

Amin Maalouf, *Leo the African*[1]

A woman [in Constantinople/Istanbul] called Suna Suzer – wife of the owner of the Pera Palace Hotel – caters for the Jewish club on Prince's Island. Under the supervision of a rabbi, she cooks Jewish specialties learned from elderly Jewish ladies. For the quincentenary celebrations of the expulsion of Jews from Spain, she made a giant cake that was a model of the first Turkish ship that went to pick up the Jews from Spain when they were banished. Lately, there has been a revival of interest in Sephardi culture and food within the community. ... Many of the dishes popular in the community are the same as those of the non-Jewish population, but in the minds of its members the Spanish heritage is all-important, and indeed it is obvious. Cookbooks recently published in France on the cooking of the Jews of Turkey are entitled *Cuisine judeo-espagnole*. ... One of their strong points is a range of vegetarian egg and cheese dishes, because it was usual to have a meat meal at lunch and a dairy one in the evening. Amongst these is almodrote de berengena – roasted and mashed aubergine mixed with cheese and egg. A similar dish is mentioned in the records kept by the Court of the Inquisition in Toledo in which a woman was accused of keeping Jewish traditions because she cooked this dish to be eaten cold on Saturday....

Claudia Roden, *The Book of Jewish Food*[2]

... a Jew is never the simple creature the Christians have always wanted us to believe. And a Jewish heretic is never so single-minded as our rabbis would

claim. We are all of us deep and wide enough to welcome a river of paradoxes
and riddles into our souls.

Richard Zimler, *The Last Kabbalist of Lisbon*[3]

Western narratives about the Orient, Edward Said suggests in his introduction
to *Orientalism*, are truly numberless.[4]

Allegorical narratives in world literature about the implications of '1492' are
also becoming impressive not only in number but also in the quality of
textuality being displayed and offered.

'1492' has become the historical and mythological moment when in January
of that year Boabdil, last of the Nasrid amirs, surrendered Granada and the
Alhambra to the besieging Christian forces led by the Catholic monarchs
Ferdinand and Isabella. Boabdil left sighing over what had been the last
dazzling remnant of that remarkable society, Moorish Spain, held in
subsequent narrative and legend and desire to be open, heterogeneous,
tolerant of difference, pluralistic: multi-ethnic, multi-religious, multicultural.
From 712 to the fateful fall of Granada, Muslim and Christian and Jewish
communities lived side by side in the Iberian peninsula, clutched in a long,
intimate embrace, sharing a land, learning from one another, trading,
intermarrying, misunderstanding, squabbling, fighting: a historical scene
diverse, boisterous, crowded with life, in a pattern of peoples already
palimpsestial, the Arab and Berber Moors overlaying a society of Hispano-
Romans, Basques, Visigoths, Jews; until in the *Reconquista* the triumphal
Christians enforced a future, extending from Spain to the New World, of
sinister intolerance and xenophobia.[5]

'1492' focuses the three key events that occurred within a very short time
near its beginning: Columbus sailing for the Americas, eight centuries of
Muslim Spain ending in the surrender of Granada, and the expelling of the
Jews of Spain.

In this chapter and the following I will focus on contemporary historical
novels that invoke '1492' as a frame story, as a way of leading into some
general reflections on the significance of '1492' for world history: its
implications, consequences, aftermaths, the further diasporas and exiles it
created.

In this chapter I will discuss Amin Maalouf's *Leo the African* (1986) and
Richard Zimler's *The Last Kabbalist of Lisbon* (1998); in the next I will home in
on Salman Rushdie's *The Moor's Last Sigh* (1995).

There is desperation in this '1492' literature; edge, *attaque*, urgency,
sombreness, fatefulness, cynicism, resignation, despair, anger. The apocalyptic
moment of half a millennium ago speaks to humanity at the new millennium, as
moment of choice, between hope through openness and generosity towards

the Other and Others, the Stranger and Strangers, or the familiar reverse of that hope; a haunting choice for many cultures, many peoples, many lands.

These texts seek our attentiveness to millennial questions: Is humanity doomed to repetition of a fatal iconic moment in history? Are we in humanity's twilight? Has the owl of wisdom flown through dusk into darkness, unperceived, unheeded, unrecognized?

These texts explore the *idea* of '1492' in ways that recall the kind of aesthetic philosophy that Walter Benjamin evokes in the prologue to *The Origin of German Tragic Drama*. Benjamin writes that the artist shares with the philosopher the task of representation of ideas, where representation proceeds by digression, the absence of an uninterrupted purposeful structure. Representation as digression, as interruption, will work through the unique and the extreme. 'Just as', Benjamin writes as is his wont in enigmatic parable, 'a mother is seen to begin to live in the fullness of her power only when the circle of her children, inspired by the feeling of her proximity, closes around her, so do ideas come to life only when extremes are assembled around them.' Representation 'looks for that which is exemplary, even if this exemplary character can be admitted only in respect of the merest fragment'. Representation seeks out 'the most singular and eccentric of phenomena, in both the weakest and clumsiest of experiments and in the overripe fruits of a period of decadence'. The representation of an idea cannot be considered successful unless the whole range of possible extremes it contains has been virtually explored. Representation in the investigation of a phenomenon is not satisfied until it has absorbed all its history; and in such investigation this historical perspective can be extended, into the past or the future, without being subject to any limits of principle. [6]

Benjamin is concerned in *The Origin of German Tragic Drama* with the Baroque theatre, literature and art of the seventeenth century, which he compares to the aesthetic of modernity, especially early twentieth-century German Expressionism. Appearing to be a caricature of classical tragedy, everything about the German Baroque was offensive, even barbaric, to refined taste. Baroque theatre reveals an agonizing violence of style; it is replete with bombast and excess; it is an eccentric drama that revels in its own visuality and theatricality, in the extravagance of its technique, in exaggeration; it delights in an arbitrariness of language, in neologisms, archaisms, coinings. Its spectacles create a characteristic feeling of dizziness. [7]

To adapt Benjamin's brilliant evocation: the idea of '1492' comes to life when extremes are assembled around it, in historical perspectives stretching from past to future, in literary art that can be agonizing in its representational violence, unsettling in invoking other languages beside the European, digressive, fragmentary, extreme, singular, eccentric, in imagery and styles so extravagant they often induce vertigo, even gasps of admiration and smiles of delight for the boldness of such excess.

The Wandering Moor

A strand of Western literature, thought, folklore and fantasy has focused on the figure of the Wandering Jew, in changing ways and for benign or malign reasons. Much less has Western attention been brought to bear on the possibility and historical presence of a corresponding figure that I will discuss here as the Wandering Moor: in a lingering Orientalist image, the Muslim in modern history is conceived as frozen within an inherited Islamic culture, unable to change it, indeed not wishing and never wishing to change it, to renovate it, break out of it, go beyond it, to imagine different worlds and new ways of being and new modes of representation in art and ideas, to defy the cages and chains of history.

The Orientalist image of the Muslim caught desiccated like a moth in time and history is explored in Amin Maalouf's great novel *Leo the African* (first published in French in 1986, translated into English in 1988). Maalouf is a prize-winning Lebanese journalist and writer living in Paris since 1976, whom I'd encountered before as the author of the remarkable *The Crusades Through Arab Eyes* (1983). *Leo the African* is based on the life and adventures of an actual historical personage, Al-Hassan Ibn-Mohammed al-Wezaz Al-Fasi, a Moor born in Granada in the 1490s, later baptized in Rome as Giovanni Leone, now usually referred to as Leo Africanus, an early sixteenth-century merchant, traveller, diplomat, writer, poet, ethnographer, at times a Muslim, at times a Christian, known to posterity as author of *The History and Description of Africa*. [8]

Leo the African observes the convention of the recently discovered lost manuscript. It is supposedly the chronicle of his life that Leo writes on board the ship that in 1527 is taking him and his conversa wife Maddalena and their baby son Giuseppe away from Rome to what he hopes will be his final place of exile, in Tunis, back in the Muslim world of North Africa; though a North African Barbary coast increasingly threatened by European colonial expansion, at that time by the Spanish and Portuguese. Leo addresses the chronicle to his son when he will be old enough to read and profit from its wisdom earned through extraordinary adventures and sufferings in the early modern Mediterranean.

The novel partakes of another convention, that of *The Thousand and One Nights*, with multiple stories, multiple narrators; an interlacing, a tracery. It is in the Granadan and Andalusian exile community in the Maghreb, in Fez, that the young Leo hears the stories told by his mother Salma and father Muhammad and his maternal uncle Khali of the last days of Moorish Granada in late 1491, early 1492.

These stories, he soon appreciates, are not mere apologetics for the defeated Muslim regime. They tell of how the old sultan, some ten years before 1492, had foolishly decided to make war on the neighbouring and militarily much stronger Christian powers; Aragon and Castile were now combined because of the marriage of Ferdinand and Isabella. Granada was subsequently divided by civil war, between the old sultan and his son Boabdil; and Boabdil in these family stories does not emerge as a figure of pathos, but as weak, venal, selfish, 'born a vassal', unheroic, small-minded, petty, desperate only to save himself and eager to negotiate with the Catholic Kings Granada's final defeat.[9]

Leo Africanus's journey begins as Hasan the son of a high-born family in Granada of officials (his father the weigh-master), court scribes (his uncle), booksellers (his grandfather), men who are close to power but also detached from it and towards it; educated cultivated men like his uncle who are poets and can be asked to make ambassadorial visits on behalf of ruling sultans to other rulers (who require to be praised in verse). The first part of the novel evokes Moorish Granada's final desperate years, months, days, hours, the despairing death of a city. At a crisis meeting in the Hall of Ambassadors at the Alhambra, Boabdil's vizier tells the assembled notables that the Moors must now capitulate to superior military power: 'Let us look the truth in the face, even if it is hideous, and let us scorn untruth, even if it is decked out in jewels.' The vizier urges that Granada surrender peaceably to the Catholic Kings: 'I wish to save you from the bitter cup of humiliating defeat, from massacre, the violation of women and young girls, from dishonour, slavery, pillage and destruction.' At the meeting the lean and choleric preacher Astaghfirullah speaks, declaiming that the impending loss of Muslim Spain is God's judgement on the Muslims for their lax ways, their drinking of wine and visits to prostitutes, their reversion (especially among the women) to a pre-Islamic culture of amulets and magic and idolatry, and their reading of secular books. In the final days of the city there is a resurgence of fundamentalism, the emptying out of the taverns, and books being publicly burnt.[10]

Also at the meeting Abu Khamr the doctor speaks, plump and ironic towards the absurdities of life, and very well known in the city for his associating wine drinking with the pursuit of secular knowledge (in his learned circle they discuss topics like 'mithridate, the astrolabe and metempsychosis'). He is keenly interested in art and architecture as in the wondrous grace of the Alhambra itself, which he sees as the last reminder of the great heritage of eight centuries of Moorish presence in Europe. The doctor had 'studied medicine from the old books, from the works of Hippocrates, Galen, Averroes, Avicenna, Abu'l-Qassis, Abenzoar and Maimonides'. His scientific interests ranged from astronomy to botany, alchemy to algebra. The doctor would order rare books from Hasan's grandfather, from Cairo and Baghdad, sometimes from Barcelona, Rome, Venice. The doctor would bemoan that intellectual culture in the Muslim lands had almost ceased; he recalled the first centuries of Islam when so many treatises on philosophy, mathematics, medicine and astronomy were written, and how then the poets were numerous and innovative, in both style and content.[11]

The doctor can see no point in living once this glorious heritage finally dies with the death of Granada, even if the Golden Age of Moorish Spain – of philosophy, medicine and literature that included great Jewish scholars like Maimonides and reached back to the classical Greeks – was some centuries before, whereas now all that remained of al-Andalus was the small pocket around them.

The Granadans in general fear that the terms of the treaty guaranteeing safety for the defeated Moors will not be kept by the victorious Christians, that they will be sold into slavery like the people of Malaga, who had also surrendered. They fear that what has happened to the Jews of Spain will now happen to the Muslims: 'See how the Inquisition has raised pyres for the Jews of Seville, of Saragossa, of Valencia, of Teruel, of Toledo! Tomorrow the pyres will be raised in Granada, not just for the people of the Sabbath but for the Muslims as well!' The opening episodes of *Leo the African* establish how close are daily relationships between Muslims and Jews in the city, especially among the women facing similar problems of powerlessness in patriarchal religions. In Granada Hasan's mother Salma is often visited by Gaudy Sarah, who would come to sell amulets and bracelets, perfumes made from lemon, ambergris, jasmine and water lilies, and to tell fortunes; Sarah the pedlar-clairvoyant also doubled when necessary as midwife, masseuse, hairdresser and plucker of unwanted hair. Such close relationships persist in the Andalusian exile communities in North Africa, for Jews like Gaudy Sarah also choose exile there, as do Hasan's uncle and his mother and father.[12]

It is also stressed throughout the novel how much Islam shares with Christianity and Judaism common figures and features, since they are all Peoples of the Book. The Muslims in daily life and thoughts in Granada and North Africa invoke biblical figures like Noah and the Flood; the fires of Gehenna; Eden (its gardens compared to those of the Alhambra); Abraham and the sacred crime he was poised to commit 'in which the revealed religions meet' and that is praised 'each year in the feast of al-Adha'; 'Our Lady Eve, mother of mankind'; Isaac and Jacob and the twelve tribes and the Books given to Moses and Jesus and the prophets. In Granada the Muslims celebrate events not only in the Islamic and Persian calendars but also in the Christian, providing numerous occasions for feasting. The first day of the Christian year was a time for celebrations which children would wait for impatiently; they would 'sport masks, and would go and knock at rich people's houses, singing rounds, which would win them several handfuls of dried fruit, less as a reward than as a way of stopping the racket'.[13]

It is this plural society that will now cease to be when Boabdil surrenders to Ferdinand and Isabella. As it turns out, as evoked in the early chapters of *Leo the African*, the initial strange quiet of the surrender, with Christian troops and officials stationed in the city, is soon broken. Unpleasant incidents occur. Once important citizens (including Hasan's father) are humiliated in front of their neighbours; resistance here and there leads to killing some of the Christian occupiers, which in turn leads to a massacre of Muslims and a demand they submit to baptism or be exterminated. Some court officials quickly betray their fellow Muslims, suddenly turning converso and enthusiastically joining in with the conquering forces; the vizier himself has secretly earned vast estates through negotiating the surrender. Faced with torture if they oppose or are suspected of opposing the conquest, and denial of their identity as a religion, many Moors choose exile, taking to ships

7 September 1999: as I write these lines, the conversos of East Timor (part of the long history of Portuguese Catholic occupation of the archipelago island) are being massacred by the Indonesian military and militias. What a familiar story in history, to feel powerless while a people is slaughtered. I write this chapter with heavy heart: this terrible century remains terrible even to its very end.

in desperate scenes, and becoming part of diaspora exile communities in North Africa which are often only uneasily accepted and frequently suspected of possible treachery.

The Muslims in Granada who had been forcibly converted refused to repudiate their religion, continuing it in secret. In the Andalusian exile communities in North Africa, wise men discussed the anguished dispatches they were receiving from the newly baptized in Granada requesting advice. The sages agreed that in this desperate situation affecting hundreds of thousands of their fellow Muslims great daring of interpretation was necessary. One of these sages, the mufti of Oran, advised his Muslim fellows in Granada to teach the principles of Islam to their sons, but not before puberty, not before they are old enough to keep a secret; prudently, to escape notice and persecution, they will have to show themselves prepared to drink wine and to eat pork and even publicly insult the Prophet. The mufti said that their secret co-religionists in Catholic Granada will now be sadly known as *Ghuraba*, Strangers, yet blessed are the outsiders, for isn't that how Islam began?[14]

From Fez, Hasan when 17 accompanies his uncle on a caravan journey into

sub-Saharan Africa, trading and bringing diplomatic greetings to various local
rulers. During this journey an African ruler gives to Hasan a precious gift,
Hiba, a young slave girl from the Numidian desert, with whom he falls deeply
in love and treasures her memory to the end of his days. As a young man he
becomes involved in various misadventures not of his own making, and is
exiled by the sultan of Fez to Cairo, wherein he meets the Circassian princess
Nur, consumed by her desire to establish her baby son on the Ottoman throne.
In Cairo he sees with his own eyes the gruesome death of the Mameluke
dynasty, massacred by the Ottomans as the Grand Turk establishes a new and
powerful empire around the eastern Mediterranean and across North Africa.
He journeys to Mecca to feel the anthropomorphic presence of God. On board
a ship on the way back to the Maghreb he is kidnapped by an Italian corsair
and taken in chains to the palace in Rome of Pope Leo X, part of the Medici
family accused, especially by the rising force of Lutherans in Germany, of
luxury and corruption; Lutherans who are in league with the Catholic Spanish.
The Medicis wish to train an educated Moor like Hasan — they baptize him
John Leo — in order for him one day to become an ambassador for them to the
Ottoman court. Hasan is now Leo Africanus. It is in Renaissance Italy that he
writes in Latin his *Description of Africa* and witnesses what he perceives as the
Lutheran and Spanish sacking of the Eternal City. [15]

Leo Africanus's life spans turbulent times; so turbulent that he concludes
that life is ruled by a fate and destiny that is unpredictable, where fortune may
smile and bring joy, prosperity, passion, love, which are always threatened by
destruction, ruin and desolation. Such is the life of the exiled individual and
exile community: victim of disaster, eager for adventure, resigned to further
disaster and further exile.

Leo does not, however, believe that the individual is totally determined by
fate or that the individual is passive before fate. Part of the wisdom he acquires
in contemplating his life is his view that the individual, in being ignorant or
arrogant or impetuous or misreading people and events or accepting
appearances and illusions or lacking humility in desiring riches and power or
arranging vengeance or plunging heedlessly into love and passion, brings on
his own fate. He is fated, yet he also makes his own fate. [16]

The family stories of the death of Granada that Hasan listens to as he grows
up establish questions for him he will all his subsequent life try to answer;
establish choices he will have to make which the novel feels are important not
only for Hasan/Leo the African himself but for the future of Islam in world
history, as well as for writers and intellectuals in modernity.

A key question is: how much should a writer and intellectual serve power
when sultans and princes and every ruler he encounters are almost invariably
venal and corrupt, taxing their citizens and lands to the point of ruin, wish only

to glorify themselves, and make war ceaselessly? Hasan admires the Medici Popes and cardinals and indeed when baptized as a Christian is adopted as a Medici, yet he also recoils from them, noticing that every prince and even ruler-Popes kill and are involved in alliances that lead to wars and never-ending violence. Leo will decide that the writer and intellectual owes his being to his being a writer and intellectual; he must stay sceptical and critical of and detached towards and if possible free of power and rulers. Here Leo Africanus is created as presaging the productive scepticism of another eventual product of exile from '1492', son of Portuguese marranos, the great heretic Baruch (Benedict) Spinoza.

Another key question: should a writer and intellectual serve a particular religion? Leo can choose the way of religious purity, like the preacher Astaghfirullah (who also becomes an exile in Fez), or as in the kinds of religious fanaticism and intolerance he encounters in Europe, amongst Spanish Inquisitors spreading across Italy or demented Reformation Protestants like the Lutherans who loathe those who follow the Medici Popes as idolaters. Just as Spinoza decried the violence and intolerance created by religious sectarianism in Europe in the seventeenth century, Leo in Europe a century before makes his life choice: he decries religious fanaticism, whatever its source. Even Clement VII, one of the worldly cosmopolitan Medici Popes he admires and who admires him, exclaims to Leo: 'There must be one true faith!' [17] And in drawing back from that call, Leo is suggesting that writers and intellectuals should sever themselves from the obsessive and fantastical demands of monotheism in all its forms.

The writer with a relationship to Islam has to explore the boundaries of thought just as philosophers and poets were permitted to do in the Moorish Golden Age. Leo throws out a challenge to present-day Islam to innovate, to break with post-Golden Age traditions, even if this means learning from Christian Renaissance Europe with its great artists, sculptors, poets, writers and thinkers. Leo suggests that Islam is in a long period of decline, where the radiance of culture as in the time of the caliphs has been replaced by the culture of force of the sultans. For Leo, Islam is now in 'the age of decadence'. [18]

Yet Leo himself does not find it easy to challenge some of the deepest tendencies within Islam; he is torn and divided. We see him in Renaissance Rome, where Medici patronage has attracted so many artists, at first disagreeing with Raphael of Urbino in a comparative discussion of art and culture. Raphael says: is it true that in the world of Islam there are neither painters nor sculptors? Leo replies that there is indeed painting and sculpting, but 'all figurative representation is condemned' as it is 'considered as a challenge to the Creator'. In another discussion in Rome Leo recognizes a similarity between Protestantism, as with Luther, and Islam in a repudiation of statues in places of worship, a common condemnation of Roman Catholicism as idolatrous that he can sympathize with. He is shocked by Michelangelo's ceiling in the Sistine Chapel, and at first agrees with a zealous new Pope, Adrian VI, that such blasphemous figures should be whitewashed. It is not long, however, before Leo is appalled at the bigotry and hatred, the desire to persecute and destroy, that both Adrian VI and his allies the Lutherans display. The repressive Adrian, says Leo, in a few weeks had made a 'complete Medici' out of him, for Adrian fulminates against art, that of the Ancients as well as of contemporaries, and proclaims against feasting, pleasure, and the expenditure that goes with patronage of art. Renaissance Rome becomes a dead city; its artists and writers flee to still hospitable cities like Florence.[19]

The implication – I think – is that Leo will now revise his suspicion of figurative art, including its presence in sacred places; for to continue to support its repudiation is to align oneself in history with those who place limits on mind and creativity. He now accepts, indeed now possibly delights in, the Italian Renaissance.

Leo by his life's journey's end will tell his son that Islam has to draw on other cultures, learn from other civilizations, and that his own wisdom 'flourished in Rome'. In connecting the lost glory of Islam and Moorish Spain's Golden Age with the Renaissance of the Medicis, Leo suggests to his son that Muslims, Christians and Jews can participate in a common culture, a culture secular, freethinking, innovative, experimental, unpredictable; can be open to the daring of figurative painting, the nude, and Renaissance-type sculpture.[20]

In various mentions *Leo the African* records how Islam as a monotheism has tried to erase the pre-Islam figurative art that used abundantly to exist in the territories it conquered, though sometimes this art continues to live in popular religious practices. In Granada before its fall the preacher Astaghfirullah had railed against household practices of the Muslims in keeping marble statues and ivory figurines that reproduce in his reproving eyes 'the male and female and animal form in a sacrilegious fashion'.[21] Well might we think here of the injunctions in the Hebrew Bible against the pagan religious and aesthetic practices of the Canaanites with their worship of gods and goddesses like Baal and Astarte.

Leo by his life's journey's end will, again like Spinoza, dissociate himself from membership of any specific religion, declaring to his son the desirability of a freedom, an adventurousness, of identity:

I, Hasan the son of Muhammad the weigh-master, I, Jean-Leon de Medici, circumcised at the hand of a barber and baptized at the hand of a pope, I am now called Leo the African, but I am not from Africa, nor from Europe, nor from Arabia. I am also called the Granadan, the Fassi, the

Zayyati, but I come from no country, from no city, no tribe. I am the son of the road, my country is the caravan, my life the most unexpected of voyages. ... From my mouth you will hear Arabic, Turkish, Castilian, Berber, Hebrew, Latin and vulgar Latin, because all tongues and all prayers belong to me. But I belong to none of them.[22]

Leo at one point breaks off his narrative to address Giuseppe his son directly, urging him to embrace a Granadan-style openness to all experiences, even the erring, even following love and passion to the point of tyranny. He hopes his son will risk becoming 'lost' in his turn: will always refuse certainty. And he tells his son not to forget that in the drama of history disaster and absurdity mix, as in the freethinking doctor in Granada acquiring a cannon (he felt the Muslims were falling behind in military technology) for the defence of the city which no one, least of all the doctor, knew how to operate.[23]

He rejoices in Giuseppe being born of mixed ancestry, Moor and Jew and Christian. In Rome in 1520–21 Leo meets and marries the young and spirited Maddalena, who says to Leo when they first meet 'Is it true that you are from Granada, like me, and that you are also a convert, like me?' Maddalena tells Leo her story. She starts out in life as Judith, from a poor Jewish family which after the edict of expulsion in Spain in 1492 emigrated to Tetouan. Her parents decide to leave North Africa and set themselves up in Ferrara, where they have cousins. Plague, however, breaks out on the ship, which manages to land at Pisa. Only 8, Judith has now been made an orphan. She is taken into a convent by its head, an old nun. Baptized, she is called Maddalena and for some seven years becomes a fervent Christian. But the old nun dies and is replaced by a tyrant, a natural daughter of a Spanish grandee, who singles out Maddalena for humiliation because she is a New Christian. Under such battery of humiliation, Maddalena finds herself returning in her heart to her inherited Judaism, finding the pork she has to eat nauseating: in effect, she becomes like the converted Moors and Jews of sixteenth-century Portugal, the Moriscos and marranos. When one of the Medici cardinals happens to visit the convent, Maddalena pleads with him to be allowed to leave, and he takes her to Rome in order to marry her to their captive Moor, now a friend and confidante. Maddalena and Leo, entranced by a historical kinship, conversa and converso, fall immediately in love.[24]

Giuseppe the son of Maddalena and Leo is, then, born into multiple identities. Leo on the last page of his chronicle gives advice to Giuseppe that could have come from Spinoza's life and work: 'Wherever you are, some will want to ask questions about your skin or your prayers. Beware of gratifying their instincts, my son, beware of bending before the multitude! Muslim, Jew or Christian, they must take you as you are, or lose you. ... Never hesitate to go far away, beyond all seas, all frontiers, all countries, all beliefs.'[25]

In *Leo the African*'s assembled narratives, there is a common enemy of cultural syncretism and plural identities, of intellectual innovation and political tolerance. The novel envisages, hopes despairingly for, a Mediterranean culture where Muslims, Jews and Christians freely relate and converse. But such hopes are continuously threatened or destroyed by Catholic Inquisitional Spain and its representatives and allies. In formerly plural Spain the *Reconquista* imposed a militant demand for an homogeneous society, and now the Spanish attempt to make such homogeneity universal in an empire stretching from Naples to the New World. Wherever they are in Europe the Spanish are violent towards former Moors and Jews. It is the Spanish head of the convent who detests Maddalena as a *conversa* of impure blood; when Maddalena tries on one occasion to escape, she is caught, thrown into a dungeon and whipped until the blood comes. The Inquisitional Spanish dream of making Rome submit to their will. Adrian VI, the Pope who attempts to repress the Renaissance Medicis (including Leo, whom he jails) had been an inquisitor in Aragon and Navarre before his arrival in Rome, and he would like to launch a new crusade against the Muslims. It is Spanish monks who most violently persecute those in Rome who try to practise a Renaissance freedom of mind.[26]

When Leo, Maddalena and Giuseppe manage to escape and take ship to Tunis, Renaissance Rome is under attack and dying from what Leo refers to as the combined forces of the Spanish and their allies in fanaticism the Protestant Lutherans. Leo reports the raping and then strangling of nuns on the altars of churches, the sacking of monasteries, burning of library manuscripts, frenzied looting, and the massacre of some 8000 Roman citizens. 'I have never', says the veteran viewer of carnage and cruelty, 'encountered such bestiality, such hatred, such bloody destruction, such pleasure in massacre, destruction and sacrilege!'[27]

As Leo and his family sail towards an uncertain future in North Africa, they leave behind a Europe plunged into darkness by the heirs of those who prosecuted the disaster of '1492'.

Leo the African is a remarkably rich novel. There are many things in it I haven't had time to explore, as in its observations of a popular female culture shared by Moorish and Jewish women, or its fragments on slavery and slaves in the lands of Islam. It does not glorify the position of Jews in the early modern Muslim world, mentioning daily prejudice and occasional massacres. It suggests the value of journeying in travel and adventure, in mind and spirit, but also stresses the eternal value of love in quiet places of refuge, of meditation in stillness and in humble surrounds, or enjoyment of a particular city like Cairo, which Leo feels quickly welcomes the stranger and foreigner.[28]

As in Benjamin's evocation of Baroque excess, its style is frequently one of grandiloquence, breaking into extraordinary aphorisms and declarations from the mouths of various characters:

'An exhilarating rumour, a vessel which sails through storm after storm, and which is sometimes wrecked, is that not what a city is?'[29]

'... my eyes have seen cities die and empires perish.'[30]

'I never ask from God that He should preserve me from calamities; only that He should keep me from despair.'[31]

'... all religions have produced both saints and murderers, with an equally good conscience.'[32]

'In the face of adversity, women bend and men break.'[33]

In *Leo the African* we see Leo living through times of transition. The Ottomans are forging a powerful wide-flung empire around the Mediterranean, where they contest the power of the new maritime European empires of Spain and Portugal. *Leo the African* records – here reminding us of Amitav Ghosh's *In an Antique Land* – how, while Leo was in Cairo in 1513–14, the Mameluke sultan had received a Hindu emissary, who was 'particularly concerned about the sudden interruption of trade between the Indies and the Mameluke Empire brought about by the Portuguese invasion'. The Portuguese, attacking even in the Red Sea, landing troops on the coast of Yemen, were destroying the trade routes between the Islamic Mediterranean and India, hemming the Muslim Middle East in, constricting it.[34]

The disaster of East Timor, September 1999

14 September 1999: in the last week the Indonesian military and militias, enraged at a UN plebiscite which showed overwhelming support for independence from Indonesia, have attempted to reduce the ex-Portuguese colony of East Timor, with its largely Catholic population, to scorched earth. In planned manoeuvres, international observers of various kinds and UN personnel were forced from the province by violence or threat of violence. The Indonesian military and militias wished to have no witnesses. The capital Dili has been sacked and burns. Catholic churches and aid organizations have been attacked, nuns and priests and church workers have been executed. UN compounds sheltering refugees have been fired on with automatic weapons. Those who could amongst the East Timorese have fled to the hills (an estimated 300,000 people), where they face starvation and outbreak of fever. Those who could not flee have been subject to mass deportation to concentration camps in Indonesian West Timor, and massacre throughout towns and villages in East Timor. There are reports of refugees being herded onto boats and those boats returning from the sea empty; there are reports of piles of bodies being burnt on the streets of Dili *(Sydney Morning Herald*, 14 September 1999).

The disaster of Portugal: late 1490s, early 1500s

In July of 1999 as I was gathering further material and writing more for and doing what I thought were the final revisions on this chapter, Ann Curthoys and I took time out from university life in Canberra for a visit to Sydney to attend a media history conference. We naturally visited our favourite bookshop, Gleebooks. As I wandered aimlessly about (perversely, when writing I don't like reading), Ann came up to me and said: 'Have you seen this book? It might be relevant for what you're doing.' I looked at it with slight wonder and raised eyebrows: a paperback novel called *The Last Kabbalist of Lisbon*, by Richard Zimler, with the back cover saying that it was set in 1506 in Lisbon at a time of peril for the Jews, or rather New Christians, of Portugal. On the inside cover it said the novel was published in 1998 and reprinted four times in 1999. The back cover said nothing about the author, nor did the inside cover with its mandatory publication details suggest the author's birth date. I glanced quickly at an Author's Note which said the novel was based on the discovery in Constantinople in 1990 of a previously unknown manuscript. I said to Ann, 'Yes, indeed, I think this book might be relevant.' Ann already had a pile of books to buy and I included this one with hers when we paid. Yet even from those initial glances (as I murmured to Ann in Otto's, a nearby Glebe café, soon after) I was worried by the lack of information about the author. I thought nervously of a controversial 1997 publication, *The City of Light*, which claimed to be a history based on the discovery of a previously unknown manuscript of a supposed actual traveller (Jacob D'Ancona) who journeyed, four years before Marco Polo's arrival in Xanadu in 1275, from Italy to China.[35] But, I thought reassuringly, *The Last Kabbalist of Lisbon* claims only to be a historical murder mystery and thriller novel.

Back in Canberra, because of my shameful technological incompetence (which, painfully slowly, I'm trying to remedy), Ann looked up the Amazon.com discussion of *The Last Kabbalist of Lisbon* to see if it offered knowledge of the book and its author. And indeed it did. The time of looking was Friday 30 July 1999. The author Richard Zimler was quoted as saying that he had spent three years of his life working on the novel, one year doing research in the USA and Portugal, and another two years writing it. He was very pleased by the reviews and reactions so far, and welcomed hearing comments from Amazon.com customers. Then there followed a sampling of customer comments and questions, almost all very favourable though with some doubts and questions. A reader from California liked the mix of mystery, religion and historical fiction, and said that s/he has a Brazilian friend who is descended from Portuguese Jews forced to convert who later emigrated to Brazil. A reader from Lisbon in Portugal felt that this is 'the book of my life'. Some readers (one from Australia) were puzzled by the identity and motive of the killer, but felt that this was not important, because the book was so rich in history, poetry and texture. A reader from Columbus, Ohio reported that in her or his book club there was quite a debate on whether the manuscript was truly a discovery or was this the author's liberty in a work of fiction: 'Is there any truth to the discovery of the manuscript?' A tough-sounding reader from New York, however, felt the novel considered as history to be cartoonlike, with a simple opposition between the Jews in the story as wholly good and Christians as wholly bad; this disgruntled customer was also irritated by the thriller aspect: 'As far as the mystery is concerned, I found it incomprehensible. Having finished the book, I still have only the vaguest notion of who the killer is and no idea at all of the motive.' These are all interesting comments.

The puzzlement about the identity and motives of the killer surprised me, however, for on reading *The Last Kabbalist of Lisbon* with pleasure and admiration for its art I felt identity and motive were very clear. Though of course I'm not going to reveal who I think the killer is!

On beginning my reading I immediately liked the Author's Note, which is what we might call Postmodern Playful, announcing the kind of tradition the novel is reprising. It is clear at least to this reader that it offers itself as part of the mystery tradition that is prominent in nineteenth-century texts like Henry James's *The Turn of the Screw*, Bram Stoker's *Dracula*, Wilkie Collins's *The Woman in White*, Charles Maturin's *Melmoth the Wanderer*.[36] In such texts the author makes it clear that he is merely a kind of Arranger of recently discovered manuscripts and testimonies by other people which he urgently wishes to bring to the attention of the reading public.

In postmodern fashion, in *The Last Kabbalist of Lisbon* a popular genre is unexpectedly crossed with evocation of tragic historical events and religious and theological motifs of great intensity.

In the Historical Note and the Author's Note, the author explains as much. He tells us that in 1990 he'd gone to Constantinople to do some research on Sephardic poetry, knowing that many Sephardim had, from 1492 onwards, gone to the Ottoman capital. The house he stays in, once owned by a Sephardic Jew, is being renovated, and the author comes upon a lucky discovery, long hidden from view, a set of leather-bound handwritten manuscripts. The manuscripts turn out to be written by a Berekiah Zarco, during the period 1507 to 1530. Six of the manuscripts concern various aspects of the Kabbalah. Three of the manuscripts, however, focus on the fate of the Jews who fled Spain in the 1490s hoping for refuge in Portugal. These manuscripts relate that in 1497 the Jews of Portugal (those fleeing from Spain, those already there like Berekiah's family) are forcibly baptized as New Christians, and given some twenty years by the Portuguese king to forgo their Jewish ways and become true Catholics. Their presence in Portugal, however, meets with massive hostility from those who consider themselves superior as Old Christians. In April 1506, during a time of drought and fear of plague, Dominican friars in Lisbon inspire and lead a massacre during which some 2000 New Christians, screamed at and derided as marranos and Jews, die, often gruesomely dismembered, with women raped. Many are burnt in the square that still centres the Portuguese capital. [37]

The author realizes that these three manuscripts not only evoke the massacre but also concern Berekiah Zarco's search in those desperate days for the killer of his beloved uncle Abraham, who has been his master in Kabbalistic knowledge, teaching his young nephew its major texts (the Bahir and the Zohar), wisdom practical and spiritual, numbers mystical, concepts primary, and various necessary recitations and chants. Our author decides to reshape for a contemporary readership the three old manuscripts into a modern mystery novel, to use late twentieth-century colloquial language, and to exclude the abundant presence of extended prayer recitations and chants as well as arcane disgressions on finer points of Kabbalistic belief. The author also points out that these manuscripts written by Berekiah − in his daily life in the Jewish quarter of Lisbon not only an apprentice Kabbalist but also a manuscript illuminator and fruit seller − differ from the Spanish picaresque novel in that Berekiah's tone as narrator is hardly ever ironic and never slapstick.[38]

In my view, *The Last Kabbalist of Lisbon* explores many things pertinent to this my book. The novel explores the fatal impact of the development in early modern Europe of exclusive conceptions of ethnicity and culture. The novel questions Zionist assumptions that are Eurocentric and contemptuous of Arab and Islamic traditions; indeed, it challenges what the Israeli philosopher Igor Primoratz has critically referred to as the deep suspicion of and hostility to Islam and Muslims in general that characterize both Israel's political establishment and large sections of Israeli society.[39] The novel is also a kind of *Bildungsroman*, a story of moral formation and developing sensibility, creating the moment of the historical rise of marrano consciousness in Berekiah Zarco's thoughts and passions, with the author in his opening Note himself drawing attention to similarities between Zarco and 'another Jew of Portuguese extraction a century later, Baruch Spinoza'.

In the novel Berekiah Zarco is a recognizable detective figure, possessed by the search for Uncle Abraham's murderer, using his drawing abilities to make photo-like illustrations to show to people, engaging in confrontations with suspects, risking love and family by his relentless pursuit of justice and revenge. As in detective fiction, events occur in a rush. Berekiah, known in his family and to friends as Beri, follows clues (good or misleading or false), makes guesses, has hunches, interviews people, his appearance becoming wilder and wilder, his manner obsessed. As he explores the crime, the young Berekiah journeys within himself, discovering and shaping his sensibility into a new kind of Jew, a Jew prominent in modernity, secular, sceptical, doubting, heretical.

In *Leo the African* Leo from Granada marries Maddalena, also from Granada, a converso and conversa of Muslim and Jewish descent.

In *The Last Kabbalist of Lisbon* there is similar friendship, indeed love, between Moor and Jew. From childhood in Lisbon, Beri has grown up with Farid, son of Samir, a neighbouring Muslim family; or rather, Morisco family, for the Muslims too in Portugal have had to keep their mosques and sacred texts underground and secret, and in the riots of 1506 the homes of the Moriscos are also looted and many Moriscos die, including Farid's beloved father Samir. Young Farid is deaf and mute from birth, but growing up together he and Beri share a complex eloquent sign language that only they can understand: 'we were born just two days apart and grew up holding hands'; 'he and I were twins gifted to different parents'. Farid, of green eyes and soft olive skin, composes poetry very much admired by Beri. Beri also admires Farid's breathtaking beauty. Farid has hypersensitive capacities to see and smell, qualities which make him a key player in the novel's dramas. For a period during the riots Farid is ill, and Beri looks after him tenderly, realizing his love for his boyhood friend, and capably deploying expert medical knowledge that is part of his Sephardi inheritance. Farid recovers, and becomes with Beri his co-detective, often perceiving, sensing, sniffing clues that Beri can't. They face danger and peril together. Farid looks after Beri and saves his life from an assassin. Their trust in each other is absolute. In interviews with Jewish suspects in the crime – for Beri believes his uncle was murdered by a fellow Kabbalist in their secret cellar, with its geniza storehouse of sacred documents – Beri insists that anything can be said in front of his friend Farid. At the end of the novel, Farid travels into exile in Constantinople, as do Beri and his family a little later, taking up a house in the Jewish quarter that Uncle Abraham had already put a down payment on. Farid, become a successful poet, with his male lover and Beri with his new wife live near each other. Beri knows some Arabic and can recite suras from the Koran. In Constantinople the two families of Farid and Beri eat together every night. [40]

At novel's end, Beri decides to return to Portugal and warn the Jews of Europe to leave that accursed continent.[41] Yet, *contra* Zionism, Beri does not suggest that Jews should return to a lost Palestine as a separate and ethnically pure Jewish-only nation.

Beri frequently declares his hatred for Christian Europe, not surprising given his detailing of the anti-semitic frenzy of the riot against the New Christians, who are proclaimed by the demented Dominican friars to be heretics, devils, vampires of Christian children, only half-human. During the riots the New Christians are accused of summoning the drought with witchcraft, of having 'prehensile tails', and emitting a body odour similar to 'rotting whale meat'. His little brother Judah disappears never to be seen again, his aunt Esther is raped, friends and acquaintances die horrible deaths.[42]

Beri also creates an Iberian Inquisitional world of suspicion, treachery, betrayal and possible blackmail that taints every relationship and situation, even amongst the New Christian conversos themselves. Everyone is brutalized, including the New Christians, anyone might kill just to survive when faced with possible torture by the officers of the Inquisition. (Herein lies the motive for the murder of his uncle.)[43]

Beri also observes extreme brutality and cruelty directed against African slaves who work in Lisbon and Portugal.[44]

The events of the novel, the massacre and aftermath as Beri and Farid hunt and close in on the killer, occur during the rituals of Passover, commemorating the flight of the Israelites from Pharaoh and Egypt. Beri recalls that as a child he 'read about the sacred ibises who helped Moses cross an Ethiopian swamp riddled with snakes'. Beri sees his uncle Abraham (of 'warm green eyes') as a kind of Moses, with his ibis ring, and Beri too is created as a kind of Moses, signing his manuscripts 'in the form of an Egyptian ibis', symbol of Judaism's 'divine scribe'.[45]

Both uncle and nephew nonetheless oppose a central teaching of Moses and the Book of Exodus: that the Israelites should ingather in an actual Promised Land, the land of Canaan. Abraham while still alive and Beri writing his history many years later of the massacre believe that the Jews of Iberia and of Europe as a whole should leave Europe behind and seek safety in the Orient, in the Ottoman Empire, in particular Constantinople. Jews should live in diaspora, preferably in the East with its multiplicity of different communities. In diaspora Jews can observe the 'hidden core' of the Passover story, the 'story of the spiritual journey each of us can make, from slavery to sanctity'. Jews, Beri exhorts, 'always remember that the Holy Land is in you!'[46]

Beri grows into full independence of spirit and outlook after his uncle's death. Yet Beri's relationship with his Jewish community, both during the riots in Lisbon in 1506 and subsequently in Constantinople, is increasingly fraught.

He becomes an outsider, a stranger to his own, considered an eccentric and possibly a heretic: here is the comparison with that great descendant of marranos, Baruch Spinoza. We see in Beri the moment of formation, in Portugal in the beginning of the sixteenth century, of marrano consciousness and phenomenology.

For Beri, the death of his uncle is the death of a certain kind of Jewish traditional life. Abraham, he learns, was smuggling books and manuscripts out of the Christian Iberian world which was intent on destroying the literary and philosophical heritage of Moorish Spain. Beri agrees with this desire to preserve and pass on to future generations that great archive of learning sacred and secular (including works by Gabirol the eleventh-century poet, Abulafia the Kabbalistic mystic). But he also realizes that Abraham belongs to a time when the Jewish community was unified and self-governing. For Beri, with the destruction of rabbinical authority by Christian Spain and Portugal, that community was splintered and near-destroyed, and individuals now had to make their own assessments of history, judgement of events, interpretation of texts.

Given the horror of the Lisbon massacre and the death of his mentor and life's guide, Beri begins to voice to himself and others his scepticism about the existence of God: 'So much of my faith flowed away with my master's blood.' At one point as he thinks of all the New Christians he knows who have been killed, dismembered, burnt, he begins to chant a consoling prayer. 'Yet into the breathing spaces of my prayer burst the question: why has He allowed any of His self-portraits to be so desecrated?' Beri feels that he and Farid can trust only themselves in the world: 'We've been abandoned by Moses and will have to get to the other shore of the Red Sea by ourselves. We're all alone.' He is suddenly 'pervaded by the sensation that history had taken off on an errant path unforeseen by God Himself'. He is chilled by the thought that he 'no longer trusted God', indeed that there might be no beneficent God watching over us, that even at its Kabbalistic core the Torah is simply fiction, that there is no covenant, that he has dedicated his whole life to a lie. He feels that Jews are emerging into a 'new era', a world defined by history texts, not the works of God; a world where rabbis and Kabbalists could become obsolete. He realizes that he has lost faith in the coming of the Messiah: 'what if our faith in His coming is nothing but the hope of the forever shipwrecked?'[47]

'I'm not sure', he even declares to another converso, 'if I'm Jewish anymore.'[48]

Beri begins to reflect on history and faith in terms that anticipate Spinoza: 'A new landscape is forming, a secular countryside that will give us sanctuary from the burning shores of religion.' This landscape will, he feels sure, be inhabited by mystics and sceptics: 'But neither priests nor friars, nor deacons nor bishops nor Popes will find a home there', and, he adds: 'no didactic rabbis, either' with their 'scroll of commandments'. He realizes that one of the journeys he has made this Passover is that 'at long last' all the 'self-righteous rabbis the world over' have lost their power over him. The key Kabbalistic concept that Beri thinks he might retain amidst his new scepticism and secularism is *Ein Sof*, 'an unknowable God without any recognizable attributes'.[49]

In the landscape Beri envisages, women are more powerful, recalling for us perhaps the figure of Rebecca in Scott's *Ivanhoe*. Beri's wife in Constantinople, Leci of the green eyes, makes love as woman-on-top. Beri's daughter Zuli, now 18, wants to be a scribe like Aunt Esther.[50]

In the cultural mixing of Constantinople, Aunt Esther does indeed resume her profession as a scribe, work in 'Hebrew, Arabic, Persian, Castilian and Portuguese' that continues, says her nephew proudly, 'to be without equal'. Beri says that Aunt Esther and he recently completed an illuminated text 'for Sultan Suleiman the Magnificent, may God bless him each and every day'.[51]

Beri now feels that religious differences of the past, as between Jews and Muslims, should no longer matter.[52]

Europe, the New World and Zionist historiography

Leo the African and *The Last Kabbalist of Lisbon* explore in fictional form issues discussed in recent cultural history and theory like Ammiel Alcalay's *After Jews and Arabs: Remaking Levantine Culture* and essays by Ella Shohat, work which brings together into the one conversation different world histories, of Europe, the Mediterranean Orient, the New World, and the world monotheistic religions, the Islamic, the Jewish, the Christian.

Perhaps the most eloquent theoretical essay written on '1492' is Ella Shohat's 'Staging the Quincentenary: the Middle East and the Americas', part of a wave of thinking stimulated by the commemoration in 1992 of Columbus's voyage to the New World, with all its momentous consequences both for the New World and for Europe itself. Shohat observes that in 1492 the *Reconquista* of Moorish Spain by the Spanish Catholics – begun in the eleventh century with the fall of Toledo and completed in the surrender of Granada in January 1492 – coincided with the *Conquista*, the invasion of the New World. Columbus's leaving for what he thought was India in order to convert its inhabitants to Christianity occurred almost at the same moment as the final defeat in Spain of the (three million) Muslims and Spain's expulsion of (300,000) Sephardi Jews. Colombus's voyages themselves were largely financed, Shohat points out, by wealth taken from the defeated Muslims and confiscated from Jews through the Inquisition.[53]

The gradual institutionalizing of expulsions, conversions and killings of Muslims and Jews in Christian territories prepared the ground, Shohat notes, for subsequent similar *conquista* practices in the New World: in a fearful continuum the conquistadors of the Americas were the direct heirs to the *Reconquista* in Spain. Shohat points out that the Crusades, which inaugurated the idea of 'Europe' as a geopolitical entity, had already linked Muslims and Jews: the campaigns against the Muslim infidels in the Eastern Mediterranean were accompanied by anti-semitic pogroms in Europe itself (especially in Germany and France). Anti-semitism was directed against both Muslim and Jew.[54]

Shohat argues that in Spain the constant campaigns against Muslims and Jews, as well as against heretics and witches, provided a repertoire of gendered racial discourse which could immediately be applied in the Americas, in the developing Spanish and Iberian Empires. The conceptual and disciplinary apparatus that was turned against Europe's immediate or internal others, in the Crusades and the Inquisition, was projected outward against Europe's distant or external others. Just as the Muslims and Jews were demonized as drinkers of blood, cannibals, sorcerers, devils, savages, so too were the indigenous Americans and the Black Africans. The practices of the Inquisition, where Muslims and Jews were either killed, expelled, or forced to convert, were extended to the New World: the indigenous peoples were officially protected from massacre only after they had converted to Christianity. Like the Jews and Muslims in Christian Spain who remained, the indigenous peoples of the Americas had to feign allegiance to Catholicism, had to become conversos.

Shohat argues that the Eurocentric configuration of Zionist historiography obscures important linkages in the events and effects of 1492 between Spain, the Americas and the Middle East. Zionist historiography, she feels, is not interested in linking the practices of the Inquisition in Catholic Spain and the expulsion of Sephardi Jews to the genocide of the indigenous peoples of the Americas and the devastation of African peoples. Nor will such historiography relate the history of Sephardi conversos to that of other conversos, especially of the Moriscos, the Spanish Moors who converted to Christianity. Zionist historiography views the Inquisition as directed solely against the Spanish Jews. But, Shohat points out, the Inquisition, institutionalized as a tool of the state in 1478, also occupied itself in disciplining Muslims. In 1499 there were mass burnings of Islamic books and forced conversions; in 1502 the Muslims of Granada were given the choice of baptism or exile, a decision forced in 1525–26 on Muslims in other provinces. The same Inquisitional measures taken against Jewish conversos who were discovered practising Judaism in secret were taken against the Moriscos found to be secretly practising Islam. Between 1609 and 1614 there were edicts of expulsion against the Moors, and about half a million are estimated to have had to flee to North Africa.[55]

Zionist historiography, Shohat feels, attempts always to construct a singular Jewish identity and an homogeneous Jewish history. Thus the Inquisition against Spanish Jews is viewed as a mere foreshadowing of the Holocaust of largely Ashkenazi Jews. The expulsion of the Sephardi Jews is assimilated to the Wandering Jew motif, and the distinctive history and experiences of Sephardi Jews are subordinated to that of Christian–Jewish history, in particular the European-Ashkenazi *shtetl*, with its relentless persecution presented as a universal Jewish experience. A Muslim context for Jewish history and identity is rejected or submerged. Sephardi Jews are removed from their symbiotic Judeo–Islamic history and culture, in the Middle East and North Africa as well as pre-1492 Moorish Spain, where they, along with other religious and ethnic minority communities, lived relatively comfortably. At the time of the 1492 expulsion there were, Shohat argues, flourishing Jewish communities all over the Islamic Middle East and North Africa. When the Sephardi Jews were expelled by decree of King Ferdinand and Queen Isabella, they were welcomed to the Ottoman Empire, with Sultan Beyazid II ordering his governors in 1492 to receive Jews cordially.[56] The Sephardim of Asia, Africa and the Mediterranean led for the most part stable, non-wandering lives. They moved about the Islamic world more for commercial, religious or scholarly reasons than for reasons of persecution.

The major medieval Sephardi texts in philosophy, linguistics and medicine were written in Arabic, and reflect specific Muslim influences: the Jews in Iberia formed part of a larger Judeo–Islamic culture in North Africa and the Middle East and throughout the Ottoman Empire. When they fled the Inquisition or were expelled they returned to this world, settling in Morocco, Tunisia, Egypt and the Ottoman Balkans.[57] Over 70 per cent, Shohat says, returned to the Ottoman Empire regions while the rest went to Western Europe and the Americas.

The history of the Jews of Islam remains, Shohat feels, a contradiction, still living in the experience of Sephardim in Israel, to the Zionist representation of Jews as possessing a single Jewish experience, where all Jews are defined as closer to each other than to the cultures of which they have been or are a part; a mode of representation which denies overlapping or hyphenated identities, especially that of Arab-Jews or Jewish-Arabs.

Conclusions: a disaster for world history

'1492' is a date with disaster for Europe, because it enforced a notion of the emergent modern nation-state as ideally unified in ethnicity, religion, culture and mores. Such a notion became an assumption, and frequently led to the further notion that the nation-state should be based on ethnic superiority, separateness and contempt or hatred for other nation-states.[58]

'1492' created the European and Western nation-state as a metaphysics of desire. To be truly human, truly civilized, people have to live in a strong and organized nation-state. Those peoples who don't have a strong state and unified nation are lesser in the scale of humanity and perhaps less than human. Those from within and without who threaten the ideal unity of the post-1492 nation-state are to be regarded as the foreigner, the stranger, the outsider.[59]

Such a metaphysics met with opposition within Europe from the universalist ideals of the Enlightenment. Yet the European Enlightenment betrayed those non-Europeans who tried to oppose European colonial domination and control in the name precisely of the Enlightenment ideals of human equality and inclusiveness.[60]

Such a metaphysics led to the catastrophe of nineteenth-century European racism and its culmination, Nazism and the Holocaust.

By a devastating irony so abundant in history, the very same ideals of '1492' that a nation-state be ideally unified in ethnicity, religion, culture and mores inspired the nineteenth-century European nationalism that inspired European Zionism from the 1890s onwards; a movement which set about creating in Palestine, the land of Canaan, an ethnically absolutist state accompanied by persecution and mass expulsions of the Canaanites, the Palestinians.

'1492' was a double movement in early modern and modern history: the development of a desire for a unified culture and strong nation-state, accompanied by imperial and colonial expansion. '1492' as an idea and series of events linked Europe and the rest of the world which Europe wished to subdue. '1492' offered to Europeans the idea and assumption that wherever they went in the world that part of the world was theirs by right to own, settle, inhabit, change, convert, transform, work and work over; theirs by right to enforce an ideal racial and ethnic and cultural unity, and expel and persecute those they considered strangers on a colonial land which they, the Europeans, might have only reached moments or days before from distant parts of the world. The indigenous of the world were made strangers in their own lands. Non-Europeans who might also be wishing to settle in or visit new lands were also automatically strangers.[61]

'1492' was and is an impossible project – to try to impose notions of unity in terms of ethnicity and culture on world histories, within Europe and without, histories of almost infinite difference, complexity, conflict and layering.

Notes

1. Amin Maalouf, *Leo the African*, trans. Peter Sluglett (1986; London: Abacus, 1995), p. 258.
2. Claudia Roden, *The Book of Jewish Food* (London: Viking, 1997), pp. 451–2.
3. Richard Zimler, *The Last Kabbalist of Lisbon* (1998; London: Arcadia, 1999), p. 21.
4. Edward Said, *Orientalism* (London: Routledge and Kegan Paul, 1980), pp. 14, 16, 22, 24.
5. Richard Fletcher, *Moorish Spain* (London: Phoenix, 1994), pp. 6–10, 172.
6. Walter Benjamin, *The Origin of German Tragic Drama*, trans. John Osborne (London: Verso, 1996), 'Epistemo-critical prologue', pp. 28, 32, 35, 44–7.
7. *Ibid.*, pp. 49–51, 54–6.
8. See Leo Africanus, *The History and Description of Africa*, three volumes (originally published New York: the Hakluyt Society, 1896; this edn New York: Burt Franklin, 1963?).
9. Maalouf, *Leo the African*, pp. 23–8.
10. *Ibid.*, pp. 36, 45, 47.
11. *Ibid.*, pp. 36–7.
12. *Ibid.*, pp. 6, 8, 25.
13. *Ibid.*, pp. 14, 63–4, 174, 197, 240, 245, 279–80, 336.
14. *Ibid.*, pp. 116, 123.
15. *Ibid.*, pp. 169, 296–7, 338, 353. For historical context of the times Leo Africanus lived in, see Andrew C. Hess, 'The Mediterranean and Shakespeare's geopolitical imagination' in Peter Hulme and William H. Sherman (eds), *'The Tempest' and Its Travels* (London: Reaktion Books, 2000).
16. *Leo the African*, pp. 187, 194, 196, 200, 218, 221, 349.
17. *Ibid.*, pp. 326, 330.
18. *Ibid.*, pp. 292, 298.
19. *Ibid.*, pp. 295, 305, 312.
20. *Ibid.*, pp. 1, 312.
21. *Ibid.*, pp. 33–4, 154–5, 278.
22. *Ibid.*, p. 1.
23. *Ibid.*, pp. 39, 82.
24. *Ibid.*, pp. 306–9.
25. *Ibid.*, pp. 349, 360.
26. *Ibid.*, pp. 49, 59, 290, 293, 307, 312, 316, 328.
27. *Ibid.*, p. 353. Cf. Hubert Jedin and John Dolan (eds), *History of the Church*, vol. 5: *Reformation and Counter Reformation*, trans. Anselm Biggs and Peter W. Becker (London: Burns and Oates, 1980), ch. 20, pp. 237–41, esp. p. 240: '... the old and deep-seated anti-Roman sentiment of the Germans and the new talk about the Antichrist in the Roman Babel stirred the desire of punishing rich and wicked Rome. Charles of Bourbon fell at the very start of the attack on the Eternal City on 6 May 1527, with the result that the murder and pillage on the part of the leaderless soldiery became all the more unrestrained.' The authors then piously add: 'The *Sacco di Roma* became a judgment on Renaissance Rome.' (My thanks to John Moses for the reference to Jedin and Dolan.)
28. *Leo the African*, pp. 8, 51, 164, 226, 232–3, 253, 318.
29. *Ibid.*, p. 84.

30. *Ibid.*, p. 1.
31. *Ibid.*, p. 288.
32. *Ibid.*, p. 330.
33. *Ibid.*, p. 250.
34. *Ibid.*, pp. 231, 279.
35. See David Selbourne, *The City of Light* (London: Little, Brown and Company, London, 1997). Cf. Albert E. Dien, 'Jacob of Ancona: a review of reviews', Silkroad Foundation Home Page (1997) (my thanks to Benjamin Penny for showing me this Net review).
36. Cf. John Docker, *Postmodernism and Popular Culture: A Cultural History* (Melbourne: Cambridge University Press, 1994), pp. 68–71.
37. Zimler, *The Last Kabbalist of Lisbon*, pp. 11–12. Cf. Jane S. Gerber, *The Jews of Spain: A History of the Sephardic Experience* (New York: The Free Press, 1992), pp. 142–3; Haim Beinart, 'The conversos and their fate' in Elie Kedourie (ed.), *Spain and the Jews: The Sephardi Experience, 1492 and After* (London: Thames and Hudson, 1992), pp. 92–3, 115–17.
38. *The Last Kabbalist of Lisbon*, pp. 13–14.
39. Igor Primoratz, 'Israel and the war in the Balkans', *Mediterranean Politics*, 4(1), 1999, p. 92.
40. *The Last Kabbalist of Lisbon*, pp. 27, 62, 68, 76–8, 83–6, 88, 94, 97, 108, 137–8, 147, 153, 175, 180, 184, 203, 250, 262, 301, 303–5, 308.
41. *Ibid.*, pp. 312–13.
42. *Ibid.*, pp. 86, 89, 106, 115, 190, 216.
43. *Ibid.*, pp. 264, 267, 279–80, 287, 289, 300, 312.
44. *Ibid.*, pp. 43, 109–10, 132, 150, 191, 286, 292.
45. *Ibid.*, pp. 12, 18, 23, 34, 311.
46. *Ibid.*, pp. 48, 70, 87, 253, 298.
47. *Ibid.*, pp. 81, 86, 97, 104, 127, 199, 224, 302.
48. *Ibid.*, p. 218.
49. *Ibid.*, pp. 218–19, 267.
50. *Ibid.*, pp. 305, 307–8.
51. *Ibid.*, p. 306.
52. *Ibid.*, p. 221.
53. Ella Shohat, 'Staging the Quincentenary: the Middle East and the Americas', *Third Text*, 21 (1992–93), pp. 95–105.
54. Cf. Amin Maalouf, *The Crusades Through Arab Eyes*, trans. Jon Rothschild (London: Al Saqi Books, 1984); Gerard Delanty, *Inventing Europe: Idea, Identity, Reality* (New York: St Martin's Press, 1995), pp. 28, 34–5.
55. Fletcher, *Moorish Spain*, pp. 166–9, also relates that the Moriscos were subject to continuing suspicion, persecution, suppression, forcible resettlement, and finally between 1609 and 1614 mass expulsion. They were famous for their industry and thrift and their expulsion cost the sagging economy of seventeenth-century Spain very dear. Cardinal Richelieu described the expulsion as this 'most barbarous act in the annals of mankind'. Cf. also Rana Kabbani, 'Behind him lay the great city of Cordoba', *Third Text*, 21 (1992–93), pp. 67–70.
56. For the long tradition of the Ottoman Empire as a refuge for the persecuted, see Andrew Wheatcroft, *The Ottomans* (London: Viking, 1993), pp. 73, 75.
57. Sephardi Jews, for example, formed for centuries the largest community in

Salonika, a thriving port city in the northern Aegean that was for a very long time part of the Ottoman Empire, but captured by nationalist Greece forces in 1912. The Sephardi Jews of Salonika still spoke Judeo-Spanish (or Ladino). Early in 1943, in Nazi-occupied Greece, almost the whole of Salonika's Sephardi Jewish community, some 46,000 people, approximately one-fifth of the city's population, was deported to Auschwitz. The community, once known as *Malkah Israel*, Queen of Israel, was destroyed. See Richard Clogg, *A Concise History of Greece* (Cambridge: Cambridge University Press, 1992), pp. 81, 83–4, 129–31.

58.   Cf. Peter Hulme, 'Dire straits: ten leagues beyond', paper given to conference on 'National Culture(s)', University of Casablanca Ain Chok (November 1998); *Leo the African* is highlighted in this paper.

59.   Cf. William E. Connolly, *The Ethos of Pluralization* (Minneapolis: University of Minnesota Press, 1995), pp. 147–8.

60.   Cf. Gerhard Fischer (ed.), *The Mudrooroo/Müller Project: A Theatrical Casebook* (Sydney: New South Wales University Press, 1993).

61.   Cf. John Docker and Gerhard Fischer (eds), *Race, Colour and Identity in Australia and New Zealand* (Sydney: University of New South Wales Press, 2000), pp. 10–11.

11

The disaster of 1492: Europe and India

Beyond the embowered region of the Vega you behold to the south a line of arid hills, down which a long train of mules is slowly moving. It was from the summit of one of those hills that the unfortunate Boabdil cast back his last look upon Granada and gave vent to the agony of his soul. It is the spot famous in song and story, 'The last sigh of the Moor'.

Washington Irving, *The Alhambra*, 1832[1]

... in January 1492, while Christopher Columbus watched in wonderment and contempt, the Sultan Boabdil of Granada had surrendered the keys to the fortress-palace of the Alhambra, last and greatest of all the Moors' fortifications, to the all-conquering Catholic Kings Fernando and Isabella, giving up his principality without so much as a battle. He departed into exile with his mother and retainers, bringing to a close the centuries of Moorish Spain; and reining in his horse upon the Hill of Tears he turned to look for one last time upon his loss, upon the palace and the fertile plains and all the concluded glory of al-Andalus ... at which sight the Sultan sighed, and hotly wept –

The Moor's Last Sigh, 1995[2]

His family had lived in the fortress from generation to generation ever since the time of the conquest. His name was Mateo Ximenes. '... We are the oldest family in the Alhambra, – *Christianos Viejos*, old Christians, without any taint of Moor or Jew.'

Irving, *The Alhambra*[3]

The presence of the colonizing Portuguese in the Indian Ocean from late in the fifteenth century, and the continuing influence of the events in Spain in 1492, figure prominently in the Salman Rushdie novel I will now evoke.

Rushdie's extravagant historical novel *The Moor's Last Sigh* spectacularly appeared in 1995, emerging as it were between Amin Maalouf's *Leo the African*

(1986) and Richard Zimler's *The Last Kabbalist of Lisbon* (1998), three contemporary novels of baroque excess forming a kind of '1492 lineage'. Like its kin in this lineage, *The Moor's Last Sigh* mines and transforms diverse cultural histories. I will take up the suggestion Rushdie made to an Indian newspaper that his novel draws on a 'European Muslim myth, the myth of The Moor's Last Sigh'; that it connects European, Middle Eastern, and Indian mythologies and literatures. To effect this entwining, Rushdie's novel looks to the famous framing story of that wonderful sprawling text which since the early eighteenth century has assisted interactions between Orient and Occident: *The Thousand and One Nights*, where, we recall, the Princess Shahrazad, in order to defer her imminent death by her husband the king Shahryar, nightly unfolds yet another story to entertain him. In *The Moor's Last Sigh*, the narrator and his narratives are also shadowed by death and destruction.

Like his provocative previous novel *The Satanic Verses*, *The Moor's Last Sigh* immediately created and attracted controversy, literary and political. In England the 1995 Booker Prize, which it was favoured to win, went instead to *The Ghost Road* by the English novelist Pat Barker. In India there were distribution troubles. Fundamentalist groups, reported *The Hindu* in the latter part of 1995, were mounting a campaign against the importation of the novel. *The Hindu* noted nevertheless that while India had the dubious distinction of being the first country to ban *The Satanic Verses*, *The Moor's Last Sigh* was not officially banned there, though it was being distributed with some restrictions. The novel, it appears, was selling freely in Delhi and other major cities, though Customs and Excise had issued notices to some bookshops in smaller towns directing them not to sell stock until further notice, a kind of informal ban. *The Hindu* speculated that Customs and Excise were reacting to the anger expressed by Mrs Sonia Gandhi that Rushdie had named a pet bulldog in the novel after Jawaharlal Nehru. [4]

In Bombay the novel had not been released, apparently at the instigation of the company distributing it, because of fear of a Hindu fundamentalist backlash, given its by now notorious references to Mr Bal Thackeray, chief of Shiv Sena. Mr Thackeray, who is lampooned in *The Moor's Last Sigh* as Raman Fielding, nicknamed Mainduck ('frog' in Marathi), said that he would get the book banned in his state (Maharashtra), and that he would not brook the implication in the novel that he was the instigator of riots in Bombay. [5]

The novel stands accused, in its attack on a religious personality like Mr Thackeray, of recklessly risking, even deliberately provoking, violence, for the religious sensibilities of millions of people are involved. Rushdie, in this view, considers nothing sacred. He was culpably out of touch with Indian society. [6]

Rushdie in turn replied that in his satirical portrait of Mr Thackeray he attacks the forces which are trying to undermine India's liberal, tolerant and secular traditions, that his novel is a defence of 'the Nehruvian ethos', now besieged. Rushdie also argued that in this portrayal of a fundamentalist he was satirizing other prominent nationalists in world politics like the Russian politician Zhirinovsky. As for Sonia Gandhi's reported anger, Rushdie felt this was bizarre, for the character who calls his pet dog Jawaharlal is a pro-British pro-Raj *chamcha* trying to annoy his nationalist younger brother. The novel, Rushdie pointed out, was quite clearly not on that character's side. The naming of the canine was entirely ironical, and did not in any way represent his own views: 'let's not', Rushdie said, 'get sidetracked by a dog'. *The Hindu* itself, while it felt that Rushdie's choice of name for the dog 'must offend every Indian', strongly opposed censorship of the novel as an undermining of India's liberal democratic traditions.[7]

To the charge that his novel would provoke violence Rushdie replied that he was indeed concerned by incidents of terrible murder and slaughter in India's recent history: 'One of the things that struck me', Rushdie commented, 'was that it is not like a war where the murderer is a stranger. I have tried to understand the relationship between the apparent harmony of people living together and such violence.' He also felt that Thackeray's Shiv Sena – satirized in the novel as 'Mumbai's Axis' – was not purely a religious organization, but was acting as a new and dangerous political force. The Bombay-born Rushdie insisted as well on his continuing links with India: 'I still speak Hindi and Urdu, I still read and write those languages ... my family lives there, my friends live there. Because I chose to live in England, it does not mean I've divorced myself from India.'[8]

I begin with this context, because I feel that the controversy *The Moor's Last Sigh* attracted made it appear that the novel's provenance, its urgent field of attention, lay wholly in its political reception in contemporary India. In his irritation and mystification at this reception Rushdie has drawn attention to his novel, to any novel, as *not* the expression of the author's supposed ethnicity or inherited community and religion:

> In this novel, I deliberately decided to use as central characters and the point-of-view character from a different Indian community than my own. First of all, it was a way of saying that I am also that. Just because I come from the Indian Muslim background does not mean that I can use only Indian Muslim characters.
>
> One of the great pleasures for me was to be able to use a European Muslim myth, the myth of The Moor's Last Sigh, and to use it as a way of describing the fate of a Jewish and Christian family. There was no problem because one story is relevant to the other.[9]

In his reference to 'the point-of-view character' Rushdie was wishing to stress that his novel, that any novel, possesses characters, narrators and narratives that express their own varied conflicting viewpoints, with which the novelist may not necessarily agree, indeed which he might sharply oppose. Clearly, Rushdie thinks such is obvious, but he also knows, would know more than any contemporary writer, that in the international public sphere of political and ethical debate, whatever appears offensive or objectionable in a controversial novel is usually directly attributed to the author.[10]

The Moor's Last Sigh features stories about what might be regarded as minute fragments of Indian history and unusual or extreme characters, not Hindu or Muslim but Jewish and Christian and entwined Jewish–Christian. Here, I suggest, *The Moor's Last Sigh* draws on the aesthetic philosophy outlined in Walter Benjamin's prologue to *The Origin of German Tragic Drama* and which it shares with its kin in the '1492 lineage': representation can productively work through extremes and fragments, through the most singular and eccentric of examples, in an agonizing violence of style, to the point of vertigo.[11]

To baroque intensity *The Moor's Last Sigh* adds carnivalesque parody and self-parody.

Granada–Bombay–Granada

The Moor's Last Sigh begins not in India but in Europe, in Spain, in Andalusia, near Granada, near the Alhambra. At the beginning of *The Moor's Last Sigh* we see the narrator, Moraes Zogoiby, called Moor all his short life, by family lore of mixed Christian, Moorish and Jewish ancestry, clutching the manuscript of the novel that we are about to read. In this framing story of a few pages, we learn that the Moor has just fled imprisonment from a 'mad fortress' in an Andalusian mountain village, leaving, like Luther, a message nailed to its door. In his hand he holds the story of the generations of his spice-trading family in Cochin India and then Bombay, the story as well of his mother Aurora and his love Uma, both now dead. His life, all life, feels like a 'crucifixion'. Yet, when young, he was told by the Goan painter Vasco Miranda, then a family friend, even father figure, that as the offspring of the 'daemonic Aurora', India's most famous painter, he will be a 'modern Lucifer'. It is the same Vasco Miranda who, gone mad and vengeful, will imprison the Moor in Spain.[12] In this opening frame story the Moor calls on Virgil and Dante, that he is sitting in a dark wood in what ought to be the middle passage of his life. Has the Moor's journey been through an underworld, yet finally achieving light? Is the Moor a Christ figure, a Luther, or is he Luciferian? Is he prophet or fool?

And why does he end his life and storytelling in Europe, far from the Bombay in which, amongst famous painters and zealot politicians, he was raised and lived such an eventful life?

I naïvely ask this last question because *The Moor's Last Sigh* reverses the movement of *The Satanic Verses*, which had ended with Saladin Chamcha's return from Europe to India, India as home, and more specifically Zeeny Vakil and Bombay, telos of an ideal desire, of heterogeneity and tolerance, of a 'culture of excess'.[13] There is, I think, an active relationship between the two novels, of carnivalesque and Gothic, utopia and dystopia. Not least in *The Moor's Last Sigh*, Zeeny Vakil recurs as a character, but is far less joyously involved.

In its witty fantastical language and metamorphoses, *The Moor's Last Sigh* traces a history of India as diasporic, as palimpsestial, as heterogeneity entwined with violence, a history that comes to an apocalyptic end. The Moor is the last surviving male heir of a spice dynasty. On his mother's side he is descended from the da Gama family, which had come from Portugal centuries before and had settled in Cochin as increasingly wealthy spice growers and traders, of peppercorns, cardamoms, cashews, cinnamon, ginger, pistachios, cloves, cumin, fenugreek, as well as coffee beans and tea leaf. The Catholic da Gamas become part of India's overlaying fabric of peoples, cultures and religions, and the first part of the novel is chiefly concerned with them, a story of a family often bitterly divided, a story in which women become increasingly powerful, almost Medusan, culminating in the coming of Aurora, who, in 1939, at a young age falls in love with the duty manager of the family warehouse, Abraham Zogoiby, many years older than herself, and a member of the Cochin Jewish community: Abraham, the father of the Moor, the son who will later see himself as a 'high-born cross-breed'.[14]

Abraham Zogoiby's family history, at least in terms of 'legend' and 'yarn', draws on stories of the fall of Moorish Spain and the melancholy figure of Boabdil its last Sultan. The Jews of Cochin India had come as exiles from Babylon, Persia and Palestine from well before as well as during the Christian era, as soldiers then as spice growers, their numbers augmented by Sephardim expelled from Spain in 1492. When Abraham tells his mother Flory that he is going to marry a Catholic spice heiress, she becomes enraged: it was unheard of for a Cochin Jew to marry outside the community, a major reason why, the novel notes, it was sadly dwindling in the twentieth century and why its younger members almost all finally left for Israel. The Cochin Jews had long resented the ex-Portuguese Catholics, who had supplanted them in the spice trade and destroyed their prosperity. Flory also doesn't like Moors, whom she calls 'Othello-fellows'. In the face of his mother's vehement opposition Abraham angrily recounts the story of their curious name. Why, he demands, when other Cochin Jews have names like Cohen and Castile, are we called by an Arab name, Zogoiby, which Flory herself concedes is Andalusian? As other members of the community gather around, Abraham publicly relates the shameful secret of his mother's lineage, that a female ancestor had left with Boabdil in 1492 as his lover, and had stolen away from him, pregnant, taking his crown and silver dagger. She came to India, assuming the name El-zogoiby, the name of Boabdil after his fall, Boabdil the Misfortunate. Abraham publicly declares that he is a 'bastard Jew', a product of 'miscegenation', both Moor and Jew.[15]

Thirty-six-year-old Abraham and 15-year-old Aurora try to marry, and he promises to convert to Catholicism. But the local Catholic authorities won't permit the marriage, the very rumour of which has stimulated threats of riots. Abraham evidently tells his young bride the legend of Boabdil's Indian Jewish connection, for she is fond of telling the story later when she and Abraham move to Bombay. They live on Malabar Hill overlooking the city, where she has four children including the Moor, and she becomes an illustrious artist, friend of Nehru, and famous for her championing of India as secularist, pluralist and cosmopolitan.

Aurora becomes preoccupied in a series of paintings with linking the history of Granada to the fate of India. She begins to conceive her mansion on Malabar Hill as the Alhambra. Her allegorical art blends the red fort of the Alhambra with India's own red forts, the Mughal palace-fortresses in Delhi and Agra, fusing Mughal splendour with the Spanish building's Moorish grace. Aurora tells her son the Moor that she thinks of what she has painted as 'Mooristan', or 'Palimpstine', a place 'where worlds collide, flow in and out of one another, and washofy away'. In her son's view, these paintings were polemical, even didactic, idealized and sentimental, using Arab Spain to re-imagine India as a golden age, a miraculous crowded composite of Jews, Christians, Muslims, Hindus, Parsis, Sikhs, Buddhists, Jains, mixing in fancy-dress balls with Boabdil as a masked harlequin. She was attempting, he feels, to create a romantic myth of the plural, hybrid nation. In these early paintings of the Boabdil sequence, the gloom of the future, the reconquering armies of Ferdinand and Isabella, were hardly in sight. In the late paintings of the cycle, however, that gloom came, culminating in 'apocalyptic' pictures of exile and terror. In one work, the harlequin Moor looks down 'at the tragedy, impotent, sighing, and old before his time'. Then, in her last, unfinished work, *The Moor's Last Sigh*, there is a 'stark depiction of the moment of Boabdil's expulsion from Granada', with 'horror, weakness, loss and pain' pouring like darkness from the Sultan's face, 'a face in a condition of existential torment reminiscent of Edvard Munch'. (We might also recall here Benjamin's prologue to *The Origin of German Tragic Drama*, linking the Baroque to German Expressionism.) The painting became lost after Aurora's own death, Aurora as Cassandra foretelling doom to her unheeding nation.[16]

Aurora dies falling from her cliff-top house onto the rocks below, dancing her annual dance against the gods, against the hold of religion. Later, near the end of the novel, Bombay will be destroyed in a series of bomb explosions in which Zeeny Vakil, reappearing cameo-fashion from *The Satanic Verses*, is killed. In *The Moor's Last Sigh* Zeeny Vakil bounces onto the page as 'a brilliant young art theorist and devotee of Aurora's oeuvre', who has begun a critical appreciation of her work called *Imperso-Nation and Dis/Semi/Nation: Dialogics of Eclecticism and Interrogations of Authenticity in A.Z.*, a parodying reference to the kind of postcolonial theory, especially that of Homi Bhabha, heralding a kind of utopian hybridity.[17]

Zeeny was particularly scornful of Raman Fielding's Hindu fundamentalist rhetoric, exclaiming that it narrowed and distorted Hindu culture, 'its many-headed beauty, its peace', selecting as if monotheistically only the one martial god Lord Ram for devotion and exclusive attention.[18]

The death of Zeeny Vakil is the death of Bombay as India's — and perhaps the world's — last hope of recreating the fluidity, heterogeneity and hybridity of Moorish Spain. Now, at India and the world's gates, stands the barbarism of fundamentalism, of ethnic nationalism and exclusivism: 'the tragedy of multiplicity destroyed by singularity, the defeat of Many by One'. Now might conquer figures like Raman Fielding, who was 'against unions, in favour of breaking strikes, against working women, in favour of sati, against poverty and in favour of wealth'. He was against those he referred to as immigrants to Bombay, by which he meant all non-Marathi speakers, including those who had been born there, being in favour of its 'natural residents', which included Marathi-types who had just stepped off the bus. He was for paramilitary activity in support of his political aims, lauded the Hindu preference for the eternal stability of caste, and spoke of a golden age 'before the invasions', the true Hindu nation buried beneath the layers of alien empires. When the mosque at Ayodhya, claimed to be built on the same site as the mythical home of Lord Ram, was destroyed, and four paintings of Aurora's Moor Cycle were stolen from their Bombay gallery, Raman Fielding connected the two events. Let no man mourn when such alien artefacts disappear from India's holy soil, for, he declared, there is much such invader-history that may have to be erased.[19]

The Moor becomes enraged at this insult to his mother's memory. 'So', he asks, 'we were invaders now, were we? After two thousand years, we still did not belong.'[20] Yet the Moor continues traditions of violence in Indian history by then killing Raman Fielding, his erstwhile employer.

The Moor himself escapes the catastrophic destruction of Bombay, flying away to Spain and thence to Andalusia, only to find himself imprisoned by the mad Vasco Miranda, who is attempting to recreate his own mock-vision of the Alhambra. The novel's end returns to its beginning. We see the Moor imprisoned in Miranda's Gothic house, his death postponed as long as the tale of the Zogoiby family history holds Miranda's interest: 'He had made', says the Moor, 'a Scheherazade of me.' It is only at the end of the novel that we realize that the occasional invocations to 'Dear Reader' (including 'O my omnipotent reader') are ironically addressed to the Moor's jailer. He has to make his language and narrative interesting if he hopes to live: yet he is dying anyway.[21]

The Moor

I must talk more of the Moor. He is a kind of carnival-monster figure. If Gargantua stayed too long in his mother's womb, the Moor's duration was not long enough: he emerged after only four and a half months, a 'generous erection serving somewhat to impede his passage down the birth canal'. He refers to himself as Baby Gargantua Zogoiby. He is also born with a 'deformed right hand like a club'. He ages twice as rapidly as his fellows, being sexually mature and enticing when still only 7. He becomes a giant, six foot six at 10. As in a 'werewolf movie', his feet and hair grow almost visibly. He feels like Gulliver, or, in a Hollywood image in a novel that refers frequently to Hollywood images, like the Incredible Hulk. But his life's span is only 36 years, by which time he has white hair and is old and gaunt. He feels 'ugly; malformed, wrong'. He is 'a freak of nature', 'alone in the universe'. How could he, he pleads, 'have turned out to be anything but a mess?'[22]

The Moor tells his story, as he must, from bits and pieces of information, old family yarns, reminiscences, private journals, rumours, guesses, hunches, jokes, tall stories, reported dreams. He breaks with his mother, and blames her for it, for expelling him from the family circle. Yet it is by his own choice that he has taken up with the beautiful young sculptor Uma Sarasvati, whom Aurora sees as an impostor come to destroy the Zogoiby family, which she ruthlessly does: Uma, who turns out to be a follower of Lord Ram, principal deity of the fundamentalists; Uma, who manipulates the Moor to betray his mother and everything she stands for. The Moor then goes to work for Mainduck's goon-squad as a Mumbai's Axis enforcer, brutally beating up strikers and suchlike with his Cain-like mark, his club-fist. History, Marx noted in *The Eighteenth Brumaire*, repeats itself, the first time as tragedy, the second time as farce. If the stories and legends of Boabdil at times create him as a tormented tragic figure, his descendant the Moor confesses himself to be 'this damaged young-old fool'.[23]

As the Moor says:

Tragedy was not in our natures. A tragedy was taking place all right, a national tragedy on a grand scale, but those of us who played our parts were – let me put it bluntly – clowns. Clowns! Burlesque buffoons, drafted into history's theatre on account of the lack of greater men. Once, indeed, there were giants on our stage; but at the fag-end of an age, Madam History must do with what she can get. Jawaharlal, in these latter days, was just the name of a stuffed dog.[24]

The Moor himself had helped destroy Bombay, 'the inexhaustible Bombay of excess' which he loves, the smouldering city he looks back on, in a characteristic dystopian topos, from his plane as it turns towards Spain.[25] He is, that is, a classically unreliable narrator, betraying, treacherous, and we certainly can't reproduce his observations, interpretations, judgements, as the novel's or author's own.

Millennial unease

Patterns of meaning in *The Moor's Last Sigh* are not at all that easy to divine. I've selected only a few things to nudge about, and I'm very aware that the novel's language is ever hyperbolic, parodying and self-parodying, elusive, letting no simple or unqualified meanings stand.

The novel suggests an opposition between ethnic nationalism and secular cosmopolitanism, yet also never lets that opposition settle. Raman Fielding, for example, as ethnic nationalist propagates a view of Indian history and the future as a necessary hierarchy, where Hindu religious and cultural values are to reign supreme, other religions and cultural values designated as minority and subordinate. In the new order, he says, they'll know their place: 'Mainduck's vision of a theocracy in which one particular variant of Hinduism would rule, while all India's other peoples bowed their beaten heads.' Yet Mainduck himself, the Moor observes while in his dubious employ, enjoys a plurality of tastes and values. In terms of food, Mainduck savoured 'many non-Hindu tastes'. Bombay's meat-eating Parsis, Christians and Muslims, for whom in so many other ways he had nothing but contempt, were often applauded by him for their non-vegetarian cuisine. Indeed, he 'loved meat': 'couldn't get enough of it', of lamb, mutton, keema, chicken, kababs. He cultivates a façade of philistinism, yet reveals a genuine interest in Indian high culture. When his followers expressed their contempt for the culture of Indian Islam, he was stirred to recite Urdu poetry and spoke of the moonlit splendour of the Taj.[26]

There is always a kind of bad faith in ethnic nationalism, the violent insistence on an ethnic purity it always wishes to exceed.

Yet the novel suggests doubts about the postmodern ideals of hybridity and cosmopolitanism as absolutes. For one thing, Aurora Zogoiby and her family, wealthy for generations, are hardly presented as wholly admirable. An ancestor, Francisco da Gama, had been interested in European modernist thought and aesthetics, 'the virtues of nationalism, reason, art, innovation, and ... protest'. He had invited a young French architect, M. Charles Jeanneret, who would call himself Le Corbusier, to build 'Western-style' structures in their gardens. Much later, Abraham would conduct his business high above the New Bombay in a soaring I. M. Pei tower.[27] Secularism here is associated with twentieth-century architectural modernism and its metaphysics of purity and restraint, its desire to steer clear of the past, of all customary culture and traditional ways, of any arabesques of excess.[28]

Because of Abraham's business activities Aurora maintains the family wealth in style in Bombay on the slopes of Malabar Hill. Vasco Miranda, in a drunken rage, shouts at Aurora and her friends '*You don't belong here*', that their 'secular-socialist' beliefs and vision grow from 'foreign roots', not the soil of religious India. Aurora has a house full of servants, and a man at their gate, Lambajan, yet knows, as Raman Fielding points out – getting in a good dig – almost nothing of their lives, nor of the poor who were following Fielding and Mumbai's Axis in increasing numbers. Uma points out that the Moor comes from a tiny minority, compared to the 'gigantic Hindu nation'.[29]

The novel probes the notion of cosmopolitanism as always ideal. At one point the Moor ponders his upbringing on Malabar Hill, where 'all communal ties had been deliberately disrupted; in a country where all citizens owe an instinctive dual allegiance to a place and a faith, I had been made', he feels, 'into a nowhere-and-no-community man'. He was raised, he says (in language reminiscent of Mr Leopold Paula Bloom in *Ulysses*), 'neither as Catholic nor as Jew: I was both, and nothing: a jewholic-anonymous, a cathjew nut, a stewpot, a mongrel cur. ... Yessir: a real Bombay mix.' Because his parents weren't married, he refers to himself as a bastard, a 'smelly shit'. Usually he feels 'proud' of his lack of allegiance to any community, but one day surprises himself, in conversation with his father Abraham, by declaring 'excuse me, but I find that I'm a Jew'. Abraham himself has lost any anchoring in inherited values of any kind, any residual loyalty to his Jewishness, at one stage joining in a project to finance a 'so-called Islamic bomb' for the Middle East intended to destroy Israel. The Moor rebukes his father for this venture, saying Abraham has betrayed his descent from the Cochin Jews. Abraham replies that many of 'our Cochin Jews, by the way, complain of the racism with which they are treated in your precious homeland across the sea'.[30] Israel, in this suggestion, is no ideal Palimpstine.

Cosmopolitans like Aurora are shadowed by doubles, sinister *doppelgängers*.

Vasco Miranda becomes famous as a painter for airport lounges, yet also enjoys creating scenes of the Moor's last sigh. Uma Sarasvati is so fatally beguiling because she can perform any identity. The young Adam Braganza, whom Abraham adopts as his heir and business partner, talks an international argot, a verbal pickle of references to the world of multinational capital, while destroying his new father's company and wealth. Is Uma Sarasvati the new woman of postmodern hybridity? Is Adam Braganza the new man of postmodern capitalism? What, the novel appears to be asking, is the value of cosmopolitanism if it can assist the operations of those who effortlessly manipulate identity and masking for their own destructive ends?

In *The Moor's Last Sigh* the last hope for cosmopolitanism, for the valuing of diversity and difference, would appear to lie with the former Miss India, the Parsi beauty queen Nadia Wadia, who later becomes Miss World at the beauty finals in Granada, Spain. Nadia Wadia, 'true creature' of Bombay, survives its bombing, then appears on television to appeal to her nation, that the old spirit of Bombay, as the confluence of all the waters, will revive and still thrive.[31]

But is Nadia Wadia also a clown figure? Is history, once a tragedy, again repeating itself as burlesque foolery?

Veiled Stranger: You haven't admitted your misgivings about *The Moor's Last Sigh*, that you don't think it's as good as *The Satanic Verses*, whatever 'as good' means. Remember what Benjamin says in the prologue to *The Origin of German Tragic Drama*, that a 'major work will either establish the genre or abolish it; and the perfect work will do both'.[32] I think you think *The Moor's Last Sigh* is too much within its (dystopian) genre; its structure is too purposeful, not interrupted, not digressive, enough ... I also think you think that the character of the Moor is just a little uninteresting, compared to the main characters of *The Satanic Verses*. Indeed, none of the characters are anywhere near as interesting (whatever 'interesting' means) as those of *Satanic Verses*.

Do you think there is something just faintly slightly superficial about *The Moor's Last Sigh*? Does it register enough the terribleness of history? Isn't its parody too relentless, too driving, creating the novel in one tone only?

Notes

1. Washington Irving, *The Alhambra* (London: Henry G. Bohn, 1850), p. 26. My thanks to Jill Matthews for her gift to me of a later edition of Irving's book.
2. Salman Rushdie, *The Moor's Last Sigh* (London: Jonathan Cape, 1995), pp. 79–80.
3. Irving, *The Alhambra*, p. 18.
4. *The Hindu* (2 September 1995; 14 September 1995; 2 October 1995). My thanks to Subhash Jaireth for providing me with material from *The Hindu*.

5. *Ibid.* (11 September 1995; 2 October 1995).
6. *Ibid.* (9 September 1995; 20 September 1995).
7. *Ibid.* (7 September 1995, 9 September 1995; 14 September 1995; 2 October 1995).
8. *Ibid.* (9 September 1995; 20 September 1995).
9. Rushdie, quoted by Asghar Ali Engineer, 'Rushdie: last sigh?', *The Hindu* (20 September 1995).
10. Cf. in relation to another literary controversy, Andrew Riemer, *The Demidenko Affair* (Sydney: Allen and Unwin, 1996); John Docker, 'Debating ethnicity and history: from Enzensberger to Darville/Demidenko' in Gerhard Fischer (ed.), *Debating Enzensberger: 'Great Migration' and 'Civil War'* (Tübingen: Stauffenburg Verlag, 1996), pp. 213–24.
11. Walter Benjamin, *The Origin of German Tragic Drama*, trans. John Osborne (London and New York: Verso, 1996), 'Epistemo-critical prologue', pp. 28–9, 35, 44–6.
12. *The Moor's Last Sigh*, pp. 4–5.
13. Salman Rushdie, *The Satanic Verses* (London: Viking, 1988), p. 355.
14. *The Moor's Last Sigh*, pp. 4–5, 68–9.
15. *Ibid.*, pp. 70–2, 78–83, 119.
16. *Ibid.*, pp. 218, 225–7, 236, 408.
17. Cf. Homi K. Bhabha (ed.), *Nation and Narration* (London: Routledge, 1992), ch. by Bhabha, 'DissemiNation: time, narrative, and the margins of the modern nation'.
18. *The Moor's Last Sigh*, pp. 315, 351, 337–8. Cf. Jon Mee, review of *The Moor's Last Sigh*, *The Age* (Melbourne), 16 September 1995.
19. *The Moor's Last Sigh*, pp. 298–9, 364, 372, 408.
20. *Ibid.*, pp. 363–4.
21. *Ibid.*, pp. 145, 374, 421.
22. *Ibid.*, pp. 144–6, 152–4, 161–2, 188, 197, 219.
23. *Ibid.*, pp. 248, 262, 305–7, 314, 408.
24. *Ibid.*, p. 352.
25. *Ibid.*, pp. 193, 376.
26. *Ibid.*, pp. 234–5, 297–9, 332.
27. *Ibid.*, pp. 15–19, 22, 37, 65, 99, 104, 187.
28. Cf. John Docker, *Postmodernism and Popular Culture: A Cultural History* (Melbourne: Cambridge University Press, 1994), ch. 1.
29. *The Moor's Last Sigh*, pp. 60, 165–6, 230, 261–2, 294.
30. *Ibid.*, pp. 104, 336–7, 341.
31. *Ibid.*, pp. 322–12, 352.
32. Benjamin, *The Origin of German Tragic Drama*, p. 44.

12

The fictionality of identity and the phenomenology of the converso: Sally Morgan's *My Place*

'Aboriginality', therefore, is a field of intersubjectivity in that it is remade over and over again in a process of dialogue, of imagination, of representation and interpretation. Both Aboriginal and non-Aboriginal people create 'Aboriginalities'....

Marcia Langton, 'Aboriginal art and film ...'[1]

In the last quarter of the twentieth century contemporary Australian Aboriginal visual and performing artists, film-makers and musicians (as with Yothu Yindi) gained a world-wide reputation and acclaim. The cultural critic and leading Aboriginal spokesperson Marcia Langton suggests that traditional Aboriginal visual and oral expression, along with multilingualism and dance, were always more elaborate than the material culture used in everyday life. Langton argues for continuity between old and new, that in recent art and music the non-Aboriginal world is continuously incorporated into the Aboriginal worldview and cosmology. What is made available for the West to appropriate in Aboriginal painting is only exterior decorative features, not the body of hidden meaning and sacred secret knowledge that remains inaccessible behind the abstraction (secret knowledge which is in any case restricted within Aboriginal society).[2]

My Place (1987), the autobiography of Western Australian writer and artist Sally Morgan, evoking the upbringing of a young woman told by her mother and grandmother from childhood that she was Indian not Aboriginal, also has earned a world-wide reputation and remarkable sales, becoming a bestseller. Yet its scholarly reception has been rancorous, angry, passionate and bitter. Success with a national and international readership has been matched by hostility from many critics, non-Aboriginal as well as Aboriginal (including Marcia Langton).[3] As is not unusual in the history of literature, particularly in the modernist construction of popular genres as the low, other and female, its very popularity appears to have provoked immediate suspicion, patronizing disdain, cold dissection; repudiation was accompanied by lofty speculation on the motives and intentions of both the writer and her readers.[4]

I encountered the international reputation of *My Place* in mortifying circumstances in the early 1990s, while talking as a guest to a university class taking Australian Studies in Budapest. What, the students eagerly asked, did I think of *My Place*? which they'd all read and enjoyed and felt moved by. I will never forget, and always regret, the shadow of disappointment that passed over their young faces when I admitted I hadn't yet read it.[5]

I think I hadn't then read *My Place* and caught up with the surrounding acrid controversy because I hadn't seen ways of connecting the text and its reception to my own research and theoretical interests in diaspora and exile.[6]

Talking with people later about *My Place*, I at last sensed that it might indeed connect to what was obsessively interesting me.[7]

Concepts of diaspora and exile are now being productively deployed in relation to Aboriginal histories of dispossession and displacement.[8] Here I would like to explore notions of diasporic sensibility in relation to *My Place* as a literary text; I would like to draw in and spread out surprising analogies to European and Jewish cultural history. By so doing, I wish to alter the terms of the debate so far.

It's worth reprising the historiography of the debate at this distance to observe the pattern and shape it assumed. In an early shot replete with influential moves, the ethnographer and cultural theorist Eric Michaels consigned Sally Morgan and *My Place* to a certain tradition of popular textuality, especially that of television serials like *Return to Peyton Place*, *Dallas* and *Dynasty*. In Michaels's view, such serials are a variation on the *roman à clef*, because their narrative strategy, driven by genealogies of kin and exchange, constantly reproduce gossip and revelation which lure the reader/viewer into a detective-novel kind of relationship, attempting to match characters with identities in a community. Michaels urges that we avoid the trap set by this subgenre, of being drawn into treating characters as if they have documentary reality, rather than viewing them as constructed and interpreted. In another formative move, Michaels sees no point in distinguishing between Sally Morgan and her text: to talk of one is simultaneously to be talking of the other. In these terms, *My Place* is a journey of discovery that culminates in her ancestral country: 'she traces relatives there and completes the picture'; she claims the 'discovery' of an 'authentic, lineally descended Aboriginal identity'. In contrast, Michaels reminds us of the capacity of the ethnographer always to be suspicious of an informant's words as data – a capacity for and training in forensic detachment of which a popular readership is apparently incapable. Michaels will unmask *My Place* by pointing out that we should pay attention to non-documentary features like its Peyton Placeish narrative frame and its literary conventions, features which textually invent identity. Then we will see that *My Place* is constructing a modern autobiographical notion of personhood that is culturally syncretic. It is Christian and more precisely Protestant, as well as drawing on elements of theosophy and New Age astrology. In terms of Aboriginality, such individual literary invention can be contrasted to Western Desert oral traditions of storytelling that are collective and culturally constrained.[9]

In classic modernist fashion, Michaels makes a comforting distinction between an avant-garde of theorists like new-style self-reflexive anthropologists, and a credulous popular readership that innocently takes *My Place* as documentary realism; a popular readership whom he can readily psychologize. Oddly, he asserts *My Place* to be part of generic works like *Dallas* and *Dynasty*, which he says do not observe 'any classical form of plot'. Michaels is himself innocent of a large body of cultural studies work theorizing the history and aesthetic of melodrama and serial fiction as genres which aim for the reverse of realism; genres calling attention to themselves as melodrama and fantasy, as a poetics of excess.[10]

In a 1988 essay and again in his *Textual Spaces* (1992) the cultural critic Stephen Muecke took upon himself the burden of advising and admonishing on behalf of the Other. Travelling in Eric Michael's tracks, Muecke praised *My Place* in Bakhtinian terms as polyphonic, because the inclusion of the directly told stories of Arthur Corunna, Daisy Corunna and Gladys Milroy made the book into an occasion of collective narration, thus deferring to traditional textual conventions, where there is deferment of narrative authority to the correct custodians of parts of stories. Here, *My Place* is open, Muecke approvingly nods, to Aboriginal or Aboriginalizing readings. But, he feels, in too many other ways the book is over-determined by available reading strategies of a European kind: as quasi-documentary autobiography promising historical truth-effects; its detective narrative; its romance of overcoming repression of identity in self-expression and self-discovery; and in its pursuit of the grandmother to confess, while Daisy herself resists such importuning as Aboriginal people in general must resist missionaries and anthropologists and suchlike who try to secure confessional knowledge from them. Muecke recommends to writers like Morgan, and to practitioners of Aboriginal literary politics in general, that they pursue an Aboriginal discursive strategy of non-disclosure, and an observance of traditional Aboriginal genres.[11] For Muecke, writers, if they wish to be truly Aboriginal, should abide by their own traditions, of which he is a kind of non-Aboriginal guardian, a supportive scholar at the gate of authenticity, a watchful cultural guide armed with canonical criteria of indigeneity.

In another important intervention the historian Bain Attwood in 1992 acknowledged and followed Eric Michaels and Stephen Muecke in suggesting in Foucauldian fashion that Morgan's Aboriginality is really but an assemblage of effects of European discourse. Like Muecke, Attwood is drawn to the trope of over-determination: Morgan's book 'mirrors' pretty well everything that surrounds her, the bourgeois individualism of the age in general as well as institutional frameworks, epistemologies such as traditional anthropology, radical and oral history and behavioural psychology, numerous literary genres (not only detective but classic realism, quest, autobiography, family saga, Gothic novel, family history, genealogy, genesis story and Aussie-battler), and the counter-culture of the 1960s and 1970s.[12]

Amidst an agitated wave of responses, Tim Rowse pointed out that Attwood identifies *My Place* with the presumed biography and subjectivity of the author, which Attwood claims to know more intimately than she does. Attwood's magisterial rhetoric and reflectionist methodology ('mirrors' indeed!) are moved by a desire to master Morgan and her text, to explain her biography and her consciousness and unconsciousness totally, to leave her and *My Place* no mystery, no refuge, no freedom, no dignity; no place beyond the contexts he has chosen.[13] Indeed, throughout Attwood's panoptic analysis there is a faint but discernible tone of near-derision of Morgan for being a kind of second-hand European, a predictable simulation, a mere Same.

In her impassioned *testimonio* Jackie Huggins, writing as one of those who 'never ceded their identity no matter how destructive, painful or bad the situation was', substantially agreed with Attwood in doubting Sally Morgan's claim to Aboriginal heritage, values and identity beyond a genetic inheritance. *My Place*, Huggins feels, reads like the story of a middle-class Anglo woman, and its only strength lies in the family testimonies, which should have been placed at the front. Writers like Morgan have jumped on the bandwagon, naïvely thinking they can instantly acquire Aboriginality. They are individuals who have not earned the right, through years of sensitivity, hard work, effort and attention to protocols and ethics, to be accepted back into the community. The greatest weakness of *My Place*, Huggins writes, is that it presents Aboriginality as something that can be easily understood by a white audience and white literary world. It therefore represents an act of passing which is a horrendous crime in Aboriginal circles: 'We vindictively remember those who have passed and ... can never forget nor forgive these traitors.' Sally and her mother and grandmother have co-operated with the enemy. Jackie Huggins is also disappointed that overseas readers assimilate *My Place* to a North

American slave narrative and also that Alice Walker could acclaim it as representative of the oneness of all Australian Aboriginal people: 'It might', Huggins responds, 'be the oneness of slaves and Afro-Americans but how do the Native Americans deal with *My Place*?'[14]

Subhash Jaireth took issue with earlier contributors to the debate like Attwood and Huggins for what he saw as lack of attention to the textuality of *My Place*. He quotes Bakhtin to the effect that even in autobiography the author is other to the 'I' who is constructed in the text, who belongs to narrative not biography. He also agrees there is a certain degree of heteroglossia in the independence of the testimonies from the principal narrator. Nevertheless Jaireth's judgement is firm: *My Place* is not polyphonic because her voice is a monologic force that frames and controls the text. There is insufficient difference between the consciousness of the author and the subjectivity of the principal character, who is created as one who discovers herself during the course of the narrative as complete, rounded and essentialized.[15]

It was an interesting debate, revealing perhaps how debates flow and ebb, their start–stop rhythm, their tidal movement. The controversy seemed to settle in the sand because its participants and contestants agreed that *My Place* is occupied by the desire for and uncovering of the principal narrator as a homogeneous, unitary and unified subject; the apparent heart of the book is her quest for her true identity, her authentic Aboriginal heritage, a pilgrimage towards her real self, an absurd return to her original being while ontologically she belongs to European modernity.[16] The debate was also freely prescriptive, anxious to tell Sally Morgan what she should have done. Eric Michaels felt she should have 'more frankly' acknowledged the duality and contradictions of her story and history, she should have described the part played by the whites in her ancestry, upbringing and present life. Sounding like a Marxist of old, Stephen Muecke also felt her work should have dealt with 'social contradictions', in particular, to confront European agency. Attwood, too, believes she should have addressed her white heritage, for she discusses her past only in terms of the prism of Aboriginality. Huggins called on Morgan to pay recompense to her community rather than being a self-centred self-serving ego. Jaireth asked her to pay heed to the messy fragmentary nature of one's subjectivity and to the necessity of a more ruptured narrative.[17] The debate also agreed that, despite the inserted stories of Arthur, Gladys and Daisy, text and author, *My Place* and Sally Morgan, are substantially one; her particular use of autobiography had closed off the possibility of disjunction and so of decentring and polyphony in the main narrative.

The question I'd like to ask the participants in the debate is: why did *they* marginalize the non-Aboriginal narratives in the text?[18] In what follows I will deploy Walter Benjamin's allegorical method, fragmenting the object of analysis to reconstitute *My Place*'s narratology as dispersed, complex and densely intertextual. The novel explicitly and openly suggests that the ethnic and cultural identities of the narrator and her family are multiple, and here *My Place* can reprise by analogy the historical experience of forced assimilation and conversion in Europe of Moors and Jews, especially in the history of the conversos and marranos of medieval and early modern Spain, Portugal and Holland; and in European colonizing across the globe, beginning with the Catholic Spanish in the Americas.[19] I do not see the novel's generic connections and literary conventions as a sign of the failure of her alleged claim to authentic Aboriginal identity. Rather, such textuality and intertextuality constitute a major part of its interest and richness as an autobiographical novel, a novel which is no less a novel for referring to actual names, a novel which foregrounds and highlights rather than attempts to mask and conceal cultural syncretism.

A new look

Since the narrator of *My Place* grows up conscious of herself as a storyteller and artist, the novel is a kind of *Kunstlerroman*, where the text maintains a more or less gentle distance from the narrator. Certainly Sally Morgan is the author and she is the principal narrator of her childhood and growing up and of interactions with various characters and events. Even so, the novel is not necessarily to be equated with her consciousness: in Bakhtin's terms, there cannot be a coincidence of author and hero, they belong to different moments of time and space, and they represent different constitutive aspects of the text.[20]

Sally, for example, more than once tells us that as a child she was an outsider figure who missed school if she could. To her surprise in her last year at primary level, in Grade Seven, she wins the 'coveted Dick Cleaver Award for Citizenship': 'The whole school', she notes with surprise, 'voted, and, for some reason, I won.' Sally sillily wonders if her sister Jill has bribed someone.[21]

The novel is suggesting that there are gaps between Sally's perceptions of herself and the perceptions of others: she can misperceive, her self-knowledge is suspect, the explanations she reaches for can be obviously unsatisfactory. She thinks of herself when a schoolchild as an idler, a romantic dreamer, and is perplexed when others see her as clever. When she is 15, after an outburst from Nan, she finally becomes conscious of her grandmother's colouring. Jill chides her for her naïvety in ever thinking they were not Aboriginal rather than Indian. Paul, her future husband, himself the son of missionaries who had been brought up with Aboriginal people, implies to Sally that some of her attitudes 'were very immature'.[22] *My Place*, then, in various places offers enough clues to establish that her attitudes, opinions and self-knowledge can be questioned: she is not a wholly reliable narrator.

Narratives abound in *My Place* of white people who are recognized as significantly influencing Sally's formation and character, not least her father Bill the returned soldier. Bill is a major figure in the novel. There are descriptions of visiting him in his long stays in hospital; his aversion to killing anything, including the chook for Christmas (Nan would have to do it); his not caring what the neighbours or anyone else think; his drinking himself to an early death, and his suicide. Sally's mother Gladys says that Bill was 'more worldly' than other men she'd met when she was young. Bill will never tell Gladys all that happened to him during the war. He'd have nightmares: 'He'd scream and scream at night.' In better times he enjoyed mixing with and talking Italian with the Italian market gardeners in Perth, often doing plumbing jobs for them free of charge.[23]

In terms of a narratology of stories within stories – recalling eighteenth-century decentred narration rather than the narrative of unified self-becoming of the nineteenth-century *Bildungsroman* – Gladys's testimony interpolates an account of Bill's wartime experiences constructed from what he had told her. Bill, it appears, fought in the desert in the Middle East, was captured at El Alamein and survived a torpedoing to the ship that transported him to Greece and Italy, where Allied prisoners like him were publicly humiliated. In Italy Bill escapes, hides out with a family supportive of the partisans, and learns to speak Italian fluently and drink vino while trying to keep out of sight of the Germans. He is captured and handed over to the SS, who question and torture him for days, and then is transferred to Germany to camps where he is again mistreated. In the end Gladys realizes that the Nazis had broken not his spirit or will to live but his mind: 'He had a sensitive side to him; they'd destroyed that, degraded him. ... He couldn't escape from his own memories.' Unless it was the shock treatment the doctors in Perth hospital gave him.[24]

Compared to the public timidity of her grandmother and mother, where does Sally acquire her boldness, independence, forthrightness, lack of dread in relation to society? In her childhood Sally, more than the other children, feels an affinity with her father, an affinity he recognizes even in her speaking back to him, as do Gladys and Nan. When he has drinking bouts that sometimes end in rages with the family fleeing to a neighbour's house, it is Sally who is sent to talk to him.[25]

The portrait of the father involves sympathy and empathy, for Sally feels he is part of her, she entwines aspects of her father's will and spirit into her will and spirit, though she rejects his drinking. At school Sally regards the teachers as akin to the army officers her father disliked; like him she feels herself to be a nonconformist opposed to regimentation, comparing herself to her more conventional sister Jill. She listens eagerly to his stories of precarious life with the partisans in Italy and his friendship with the Italian family that sheltered him; she learns to share his tastes that were a wartime legacy, a love of seafood and vinegar. Bill teaches her to sing the Communist anthem in Italian, and she later stuns her teacher and class not only by singing 'The Internationale' in that tongue, but by her 'sudden show of theatrical talent'. She feels cursed for being a girl and not being able to be a soldier, but she is proud that she can defy authority just as her father defied the Gestapo, not telling them anything. As Gladys says of Sally and her father: 'In some ways, they were similar, they were both rebels.'[26] It is because of the public insouciance and worldliness Sally absorbs from her white father that she feels impatient with the timidity of her mother and grandmother and is so confident in launching her quest for knowledge of her Aboriginal ancestry.

Sally may also have derived from her father some of her theatricality, her desire to dramatize her story as scenes of fragmented identities. Her talent here suddenly emerges on the occasion when she sings 'The Internationale' in class. Sally and the other children also love going to the local outdoor theatre to see films; on television they are fascinated by 1920s, 1930s and 1940s movies. Enraptured by the magic of performance, Sally at high school had 'very romantic notions about running away to join a circus'. Jill and her mother think that Sally is always being 'dramatic', she 'should have gone on the stage', so excited does she become by her new awareness of an Aboriginal heritage.[27]

Other white people, the wealthy 'upper class' colonial pastoralist family the Drake-Brockmans, are major obstacles in Sally's path towards knowledge of that which she seeks, the history of her body. The female Drake-Brockmans, Aunty Judy in Perth and Alice in Sydney, whom Sally talks to about who might have fathered Nan and Gladys, construct for Sally an imaginary kinship involving a cook called Maltese Sam and an Englishman called Jack Grime. The Drake-Brockman women brutally disavow any kinship with Sally, though the strong suggestion emerges through the various stories and evasions, feints and lures, that the owner of Corunna Downs station in the north of Western Australia, Alfred Howden Drake-Brockman, both fathered Nan and later when she was a teenager forced incest on her to produce Gladys.[28] Here is a story common in the history of European colonialism and its associated literature, a continuation in new situations of aristocratic desire for the low and other, their female servants, yet explosively intensified in colonial situations of an erotics of the exotic.

My Place is part of a contemporary literature that explores how fictional kinship can be in human societies, how much it involves silences, gaps, creation of kin, hierarchy, exclusions, violence – that kinship is always torn, always wounded.[29] What wounds Sally is that in her family it is not only the white women who refuse knowledge but her immediate matrilineage, her mother and grandmother. Her mother is reluctant to find out who fathered her, while Daisy insists on withholding unto her death what she regards and guards as her secrets, presumably the horror of incest, rape and sexuality with and by her own father.

Scott's *Ivanhoe*

In Sally's consciousness, it is the women in her family, black and white, who should maintain, preserve and transmit genealogical knowledge. As Sally says to a reluctant Gladys: 'You're as bad as Nan, sometimes! You've got to help me, you're my mother, it's your duty.' Yet race and racism have created in *My Place* a tension between women as bearers of family history and women forced to conceal kinship connections or create false genealogies. Curiously, it is Uncle Arthur who provides crucial genealogical information, not Sally's female line.[30]

Daisy's withholding of such knowledge suggests an interesting intertextual relationship with *Ivanhoe* (1819). In *My Place*, the name Ivanhoe occurs often; it refers to 'a grand old house' in Claremont on the banks of the Swan River in Perth where Daisy as a young girl of 15 or 16 is taken by Howden Drake-Brockman and where she spends most of her working life as the family nursemaid, servant and cook, feeling like the white family's captive and slave: the family that was also her family but was never acknowledged as her family.[31] One might hazard that it was because of the remarkable popularity of Scott's *Ivanhoe* in the nineteenth century, in literary imitations as well as paintings, dramatizations and operas, that it spread as a house name across the British Empire.[32]

Ivanhoe is a predecessor novel concerned with invasion, colonial relations of domination and subordination, race, and destructive desire for the other. Recall in *Ivanhoe* (the novel being set in the late twelfth century) the dramatic scenes in Sir Reginald Front-de-Bœuf's castle, to which the Jewess Rebecca and her father Isaac, and Wilfred of Ivanhoe and the other Saxons, captured in the forest, are led by a party of predatory Norman knights. In the castle is an old servant called Urfried. Urfried tells her story, briefly to Rebecca and later more fully to Cedric, the Saxon patriot who is still smarting under Norman rule. Urfried says that in a previous generation the Norman invaders had stormed this castle, and after killing all the Saxon male nobles had raped the women, including herself, who was once a Saxon noblewoman. Urfried is the Norman

name the invaders gave her; once she had a Saxon name, Ulrica, the daughter
of Cedric's old friend the Thane of Torquilstone. But once her beauty had
gone, she was no longer the sport of her masters' passions and was treated
henceforth as servant and slave, object of their contempt, scorn and hatred; she
in turn despises the Normans, and hates and despises her wretched self. Cedric
the Saxon is repulsed by her story of 'horror and guilt', that she should have
survived and slept with the enemy while her male relatives in the very same
castle had been brutally slain. He reviles her, tells her she should have killed
herself, that she deserves the 'hate and execration' of 'each true Saxon heart'.
He can only look upon Ulrica, in her guilt, wretchedness and despair, with
'abhorrence' and 'disgust', accusing her of possessing a 'leprosy of soul'. He
must get away from her presence. In a moment of high melodrama, Ulrica will
die having set alight the accursed castle with its encrypted stories of spilt
blood and shameful secrets.[33]

In *My Place* it would appear that Howden Drake-Brockman the white
station owner took Daisy to Ivanhoe in Perth for his sexual pleasure, even
though he'd also fathered her back in the north where Daisy had been born
with and was known by her Aboriginal name Talahue. There is mention, too,
of Daisy giving birth to another child who died, possibly also fathered by
Howden. Daisy at the end of her life warns Sally to be watchful of Sally's
daughter Amber: 'Some men can't be trusted. They just mongrels. They get
you down on the floor and they won't let you get up. ... You watch out for
Amber. You don't want her bein' treated like a black woman.' Howden may
have had affection for Daisy. He insisted on holding his and Daisy's daughter
Gladys just before he died; Howden had also promised money to Daisy and
her brother Arthur, and sent photos to Arthur.[34]

Does Daisy formerly Talahue fear that she can never face her Aboriginal kin
back in the north nor her daughter and grand-daughter in Perth, with a
narrative of sexuality that will repulse and disgust them as Cedric the Saxon
was repulsed and disgusted by Urfried formerly Ulrica? Isn't her grumpiness
and temper when Sally, and her siblings are growing up reminiscent of Urfried
in the castle? Does she, like Urfried, despise herself?[35] Daisy appears to fear her
story will blight them, will extinguish hope in and bring horror to their young
eyes. She can't seem to believe that Sally, her bold young grand-daughter who
has already heard her father's war stories, will not be horrified.

Conversos and marranos

As historical romance Scott's *Ivanhoe* draws on both Gothic and melodrama,
related genres that evoke allegories of desire in relation to secret knowledge, in

stories that strain both to conceal and to release the repressed into open theatre and theatricality; the kind of melodrama that Sally and her family relish in transformed form in Hollywood movies on television. Gladys relates that in her schooling (her mother Daisy had never been taught reading and writing), she had fallen asleep while the teacher read Jane Austen to the class. Gladys recalls the same teacher, whose fiancé had been killed in the First World War, becoming tearful as she read out 'old romantic novels, especially Wuthering Heights'.[36]

Indeed, rather than in Jane Austen's gentler narrative toning, Gladys's narration does construct key moments of crisis in her life in heightened ways reminiscent of the Gothic melodrama of that incest novel *Wuthering Heights*, with its fantastical happenings and uncanny visions. Such is especially so in the nightmares she reports having about her future with Bill before she marries him, and his own nightmare attempted stranglings of her later when, suddenly a terrifying stranger, he screams 'SS, SS' with his hands around her throat, imagining she was a particularly brutal Gestapo officer. The year before Bill dies, Gladys wakes suddenly, seeing a light in her bedroom, which she interprets as the spirit of Christ, His arms outstretched as though He'd come for someone: 'I screamed and told him to go away, I knew I was looking at death.' Later the following year she thanks God for giving her and Bill extra time together, feeling that God was preparing her for his death. After he dies she begs God to tell her where Bill had gone. She closes her eyes, and opens them to see herself surrounded by light, and then notices Bill being beckoned by Jesus in a long white robe to join others seated on a lawn: 'When that vision finished, I was surrounded by a glow of pure love, I was so happy. I knew Bill was all right.'[37]

If in Scott's *Ivanhoe* there's a prominent Jewish narrative concerned with the exclusion, violence and othering faced by Rebecca and Isaac in medieval Christian England, in *My Place* there's also a Jewish narrative, though one threaded through scattered references, and apparent also in certain similarities – so in any case I'm now going to argue – to the conversos of sixteenth- and seventeenth-century Catholic Portugal. Recall from discussion in previous chapters that those conversos were descended from the Sephardic Jews of Spain expelled in 1492, who had come to Portugal and were forcibly mass-baptized in the late 1490s; for the next several generations, now formally Catholic and frequently rising to high positions in the society (until discriminated against as New Christians), the conversos could also be marranos, or secret Jews. Because, however, of the watchful care with which the Inquisition policed identities, the marranos possessed only fragmentary, distorted memories of Judaism, and they often mixed Jewish with Catholic beliefs and cosmologies in individual, distinctive, idiosyncratic, imaginative ways. The marranos experienced a double consciousness, both Catholic and Jewish, both participating in and conforming to the society about them yet sustaining a secret consciousness of difference. They were suspicious of any institutional authority, religious system and church bureaucracy, trusting to their own inner journeys of thought and reason, their own inner awareness, one's own spirituality, your own path, however eccentric.

Justifiably afraid of persecution, the marranos were ever cautious and prudent in their accommodations to the society they found themselves in, as they managed and negotiated dualities of public and private, outer and inner.[38]

I wish to set into play a metaphoric relationship between converso and marrano diasporic culture, a culture that was neither Jewish nor non-Jewish, and Sally Morgan's family history and upbringing, that was neither Aboriginal nor non-Aboriginal.[39] Nan surprises Sally one day by saying to her: 'You don't know nothin', girl. You don't know what it's like for people like us. We're like those Jews, we got to look out for ourselves.' Sally feels she knows 'a lot about the Jews because of the war and Dad'. Some of Bill's wartime stories concerned being in POW camps near Jewish concentration camps, and his also teaming up with a POW who was 'half-Jewish' and was badly treated by the Nazis. In response to her eccentric grandmother's outburst of affinity, Sally thinks to herself that there 'was no possible comparison' between Jews and her family.[40] The novel as a whole, nevertheless, does create Sally's matrilineage as comparable to the culture and consciousness of the conversos and marranos.

Sally's mother and grandmother had led lives of fear and caution, always attempting to conform to the white colonialist society around them in Perth so that the Inquisition-like government would not declare them to be Aborigines who would be subject to curfew, surveillance and apartheid-like restrictions. They wish to be whites, to succeed in the society, and for Sally and the other children to do well at school and university, which indeed they will do, qualifying to become part of the professional middle class (in psychology, medicine, law).[41]

Yet their attempted conformity never quite works, reminding us of the conversos, who even when they disavowed the Jewish religion and sincerely sought to assimilate into Christian society, found they were still discriminated against because of their ancestry and taint of blood, however much they might attempt to conceal their own history.[42] When as a teenager Sally, after a vision of God, becomes a churchgoing Christian (though she dislikes the regimentation of church) and joins a local youth group, she is told by a friend's father, one of the deacons of the church, to stay away from his daughter: 'I don't want her mixing with you', says the deacon with a quiet sinister smile, 'in case she picks up any of your bad habits.' On one occasion at school Sally ingenuously tells one of the girls in her class how ordinary her family is. Her classmate bursts out laughing, happy to confide to Sally that she has 'the most abnormal family' she'd ever come across: 'Don't get me wrong, I like your mother, I really do, but the way you all look at life is weird.'[43]

Gladys shares a converso and marrano interest in masking and personae: 'Mum always worried about what to tell people. It was as if the truth was never adequate, or there was something to hide. ... She had been inventing stories and making exaggerated claims since the day she was born.' Gladys's Christianity, seeing Christ as both a frightening figure of death and a deliverer of Bill her suicide husband into paradise, has the idiosyncrasy of marrano religious phenomenology. Nan, brought up as a child in her own people's country, though forced to be a 'house native' separated from the 'camp natives', maintains notions of what she feels are Aboriginal beliefs, in her love of nature and her non-perspectival drawing skills (which Sally learns from her for her own conceptions of art that will scandalize her teachers).[44]

Yet Nan mixes such memory and imagining of traditional knowledge with other kinds of consciousness. Sally observes that Nan is suspicious of any kind of authority, including that of doctors, and that her 'view of the physical world was a deeply personal one'. Her obsession with observing the weather revealed Nan's 'rather pessimistic view of the frequency of natural disasters'.

> Daily, she checked the sky, the clouds, the wind, and, on particularly still days, the reactions of our animals. Sometimes, she would sit up half the night, checking on the movement of a particular star, or pondering the meaning of a new colour she'd seen in the sky at sunset.[45]

Nan's consciousness here, her fear of storm and earthquake, a fear that terrifies the children when young, is akin to a strand of Jewish messianic consciousness. I'm thinking of Adorno's comment on Benjamin: 'Sadness ... was his nature, as Jewish awareness of the permanence of danger and catastrophe.'[46]

It is also akin to the philosemitic radical and Romantic millennial culture towards the end of the long eighteenth century that Iain McCalman discusses, in enthusiasts and seekers ranging from Joseph Priestley to William Blake. Appearing dangerously deranged to their conservative opponents, millenarians focused on apocalyptic biblical prophecies that the end of days would come with the restoring of the Jews to Palestine, though they agreed that the millennium would not arrive without cataclysm and violence. Millenarians would devote much time to studying the world's phenomena for allegorical hints, equivocal figures, enigmatic signs.[47]

It's her grandmother's fear of history as the nightmare that is always near that Sally fights to overcome, finally insisting the rest of the family, though Nan tries to sabotage the trip, travel north to find their Aboriginal relatives (the Mulbas of the Port Hedland/Marble Bar area of Western Australia). Just how much the family had lived as conversos and assimilados becomes clear when Sally reports that her children were convinced that 'going north was as adventurous as exploring deepest, darkest Africa'. It is during this journey that Sally makes the annunciatory statements that have so angered her critics, that she instinctively knew her kin, that she and her family had come home, that they now had a sense of place and belonging: 'We had an Aboriginal consciousness now, and were proud of it.' They would have survived, 'but not as whole people'.[48]

Sally, we might say, is as grand-daughter influenced by Daisy's messianic consciousness, though in an apocalyptic way. Out of disaster – the disaster of her family history, with its forced removal, forced sexuality, forced separation of mother and child (Gladys from Daisy), forced conformity, white relatives who refuse to be kin, incest, suicide and deception – may come annunciations of the new. From such disaster may come rebirth in the journey to the north and knowledge of her Aboriginal genealogy, just as English radical dissenters like Priestley looked for signs of catastrophe followed by hoped-for rebirth in Palestine. In this reading the north of Western Austraia is her redemptive Palestine, her New Jerusalem, with which, living in the city far away, she will now have a diasporic relationship.

Sally, I suggest, can be compared to the marranos who – like Spinoza's parents – managed in the seventeenth century to leave Portugal, coming to a newly liberalized Amsterdam, where they attempted to rejudaize, becoming known as New Jews. But it was a process more tortuous than smooth. Some of the returning marranos posed problems for Amsterdam's Jewish community and leadership, concerned to assist the marranos recover their torn religion and a stability of faith and identity rooted in daily observance of the ancient customs of Israel.[49]

Some marranos, however, wished both to rejoin the community yet continue, if with difficulty and anguish, their own inner journeys, their distinctive consciousness. Such marranos, or children of marranos like Spinoza, were excommunicated by the community. Here is the wording of the *herem* (ban) on Spinoza, then in his twenty-fourth year:

> By the decree of the Angels and the word of the Saints we ban, cut off, curse and anathemize Baruch de Espinoza. ... Cursed be he by day and cursed by night, cursed in his lying down and cursed in his waking up, cursed in his going forth and cursed in his coming in. ... We warn that none may contact him orally or in writing, nor do him any favour, nor stay under the same roof with him, nor read any paper he made or wrote.[50]

Now think of the excommunicatory harshness of Jackie Huggins's response to *My Place*, accusing Sally Morgan of co-operating with the enemy and a traitorous individualism, a refusal to observe continuing ancient custom and tradition, acts that will be neither forgotten nor forgiven.

Conclusions

I believe such harshness involves a misreading of the textual movement of *My Place*. Like the marranos in relation to their receding Jewish heritage, Sally at the beginning of the novel knows little to nothing about Aboriginality and Aboriginal people: 'What did it really mean to be Aboriginal? ... I'd lived all my life in suburbia and told everyone I was Indian.' Like the marranos, she distrusts the authority of state institutions. Yet she has what the marranos had, confidence and pride in her own capacity to think independently. Like the marranos, she grows up in a family that, she learns, puzzlingly mixes Christian beliefs and visions with other beliefs and visions that suggest hidden histories. Like the marranos, she knows that pasts are being kept secret because of a fear of racism and state surveillance. Like the marranos, she experiences ruptures of identity, now Indian, now New Aboriginal.[51]

Launched on her quest, she is moved by finding her lost ancestry, discovering much about the Aboriginal history of her family. It brings her great joy. She makes excited, exaggerated claims. But such excitement and knowledge is not the telos, the consummatory end, of her journey, the acclamation of a rounded essentialized Aboriginal identity. The joy and genealogical knowledge are a vital addition to her identity in process, as process; her identity as a verb not a noun (to adapt Judith Butler). In terms of the novel as a whole Sally develops a complex diasporic sensibility that is not centred on recovering a single totalized ersatz Aboriginality. She continues to belong to more than one place, more than one chronotope, more than one history, more than one genealogy. The textuality of the novel does precisely what Eric Michaels and its other critics said it should do. It creates Sally's identity as always involving the exploring, probing, negotiating of multiplicity. It creates the autobiographical theatre of observing diverse contradictory elements and fragments of herself. Sally Morgan the author looks with great interest at the 'I' called Sally Morgan: someone who is at once both Same and Other, someone who is Many rather than One, someone who is always between the Many and the One.

My Place raises in disturbing ways the difficult, baffling issue of the relationship between notions of biological or genetic inheritance and constructions of cultural identity. In 1990s Australia the relationship was brought to public notice and controversy by the suggestion that the prominent Aboriginal writer, critic and dramatist Mudrooroo (born Colin Johnson) has no Nyoongah ancestry and kin.[52] According to a newspaper report, Mudrooroo's sister publicly stated her belief that their grandfather was an American migrant from North Carolina, apparently of African-American descent. The same report quotes Mr Robert Eggington, the co-ordinator of the Dumbartung Aboriginal Corporation in Western Australia, expressing his anger at Mudrooroo's long-held claim to Aboriginal identity: 'His deception is an example of the on-going and continued spiritual colonisation of our people ... a continuation of genocide.' Mr Eggington felt that any determination of Aboriginality must include analysis of bloodlines as well as acceptance of the person by the elders (whom, he suggests, Mudrooroo was unwilling to face). 'Unless you've got Aboriginal blood, you can't claim to be Aboriginal. ... I, as an Aboriginal person, with English blood as well, can't declare myself to be Japanese.'[53]

In his turn Mudrooroo suggested that his identity had always been textually created by others, a designating by whites and the white government ('I had to go along with that'). He feels that the Nyoongah people who now repudiate his Aboriginality and call on a language of blood are speaking in the violent accents of Western race classifications that culminated in Nazism.[54] In this defence Mudrooroo comes perilously close, I think, to constructing a victimological narrative, claiming the status of a passive victim.[55] Such a claim is all the more odd given that in his past critical writings Mudrooroo appeared very actively, not least in disdainful comments on Sally Morgan's *My Place*, to be policing the white/black borders of who was truly authentically Aboriginal, who had the right to speak; the claiming of certain knowledge of essential Aboriginality by which he could judge, evaluate and condemn degrees of Aboriginality in others.[56] As an act of self-making he also very actively constructed a Nyoongah genealogy of descent and cultural knowledge transmitted matrilineally ('It was from my mother that I got most of my culture ...').[57] Mudrooroo's sister, however, claims that their mother comes from a family of white settlers who arrived in Western Australia from Britain in 1829.[58]

In further destabilizing incidents it has been publicly claimed that the writer Archie Weller, born into a Western Australian pastoralist family, also apparently bases his claim to Aboriginality on a photo suggesting that his paternal great-grandmother may be Aboriginal (his mother Helen Weller has said that she used to think the great-grandmother in the photo was Malaysian).[59] Controversy has also been inspired by the elderly white artist Elizabeth Durack's creation of an Aboriginal painter, Eddie Burrup, in whose name she has chosen to exhibit.[60]

There is also the very interesting autobiography *An Australian Son* (1996) by Gordon Matthews, an Australian diplomat. As he tells it, Matthews was adopted as a baby, brought up by a white professional family, and educated in middle-class schools in Australia and England. Dark of skin, he was subject to racist abuse when young, and grew up thinking he must be Aboriginal; he was so believed, and became part of the Aboriginal community. In his early thirties, however, he discovered through a genealogical search that his father was Sri Lankan. Matthews' memoir is in many ways a tragic story of the effects of colonialism, of how brutal and disruptive and dislocatory its racism can be. Matthews no longer feels he can call himself Aboriginal; he wishes actively to acknowledge that his ancestry on his father's side is Sri Lankan (his mother is white Australian). Torn and tortured, Matthews nevertheless does not retreat into claiming the status of victim. Rather, more in the spirit of Benjamin's allegorical method, he fragments his relationship to identity in terms of various histories, genealogies and tense, tentative, perhaps failing, relations with his biological family that he has discovered living in the United States: his identity is now the writing of the narrative.[61]

In this context of revelation and controversy, of identity as performance and adventure, of vigorous claim and counter-claim, of hurt and bewilderment, amidst heated media attention, Sally Morgan's *My Place* remains in the new millennium a flashpoint and a challenge, not only to local Australian arguments concerning the body, ethnicity and identity, but to the wider unresolved centuries-long post-1492 colonial and postcolonial histories of conversion and assimilation, exile and diaspora.[62]

Notes

1. Marcia Langton, 'Aboriginal art and film: the politics of representation', *Race and Class*, 35(4) (1994), pp. 89–106.
2. *Ibid.*, pp. 89–93.
3. *Ibid.*, pp. 97–8. Cf. Mudrooroo Narogin, *Writing from the Fringe* (Melbourne: Hyland House, 1990), p. 149.
4. Cf. Andreas Huyssen, 'Mass culture as woman: modernism's Other' in Tania Modleski (ed.), *Studies in Entertainment* (Bloomington: Indiana University Press, 1986).
5. For another account of this journey to Hungary, see John Docker, 'Rethinking postcolonialism and multiculturalism in the *fin de siècle*', *Cultural Studies*, 9(3) (1995), pp. 419–22.
6. Cf. James Clifford, *Routes: Travel and Translation in the Late Twentieth Century* (Cambridge, MA: Harvard University Press, 1997), ch. 10, 'Diasporas', pp. 244–77; Edward W. Said, *Representations of the Intellectual: The 1993 Reith Lectures* (London: Vintage, 1994), ch. 3, 'Intellectual exile: expatriates and marginals', pp. 35–47.

7.   A different version of this chapter appeared as 'Recasting Sally Morgan's *My Place*: the fictionality of identity and the phenomenology of the converso', *Humanities Research*, 1 (1998), pp. 3–22. My thanks to Radhika Mohanram in particular for conversation about the novel, and also to Deborah Bird Rose for e-mail comments.

8.   Cf. the video documentary *Dhuway: An Australian Diaspora and Homecoming* (1996) concerning the forced dispersal of the Yiidhuwarra people of Cape York from their homelands, and their desire to return. See also Deborah Bird Rose, 'Rupture and the ethics of care in colonized space' in Tim Bonyhady and Tom Griffiths (eds), *Prehistory to Politics: John Mulvaney, the Humanities and the Public Intellectual* (Melbourne: Melbourne University Press, 1996); Ann Curthoys, 'Entangled histories: conflict and ambivalence in non-Aboriginal Australia' in Geoffrey Gray and Christine Winter (eds), *The Resurgence of Racism: Hanson, Howard and the Race Debate* (Melbourne: Monash Publications in History, 1997) and 'Expulsion, Exodus, and Exile in white Australian historical mythology' in Richard Nile and Michael Williams (eds), *Imaginary Homelands: The Dubious Cartographies of Australian Identity* (St Lucia: University of Queensland Press, 1999).

9.   Eric Michaels, *Bad Aboriginal Art: Tradition, Media, and Technological Horizons* (Minneapolis: University of Minnesota Press, 1994), pp. 165–76. The essay was originally published in *Art and Text*, 30 (1988).

10. Cf. Docker, *Postmodernism and Popular Culture: A Cultural History*, ch. 18.

11. Stephen Muecke, 'Aboriginal literature and the repressive hypothesis', *Southerly*, 48(4) (1988), pp. 405–18, and *Textual Spaces: Aboriginality and Cultural Studies* (Sydney: University of New South Wales Press, 1992), pp. 119–38.

12. Bain Attwood, 'Portrait of an Aboriginal as an artist: Sally Morgan and the construction of Aboriginality', *Australian Historical Studies*, 25(99) (1992), pp. 302–18.

13. Tim Rowse, 'Sally Morgan's kaftan', *Australian Historical Studies*, 25(100) (1993), pp. 465–8.

14. Jackie Huggins, 'Always was always will be', *Australian Historical Studies*, 25(100) (1993), pp. 459–64. Concerning the difficulties of acceptance by Aboriginal communities of the stolen generations, cf. Peter Read, obituary of Burnum Burnum, *The Australian* (20 August 1997).

15. Subhash Jaireth, 'The "I" in Sally Morgan's *My Place*: writing of a monologised self', *Westerly*, 3 (1995), pp. 69–78.

16. Michaels, *Bad Aboriginal Art*, p. 168; Muecke, *Textual Spaces*, pp. 126, 129; Attwood, 'Portrait of an Aboriginal as an artist', pp. 305–8; Jaireth, 'The "I" in Sally Morgan's *My Place*', pp. 70, 75, 77; Rowse, 'Sally Morgan's kaftan', p. 466; Huggins, 'Always was always will be', p. 461.

17. Michaels, *Bad Aboriginal Art*, p. 169; Muecke, *Textual Spaces*, p. 126; Attwood, 'Portrait of an Aboriginal as an artist', pp. 315, 318; Huggins, 'Always was always will be', p. 460; Jaireth, 'The "I" in Sally Morgan's *My Place*', pp. 70, 77.

18. Cf. however, Elizabeth Reed, 'Sally Morgan: a tall black poppy?', *Australian Historical Studies*, 25(101) (1993), pp. 637–9. See also Rosamund Dalziell, 'Religious experience and the displaced child: autobiographies of illegitimacy and adoption', *St Mark's Review*, 170 (1997), pp. 25–6.

19. Cf. Ella Shohat, 'Taboo memories and diasporic visions: Columbus, Palestine and Arab-Jews' in Mary Joseph and Jennifer Natalya Fink (eds), *Performing Hybridity*

(Minneapolis: University of Minnesota Press, 1999), pp. 131–56.

20. See Mikhail Bakhtin, *The Dialogic Imagination*, ed. Michael Holquist (Austin: University of Texas Press, 1981), 'Forms of time and of the chronotope in the novel', p. 256, and *Art and Answerability: Early Philosophical Essays*, ed. Michael Holquist and Vadim Liapunov, trans. Vadim Liapunov (Austin: University of Texas Press, 1990), p. 151.

21. Sally Morgan, *My Place* (Perth: Fremantle Arts Centre Press, 1987), pp. 23, 78.

22. *Ibid.*, pp. 83, 97–8, 112, 132.

23. *Ibid.*, pp. 31, 33–5, 52, 275, 277, 288.

24. *Ibid.*, pp. 285, 295.

25. *Ibid.*, pp. 31–2, 44, 135.

26. *Ibid.*, pp. 24, 27–8, 30–1, 34–5, 40, 86–7, 89, 138, 298, 309.

27. *Ibid.*, pp. 40, 55, 83, 134, 138, 149.

28. *Ibid.*, pp. 152–3, 155–6, 327.

29. Cf. Regina M. Schwartz, *The Curse of Cain: The Violent Legacy of Monotheism* (Chicago and London: University of Chicago Press, 1997), pp. 6, 78–83.

30. *My Place*, pp. 149, 173.

31. *Ibid.*, pp. 149, 152, 158–9, 247, 263, 267, 325.

32. A. N. Wilson, Introduction to Sir Walter Scott, *Ivanhoe* (London: Penguin, 1986), p. xx.

33. *Ivanhoe*, chs XXIV, XXVII, XXX.

34. *My Place*, pp. 200, 234, 317, 329, 332, 335.

35. Cf. Dundi Mitchell, 'Sickening bodies: how racism and essentialism feature in Aboriginal women's discourse about health', *The Australian Journal of Anthropology*, 7(3) (1996), pp. 258–67. (I owe this reference to Deborah Bird Rose.)

36. *My Place*, pp. 108, 268–9.

37. *Ibid.*, pp. 274, 288–9, 296–7.

38. Yirmiyahu Yovel, *Spinoza and Other Heretics*, vol. I: The *Marrano of Reason* (Princeton, NJ: Princeton University Press, 1989).

39. My thanks to Marsha Rosengarten for the wonderful phrase 'neither Jewish nor non-Jewish'.

40. *My Place*, pp. 105, 283.

41. *Ibid.*, pp. 80, 88, 104, 107, 111, 114, 121, 135, 140, 146, 299–300, 304.

42. Yovel, *The Marrano of Reason*, p. 189. Cf. Haim Beinart, 'The conversos and their fate' in Elie Kedourie (ed.), *Spain and the Jews: The Sephardi Experience, 1492 and After* (London: Thames and Hudson, 1992), pp. 92–122.

43. *My Place*, pp. 102–3, 106–7.

44. *Ibid.*, pp. 96, 99, 135, 323.

45. *Ibid.*, pp. 61–3, 67, 74.

46. Theodor W. Adorno, 'Introduction to Benjamin's *Schriften* (1955)' in Gary Smith (ed.), *On Walter Benjamin: Critical Essays and Recollections* (Cambridge, MA: MIT Press, 1991), p. 15. See also Max Pensky, *Melancholy Dialectics: Walter Benjamin and the Play of Mourning* (Amherst: University of Massachusetts Press, 1993), p. 18.

47. Iain McCalman, 'New Jerusalems: prophecy, Dissent and radical culture in England, 1786–1830' in Knud Haakonssen (ed.), *Enlightenment and Religion: Rational Dissent in Eighteenth-Century Britain* (Cambridge: Cambridge University Press, 1996), pp. 312–35.

48. *My Place*, pp. 214, 217, 224, 227, 229–30.

49. Yovel, *The Marrano of Reason*, pp. 12, 64–5, 67, 71.

50. *Ibid.*, pp. 3, 6, 42–50, 57–80, 178.

51. *My Place*, pp. 100, 102, 112, 134, 139, 259, 296, 336, 341.

52. The following thoughts on Mudrooroo and also on Gordon Matthews owe a great deal to discussions with Gerhard Fischer, and reading of his essay 'Performing multicultural and post-colonial identities. Heiner Müller "aboriginalized" by Mudrooroo (with a postscript on Mudrooroo's dilemmas)' in Wolfgang Kloos (ed.), *Across the Lines: Intertextuality and Transcultural Communication in the New Literatures in English* (ASNEL Papers No. 3), (Atlanta, GA; Amsterdam, 1998), pp. 215–36.

53. *The Weekend Australian* (5–6 April 1997).

54. Mudrooroo, ' "Tell them you're Indian" ' in Gillian Cowlishaw and Barry Morris (eds), *Race Matters* (Canberra: Aboriginal Studies Press, 1997), pp. 259–68.

55. On the importance of a victimological narrative in white Australian history, see Curthoys, 'Expulsion, Exodus, and Exile in white Australian historical mythology'.

56. Cf. Mudrooroo's comment in *Writing from the Fringe*, p. 149, that *My Place* is 'an individualised story and the concerns of the Aboriginal community are of secondary importance', and that it is now 'considered O.K. to be Aboriginal as long as you are young, gifted and not very black'.

57. 'Mudrooroo Narogin: writer' in Liz Thompson (ed.), *Aboriginal Voices: Contemporary Aboriginal Artists, Writers and Performers* (Sydney: Simon and Schuster, 1990), p. 55, quoted in Fischer, 'Imagined identity: on Mudrooroo's dilemmas'.

58. *The Australian Magazine* (20–21 July 1996), pp. 28–31.

59. See Debra Jopson, 'Now a black writer confesses: I can't prove that I'm Aboriginal' and 'Mystery over writer's black ancestry stranger than fiction', *The Sydney Morning Herald* (24 March 1997); and Weller's reply in letters page, *The Sydney Morning Herald* (29 March 1997). See also Sian Powell, 'Author chose Aboriginality', *The Australian* (25 March 1997).

60. Debra Jopson and Kelly Burke, 'Painting hoax has art world divided', *Sydney Morning Herald* (8 March 1997); Susan McCulloch, 'Blacks blast Durack over art of illusion', *Weekend Australian* (8–9 March 1997).

61. Gordon Matthews, *An Australian Son* (Melbourne: William Heinemann Australia, 1996). Cf. Dalziell, 'Religious experience . . .', pp. 27–8. See also Gerhard Fischer, 'Mis-taken identity: Mudrooroo and Gordon Matthews' in John Docker and Gerhard Fischer (eds), *Race, Colour and Identity in Australia and New Zealand* (Sydney: University of New South Wales Press, 2000), pp. 95–112.

62. See Ella Shohat, 'Staging the Quincentenary: the Middle East and the Americas', *Third Text*, 21 (1992–93), pp. 95–105.

Concluding Mosaic

I

I'd like to shape my Concluding Mosaic in the genre of the anti-conclusion, in the spirit of the closing lines of *The Waste Land*, lines that have haunted me and that I recount in my head and misremember (because I don't go back and check) ever since I did a thesis on Eliot's great poem in the fourth year of my undergraduate life, in 1966: these are the fragments, these are the fragments that shore up my ruins. I also think of Montesquieu's *Persian Letters*, where the letters are in no sequential order at all.

I've loosely envisaged this book as similar to a trading voyage in the medieval Judeo–Islamic world, a ship visiting ports in Western Europe, travelling through the Mediterranean, journeying across oceans to India and beyond. These concluding fragments are the many side journeys the ship didn't manage to take.

The method of writing I kept thinking of involved Benjamin's suggestions in the prologue to *The Origin of German Tragic Drama*. Ideas, says Benjamin, are the object of his investigation. But ideas always have to be represented. Method works by representation, and representation involves digression, fragmentation into capricious particles that are distinct and disparate, a focus on minute details of subject-matter, the seeking out of extremes, an awareness of discontinuity, of irreducible multiplicity. The representation of ideas involves consideration of the formal language of the works being contemplated, indeed the metaphysics of form. The representation of ideas requires an approach that is always historical, indeed a history of forms that is at the same time a philosophical history. Benjamin compares such contemplation to the medieval mosaic. [1]

My previous book, *Postmodernism and Popular Culture: A Cultural History*

(1994), is a kind of defence of poststructuralism and postmodernism in contemporary cultural theory. It is often said by their critics that poststructuralism and postmodernism deny truth, they have abandoned truth as the goal of knowledge. Not so. The poststructuralists and postmodernists have only said that truth is deferred, it is never arrived at by knowledge, for knowledge works through language, and language always involves that which creates irrepressible uncertainty: metaphor, rhetoric, particularity, anecdote, example, theatricality, performance, parables, stories, allegories. I do believe in truth. I search for truth. It is that search which inspires my reading and thinking and writing. I want to find out, seek deeper, go further. But I'm fascinated by a parable Benjamin tells in the prologue to *The Origin of German Tragic Drama*. Benjamin muses on the Platonic declaration that truth is beautiful. Truth, Benjamin ponders, is not so much beautiful in itself, as for whomsoever seeks it: the inescapable irresolvable problem of historical relativism. Though truth as beauty provokes pursuit by the intellect, 'beauty will always flee: in dread before the intellect, in fear before the lover'.[2] Truth will resist being possessed by knowledge, when knowledge grimly presents itself to truth as that which tries to possess it absolutely, as epistemology, as concepts that are supposed to be universal and objective, supposed to have transcended the dance of representation and to be purified of particular aesthetic and cultural forms. Yet truth will not, I think Benjamin is saying, flee as much when approached by the method he proposes, the representation of ideas, representation aware of itself, self-reflexive, unsure, lost. As Benjamin says at the end of the prologue, the mind that enquires knows itself in a state of apprenticeship, and perhaps truth as beauty will not flee the apprentice as much as she will flee the enquirer offering himself or herself as he or she who can master a field of knowledge.

Truth never reaches Ithaca, never arrives home. Adapting a phrase from Paul Celan's poem 'Die Gauklertrommel' (The Jugglerdrum), we might say that truth is unplayable. We should wish truth her freedom, not wish to capture and possess. We must remain apprentices, who can be king only for a day, like the fool and clown in carnival.

II

One method I've resisted (easily) is any kind of deployment of psychoanalysis. Sometimes I think psychoanalysis is simply something I don't do: it can be wonderful and illuminating, it's just not for me. At other times I think psychoanalysis is to be deeply suspected, not least when it features in Canonical Postcolonial Theory. In such theory, which is supposed to derive its energy and inspiration in passionately resisting and opposing the universalizing of the Western theoretical gaze, psychoanalysis strangely appears as a discourse of centrality, foundation, origin, total explanation. This is not surprising, since psychoanalysis is a universalizing discourse, accessing a supposedly universal human psychic structure and drama. Universality, the repressed, triumphantly returns.

The advantage of contemporary diaspora theory is that it suggests that we can't universalize and totalize, that each and every diaspora journey is individual, particular, distinctive, and that there is no historical diaspora (Jewish, Greek, Armenian, Indian, Chinese, whatever, whosoever) that is to be regarded as a master model.[3]

However, some contemporary diaspora theory is certainly attracted to psychoanalysis (Freud, Lacan) as a way of arguing for a deep psychic structure (mourning, or the uncanny) held to be universal in the experience and phenomenology of diaspora and exile. Furthermore, when a particular diaspora desires to claim or imply that its diaspora experience and phenomenology is exemplary of all the different world diasporas, it is even more attracted to the universalizing authority of psychoanalysis.

III

In this book I've tried to evoke a utopian desire to recover in story and imagination the medieval pre-1492 Judeo–Islamic trading and social world of plurality and *convivencia* that stretched from Moorish Spain to India and China. The journey of utopian desire might well be illusion, fantasy, delusion, absurdity, derisory comedy, accompanied by an idealizing spirit. So I should make certain things clear. I don't believe that the Sephardi Jews whose history has fascinated me in this book are innocent in history. Sephardi Jews, for example, entered the New World as a particular segment of the European colonizing project. In Richard Price's *Alabi's World* (1990), there is mention of how some 200 Portuguese Sephardi Jews, refugees from religious persecution in Brazil, arrived in the Dutch colony of Suriname in the 1660s and were granted privileges that encouraged the formation of a relatively closed community, with its own religious, judicial, educational and even military institutions, a special caste set firmly within the larger colonial structure. By the 1680s, Price remarks, they owned about one-third of the colony's plantations. In 1690 there was a revolt by Suriname's African slaves, who killed a plantation owner, a Jewish man named Imanuel Machado. The Jewish plantation owners mounted an expedition which killed many of the slaves. There was also a Jewish militia that for years 'hunted down stray rebels'.[4]

I don't assume that the condition of Jews in the medieval Islamic world was idyllic. It is just that, as Maxime Rodinson, the great French anti-Zionist historian of the Middle East, has written, on the whole the situation of Jews in Muslim countries over fifteen centuries has been better than in Christian countries. Judaism and Christianity were tolerated religions, protected and enjoying a special status. But their believers were nonetheless considered enemies of the true faith, and appreciations of them were disparaging, suspicious and scornful. Jews were often slandered, there was occasional violence against them.[5] Rodinson sees neither Arabs nor Jews as a saintly people. I've quoted the following passage before in the body of this book; I must quote it again — it haunts my thoughts like the closing lines of *The Waste Land*.

> No people is saintly. No people is intrinsically good or bad eternally and by their essence. No people is destined always to be victims. All peoples have been victims and executioners by turns, and all peoples count among their number both victims and executioners.[6]

IV

My mother came to London to stay with us, Ann Curthoys and myself, in 1974. After Ann had finished her doctoral thesis (on race relations in colonial Australia) in 1973, and I had handed in the manuscript of my first book *Australian Cultural Elites*, we left on the 'overland trail' from Australia to England, via Bali and Java, Singapore, Malaysia, Burma, Thailand and India, thence by plane to London, where we stayed doing office 'temp' work during the day and almost every night going to public seminars and conferences — the bizarre energy of the young.

From my uncles' stories, as children they and my mother lived separate lives, which may have occasionally shaped divergent memories.

'Eyes of diamonds and sides of silver! Eyes of diamonds and sides of silver!' my mother kept repeating joyfully, as we strolled about and negotiated the crowd and stalls and spruikers of the East End's famous Petticoat Lane. 'That's what one of my aunts used always to say about the smoked salmon we could get at Petticoat Lane.' And indeed she insisted on buying some on the spot, choosing carefully, rejecting some, staring hard, and then pointing to an enormous piece, to be eaten later with lemon juice and black pepper at our flat in Stoke Newington in north-east London.

This was in April 1974, and my mother had flown from Sydney to London to stay with us as her last chance, she correctly thought, to come back to England and see where she had grown up. To us, Stoke Newington was rather dismal and rundown, with many empty houses and closed-down shops, though infinitely more interesting and lively than the deathly quiet middle-class suburb we'd been staying in before, Willesden Green.

My mother, however, was almost over-excited by being in a Jewish area, with Orthodox Jews in black strolling purposefully in the streets and local delicatessens where there were jars and jars of different kinds of pickled cucumbers. Almost immediately, she insisted on going into a second-hand television shop. She looked at the owner, a middle-aged man, and said 'Are you Jewish?' Ann and I almost died on the spot. But he didn't appear to mind at all. He said he was, though 'they' — pointing at some Orthodox Jews passing by — 'don't recognize me as Jewish, or anyone except themselves as Jewish'. He sold us a huge old black-and-white TV (which lasted for a few weeks), so my mother could watch the BBC at home.

Having got her home base right, my mother very soon wanted to explore other parts of London. Unknown to her and us, she was just starting to suffer from the onset of middle-age sugar diabetes that would lead fourteen years later to her early death (her mother Rose, too, had diabetes). We set about tracking down her memories; she was tireless, leaving us young people in her wake, arriving home each day utterly exhausted. Over several days, we went with her to try and locate the family house in Alfred Street, only to find (like Lew on his return visit some years later) that neither the house nor the street existed any more. Nearby, however, we found a row of houses that she said were like the house she grew up in, showing us the lower level beneath the street where the coal was delivered, and reminiscing about London's pea-soup fogs. 'Where's the Roman Road? There's a library there I used to go to.' Ann, a flawless map reader, navigated from the London street directory and we walked along the Roman Road with my excited mother and found the library she said was the one she'd gone to all those years ago. 'Forty-seven years,' she kept exclaiming. Then we found the pedestrian tunnel under the railway line, the same one, I think, that my uncle Lew remembers as Tom Thumb's Arch.

Bow Street station seemed to have a special significance for her, and we spent some time going down onto its darkened platform and talking of war and how East Londoners sheltered from bombing. She was only two when the First World War started, and six when it ended, so these were early memories indeed. And I'm still not sure what bombing she was remembering or referring to. We visited Petticoat Lane for the smoked salmon. We navigated our way to Blooms to taste 'Jewish food', and she told her story to the waiter, that she'd left London 47 years ago. We found Malmsbury Road School, and my mother shouted '47 years! 47 years ago I was here!' and rushed inside, to emerge some time later beaming, telling us, who had waited somewhat embarrassed in the school grounds, that a teacher had invited her to tell the class of her childhood experiences at the school.

Another day we took the train to respectable Golders Green (where Jews went to live when they became middle-class, leaving the East End behind) to visit one of my mother's female relatives. We were shown into a front room, the visitors' room, which looked like no one had ever been in it, and, sipping tea out of best cups, we made stiff formal conversation for a while before escaping, thinking how much we preferred the parts of inner London we and our friends enjoyed going to, especially Soho, where we went to Greek and Turkish and Italian cafés. What my mother thought of her Golders Green relative she didn't say.

Another time we went with my mother to Hyde Park, and there she suddenly exclaimed 'Bella Weiner!' and rushed over to talk to her; it's only reading Lew's reminiscences that I now realize how important Bella Weiner was in their youthful Communist and theatre days.

When I was growing up, my mother would quite frequently talk of her London life as a child, and of being called at school 'Jaw-me-dead' because she talked so much. She recalled that one particular teacher annoyed her by addressing her as 'Miss Levy' in what she thought was a deliberately anti-semitic way. She would say that Father, a very tall man, was very bad-tempered, not least around the dinner table, especially 'with the boys', her brothers, and if he got too bad-tempered she would escape and stay overnight or for a few days with her grandmother, who lived nearby. Once, she said, Lew farted at the dinner table, but looked unblinkingly at his brother and said reproachfully 'Jock!'

Like Lew and Jock, she remembered that their father would take her to the theatre, and she got used to sitting 'in the gods'. Like her brothers, she developed a lifelong love of the theatre, which has curiously passed on to her son as a dislike of live theatre but a relishing of the theatricality, extravagance, flamboyance and excess of popular television. She would recount how the family could never work out why Father insisted they migrate to Australia, not South Africa as they expected. She talked of how hard it was in the first years, and the rag-trade factories she worked at in Sydney, where you were under constant surveillance and were lucky to have time off to go to the toilet; and the number of places they had to leave because they couldn't pay the rent, before they settled in a semi-detached house in Bondi. Occasionally, she would be nostalgic for the family's London life, saying they were not that badly off, they had servants, and maybe they shouldn't have migrated, it was Father's insistence because he had lived so long away from England in South Africa. She said how sad it was that her mother never saw *her* mother again, and (something that would chime in with a comment of Lew's about their parents' level of literacy) that 'she never wrote to her once she got to Australia'.

V

The story of coffee and coffee houses is part of the long history of interactions and influences between Orient and Occident. We who every morning enjoy a coffee at home or in a favourite coffee shop benefit from a remarkable history.

In *Coffee and Coffeehouses* (1985), a book I read with delight while writing chapters for this book, Ralph S. Hattox discusses the origins of coffee (*coffea arabica*) and the coffee house in the medieval Middle East, in the fifteenth and sixteenth centuries, accompanied frequently in the early stages of its presence by controversy of various kinds, political, religious, legal, intellectual, literary. There were also occasional bannings or attempted bannings, persecutions, and pro- and anti-coffee riots. What is fascinating, Hattox feels, is to trace what happened in Middle Eastern society when something entirely new was introduced into its fabric. Coffee and the coffee house were not brought in from the lands of the unbelievers, nor by the protected Christian and Jewish minorities, always considered separate and inferior (though Jews and Christians would probably, he feels, have come to enjoy the use of coffee). They were introduced by the Muslims themselves. (Coffee was for the most part introduced to Europe by Christians from the Near East, usually Armenians or Greeks.)[7]

Coffee appeared suddenly, if at first obscurely, in history. It appears that in the mid-fifteenth century traders from the Yemen noticed coffee being consumed and enjoyed in nearby Ethiopia. Coffee was then brought to the Yemen and cultivated, and at first it was especially appreciated by practitioners in Sufi mystical orders, who used it for devotional purposes. Coffee might have aided the Sufis to attain a trancelike concentration in reaching out to God: a state of complete obliviousness to the outside world and to mundane concerns; a kind of spiritual merging with the divine, to be attained in chants and rhythmic repetition. The Sufis were not as a rule reclusive hermitic holy men, but practised ordinary crafts and vocations. It seems that it was the Sufis especially who began to spread coffee throughout the lands of Islam, fanning out from the Yemen in all directions, from Aden and thence to Mecca, Medina, Damascus, Cairo, Istanbul. Until the early eighteenth century almost all coffee consumed in the Middle East (and Europe) came from the ports of the Yemen, which served as outlets for the coffee-growing areas of the interior. Coffee quickly became common in cities, in workplaces, shops, bath-houses. From the beginning it was held to be more than a mere beverage. Coffee possessed a mystique, in particular that it stimulated and led to heightened states, perhaps driving away fatigue and lethargy, bringing to the body and mind a certain sprightliness and vigour; a kind of coffee euphoria.[8]

Coffee in the fifteenth and sixteenth centuries in the lands of Islam was quickly recognized as a stimulus to talk and sociability, and from this recognition the coffee house was born. It was, however, the association of coffee with the coffee house that also stimulated controversy. Coffee spread and spread, becoming ever more popular, in both public and private use. But there was also persistent sporadic opposition before it was finally generally accepted. For some religious leaders, its emerging widespread use for pleasure rather than piety was troubling. There were debates whether or not coffee was more than a stimulant, whether or not it was an intoxicant like wine, and so should be banned. On one occasion coffee was burned in the streets of Mecca. In the sixteenth century in Cairo there was considerable civil disturbance and fighting in the streets between rival groups of opponents and proponents. Yet the attempt to ban coffee was doomed, because of its ever-increasing popularity and because the religious community always remained divided over it. Then again the coffee house might disturb those in power, because it could be the scene of political plotting and opposition, in clandestine nocturnal gatherings; for this reason the coffee house was occasionally banned by rulers in various places and at various times. So much was coffee intensely debated on various grounds, that its reputation often preceded its actual arrival in an area.[9]

Coffee, says Hattox, in and from the sixteenth century, came to enjoy considerable influence in the urban life and economies of the Middle East. In the seventeenth and eighteenth centuries, Cairene merchants made up for much of what they had lost through European short-circuiting of the spice trade by dealing in coffee. In village and town and city throughout the Muslim Middle East a hitherto unknown social institution was born, the coffee house. It quickly became established that while coffee was drunk in the home, it enjoyed a particularly close association with its public consumption in the coffee house: the coffee house became the preferred place to drink coffee. The coffee house as a universal social institution profoundly changed the look of towns and cities. It could encompass the larger metropolitan establishment, as well as the small neighbourhood coffee house, and when the modest confines of smaller coffee houses were insufficient to accommodate all the customers, particularly on nights when a story-teller was present, patrons spilled out onto the front stoops of shops adjacent and opposite the coffee house. It added more lights to the city at night (other than those in the mosque). The pleasant smell of coffee roasting and brewing was added to other smells and odours of the street and marketplace (there were also strolling coffee sellers). The coffee house attracted men through its promise of companionship. It drew people in from all social strata. In a world where eating out was rare, that lacked a restaurant culture, coffee houses meant people could leave the home for entertainment and enjoy and cultivate the art of conversation, caffeine-stimulated. Hospitality was no longer something one offered solely in one's own home. In the coffee house coffee was usually brewed just with water, unaccompanied by sugar or milk (to the first European travellers it seemed very bitter), and drunk hot, almost scaldingly so. Occasionally cardamom was added. Serving cups were of either clay or porcelain, and usually of the same diminutive size as the standard Turkish coffee cup of the present. Biscuits were often sold outside. Because it was served hot, it was sipped slowly, the patron taking his time.[10]

The coffee houses of the larger kind in the cities of the Middle East, from Cairo to Istanbul, in Syria, in Iraq, were grand affairs, luxurious, with a park- or garden-like atmosphere, with sensuous fountains, flowers, shady trees, surrounding the patron with refreshing sights and sounds unlike those of either the city or the desert. They were often located next to rivers (the Tigris, the Nile), and outdoor and night-time settings were created, with great lamps. At night too the storytellers often appeared, performing old romances or folk-tales. There was indeed a flourishing of activities, often varying with local tastes. The coffee house became something of a literary forum; poets and writers would submit their latest compositions for the assessment of a critical public. In other corners, there might be intense discussions on art, the sciences or literature, the subject-matter secular and worldly (there were fears expressed in some quarters that the coffee house would replace scholarly study and contemplation in the mosque). In place of newspapers or public forums, the coffee house quickly became the place for discussion of public affairs and exchange of information. Popular games like chess, backgammon and manqala were played in other corners. There might also be puppet shows, sometimes tumblers and jugglers. There was ubiquitous musical entertainment (though concern was expressed about the presence of singing girls). Or men might simply sit reading.[11]

Women were excluded from the coffee house, but with time coffee came to be offered as a refreshment for women in the public bath-house, which may have provided them with much the same opportunity for socializing as the coffee house did for men.[12]

By way of general conclusion, Hattox suggests that coffee and the coffee house becoming an integral part of social life in the Muslim Middle East over the last four centuries disproves the view that Islamic society is stagnant and immutable.[13]

VI

In *The Crusades Through Arab Eyes*, Amin Maalouf comes to depressing conclusions about the state of the Arab world past and present.

Maalouf had begun his account with a harrowing evocation of the successful Crusaders entering Jerusalem on 15 July 1099 and the slaughter that followed. By book's end, Maalouf records that on 17 June 1291 the Muslim armies finally reconquered the Eastern Mediterranean coast. After two centuries of occupation, the Frankish states established in the Middle East were routed, uprooted, forced to depart back to Europe. Before long, under the banner of the Ottoman Turks, Muslim armies would seek to conquer Europe itself, in 1453 taking Constantinople, by 1529 encamping with their cavalry at the walls of Vienna. But such apparent strength was deceptive.[14]

Maalouf believes that at the time of the Crusades the Arab world, from Spain to Iraq, was still the intellectual and material repository of humanity's most advanced civilization. Yet by the end of the Crusades, even though the Crusaders were beaten, the centre of world history had decisively shifted to the West. Maalouf feels that during the times prior to the Crusades, the Arabs suffered from certain weaknesses that the Frankish presence exposed. In particular, the Arab world revealed a historical inability to build stable institutions. The Franj (as the Arabs called the Crusaders) created 'genuine state structures' as soon as they arrived in the Middle East and set up the Crusader states. The Crusader rulers generally succeeded one another without serious clashes; a council of the kingdom exercised effective control over the policy of the monarch, and the clergy had a recognized role in the workings of power. In Western Europe, the power of monarchs was governed by principles that were not easily transgressed. The feudal landowners, the knights, the clergy, the university, the bourgeoisie and even the peasants all had well-established rights. By contrast, in the Arab East, the arbitrary power of the prince was unbounded. Every monarchy was threatened by the death of the monarch, and every transmission of power provoked civil war. The development of merchant towns, like the evolution of ideas, could only be retarded as a result. Such a situation, Maalouf says, has scarcely altered in the Arab world to this day.[15]

The schism between the two worlds of East and West dates, Maalouf suggests, from the Crusades, which were felt by the Arabs, even today, as an act of rape, an act of barbarism still sharply remembered, rather than a mere episode of the distant past. During the Crusades the Muslim world felt assaulted from all quarters, with the result that it turned in on itself. It became over-sensitive, defensive, intolerant, sterile. Throughout the Crusades, the Arabs refused to open their own society to ideas from the West. For those under threat, to learn the languages of the invaders seems a surrender of principle, a betrayal. But such closure and self-enclosing was, Maalouf argues, perhaps the most disastrous effect of the aggression of which the Arabs were the victims. As evolution continued in the rest of the world, the Muslim world felt excluded, and began to identify progress with the West, the alien other, felt now to be the eternal enemy. In contemporary times, this means that the Muslim world identifies modernism with the West. Even today, according to Maalouf, we can observe a lurching alternation, in Iran, Turkey, the Arab world, between phases of forced Westernization and phases of extremist, xenophobic traditionalism.[16]

By contrast, though eventually militarily defeated, the Crusaders learnt much from the Arab world. For invaders, it makes sense to learn the language of the conquered people, and many Franj did indeed learn Arabic. In Syria as in Spain and Sicily, the Franj learned much from the Muslim world, knowledge which proved indispensable in the subsequent European world-wide expansion. The heritage of Greek civilization was transferred to Western Europe through Arab intermediaries. In medicine, astronomy, chemistry, geography, mathematics, architecture, the Franj drew their knowledge from Arab writings, which they assimilated and then surpassed. Similar processes of gaining knowledge by imitation and assimilation occurred in the realms of industry and agriculture. So much was this so, that the era of the Crusades ignited an economic and cultural revolution in Western Europe. In the Orient, however, the Crusades led to long centuries of decadence and obscurantism.[17]

VII

Benjamin, in his essay 'Franz Kafka' in *Illuminations*, reports a conversation Max Brod remembers having with Kafka. They were talking about modern Europe and the decline of the human race. Kafka said that human beings are nihilistic thoughts, suicidal thoughts, that come into God's head. To a pessimistic move by Brod, Kafka replied that our world is perhaps only a bad mood of God, a bad day of his. Then, said Brod, there is hope outside this manifestation of the world that we know? Kafka apparently smiled: 'Oh, plenty of hope, an infinite amount of hope – but not for us.'[18]

VIII

For the student of the frequent insanity of history, of how much human beings like to destroy other human beings in the name of God, the Fourth Crusade is of some interest. I take my account from the book of the popular BBC television series. Briefly, in 1198 a new Pope, Innocent III, was elected in Rome. He decided on the reconquest of Jerusalem. A new group of Crusaders formed. In 1201 the envoys of the new Crusade arrived in Venice and laid their plans before the old blind Doge. Could Venice make the ships that would transport the armies across the sea to the Holy Land? The Doge said, yes, certainly, but it would cost. The cost was so great that the Crusaders agreed with a plan put forward by the Doge that the Crusaders and the Venetians, to accrue funds, attack Zara, a city that used to belong to Venice but now was occupied by King Emeric of Hungary. There was a small difficulty which occasioned a minor hesitation amongst the Crusaders (though not the Venetians). Zara was a Christian city, and King Emeric was one of their own, a Crusader. Nevertheless, the Crusaders decided to join the Venetians (even the Doge came along), appearing before Zara with a great fleet. After five days the city capitulated and was duly pillaged as was the custom of the times. The Doge and the Crusaders took over all the fine houses, divided the city between them, and spent the winter there. On Easter Monday 1203, after razing Zara to the ground, the Venetians and Crusaders sailed to Constantinople in order to lay siege to the fabled city, fount of legendary wealth and holy relics. Again, there was a minor difficulty, Constantinople being a Christian city, capital of Byzantium. The Crusaders and Venetians duly conquered Constantinople, and after this and that decided to sack it, which they performed with an extraordinary frenzy of pillaging, raping (including nuns) and murder. Booty from anywhere and everywhere was carried off, not least the holy relics, which began to fill the churches of Europe, to much rejoicing. Venice in particular benefited from such looting, which to this day remains on display, including the most famous piece, the four horses from the Hippodrome (the sixth-century Quadriga), still adorning the church of San Marco.

That was voyage completed for the Fourth Crusade. [19]

IX

Edward Said, in an essay 'Raymond Schwab and the romance of ideas', writes that this scholar of interactions between Europe and the Orient does not take sufficient note of the 'sheer folly and derangement stirred up by the Orient in Europe'. [20]

One has to seek out texts, thoughts, ideas, perceptions, phenomena, follies, that derange. One has to cultivate an art of madness.

X

In his book *Dark Riddle*, Yirmiyahu Yovel recounts of Nietzsche's twilight years that early in January 1889 Nietzsche collapsed on a street in Turin. He was taken to his lodgings and, after regaining consciousness, wrote letters to close friends as well as to former teachers. In his waning hours, says Yovel, as he slipped into madness and darkness Nietzsche lashed out especially against nationalist, anti-semitic Germans and against the ideology of the new Germany; he hoped for the political unification of Europe, as a means to renewing its decadent culture. He wrote to Jacob Burckhardt, the old cultural historian who had influenced him when young. Burckhardt was reputed to be an anti-semite. In this long letter Nietzsche describes his life in Turin in detail, how he does his shopping, the room he rents, how he suffers from torn shoes.[21]

I have no letters to write to old teachers. I have always been an intellectual parricide. I don't know why.

XI

Sometimes I walk around the university here thinking: will I meet someone who looks exactly like me when I was a young postgraduate student in my early twenties? I peer at faces. They stare back at me blankly. But I keep my sunglasses on.

XII

Friday 12 February 1999. In the morning I went to see eX de Medici the artist, my tattooist. We said hullo and smiled and chatted. I was pleased to see her again. eX worked for an hour or so on the Veiled Stranger tattoo that she'd already done a year or so before on my right arm, high, near the shoulder. Now she made it more of 'an androgyne', as she put it. When she was satisfied with its reshaping, she made us strong black coffee, and began to work on what I'd now asked her to do, a tattoo of Klee's *Angelus Novus*, off a stencil, high on my left shoulder. She thinks it's in male cells that men like symmetry, and I said, yes, I would like the new tattoo symmetrically opposite the Veiled Stranger. We'd had a discussion when I first arrived that morning about my initial idea, which I'd advanced in a letter to her before Christmas, that the *Angelus Novus* painting represents for me 'the angel of modernity as demonic'. But then, I said, a couple of days ago I'd reread Benjamin's Ninth Thesis on History in *Illuminations*, where he so wonderfully evokes Klee's painting as the Angel of History. I'd sent eX in the same letter a photocopy of a page from Brodersen's biography of Benjamin with a black and white copy of the painting. eX was pleased by my change of interpretation to Angel of History, and she also wished, she told me, to draw the tattoo with more broken lines.

By so doing she wanted to suggest how quickly in postmodernity everything becomes ephemeral. Yes, I said, that's the way to go. For the three or four hours of doing both tattoos (touching up the Veiled Stranger, creating the *Angelus Novus*), eX and I talked of our enjoyment of heretical ideas of God, Jesus, Catholicism; she told me of various dramas in her life and art, especially when she was resident artist at a Catholic girls' school. I evoked Spinoza's critique of the Exodus story in *Tractatus Theologico-Politicus*. I recounted Spinoza's argument, that Moses' laws and commandments and regulations only applied to the wilderness (when the Hebrews, exhausted from their journey out of Egypt, were in a state of childlike abjection) and therefore should not hold for Judaism after that time. eX commented that it was rather like the way martial law is brought in for an emergency situation, then not repealed once the so-called emergency is over. We kept joyfully babbling, interrupting each other.

I thanked eX for telling me about Jonathan Kirsch's *The Harlot by the Side of the Road*, and that it led me to new thinking, and the conclusion that monotheism is a disaster for humanity and we should return in the new millennium to the pagan and polytheistic.

eX had been reading a book speculating that Jesus had escaped death and lived to launch a 'Nazarene church' of his own. I told her of Michel de Certeau's speculations in *The Mystic Fable* concerning the desire in Christianity to find the lost body of Christ.

eX said people become more confident with their bodies when they've got a tattoo. At the same time, people's bodies when tattooed are treated as if they are more public – people demand immediately to see a tattoo.

eX thinks the skin mediates between the body and the world.

XIII

Contemporary cultural theory is too determinedly secular. To accompany, converse with, the poetics of diaspora we need a theological poetics. [22]

XIV

In the last few years I've taken to urinating sitting down. Camille Paglia says somewhere, I think in the introduction to *Sexual Personae*, that man urinates in an arc, symbolizing his desire to create thought and culture that transcends the earth, while woman urinates directly onto the earth. [23] Can I think of my sitting down to micturate (the word for pissing I picked up from *Ulysses* and use rather tediously often in household conversation) as a protest against such essentializing of Man and Woman?

Towards the end of *Ulysses*, Mr Bloom and Stephen Daedalus, just before they part for ever, unite in pissing together outside Mr Bloom's house. Perhaps they wish, having glimpsed the shadow of Molly Bloom inside – 'wife Marion (Molly) Bloom, denoted by a visible splendid sign, a lamp' – to stress that, defiantly, as men they indeed wish to transcend women, domesticity, local concerns, the particular, embeddedness.

> At Stephen's suggestion, at Bloom's instigation both, first Stephen, then Bloom, in penumbra urinated, their sides contiguous ... their gazes, first Bloom's, then Stephen's, elevated to the projected luminous and semiluminous shadow.[24]

Later Molly will make her own caustic comments to herself on men's self-admiring ambitions, obsessive egos, little acts of defiance, and derisory fetishes they think are so interesting and give them the illusion of substance.

Micturating sitting down one can contemplate, ruminate, reverie, time passes; late at night, one is in danger of falling asleep.

XV

I would like to think of my chapters on *Ulysses* as the Bloom Quartets.

XVI

I'm a voyeur of veils. I envy female decoration.

XVII

Satendra Nandan, poet, academic, politician, exile from Fiji, old friend, suggests in an autobiographical essay that only India amongst the ancient civilizations has a continuous history: 'I feel India alone has kept the fragments of her original civilization. Arabia was overcome by Islam; Rome and Greece by Christianity; China by Communism; India, despite her horrendous problems, has kept so much of her ancient past alive.' Nandan writes that the recent vulgarity and violence of Hindu fundamentalism has dented his faith in organized religion: 'but my joy in being an Indian has been reinforced by the

Fijian coups and the outcry in India against Hindu fundamentalist *goondaism*.'[25]
I can feel no such joy in being (or seeing myself as being) any identity.

XVIII

27 September 1999. It is the first morning of a conference being held at ANU,
on Asian-Australian identities (a wonderful, vibrant, exciting conference as it
turned out, composed of writers and performers as well as academics). The
well-known and well-respected cultural theorist Ien Ang and I were (we had
been told) to stage an intellectual conversation. Ien Ang started off, giving a
fascinating paper entitled 'Can one say no to Chineseness?', where she rejected
the metaphor of the living tree, that Chineseness must have a centre, a
rootedness, either in historic China or in the Chinese diaspora.[26] I then replied
with my talk, entitled 'I have no community – dilemmas of diaspora'. I said that
Ien Ang's paper reminded me that I'd chaired a round-table discussion at ANU,
in which Ien was one of the speakers, in February 1999, on 'Reconceptualizing
the Chinese of the Southlands' (under the auspices of the ANU Centre for the
Study of the Chinese Southern Diaspora). In the audience were some
representatives of the Canberra Chinese community, and the problem came up
quite dramatically in discussion of the relation of intellectuals – and by
intellectuals here I also mean artists and writers – of the relation of intellectuals
of Chinese diasporic descent to Chinese-Australian communities. There was
tension and anger in the air, the voicing of an explicit demand that intellectuals
of Chinese descent commemorate and indeed celebrate the achievements of the
Chinese-Australian community in the difficult circumstances of Australian
history; that such intellectuals should recognize a duty to serve their
community with their particular knowledge and skills and in effect be obedient
to it. It was quite a riveting moment. In reply, Ien Ang eloquently and
strikingly questioned that demand. There the matter was left, and in my
closing remarks as chair I commented that this was an interesting discussion
indeed, which was touching on a more general problem of diasporas, the
fraught relation between diaspora intellectuals and a diaspora community that
might wish to claim them as part of its own, or which they might feel they
belong to or should belong to.

As chair I naturally couldn't then give my own view, but (I said) I'll give it
now: in my opinion, intellectuals, artists, writers should be strangers amongst
the nations. Intellectuals, artists, writers should be (to perversely adapt
Gramsci) as inorganic as possible in relation to a community. Intellectuals,
artists, writers should realize their close historical kinship in world history with
the mythological trickster figure. Intellectuals, artists, writers should be

tricksters dancing free of society and history, knowing they proudly inherit cultural traditions in many societies of the fool and clown and crank figures who engage in carnivalesque irony, mockery, laughter, directed at hierarchy, official cosmology and eschatology, conventionality, that which is constituted as normal and normative.

In the cultural history of festivals of inversion and World Upside Down, of carnivals and carnivalesque, the fool and trickster can be regarded with uneasiness and ambivalence. They can be admired for their freedom to say and do anything, to meet convention with comic derision and so stand up for those in history who are supposed to be obedient to power, authority and official wisdom. Fools and tricksters hold out the irrepressible hope for humanity that life is not necessarily preordained towards loss, failure and tragedy, that fate is not inconquerable, that new creation stories are imaginable.

Yet (I went on) tricksters and fools might also be sad clowns in their isolation, the risks they take with distance from and disagreement with a community or ordinary society. And they might be feared as not quite human because of the freedoms they take as if by the authority of unearthly powers; as if they are akin to the feared stranger, the unsettling outsider from somewhere else, from nowhere, the monster, the sorcerer, the magician, devilish, demonic, uncanny, sinister, dangerous; as if they have no place in the ordinary world, never.

In these terms, I think that in world history there is a conflict within the being of intellectuals, artists, writers, performers: they are tricksters, necessary outsiders – yet they might have an aching longing to belong. And how much more acute and intense is that conflict to be apart and yet desire to belong when the intellectual is part of a diaspora or has a diasporic history and when her or his sensibility and consciousness is inflected by the confusing phenomenology of diaspora, by multiple feelings of living in many countries of the mind, journeys of the imagination, at once.

XIX

I feel that I belong to histories, not to a place, not to a land.

XX

We should resist idealizing diasporas (that would be to continue the victimological narrative). And many intellectuals in modernity (by which I also mean writers, performers, artists) in diaspora and exile have certainly desired a close, organic relationship to a diaspora community, a leading role. A frequent contradictory aspect of diaspora communities is that they might be eloquent advocates of the multicultural and pluralist in a host society, yet support religious fundamentalism or nationalism or ethnic absolutism or even ethnic cleansing in a society of origin or claimed origin.[27]

XXI

It is loftily observed of the Sephardim that because of the fear and vulnerability created by the 1492 Expulsion, they became impatient for redemption and were peculiarly susceptible to messianic movements, disastrously so, as in the support they gave in the seventeenth century to the self-proclaimed Messiah Sabbetai Zevi.[28]

It might be commented that the Ashkenazim have for over a hundred years plunged into a far more disastrous messianic adventure, its name Zionism, its activity settler-colonialism, that brings shame and dishonour on the children of Israel.

XXII

Derrida says he looks at his (presumably circumcised) penis and doesn't register it as Jewish.[29] I agree with Derrida. If I feel Jewish from my upbringing (secular as it was), it is not because of my circumcised penis – which after all could have been part of a general post Second World War surgical procedure in Australia apparently performed for health reasons. My mother died many years ago now, it's too late to put to her a delicate enquiry of this kind. If I feel Jewish from my upbringing, it is because I knew one was Jewish through one's mother, and if I thought of my mother I thought of my grandparents we kids visited almost every day when we were young: their warmth, their poverty.

My son isn't circumcised. We didn't – I didn't – want him to go through pain, and a kind of mutilation and a limitation on sensation. Bizarrely, Ann's Christian grandmother, then very old, came to the hospital and pleaded with Ann to have our tiny baby circumcised on health grounds.

Distant memories. When we were kids, my mother and my grandmother Nan would shout at my grandfather not to fast, 'You're too old!' But he insisted. On certain days Nan would bet on the horses. In winter we'd play dominoes in front of the coal fire. Nan was a great cook of beautiful large round apple pies. But when Nan buttered the matzos, we kids would say more, more on that corner, that bit, Nan.

Notes

1. Walter Benjamin, *The Origin of German Tragic Drama*, trans. John Osborne (London: Verso, 1996), pp. 28–9.
2. *Ibid.*, pp. 30–1.
3. As James Clifford so memorably argues in *Routes* (Cambridge, MA: Harvard University Press, 1997), 'Diasporas', pp. 244–77.
4. Richard Price, *Alabi's World* (Baltimore and London: Johns Hopkins University Press, 1990), pp. 4, 9, 11. See also Natalie Zemon Davis, *Women on the Margins: Three Seventeenth-Century Lives* (Cambridge, MA: Harvard University Press, 1995), pp. 171–4 and 319 n. 143; on p. 320 n. 145 Davis refers to William Blake's engravings of punishments meted out to the slaves of Suriname.
5. Maxime Rodinson, *Cult, Ghetto, and State: The Persistence of the Jewish Question*, trans. Jon Rothschild (London: Al Saqi Books, 1983), pp. 184–5.
6. *Ibid.*, p. 182.
7. Ralph S. Hattox, *Coffee and Coffeehouses: The Origins of a Social Beverage in the Medieval Near East* (1985; Seattle: University of Washington Press, 1996), pp. x, 4–6, 95–8; also information opposite Plate 4.
8. *Ibid.*, pp. 14, 23–8, 59–60, 73–4, 115.
9. *Ibid.*, pp. 12, 28–30, 36–9, 41, 43, 46, 102.
10. *Ibid.*, pp. 72–81, 83–6, 88–9, 99–100, 125–8; information opposite Plates 5, 13 and 15.
11. *Ibid.*, pp. 81–2, 90, 101, 105–8, 121; information opposite Plates 6, 9, 10 and 12.
12. *Ibid.*, p. 124.
13. *Ibid.*, p. 129.
14. Amin Maalouf, *The Crusades Through Arab Eyes* (1983; London: Al Saqi Books, 1984), pp. 258–9, 261.
15. *Ibid.*, pp. 262–3.
16. *Ibid.*, pp. 264–5.
17. *Ibid.*, p. 264.
18. Walter Benjamin, *Illuminations*, intro. Hannah Arendt, trans. Harry Zohn (London: Fontana, 1992), pp. 112–13. Cf. Beatrice Hanssen, *Walter Benjamin's Other History: Of Stones, Animals, Human Beings, and Angels* (Berkeley: University of California Press, 1998), p. 142.
19. Terry Jones and Alan Ereira, *Crusades* (London: BBC Books, 1994), ch. 13, pp. 196–212.
20. Edward W. Said, *The World, The Text, and the Critic* (London: Vintage, 1991), p. 253.
21. Yirmiyahu Yovel, *Dark Riddle: Hegel, Nietzsche, and the Jews* (London: Polity Press, 1998), pp. 129–31.
22. Cf. William E. Connolly, *Why I Am Not a Secularist* (Minneapolis: University of Minnesota Press, 1999).
23. Camille Paglia, *Sexual Personae* (London: Penguin, 1991), p. 21: 'Male urination really *is* a kind of accomplishment, an arc of transcendence. A woman merely waters the ground she stands on.'
24. James Joyce, *Ulysses*, intro. and notes by Declan Kiberd (London: Penguin, 1992), pp. 824–5.
25. Satendra Nandan, 'Delhi: among the ruins' in Debjani Ganguly and Kavita

Nandan (eds), *Unfinished Journeys: India File from Canberra* (Adelaide: Centre for Research in New Literatures in English, Flinders University, 1998), pp. 123–4.

26. See Ien Ang, 'Can one say no to Chineseness? Pushing the limits of the diasporic paradigm', *boundary 2*, 25(3) (1998), p. 234.

27. Cf. Clifford, *Routes*, 'Diasporas', p. 252; Vijay Mishra, 'The diasporic imaginary: theorizing the Indian diaspora', *Textual Practice*, 10(3) (1996), p. 424.

28. See, for example, Jane S. Gerber, *The Jews of Spain: A History of the Sephardic Experience* (New York: The Free Press, 1992), pp. xiii, 173–5. Gershom Scholem wrote a biography: *Sabbetai Sevi: The Mystical Messiah* (1973). See also Scholem, *Major Trends in Jewish Mysticism* (New York: Schocken, 1954), Eighth Lecture, pp. 287–324.

29. Geoff Bennington (ed.), *Jacques Derrida* (Chicago: University of Chicago Press, 1993), 'Circumfession', p. 170.

Bibliography

Abu-Lughod, Janet L., *Before European Hegemony: The World System A.D. 1250–1350* (New York: Oxford University Press, 1989).

Alcalay, Ammiel, *After Jews and Arabs: Remaking Levantine Culture* (Minneapolis: University of Minnesota Press, 1993).

Alcalay, Ammiel, 'Exploding identities: notes on ethnicity and literary history' in Boyarin and Boyarin (eds), *Jews and Other Differences: The New Jewish Cultural Studies*, pp. 330–44.

Alexander, J. H., and Hewitt, David (eds), *Scott Carnival: Selected Papers from the Fourth International Scott Conference, 1991* (Aberdeen, 1993).

Ang, Ien, 'Can one say no to Chineseness? Pushing the limits of the diasporic paradigm', *boundary 2*, 25(3) (1998), pp. 223–42.

Appadurai, Arjun, 'How to make a national cuisine: cookbooks in contemporary India', *Comparative Studies of Society and History*, 31(1) (1988), pp. 3–24.

Bakhtin, Mikhail, *The Dialogic Imagination*, ed. Michael Holquist, trans. Caryl Emerson and Michael Holquist (Austin: University of Texas Press, 1981), chapter 'Forms of time and of the chronotope in the novel', pp. 84–258.

Bakhtin, Mikhail, *Problems of Dostoevsky's Poetics*, ed. and trans. Caryl Emerson (Manchester: Manchester University Press, 1984).

Bakhtin, Mikhail, *Art and Answerability: Early Philosophical Essays*, ed. Michael Holquist and Vadim Liapunov, trans. Vadim Liapunov (Austin: University of Texas Press, 1990).

Bann, Stephen, *The Clothing of Clio: A Study of the Representation of History in Nineteenth-Century Britain and France* (Cambridge: Cambridge University Press, 1984).

Beinart, Haim, 'The conversos and their fate' in Kedourie (ed.), *Spain and the Jews*, pp. 92–122.

Benjamin, Walter, *The Origin of German Tragic Drama*, trans. John Osborne (1928; London and New York: Verso, 1996).

Bennett, Jane, *Thoreau's Nature: Ethics, Politics, and the Wild* (Los Angeles and London: Sage, 1994).

Berger, Harry, Jnr, 'The lie of the land: the text beyond Canaan', *Representations*, 25 (1989), pp. 119–38.

Boer, Roland, 'The resurrection engine of Michel de Certeau', *Paragraph*, 22(2) (July 1999), pp. 199–212.

Boer, Roland, *Last Stop Before Antarctica: The Bible and Postcolonialism in Australia* (Sheffield: Sheffield Academic Press, in press for 2001).

Boer, Roland, 'Significant cuts: body building, circumcision and the phallic signifier' in William Cowling, Maurice Hamilton, Terrance MacMullan and Nancy Tuana (eds), *Returning the Gaze* (Bloomington: Indiana University Press, forthcoming 2001).

Boyarin, Daniel, 'The eye in the Torah: ocular desire in midrashic hermeneutic', *Critical Inquiry*, 16 (Spring 1990), pp. 532–50.

Boyarin, Daniel, *Carnal Israel: Reading Sex in Talmudic Culture* (Berkeley: University of California Press, 1993).

Boyarin, Jonathan, 'Reading Exodus into history', *New Literary History*, 23(3) (1992), pp. 523–54.

Boyarin, Jonathan, and Boyarin, Daniel (eds), *Jews and Other Differences: The New Jewish Cultural Studies* (Minneapolis: University of Minnesota Press, 1997).

Cagidemetrio, Alide, 'A plea for fictional histories and old-time "Jewesses"' in Werner Sollers (ed.), *The Invention of Ethnicity* (New York: Oxford University Press, 1989), pp. 14–43.

Caplan, Jane, '"Speaking scars": the tattoo in popular practice and medico-legal debate in nineteenth-century Europe', *History Workshop Journal*, 44 (1997), pp. 107–42.

Caracciolo, Peter L. (ed.), *The Arabian Nights in English Literature* (Basingstoke: Macmillan, 1988).

Celan, Paul, *Breathturn*, trans. Pierre Joris (Los Angeles: Sun and Moon Press, 1995).

Certeau, Michel de, *The Mystic Fable*, vol. I, trans. Michael B. Smith (Chicago and London: University of Chicago Press, 1992).

Chandler, James, *England in 1819: The Politics of Literary Culture and the Case of Romantic Historicism* (Chicago: University of Chicago Press, 1998).

Cheng, Vincent, J., *Joyce, Race, and Empire* (Cambridge: Cambridge University Press, 1995).

Cheng, Vincent J., and Martin, Timothy (eds), *Joyce in Context* (Cambridge: Cambridge University Press, 1992).

Cheyette, Bryan, *Constructions of 'the Jew' in English Literature and Society* (Cambridge: Cambridge University Press, 1993).

Cheyette, Bryan, and Marcus, Laura (eds), *Modernity, Culture and 'the Jew'* (Cambridge: Polity, 1998).

Clifford, James, 'Looking for Bomma', *London Review of Books* (24 March 1994), pp. 26–7.

Clifford, James, 'Diasporas', *Cultural Anthropology*, 9(3) (1994), pp. 302–38. (Reprinted in Clifford, *Routes*.)

Clifford, James, *Routes: Travel and Translation in the Late Twentieth Century* (Cambridge, MA: Harvard University Press, 1997).

Cohen, Shaye J. D., 'Why aren't Jewish women circumcised?', *Gender and History*, 9(3) (1997), pp. 560–78.

Connolly, William E., *The Augustinian Imperative: A Reflection on the Politics of Morality* (London: Sage, 1993).

Connolly, William E., *The Ethos of Pluralization* (Minneapolis: University of Minnesota Press, 1995).

Connolly, William E., *Why I Am Not a Secularist* (Minneapolis: University of Minnesota Press, 1999).

Curthoys, Ann, 'Expulsion, Exodus, and Exile in white Australian historical mythology' in Richard Nile and Michael Williams (eds), *Imaginary Homelands: The Dubious Cartographies of Australian Identity* (St Lucia: University of Queensland Press, 1999), pp. 1–18.

Curthoys, Ann, and Docker, John, 'Time, eternity, truth, and death: history as allegory', *Humanities Research*, 1 (1999), pp. 5–26.

Davis, Natalie Zemon, *Women on the Margins: Three Seventeenth-Century Lives* (Cambridge, MA: Harvard University Press, 1995).

Davison, Neil R., *James Joyce, Ulysses, and the Construction of Jewish Identity* (Cambridge: Cambridge University Press, 1996).

Deleuze, Gilles, *Spinoza: Practical Philosophy*, trans. Robert Hurley (San Francisco: City Lights Books, 1988).

Derrida, Jacques, *Writing and Difference*, trans. and intro. Alan Bass (Chicago: University of Chicago Press, 1978), ch. 3, 'Edmond Jabès and the question of the book', pp. 64–78.

Deutscher, Isaac, *The Non-Jewish Jew* (London: Oxford University Press, 1968).

Dhuway: An Australian Diaspora and Homecoming (video documentary, 1996; made in collaboration with the Yiidhuwarra people of Cape York peninsula; an OZIRIS production in association with SBS Independent, directed by Lew Griffiths, narrated by Noel Pearson).

Docker, John, 'Orientalism and Zionism', *Arena*, 75 (1986), pp. 58–95.

Docker, John, 'Blanche D'Alpuget's *Robert J. Hawke* and *Winter in Jerusalem*', *Hecate*, XIII, (1) (1987), pp. 51–65.

Docker, John, 'Jews in Australia', *Arena*, 96 (1991), pp. 145–57.

Docker, John, 'Growing up a Communist-Irish-Anglophilic-Jew in Bondi', *Independent Monthly* (December 1992/January 1993), p. 22.

Docker, John, *Postmodernism and Popular Culture: A Cultural History* (Melbourne: Cambridge University Press, 1994).

Docker, John, 'Rethinking postcolonialism and multiculturalism in the *fin de siècle*', *Cultural Studies*, 9(3) (1995), pp. 409–26.

Docker, John, and Fischer, Gerhard (eds), *Multicultural Identities: Theories, Models, Case Studies* (Tübingen: Stauffenburg Verlag, 2000).

Docker, John, and Fischer, Gerhard (eds), *Race, Colour and Identity in Australia and New Zealand* (Sydney: University of New South Wales Press, 2000).

Felstiner, John, *Paul Celan: Poet, Survivor, Jew* (New Haven, CT, and London: Yale University Press, 1995).

Feuer, Lewis S., *Ideology and the Ideologists* (Oxford: Basil Blackwell, 1975).

Fischer, Gerhard (ed.), *The Mudrooroo/Müller Project: A Theatrical Casebook* (Sydney: New South Wales University Press, 1993).

Fischer, Gerhard, 'Mis-taken identity: Mudrooroo and Gordon Matthews' in Docker and Fischer (eds), *Race, Colour and Identity in Australia and New Zealand*, pp. 95–112.

Fletcher, Richard, *Moorish Spain* (London: Phoenix, 1994).

Freud, Sigmund, 'Family romances' (1909) in *On Sexuality: Three Essays on the Theory of Sexuality and Other Works* (London: Pelican Freud Library, 1977), pp. 221–25.

Freud, Sigmund, letter dated 6 January 1935 to Lou Andreas-Salomé in Richard J. Bernstein, *Freud and the Legacy of Moses* (Cambridge: Cambridge University Press, 1998), pp. 117–18.

Freud, Sigmund, *Moses and Monotheism* (1939; New York: Vintage, 1967).

Gatens, Moira, and Lloyd, Genevieve, *Collective Imaginings: Spinoza, Past and Present* (London and New York: Routledge, 1999).

Gerber, Jane S., *The Jews of Spain: A History of the Sephardic Experience* (New York: The Free Press, 1992)

Ghosh, Amitav, *In an Antique Land* (London: Granta/Penguin, 1994).

Goitein, S. D., *A Mediterranean Society: The Jewish Communities of the Arab World as Portrayed in the Documents of the Cairo Geniza* (Berkeley: University of California Press, 1967–83).

Goitein, S. D., *Jews and Arabs: Their Contacts Through the Ages* (New York: Schocken Books, 1974).

Goitein, S. D., *Letters of Medieval Jewish Traders* (Princeton, NJ: Princeton University Press, 1974).

Goody, Jack, *Cooking, Cuisine and Class* (Cambridge: Cambridge University Press, 1982).

Hanssen, Beatrice, *Walter Benjamin's Other History: Of Stones, Animals, Human Beings, and Angels* (Berkeley, Los Angeles and London: University of California Press, 1998).

Hattox, Ralph S., *Coffee and Coffeehouses: The Origins of a Social Beverage in the Medieval Near East* (1985; Seattle: University of Washington Press, 1996).

Herrman, Irwin M., *The Arab–Israeli Conflict: Sir Isaac Isaacs and Australian Politics Today* (Annual Beanland Lecture; Melbourne: Footscray Institute of Technology, 1979), pp. 1–28.

Hess, Andrew C., 'The Mediterranean and Shakespeare's geopolitical imagination' in Peter Hulme and William H. Sherman (eds), *'The Tempest' and Its Travels* (London: Reaktion Books, 2000).

Hulme, Peter, 'Dire straits: ten leagues beyond', paper given to conference on 'National Culture(s)', University of Casablanca Ain Chok (November 1998).

Irwin, Robert, *The Arabian Nights: A Companion* (London: Allen Lane, 1994).

Israel, Jonathan, 'The Sephardim of the Netherlands' in Kedourie (ed.), *Spain and the Jews*, pp. 189–212.

Jacobs, Louis, *The Jewish Religion: A Companion* (Oxford: Oxford University Press, 1995).

Joyce, James, *Ulysses* (1922), intro. and notes by Declan Kiberd (London: Penguin, 1992).

Joyce, James, *Ulysses*, (1922), intro. and notes by Jeri Johnson (Oxford: Oxford University Press, 1993).

Kabbani, Rana, 'Behind him lay the great city of Cordoba', *Third Text*, 21 (1992–93), pp. 67–70.

Kamen, Henry, *Inquisition and Society in Spain in the Sixteenth and Seventeenth Centuries* (London: Weidenfeld and Nicolson, 1985).

Kedourie, Elie (ed.), *Spain and the Jews: The Sephardic Experience, 1492 and After* (London: Thames and Hudson, 1992).

Kenner, Hugh, *Ulysses*, rev. edn (Baltimore: Johns Hopkins University Press, 1987).

Kirsch, Jonathan, *The Harlot by the Side of the Road* (London: Rider, 1997).

Kramer, Joel L., 'Spanish ladies from the Cairo Geniza' in Alisa Meyuhas Ginio (ed.), *Jews, Christians, and Muslims in the Mediterranean World after 1492* (London: Frank Cass, 1992).

Langton, Marcia, 'Aboriginal art and film: the politics of representation', *Race and Class*, 35(4) (1994), pp. 89–106.

Levinas, Emmanuel, *Difficult Freedom: Essays on Judaism*, trans. Seán Hand (Baltimore: Johns Hopkins University Press, 1990).

Lloyd, Genevieve, *Spinoza and the* Ethics (London and New York: Routledge, 1996).

Maalouf, Amin, *The Crusades Through Arab Eyes*, trans. Jon Rothschild (London: Al Saqi Books, 1984).

Maalouf, Amin, *Leo the African*, trans. Peter Sluglett (1986; London: Abacus, 1995).

McCalman, Iain, 'New Jerusalems: prophecy, Dissent and radical culture in England, 1786–1830' in Knud Haakonssen (ed.), *Enlightenment and Religion: Rational Dissent in Eighteenth-Century Britain* (Cambridge: Cambridge University Press, 1996), pp. 312–35.

McClintock, Anne, Mufti, Aamir, and Shohat, Ella (eds), *Dangerous Liaisons: Gender, Nation, and Postcolonial Perspectives* (Minneapolis: University of Minnesota Press, 1997).

Maimonides, Moses, 'Epistle to Yemen' in Twersky (ed.), *A Maimonides Reader*, pp. 437–62.

Marks, Elaine, *Marrano as Metaphor: The Jewish Presence in French Writing* (New York: Columbia University Press, 1996).

Matt, Daniel C., *The Essential Kabbalah: The Heart of Jewish Mysticism* (San Francisco: HarperCollins, 1995).

Menacol, Maria Rosa, *The Arabic Role in Medieval Literary History: A Forgotten Heritage* (Philadephia: University of Pennsylvania Press, 1987).

Mergenthal, Silvia, 'The shadow of Shylock: Scott's *Ivanhoe* and Edgeworth's *Harrington*' in Alexander and Hewitt (eds), *Scott in Carnival*, pp. 320–31.

Mishra, Vijay, 'The diasporic imaginary: theorizing the Indian diaspora', *Textual Practice*, 10(3) (1996), pp. 421–47.

Montag, Warren, and Stolze, Ted (eds), *The New Spinoza* (Minneapolis: University of Minnesota Press, 1997).

Morgan, Sally, *My Place* (Perth: Fremantle Arts Centre Press, 1987).

Nadler, Steven, *Spinoza: A Life* (Cambridge and New York: Cambridge University Press, 1999).

Nandan, Satendra, 'Delhi: among the ruins' in Debjani Ganguly and Kavita Nandan (eds), *Unfinished Journeys: India File from Canberra* (Adelaide: Centre for Research in New Literatures in English, Flinders University, 1998), pp. 109–44.

Newman, Aubrey, 'The Sephardim in England' in Kedourie (ed.), *Spain and the Jews*, pp. 213–22.

Pagels, Elaine, *Adam, Eve, and the Serpent* (London: Weidenfeld and Nicolson, 1988).

Pandey, Gyanendra, 'In defense of the fragment: writing about Hindu–Muslim riots in India today', *Representations*, 37 (Winter 1992), pp. 27–53.

Price, Richard, *Alabi's World* (Baltimore and London: Johns Hopkins University Press, 1990).

Priolkar, Anant Kakba, *The Goa Inquisition* (New Delhi: Voice of India, 1991).

Pullan, Brian, *The Jews of Europe and the Inquisition of Venice, 1550–1670* (Oxford: Basil Blackwell, 1983).

Ragussis, Michael, 'The birth of a nation in Victorian culture: the Spanish Inquisition, the converted daughter, and the "secret race"', *Critical Inquiry*, 20 (1994), pp. 477–524.

Ragussis, Michael, *Figures of Conversion: 'The Jewish Question' and English National Identity* (Durham, NC, and London: Duke University Press, 1995).

Raz, Amnon, 'National colonial theology', *Tikkun*, 14(3) (May/June 1999), pp. 11–16.

Riemer, Andrew, *The Habsburg Café* (Sydney: Angus and Robertson, 1993).

Roden, Claudia, *The Book of Jewish Food* (London: Viking, 1997).

Rodinson, Maxime, 'Recherches sur les documents arabes relatifs à la cuisine', *Revue des Etudes Islamiques* (1949), pp. 95–165.

Rodinson, Maxime, 'GHIDHA', entry in B. Lewis, C. Pellat and J. Schacht (eds), *The Encyclopaedia of Islam*, new edition, vol. II (Leiden: E. J. Brill, 1965), pp. 1057–72.

Rodinson, Maxime, *Cult, Ghetto, and State: The Persistence of the Jewish Question*, trans. Jon Rothschild (London: Al Saqi Books, 1983).

Rose, Deborah Bird, 'Rupture and the ethics of care in colonized space' in Tim Bonyhady and Tom Griffiths (eds), *Prehistory to Politics: John Mulvaney, the Humanities and the Public Intellectual* (Melbourne: Melbourne University Press, 1996), pp. 190–215.

Roth, Cecil, *Gleanings: Essays in Jewish History, Letters and Art* (New York: Hermon Press, 1967).

Roth, Cecil, *A History of the Marranos* (New York: Herman Press, 1974).

Rushdie, Salman, *The Moor's Last Sigh* (London: Jonathan Cape, 1995).

Said, Edward W., *Orientalism* (London: Routledge & Kegan Paul, 1980).

Said, Edward W., *The World, the Text, and the Critic* (1983; London: Vintage, 1991).

Said, Edward W., 'Michael Walzer's *Exodus and Revolution*: a Canaanite reading' in Edward Said and Christopher Hitchens (eds), *Blaming the Victims: Spurious Scholarship and the Palestinian Question* (London: Verso, 1988), pp. 161–78.

Santich, Barbara, *The Original Mediterranean Cuisine: Medieval Recipes for Today* (Adelaide: Wakefield Press, 1995).

Scholem, Gershom, *Major Trends in Jewish Mysticism* (New York: Schocken, 1954).

Scholem, Gershom, *The Messianic Idea in Judaism* (New York: Schocken, 1978).

Scholem, Gershom, *Origins of the Kabbalah*, trans. Allan Arkush, ed. R. J. Zwi Werblowsky (Princeton, NJ: Princeton University Press, 1990).

Schwartz, Regina M., *The Curse of Cain: The Violent Legacy of Monotheism* (Chicago and London: University of Chicago Press, 1997).

Scott, Walter, *Ivanhoe*, ed. A. N. Wilson (London: Penguin, 1986).

Shapiro, Michael J., *Violent Cartographies: Mapping Cultures of War* (Minneapolis: University of Minnesota Press, 1997).

Shell, Marc, 'Marranos (pigs), or from coexistence to toleration', *Critical Inquiry*, 17 (1991), pp. 306–35.

Shell, Marc, 'The Holy Foreskin; or, money, relics, and Judeo-Christianity' in Boyarin and Boyarin (eds), *Jews and Other Differences*, pp. 345–59.

Shohat, Ella, 'Sephardim in Israel: Zionism from the standpoint of its Jewish victims', *Social Text*, 19/20 (1988), pp. 1–35. (Reprinted in McClintock, Mufti and Shohat (eds) *Dangerous Liaisons.*)

Shohat, Ella, *Israeli Cinema: East/West and the Politics of Representation* (Austin: University of Texas Press, 1989).

Shohat, Ella, 'Antinomies of exile: Said at the frontier of national narrations' in Michael Sprinker (ed.), *Edward Said: A Critical Reader* (Oxford and Cambridge, MA: Blackwell, 1992), pp. 121–43.

Shohat, Ella, 'Staging the Quincentenary: the Middle East and the Americas', *Third Text*, 21 (1992–93), pp. 95–105.

Shohat, Ella, 'Taboo memories and diasporic visions: Columbus, Palestine and Arab-Jews' in May Joseph and Jennifer Natalya Fink (eds), *Performing Hybridity* (Minneapolis: University of Minnesota Press, 1999), pp. 131–56.

Simmel, Georg, *The Sociology of George Simmel*, ed. and trans. Kurt H. Wolff (Glencloe, IL: The Free Press, 1950).

Simpson, David, *Romanticism, Nationalism, and the Revolt Against Theory* (Chicago: University of Chicago Press, 1993).

Spinoza, Baruch, *Tractatus Theologico-Politicus*, trans. Samuel Shirley, intro. Brad S. Gregory (Leiden: E. J. Brill, 1989).

Tales from the Thousand and One Nights, trans. and intro. N. J. Dawood (London: Penguin Classics, 1973).

Thompson, Thomas L., *The Bible in History: How Writers Create a Past* (London: Jonathan Cape, 1999).

Tulloch, Graham, '*Ivanhoe* and Bibles' in Alexander and Hewitt (eds), *Scott in Carnival*, pp. 309–19.

Twersky, Isadore (ed.), *A Maimonides Reader* (New York: Behrman House, 1972).

Waddington, Raymond B., and Williamson, Arthur H. (eds), *The Expulsion of the Jews: 1492 and After* (New York and London: Garland, 1994).

Whitelam, Keith W., *The Invention of Ancient Israel: The Silencing of Palestinian History* (London and New York: Routledge, 1996).

Yovel, Yirmiyahu, *Spinoza and Other Heretics*, vol. I: *The Marrano of Reason* (Princeton, NJ: Princeton University Press, 1989).

Yovel, Yirmiyahu, *Dark Riddle: Hegel, Nietzsche, and the Jews* (Cambridge: Polity Press, 1998).

Zimler, Richard, *The Last Kabbalist of Lisbon* (1998; London: Arcadia, 1999).

Index